RESILIENCY IN ACTION

Practical Ideas for Overcoming Risks

and Building Strengths

in youth, families, & communities

Edited by Nan Henderson,

with Bonnie Benard & Nancy Sharp-Light

Foreword by Peter L. Benson

Published by
Resiliency In Action, Inc.

ISBN: 0-9669394-3-3

Library of Congress Control Number: 2006938364

2nd Printing

(Clip art copyright © 1990-2003, RT Computer Graphics, Inc., Rio Rancho, NM. 800-891-1600, www.rtcomputer.com.)

Resiliency In Action, Inc. is a publishing and training company located in Southern California. For more information, and additional resiliency resources, visit our Web site: www.resiliency.com. We can also be contacted at:

Resiliency In Action
P.O. Box 1433
Ojai, CA 93024
800-440-5171

Acknowledgements

What a wonderful opportunity this energy-intensive but joyful labor of producing the second edition of *Resiliency In Action* has been for me. It is a privilege to convene in this book so many potent voices from so many fields of research and endeavor focused on documenting and unlocking the power of resiliency—in children, youth, families, schools, and communities.

I could not have accomplished this task without, first and foremost, my beloved support system for decades, Craig Noonan, Nancy LeBaron, and Don Henderson, as well as my new (but so powerful and appreciated) cheerleader and "book doula," Renee Mandala.

In addition, I must thank the following friends and colleagues who contributed in ways great and small—but all significantly—to the emergence of this second edition: Bonnie Sabb, Amy Bransky, Barbara Wotherspoon, Kathy Leddy, Peggy LaCerra and her "Intentional Self- Creation" group and publications, Carolyn and Michael Hernandez (who introduced me to Brain Gym), Mimi Rich and her groups of Wise Women (who in recent months provided weekly support), Janis Kling, Marcia Doty, Celeste Matesevac, Ron Pitts, Bobbi Balderman, Judy Schwocho, and Paula Pugh.

And, my deep gratitude to Ojai, whose citizens do prioritize caring and support for our children and youth, building community, and living in respect and tolerance. I must specifically thank my Taormina and Krotona neighbors (I am so blessed to live amongst you), especially the "TAPPERS"— Helene Vachet, Trina Grantham, Marqui Bury, Linda Lambert, and Virginia Moyer——and my dear Krotona friends, Joy Mills and Lakshmi Narayan.

Of course I am grateful beyond words for Bonnie Benard and Nancy Sharp-Light. The vision we mutually created a decade ago with the formation of Resiliency In Action, Inc. couldn't have materialized without you both! Living the journey of that vision has enriched my life immeasurably.

Finally, because a second edition is always built on the hard—and in this case pioneering—work of the first edition, I am also including the acknowledgements from the original edition of this book:

Thank you to Emmy Werner, Peter Benson, Steve and Sybil Wolin, Dennis Saleebey, and Glenn Richardson for your encouragement and support, your scholarship and wisdom, and—especially—for having the courage to follow where the research leads. Thank you, too, to Art Bernstein, Debra DeSantis, Tim Duffey, Donna Duffey, Don Henderson, Kelsey Henderson, Janice Janecki, Bill Lofquist, Craig Noonan, Sue Mahoney, Rich Ott, and Peter Seidman for your contributions of time, energy, talent, and advice, and for providing Bonnie, Nancy, and I with much "caring and support." In addition, thanks to Ann and Dennis Holmes, Bob Frances, Brenda Holben, Barbara Keller, Kathy Marshall, Carol Klopp, Michael Lahti, Mary Miller, Betsy Thompson, Sally Shields, Mary Vander-Wall, and all the other subscribers to our early journal, for your pioneering spirit and commitment to walking the talk of Resiliency In Action.

N.H.

GENERATION COMMUNICATIONS:

Ojai teen Paula Pugh, a Generation Communication alumni, designed this book, including the cover.

An Innovative, Resiliency-Building Program for Teens

Teenagers in the Ojai Valley have combined forces to create a resiliency-building teenage community, one that has visibility and power. Individually and as a group, teenagers contribute their talents in every aspect of the nonprofit Generation Communications, a unique media and marketing agency with the purpose of creating social change. Teen participants are involved in the professional endeavors of brainstorming, researching, writing, designing, and implementing public outreach campaigns for nonprofits and government agencies.

The Generation Communication experience creates a powerful, confident community of teens. Participants meet once a week and more often as needed to discuss issues and ideas with each other and work on campaigns. Together, they decide how to address topics ranging from water pollution to anti-tobacco use to low Latino enrollment in four-year universities. They charge and are paid "going rate" prices for their professional quality services.

What the teenagers do at Generation Communications creates real resilience, identifying and solving community problems while learning new, professionally valuable skills and creating a supportive peer community. Generation Communications is a program of the Ojai Valley Youth Foundation, and can be found on the web at www.ovyf.org/gencom.

Bobbi Balderman, Program Director
Generation Communications
A program of the Ojai Valley Youth Foundation
805 640-9555/805 640-7211 (fax)

Generation Communication teens involved in researching and solving community problems.

PREFACE

This book continues our mission, began a decade ago, of challenging a widely accepted myth about people, especially young people, who experience risks, stress, trauma, and adversity in their lives. Contrary to popular opinion, the majority of these individuals do, over time, bounce back from their problems and do well. There is a growing body of scientific research from several fields that documents this fact and yields important information as to what can be done in everyday as well as programmatic interactions to facilitate this process of overcoming.

In 1996, a middle school teacher and two social workers, convinced that the extensive national focus on risks, deficits, and pathologies obscured this truth took one of the biggest risks of their professional lives. With only a few hundred dollars, but a wealth of conviction about the need to publicize and make practical the research findings of the self-righting capacity within all, Nancy Sharp-Light, Bonnie Benard, and I founded what became a pioneering journal on moving youth, families, and communities from risk to resiliency. Little did we realize that within three short years that publication, *Resiliency In Action: Bouncing Back from Risk and Adversity—Ideas for Youth Families, and Communities,* would gain an audience of subscribers in almost every state in the country, as well as in Puerto Rico, Canada, Argentina, Australia, New Zealand, Malaysia, Samoa, Israel, and Portugal.

The first edition of this book was a direct result of the enthusiastic response the journal received. The response to the book was even more enthusiastic than to the journal, so publishing books, as well as providing training, became the focus of Resiliency In Action.

Our goal in starting the journal ten years ago, and in publishing books now, was a simple one: Share the results of the numerous scientific studies that have emerged in the past two decades showing specifically how people of all ages, families, and even organizations and communities overcome risk, trauma, and adversity to go on to life success, and do this in a practical, reader-friendly format. We wanted to make the researchers themselves human through one-to-one interviews that included their heart-to-heart advice as to how to best foster resiliency. We also wanted to spotlight the many individuals and schools and community groups that are integrating the results of this research and finding significant improvements in emotional, behavioral, and academic outcomes. Finally, we wanted to share lives of young people whose personal stories represent the reality of resilient overcoming that is more common than not.

The hopeful information about the capacity for resiliency and how to foster it has been publicized in several other leading publications since we began Resiliency In Action. It has been the cover story in many national magazines in the past decade. Extensive examination of the resiliency framework has also appeared in journals for psychologists, social workers, family therapists, educators, and other youth-serving professionals during this time. In 1998, Martin Seligman, Ph.D., a resiliency researcher and then President of the American Psychological Association, stated that the entire field of psychology is moving away from the deficit approach to a strengths-based model. The Positive Psychology movement now has its own handbooks, manuals, and research grants.

Since the publication of the first edition of this book, the tragic events of 9/11, Hurricane Katrina, and other national and international traumas have pushed the concept of resiliency even more to the forefront of public awareness. Books, magazine articles, and media stories on resiliency have proliferated. I believe, however, the reason for the growing popularity of the resiliency approach to viewing ourselves and others is an increasing awareness best expressed to me by a resilient young man who had spent most of his life in dozens of foster homes enduring tremendous risk, trauma, and adversity. What helped the most, he told me, were those people along the way who gave him the message, "What is right with you is more powerful than anything that is wrong with you."

The truth of this message, which has often been missing in the deficit-based models of the past, is at the heart of the growing embrace of the reality of resiliency and the resiliency approach. Resiliency In Action is dedicated to showing how to recognize, nurture, and utilize the "power of what is right" to transform the lives of children and youth, families, and communities. My goal, stronger than ever after 15 years of studying and communicating this approach, is that readers will not only resonate with the truth of resiliency but will also use the research, strategies, and stories in this book as a springboard to increase resiliency in their lives and in the lives of those they care about.

One of the best ways to do this, I have been told by numerous educators who have successfully motivated and facilitated resiliency-focused changes in their schools, is to start a book study group. Evidently, even if just a few people get involved, such a group has enormous power to shift culture and practices. I believe similar study groups formed in organizations and agencies would also yield such positive results. This book is uniquely suited for change-promoting study groups in that it contains three aspects of learning usually segregated: well-documented reports on the research base of resiliency, examples of "best practices" of implementing resiliency, and individual stories of resilient overcoming. My hope is that readers of this book will join with others and explore together how the ideas, practices, and stories here can further fostering resiliency within themselves, their families, schools, organizations, and the larger culture.

Nan Henderson
Ojai, CA
October, 2006

FOREWORD

As life zips by too quickly, I have decided to set certain boundaries about time. One of them is to seek to connect with people, places, and ideas dedicated to transformation. The transformation I care the most about is deep change in how American culture—through its systems, rituals, symbols, and norms—embraces and promotes the healthy development of all children and adolescents.

Such transformation will require a massive flow of human energy and spirit directed to naming and growing the inherent strengths found in each human life and unleashing the capacity of individuals, organizations, and institutions to create places and settings of support and growth. The change process begins with a transformation in human consciousness and understanding.

Resiliency is one of those consciousness-changing ideas. Grounded in decades of research and practice, the concept of resiliency causes us to think differently. With its accents on the processes of human development, the internal and external forces that promote positive growth, and conceptual and practical dimensions of change-making, resiliency becomes a way of thinking and being which changes lives. Accordingly, it is about hope and possibility.

Resiliency in Action: Practical Ideas for Overcoming Risks and Building Strengths makes this growing body of knowledge and understanding more accessible. And it does so by creating a wonderful balance of theory and practice, of head and heart. It is a unique and important compilation of core material, drawing on the work of major thinkers, writers, and practitioners. That it does so is really a testament to the quality of the Resiliency In Action journal from which [many of] these articles were gleaned.

This work and the ideas it conveys should be consumed and discussed by many—not just by the professionals who work with young people in schools, congregations, youth organizations, and agencies, but also by those who carry no formal portfolio for human development. For it may be that it is the people of our communities who have the most capacity to trigger and sustain the transformation we need.

Peter L. Benson, Ph.D.
President
Search Institute
Minneapolis, MN

CONTENTS

CONTENTS

PART ONE

THE FOUNDATIONS OF RESILIENCY

CHAPTER 1

The Foundations of the Resiliency Paradigm

by Bonnie Benard, M.S.W.

Editor's Note: Bonnie Benard was one of the three cofounders of Resiliency In Action in 1996. Years earlier, she wrote the seminal paper, "Fostering Resiliency In Kids: Protective Factors In Families, Schools, and Communities." That publication, which I encountered in 1991 before I knew Bonnie personally, changed my personal and professional life more than any other single publication I have ever read. Indeed, Bonnie Benard is an example of the power of one person—in this case a social worker "who also wanted to be a librarian" as she once told me—to change the world. Countless individuals have not only been inspired by Bonnie's research and writing, but have changed their practice with their students, young mentees and clients, and their own children, based on her writing and trainings.

More than any other single individual, I believe it is Bonnie who is responsible for the crucially important shift to viewing children and youth not as a conglomerate of risks and problems but as transcendent beings with an amazing capacity for resiliency. In recent years, it has been my great privilege to count Bonnie as a colleague; but most of all, she has been for me a life-changing mentor teaching a new way of seeing and being. And as I often tell others, I also believe Bonnie has read more resiliency studies than any other human being! The following is an updated version of her article by the same title that appeared in the first edition of Resiliency In Action. *This update incorporates much of the first chapter of her 2004 book published by WestEd,* Resiliency: What We Have Learned—*N.H.*

In the strictest sense, resiliency research refers to a body of international cross-cultural, lifespan developmental studies that followed children born into traumatic conditions such as families where parents were mentally ill, alcoholic, abusive, or criminal, or in communities that were poverty-stricken or war-torn. The astounding finding from these long term studies was that at least 50%—and often closer to 70%—of youth growing up in these "high risk" conditions did develop social competence despite exposure to severe stress and did overcome the odds to lead successful lives. In most studies, the figure seems to average 70 to 75 percent.

These studies include children who were placed in foster care (Festinger, 1984), were members of gangs (Vigil, 1990), were born to teen mothers (Furstenberg et al., 1998), were sexually abused (Higgins, 1994; Wilkes, 2002; Zigler & Hall, 1989), had substance-abusing or mentally ill families (Beardslee & Podoresfky, 1988; Chess, 1989; Watt et al., 1984; Werner, 1986, Werner & Smith, 2001), and grew up in poverty (Clausen, 1993; Schweinhart et al., 1993; Vaillant, 2002). In absolute worst case scenarios, when children experienced multiple and persistent risks, still half of them overcame adversity and achieved good developmental outcomes (Rutter, 1987, 2000). Furthermore, these studies not only identify the characteristics of these "resilient" youth, several documented the characteristics of the environments—of the families, schools, and communities—that facilitated the manifestation of resilience.

Resiliency Capacities

At the most fundamental level, resiliency research validates prior research and theory in human development that has clearly established the biological imperative for growth and development that exists in the human organism—that is part of our genetic makeup—which unfolds naturally in the presence of certain environmental attributes. We are all born with innate resiliency, with the capacity to develop the traits commonly found in resilient survivors: social competence (responsiveness, cultural flexibility, empathy, caring, communication skills, and a sense of humor); problem-solving (planning, help-seeking, critical and creative thinking); autonomy (sense of identity, self-efficacy, self-awareness, task-mastery, and adaptive distancing from negative messages and conditions); and a sense of purpose and belief in a bright future (goal direction, educational aspirations, optimism, faith, and spiritual connectedness) (Benard, 1991). The major point here is that resilience is not a genetic trait that only a few "superkids" possess, as some journalistic accounts (and even several researchers!) would have us believe. Rather, it is our inborn capacity for self-righting (Werner & Smith, 1992) and for transformation and change (Lifton, 1993).

Environmental Protective Factors

Resiliency research, supported by research on child development, family dynamics, school effectiveness, community development, and ethnographic studies capturing the voices of youth themselves, clearly documents the characteristics of family, school, and community environments that elicit and foster the natural resiliency in children. These characteristics are termed "protective factors," and appear to alter—or even reverse—potential negative outcomes and enable individuals to transform adversity and develop resilience despite risk.

Findings of resiliency research confound a core belief of many risk-focused social scientists--that risk factors for the most part predict negative outcomes. Instead, resiliency research suggests that risk factors are predictive for only about 20 to 49 percent of a given high-risk population (Rutter, 1987, 2000; Werner, 2001). In contract, "protective factors," the supports and opportunities that buffer the effect of adversity and enable development to proceed, appear to predict positive outcomes in anywhere from 50 to 80 percent of a high-risk population.

> "Despite years of promising resiliency research, popular myths about early adversity prevail. "

According to the seminal study of risk and resilience by Werner and Smith, which followed nearly 700 children born in 1955 with risk factors at birth and throughout their development, those children with risk factors grew increasingly like their peers without risk factors as the cohort of children aged. Werner and Smith report, "One of the most striking findings of our [research] was that most of the high-risk youths had staged a recovery by the time they reached midlife…They were in stable marriages and jobs, were satisfied with their relationships with their spouses and teenage children, and were responsible citizens In their community" (2001, p.167). In fact by the time the cohort reached aged 32, only one out of six of the most "high risk" group in the cohort (those born with an average of four risk factors at birth) was still doing poorly. Werner and Smith comment on the "profound" power of protective factors.

> Our findings and those by other American and European Investigators with a life-span perspective suggest that these buffers (i.e., protective factors) make a more profound impact on the life course of children who grow up under adverse conditions than do specific risk factors of stressful life events. They [also] appear to transcend ethnic, social class, geographical, and historical boundaries. Most of all, they offer us a more optimistic outlook than the perspective that can be gleaned from

the literature on the negative consequences of perinatal trauma, caregiving deficits, and chronic poverty. (1996, p. 202)

The Resilient Brain

Despite years of promising resiliency research, popular myths about early adversity prevail. Ironically, the successful public relations campaign to highlight the importance of the first three years of life misrepresents some of the brain science that was its inspiration. Lost in the media blitz are the findings over this past decade pointing to the plasticity of the human brain (Bruer, 1999; Diamond & Hopson, 1998; Eriksson et al., 1998; Kagan, 1998). (See section seven of this book, Resiliency and the Brain.) As Goleman notes in his discussion of the "protean brain," the "finding that the brain and nervous system generate new cells as learning or repeated experiences dictate has put the theme of *plasticity* [emphasis added] at the front and center of neuroscience (2003, p. 334). Unfortunately, what the public has been left with instead, warns developmental psychologist Kagan, is the "seductive" notion of "infant determinism" (1998). But as Werner and Smith explain, "[Resilience studies] provide us with a corrective lens—an awareness of the self-righting tendencies that move children toward normal adult development under all but the most persistent adverse circumstances" (1992, p. 202).

Resiliency research clearly provides the prevention, education, and youth development fields with nothing less than a fundamentally different knowledge base and paradigm for research and practice, one offering the promise of transforming interventions in the human arena. It situates risk in the broader social context of racism, war, and poverty—not in individuals, families, and communities—and asks how it is that youth successfully develop in the face of such stressors. It provides a powerful rationale for moving our narrow focus in the social and behavioral sciences from a risk, deficit, and pathology focus to an examination of the strengths youths, their families, their schools, and their communities have brought to bear in promoting healing and health.

The examination of these strengths and the acknowledgment that everyone has strengths and the capacity for transformation gives the prevention, education, and youth development fields not only a clear sense of direction—informing us about "what works!"—but also mandates we move beyond our obsession with risk identification, a statistically weaker practice that has harmfully labeled and stigmatized youth, their families, and their communities. "At risk" and "high risk" labeling is a practice that perpetuates stereotyping, classism, and racism. Most importantly, the knowledge that everyone has innate resilience grounds practice in optimism and possibility, essential components in building motivation. Not only does this prevent the burnout of practitioners working with seriously troubled youth but it provides one of the major protective factors—positive expectations—that when internalized by youth motivate and enable them to overcome risks and adversity.

Focus on Human Development

Resiliency research also offers the prevention, education, and youth development fields solid research evidence for placing human development at the center of everything we do. "Studies of resilience suggest that nature has provided powerful protective mechanisms for human development" (Maston, 1994) that "appear to transcend ethnic, social class, geographical, and historical boundaries" (Werner & Smith, 1992). This is precisely because they address our common, shared humanity. They meet our basic human needs for love and connectedness; for respect, challenge, and structure; and for meaningful involvement, belonging, power, and, ultimately, meaning.

The development of resilience is none other than the process of healthy human development—a dynamic process in which personality and environmental influences interact in a reciprocal, transactional relationship. Resiliency research validates prior theoretical models of human development, including those of Erik Erikson, Urie Bronfenbrenner, Jean Piaget, Lawrence Kohlberg, Carol Gilligan, Rudolf Steiner, Abraham Maslow, and Joseph Chilton Pierce. While focused on different components of human development—psycho/social, moral, spiritual, and cognitive—at the core of each of these approaches is an assumption of the biological imperative for growth and development (i.e., the self-righting nature of the human organism) which unfolds naturally in the presence of certain environmental attributes. Stated simply by Maston, "When adversity is relieved and basic human needs are restored, then resilience has a chance to emerge" (1994).

The major implication from resiliency research for practice is that if we hope to create socially competent people who have a sense of their own identity and efficacy,

> *"Our task is to look at the whole fabric of our society and say, 'Where and how can children be lodged in this society? Where can we find a stable psychological home for children where people will pay attention to them?'"*

who are able to make decisions, set goals, and believe in their future, then meeting their basic human needs for caring, connectedness, respect, challenge, power, and meaning must be the primary focus of any prevention, education, and youth development effort.

Emphasis on Process—Not Program!

Resiliency research has clearly shown that fostering resilience, i.e., promoting human development, is a process and not a program. In fact, Rutter encourages the use of the term protective processes which captures the dynamic nature of resilience instead of the commonly used protective factors: "The search is not for broadly defined factors but, rather, for the developmental and situational mechanisms involved in protective processes" (1987). Resiliency research thus promises to move the prevention, education, and youth development fields beyond their focus on program and what we do, to an emphasis on process and how we do what we do; to move beyond our fixation with content to a focus on context. The fostering of resilience operates at a deep structural, systemic, human level: at the level of relationships, beliefs, and opportunities for participation and power that are a part of every interaction, every intervention no matter what the focus. As McLaughlin (1994) and her colleagues found in their extensive study of inner-city youth-serving neighborhood organizations, the organizations that engaged youth and facilitated their successful development had total diversity in program focus and content, organizational structure, and physical environment. What they shared was an emphasis on meeting the needs of the youth—over programmatic concerns—a belief in the potential of each youth, a focus on listening, and providing opportunities for real responsibility and real work.

These researchers state, "We questioned the assumption that what works has to be a particular program. Our research shows that a variety of neighborhood-based programs work as long as there is an interaction between the program and its youth that results in those youths treating the program as a personal resource and a bridge to a hopeful future" (1994). Schorr's earlier exploration of successful prevention programs came to similar conclusions: Child-centered programs based on the establishment of mutual relationships of care, respect, and trust between clients and professionals were the critical components in program effectiveness (1988).

Summary

The voices of those who have overcome adversity—be they in longitudinal studies or some of the more recent ethnographic explorations—tell us loud and clear that ultimately resilience is a process of connectedness, of linking to people, to interests, and ultimately to life itself. Rutter states that, "Development is a question of linkages that happen within you as a person and also in the environment in which you live. Our hope lies in doing something to alter these linkages, to see that kids who start in a bad environment don't go on having bad environments and develop a sense of impotency" (Pines, 1984). Similarly, James Coleman claims the most fundamental task for parents, educators, and policy makers is linking children into our social fabric.

Our task is "to look at the whole fabric of our society and say, 'Where and how can children be lodged in this society? Where can we find a stable psychological home for children where people will pay attention to them?'" (Olson, 1987). Resiliency research shows the field that the blueprint for building this sense of home and place in the cosmos lies in relationships. To Werner and Smith, effective interventions must reinforce within every arena, the natural social bonds—between young and old, between siblings, between friends—"that give meaning to one's life and a reason for commitment and caring" (1982).

Ultimately, research on resilience challenges the field to build this connectedness, this sense of belonging, by transforming our families, schools, and communities to become "psychological homes" wherein youth can find mutually caring and respectful relationships and opportunities for meaningful involvement. Ex-gang member Tito sums up most insightfully the message of resiliency research: "Kids can walk around trouble, if there is some place to walk to, and someone to walk with" (McLaughlin et al., 1994).

To create these places and to be that "someone," we must, first and foremost, support our own resilience. Building community and creating belonging for youth means we must also do this for ourselves. As Sergiovanni writes, "The need for community is universal. A sense of belonging, of continuity, of being connected to others and to ideas and values that make ourselves meaningful and significant—these needs are shared by all of us" (1993). We, too, need the protective factors of caring and respectful relationships and opportunities to make decisions; without these, we cannot create them for youth.

We see learning as primarily a process of modeling; thus walking our talk is a basic operating principle of resilience work. We acknowledge this is a major challenge for educators and youth workers given we live in a society that doesn't place a high priority on children and youth nor on meeting the basic human needs of its people. This makes our work as caregivers of youth not only a challenge but a vital necessity.

Fostering resilience also requires working on the policy level for educational, social, and economic justice. As clear as it has become that all young people, indeed people of all ages, have the capacity for positive development, resiliency research should never be used to justify social and political inaction on the grounds that, *somehow*, "Most kids make it." In the face of growing global poverty, abuse, violence, and other threats to children's development, the *somehow* can no longer depend on the luck of the draw. Increasingly, healthy youth development must depend on deliberate policies, practices, and interventions designed to provide young people with developmental supports and opportunities. As we are learning, young people are resilient, but they are not invincible.

Our greatest hope for a better future lies with our youth and begins with our belief in them. We must know that when we create communities with youth that respect and care for them as individuals and invite their participation we are creating the conditions that allow their innate potential for social competence, problem-solving, sense of positive identify and self-efficacy to unfold. And, in the process, we are building a critical mass of future citizens who will, indeed, create a social covenant grounded in social and economic justice, rich with the factors that facilitate resilience for all.

> *"Young people are resilient, but they are not invincible."*

References

Beardslee, W. & Podoresfky, D. (1988). Resilient adolescents whose parents have serious affective and other psychiatric disorders: The importance of self-understanding and relationships. *American Journal of Psychiatry, 145*, 63-69.

Benard, B. (1991). *Fostering resiliency in kids: Protective factors in the family, school, and community*. Portland, OR: Western Center for Drug-Free Schools and Communities.

Benard, B. (2004). *Resiliency: What we have learned*. San Francisco: WestEd.

Bruer, J. (1999). *The myth of the first three years*. New York: The Free Press.

Chess, S. (1989). Defying the voice of doom. In T. Dugan & R. Coles (Eds.), *The child in our time: Studies in the development of resiliency* (pp. 179-199). New York: Bruner/Mazel.

Clausen, J. (1993). *American live: Looking back at the children of the great depression*. New York: Free Press.

Diamond, M. & Hopson, J. (1998). *Magic trees of the mind: How to nurture your child's intelligence, creativity, and healthy emotions from birth through adolescence*. New York: Dutton.

Eriksson, P., Perfilieval. E., Bjork-Eriksson, T., Alborn, A., Norborg, C., Peterson, D.A., & Gage, F.H. (1998). Neurogenesis in the adult human hippocampus. *Nature Medicine, 4,* 1313-1317.

Festinger, T. (1984). *No one ever asked me: A postscript to the foster care system*. New York: Columbia University Press.

Furstenberg, F., Cook, T., Eccles, J., Elder, G., & Sameroff, A. (1998). *Managing to make it: Urban families and adolescent success*. Chicago: University of Chicago Press.

Higgins, G. (1994). *Resilient adults: Overcoming a cruel past*. San Francisco: Jossey-Bass.

Kagan, J. (1998). *The seductive ideas*. Cambridge, MA: Harvard University Press.

Lifton, R. J. (1993). *The protean self: Human resilience in an age of transformation*. New York, NY: Basic Books.

Maston, A. (1994). Resilience in individual development: Successful adaptation despite risk and adversity. In Wang, M. & Gordon, E. (Eds.), *Educational resilience in inner-city America: Challenges and prospects*. Hillsdale, NJ: Lawrence Erlbaum Associates.

McLaughlin, M., Irby, M. & Langman, J. (1994). *Urban sanctuaries: Neighborhood organizations in the lives and futures of inner-city youth*. San Francisco, CA: Jossey-Bass.

Olson, L. (1987). A prominent boat rocker rejoins the fray. *Education Week, January 14,* 14-17.

Pines, M. (1984). Resilient children: Why some disadvantaged children overcome their environments, and how we can help. *Psychology Today, March.*

Rutter, M. (1987). Psychosocial resilience and protective mechanisms. *American Journal of Orthopsychiatry 57,* 316-331.

Rutter, M. (2000). Resilience reconsidered: Conceptual considerations, empirical findings and policy implications. In Shonkoff, J.P., & Meisels, S.J. (Eds.), *Handbook of early childhood intervention* (2nd ed.), (pp. 651-682.) New York: Cambridge University Press.

Schorr, L. (1988). *Within our reach: Breaking the cycle of disadvantage*. New York, NY: Doubleday.

Schweinhart, L., Barnes, H., & Wiekart, D. (1993). *Significant benefits: The High/Scope Perry Preschool study through age 27*. Ypsilanti, MI: High/Scope Press.

Vaillant, G. (2002). *Aging well: Surprising guideposts to a happier life from the landmark harvard study of adult development*. Boston: Little, Brown, and Company.

Sergiovanni, T. (1993). *Building community in schools*. San Francisco, CA: Jossey-Bass.

Vigil, J.D. (1990). Cholos and gangs: Culture change and street youth in Los Angeles. In R. Huff (Ed.), *Gangs in America: Diffusion, diversity, and public policy* (pp.146-162). Thousand Oaks, CA: Sage.

Watt, N., Anthony, E., Wynne, L., & Rolf, J. (Eds.). (1984). *Children at risk for schizophrenia: A longitudinal perspective*. New York: Cambridge University Press.

Wilkes, G. (2002). Abused child to nonabusive parent: Resilience and conceptual change. *Journal of Clinical Psychology, 58,* 261-278.

Werner, E. (1986). Resilient offspring of alcoholics: A longitudinal study from birth to 18. *Journal of Studies on Alcohol 14,* 34-40.

Werner, E. & Smith, R. (1982, 1989). *Vulnerable but invincible: A longitudinal study of resilient children and youth*. New York, NY: Adams, Bannister, and Cox.

Werner, E. & Smith, R. (1992). *Overcoming the odds: High-risk children from birth to adulthood*. New York, NY: Cornell University Press.

Werner, E. & Smith, R. (2001). *Journeys from childhood to midlife: Risk, resilience, and recovery*. New York: Cornell University Press.

Zigler, E. & Hall, N. (1989). Physical child abuse in America: Past, present, and future. In D. Cichetti & V. Carlson (Eds.), *Child maltreatment: Theory and research on the causes and consequences of child abuse and neglect,* (pp. 38 - 75). New York: Cambridge

Bonnie Benard, M.S.W., has written widely and conducted workshops and trainings on resiliency for nearly 20 years. She currently works in the Health and Human Development Program of WestEd 's Oakland, CA office, where she has helped develop a statewide survey of students' perceptions of the protective factors in their lives (www.wested.org/hks). She can be reached by email at bbenard@wested.org.

CHAPTER 2

Hard-Wired to Bounce Back

by Nan Henderson, M.S.W.

Researchers are documenting an innate "self-righting tendency" that exists in everyone. How can you use their findings to help yourself and help others be more resilient?
(This article is adapted from one of the same title published in the 2003 Prevention Researcher*)*

Can individuals learn to be more resilient, or are some just born with the ability to bounce back from adversity? Both, according to researchers, whose work suggests that human beings are born with an innate self-righting ability, which can be helped or hindered. Their findings are fueling a major shift in thinking about human development: from obsessing about problems and weaknesses to recognizing "the power of the positive"–identifying and building individual and environmental strengths that help people to overcome difficulties, achieve happiness, and attain life success.

After 15 years of studying and reflecting upon the myriad studies on human resiliency, dialoguing with thousands of people of all ages about the topic, and writing extensively about resiliency, I have come to believe that individuals are hard-wired to bounce back from adversity. I also believe everyone can expand this innate capacity for resiliency within themselves and others. People bounce back in two ways: They draw upon their own internal resources, and they encounter people, organizations, and activities that provide them with the conditions that help the emergence of their resilience. Psychologists call these internal and external conditions "protective factors" and conclude, "these buffers" are more powerful in a person's life than risks or traumas or stress. They fuel the movement towards healthy development.

I have identified four basic characteristics of resiliency building that add the power of "protective factors" to people's lives. I have observed that the most successful educators and counselors, the best parenting, and the companies identified as "the best places to work in America" utilize these approaches. They are also the best "self-help" strategies and can be used to overcome the loss of a loved one or a job, cope with a major illness, or successfully navigate the challenges of raising children.

Some resiliency researchers theorize that these conditions are actually basic human needs across the life span, that from birth to death everyone does better in environments that embody them.

1. Communicate "The Resiliency Attitude." The first "protective" strategy is communicating the attitude, "You have what it takes to get through this!" in words and deeds. I interviewed a young man a few years ago who had lived a painful life full of loss and abuse. Most of his adolescence was spent in one foster home after another. He told me that what helped him the most in attaining his own resilient outcome were the people along the way that told him, "What is right with you is more powerful than anything that is wrong."

In my trainings, people tell me that this is difficult to do. For example, a child who is skipping class and responding with anger and belligerence to any offer of help, presents a typical paradox: At the very same time a person is weighed down with problems in one area of life, he or she also has strengths somewhere else–times when obstacles have been overcome in the past; talents or skills or passions that can be focused on and developed in the present. The challenge is to both be aware of the problems and to draw upon the strengths of the person to help solve them, as well as to sincerely communicate the belief that the current problems can be successfully overcome.

2. Adopt a "Strengths Perspective." "The keystone of high achievement and happiness is exercising your strengths," rather than focusing on weaknesses, concludes resiliency researcher Seligman (2001), past president of the American Psychological Association. I recently asked a group of teenagers and adults to identify their strengths. Both ages were at a loss–neither group could name strengths, and both were hesitant to share out loud even tentative ideas about what their strengths might be. So I asked the group to identify a challenge or problem they had recently overcome in their lives.

The kids talked about having to move to another school, the death of grandparents, their parents' divorce, struggling with difficult subjects in school, being rejected by a club or social group or sports team. The adults talked about changing jobs, leaving bad relationships, stopping smoking, losing weight, and losses of friends and family, as well.

Next I asked, "List what within yourself or outside yourself helped you overcome these problems and losses." I had the group compare their lists to a list of individual strengths researchers have found are particularly useful in overcoming adversity, individual protective factors that I call "personal resiliency builders." (See list below.) Almost everyone saw that they had used two or three–or more–of these in the recent past, such things as drawing upon positive personal relationships in their lives, their sense of humor, or their spiritual faith. "How can you use these same strengths in successfully dealing with current problems in your lives?" I asked the group.

A school counselor told me recently how she applied this approach. A high school student was referred to the counselor because the girl was failing two subjects, math and science. Normally, the counselor told me, she would immediately confront the student with the problem–in this case two failing grades–after making some brief small talk. Instead, after the small talk, she opened her session with this question: "Sandy, I have learned a little about your life. Tell me, how have you *managed to do as well as you have done*?" Sandy, the counselor told me, immediately burst into tears. "Never in all my years has anyone acknowledged what it has taken just to get to school," she said. Most of the rest of the session was spent identifying all the strengths and supports Sandy had used to "do as well as she had done." Toward the end of the session, the counselor said, "Let's talk about how you can use all these things to bring your grades up in math and science."

3. Surround Each Person—as well as Families and Organizations—with all elements of "The Resiliency Wheel."

I first developed the model of The Resiliency Wheel in 1996. It is a synthesis of the environmental protective conditions that research indicates everyone can benefit from having in their lives. I realized that these six elements of environmental protection are also extremely useful in assisting families and even organizations bounce back from adversity. In the past decade, The Resiliency Wheel has been adopted as the primary organizational rubric for help-

THE RESILIENCY WHEEL

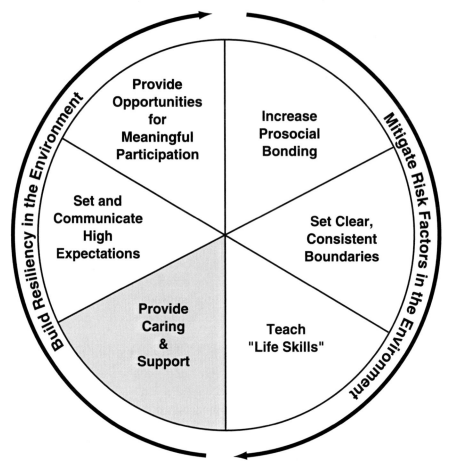

ing children, youth, adults, and families by numerous local, regional, and state agencies.

- **Provide Care and Support**. Ask yourself or assess for others, "What would be very nurturing right now?" "How can I best show compassion to myself or the person I am trying to help?" Often simply finding or providing a good listening ear is extremely resiliency-building. So is uplifting music, time in nature, or reading an inspiring book. Providing oneself and others with unconditional positive regard, love, and encouragement is the most powerful external resiliency-builder.

- **Set High, but Realistic, Expectations for Success**. Effectively using this strategy involves identifying and supporting steps in the right direction rather than demanding instant perfection. One middle school I worked with changed its "Honor Roll" program to an "On A Roll" program. In order to be recognized as "On A Roll" students need only raise their grades one letter. Everyone who does this is rewarded as "on a roll." A couple of the teachers in this school confided to me, "We were amazed at how many of our gangsters decided to participate!" Their comment reinforced the resiliency finding that people have within them, as resiliency researchers Werner and Smith (1992) state, "an innate self-righting tendency that moves them towards normal human development." It also shows the power of recognizing and rewarding small steps of progress.

- **Provide Opportunities for "Meaningful Contribution" to Others**. Paradoxically, one of the best ways to bounce back from personal problems is help someone else with theirs. Traumatized kids, for example, who are offered opportunities to be of genuine help to others who need it are often most helped themselves through this opportunity. A foster parent told me after one of my presentations that giving the boys in his care the opportunity to serve disabled vets at the local community veterans' center did more for the boys than any other strategy he'd tried to help them. Suddenly, these boys were in a new, and very healing, role. They were now resources, rather than problems. This strategy, he said, was life changing.

  In the wake of the 9/11 tragedies, a consistent message of psychologists interviewed about how to get through that time was, "Make a positive contribution in some way. Give whatever you have to give."

- **Increase Positive Bonds and Connections**. People who are positively bonded to other people (through a network of friends and family and/or clubs or organizations) and to enjoyable activities do better in life. This fact has been documented extensively by psychological and medical research. Reaching out to connect with someone, some group, or some activity that is positive is another strategy to successfully cope with adversity. In fact, several arenas of research are documenting that people who have more social connection and participate in enjoyable hobbies/activities lead physically and mentally healthier lives. As Ornish (2005) wrote:

  > Love and intimacy are at the root of what makes us sick and what makes us well. If a new medication had the same impact, failure to prescribe it would be malpractice. Connections with other people affect not only the quality of our lives but also our survival. Study after study find that people who feel lonely are many times more likely to

  get cardiovascular disease than those who have a strong sense of connection and community. I'm not aware of any other factor in medicine—not diet, not smoking, not exercise, not genetics, not drugs, not surgery—that has a greater impact on our quality of life….

- **Set and Maintain Clear Boundaries**. Feeling safe, knowing what to expect, and not being overwhelmed also builds resiliency. This means developing or encouraging in others the ability to say "no" appropriately, to stand up for oneself when necessary, and to provide whatever means are needed to feel a sense of safety. Setting and enforcing clear and consistent "family rules" or school or other organizational policies are part of this process, and are particularly powerful resiliency-builders for children and youth. Anything that increases the feeling of inner security makes it easier to bounce back.

- **Develop Needed Life Skills**. A new life circumstance, a never-before-experienced problem or crisis, a change in a job or a relationship or a familiar role almost always requires new "life skills." Good communication and listening skills, healthy conflict resolution, how to assert oneself appropriately are some of the life skills needed every day. When encountering new adversity, asking, "What life skills that I have can I use here?" or "What new life skills do I need to learn?" is another useful strategy in successfully meeting the challenge.

  When I worked in an adolescent treatment center several years ago, I used to ask drug-abusing young people how they wound up in treatment. The most common response went something like this: "I got to middle school and felt lost. I didn't have any friends. I didn't know how to navigate in this big, strange, impersonal place. So, I did the only thing I saw to do. I went out behind the gym and joined the group there lighting up and drinking. I had an instant group of friends, and my problems kind of went away." In retrospect, the kids admitted this wasn't the best way to handle things, but in the absence of having the relationship and problem-solving skills they needed, it seemed the only option available to them. Kids, and adults, need skills about how to successfully cope with new challenges each stage of our lives brings our way.

  Developing life skills, in fact, is one effective strategy that all prevention programs for youth-including substance abuse prevention, pregnancy prevention, suicide prevention, and school drop-out prevention—agree is crucial.

4. Give It Time. A resilient outcome requires patience. A few years ago, I interviewed Leslie, a young woman then 16 years old who had just finished the ninth grade on her fourth try (see chapter four for Leslie's story)! I asked Leslie how she was able to finally get through ninth grade. Leslie shared with me the two main reasons she had made it: First, her single-parent mom, who refused to give up on her, even during the years she was skipping school, using drugs, and lying. Secondly, the small alternative school her mother had eventually found for her that embodied the four strategies outlined here. "Where would Leslie be if she hadn't had at least one person who stuck with her until she finally got through ninth grade?" I thought. Stories like this one have convinced me not to give up–on myself, on children, on my friends and family going through hard times.

Collectively, these strategies represent the shift from the deficit and weakness approaches to human development prevalent in the past several decades, to what is now being called a "strengths approach." This shift is taking place in education, psychology, other social services, and in the corporate world. Saleeby, editor of *The Strengths Perspective in Social Work Practice* (2001), emphasizes the importance of this shift. "People are most motivated to change when their strengths are supported," he states.

What has transpired since September 11, 2001, including hurricane Katrina and other national disasters, will perhaps hasten this process. A silver lining to these horrific tragedies is the word "resiliency" is now constantly used in the national media. The collective national attention has at least somewhat refocused to also document the amazing goodness of human nature: the courage, the kindness, the generosity, the tenacity that is every much a part of humanity as its weaknesses. If the resiliency researchers are right these strengths, in the long run, are the most powerful. Identifying, celebrating, reinforcing, and nurturing the growth of these positive human traits is the most important skill we can collectively develop to help ourselves and others be more resilient.

Personal Resiliency Builders
Individual Protective Factors that Facilitate Resiliency

Researchers note that each person develops a cluster of three or four of these he or she uses most often in times of difficulty. *You can help yourself or help others become more resilient by reflecting on these questions:*

1. When faced with a crisis or major life difficulty, which of these do you use most often?
2. How can you strengthen your individual "resiliency builders?"
3. Can you use them now in problems you are facing?
4. Is there another one you think would be helpful for you? If so, how can you develop it?

- **Relationships** -- Sociability/ability to be a friend/ability to form positive relationships
- **Service** -- Gives of self in service to others and/or a cause
- **Life Skills** -- Uses life skills, including good decision-making, assertiveness, and impulse control
- **Humor** -- Has a good sense of humor
- **Inner Direction** -- Bases choices/decisions on internal evaluation (internal locus of control)
- **Perceptiveness** -- Insightful understanding of people and situations
- **Independence** -- "Adaptive" distancing from unhealthy people and situations/autonomy
- **Positive View of Personal Future** -- Optimism/expects a positive future
- **Flexibility** -- Can adjust to change; can bend as necessary to positively cope with situations
- **Love of Learning** -- Capacity for and connection to learning
- **Self-motivation** -- Internal initiative and positive motivation from within
- **Competence** -- Is "good at something"/personal competence
- **Self-Worth** -- Feelings of self-worth and self-confidence
- **Spirituality** -- Personal faith in something greater
- **Perseverance** -- Keeps on despite difficulty; doesn't give up
- **Creativity** -- Expresses self through artistic endeavor, or uses creative imagination, thinking, or other processes

Understanding Resiliency: A Glossary

Protective Factors

People overcome adversity through drawing upon their own internal strengths (see box) and through encountering situations in their environments that embody the recommendations described here. These internal and environmental characteristics are called "protective factors" by researchers.

Lifespan Research

Most resiliency studies are based on life span, i.e., longitudinal, research that follows a group of individuals for decades. The most famous of these studies in the US, conducted by psychologists Emmy Werner and Ruth Smith, began in 1955. These researchers continue to this day to study all the children born on the island of Kauai that year. The value of this type of research is that it does more than identify risks or problems. It documents exactly how people bounce back from their risks and problems.

Strengths Approach

Results of resiliency research are fueling a shift in psychology, other helping professions, education, and corporate management. These fields are beginning to focus not just on human weaknesses and problems but on better understanding what helps us bounce back from these problems. The American Psychological Association, under the leadership of the resiliency researcher Martin Seligman, recently established a new branch called Positive Psychology. "What is needed now," Dr. Seligman said in a 1998 speech to the National Press Club, "is the creation of a science of human strengths–how they grow and how you can maximize or minimize them. The best set of buffers we have against substance abuse, against depression, against violence in our children have to do with human strengths,...identifying [them], amplifying [them], nurturing [them], getting [people] to lead their lives around them."

References

Benard, B. (1991). *Fostering resiliency in kids: Protective factors in the family, school, and community.* Portland, OR: Western Regional Center for Drug-Free Schools and Communities.

Benson, P.L., Galbraith, J., & Espeland, P. (1994). *What kids need to succeed: Proven, practical ways to raise good kids.* Minneapolis, MN: Free Spirit Publishing.

Buckingham, M. & Clifton, D. (2001). *Now, discover your strengths.* New York: The Free Press.

Hawkins, J.D., Catalano, R.F., & Miller, J.Y. (1992). Risk and protective factors for alcohol and other drug problems. *Psychological Bulletin, 112* (1), 64-105.

Henderson, N. & Milstein, M.M. (2003). *Resiliency in schools: Making it happen for students and educators* (2nd ed.). Thousand Oaks, CA: Corwin Press.

Henderson, N. (2003). Hard-wired to bounce back. *Prevention Researcher 10,* (1), 5 – 7.

Henderson, N., Benard, B, & Sharp-Light, N. (1999). *Resiliency in action: Practical ideas for overcoming risks and building strengths in youth, families, & communities.* Ojai, CA: Resiliency In Action, Inc.

Higgins, G. (1994). *Resilient adults: Overcoming a cruel past.* San Francisco, CA: Jossey-Bass.

Meier, D. (1995). Small schools, big results. *The American School Board Journal, July 1995*, 37-40.

Noddings, N. (1988). Schools face "crisis in caring." *Education Week, December 7*, p. 32.

Ornish, D. (2005). Love is the real medicine. *Newsweek On-Line Edition, October 5*. Retrieved from: http://www.msnbc.msn.com/id/9466931/site/newsweek.

Richardson, G.E., Neiger, B.L., Jensen, S., & Kumpfer, K.L. (1990). The resiliency model. *Health Education, 21* (6), 33-39.

Seligmann, M. (2001). Book cover commentary. *Now, discover your strengths.* New York: The Free Press.

Saleebey, D. (2001). *The strengths perspective in social work practice* (3rd ed.). New York: Addison-Wesley Longman.

Werner, E. & Smith, R. (1992). *Overcoming the odds: High risk children from birth to adulthood.* NY: Cornell University Press.

Werner, E. (1999). How children become resilient: Observations and cautions. In N. Henderson, B. Benard, & N. Sharp-Light (Eds.), *Resiliency in action: Practical Ideas for overcoming risks and building strengths in youth, families, & communities.* Ojai, CA: Resiliency In Action, Inc.

Wolin, S. & Wolin, S. (1993). *The resilient self: How survivors of troubled families rise above adversity.* NY: Villard Books.

Nan Henderson, M.S.W., is an international speaker, writer, and president of Resiliency In Action, a publishing and training company in Southern CA. She has authored several articles and coauthored four books on fostering resiliency, including Resiliency In Action: Practical Ideas for Overcoming Risks and Building Strengths in Youth, Families, and Communities *and* Resiliency In Schools: Making It Happen for Students and Educators. *She can be contacted at nhenderson@resiliency.com or at by calling 800-440-5171. More information is available at www.resiliency.com.*

CHAPTER 3

How Children Become Resilient: Observations and Cautions

by Emmy Werner, Ph.D.

Editor's Note: Dr. Emmy Werner is Research Professor of Human Development at the University of California, Davis. She is known—in the words of Dr. Norman Garmezy—as "Mother Resilience" for her decades of longitudinal research on the island of Kauai that has provided a foundation for the emerging resiliency paradigm in prevention, intervention, and education, and for her understanding and discussion of the body of resiliency-focused research.

Dr. Werner presented the information below a decade ago at a conference in Albuquerque, New Mexico, sponsored by the Albuquerque Public Schools Team Action for Student Assistance (TASA) and the US Center for Substance Abuse Prevention (CSAP). Excerpts from that presentation (edited by Dr. Werner) comprise this article, in which she offers her observations about what is known about fostering resiliency, what is yet to be learned, and the urgent need for program evaluation to move the concept forward. She also offers advice for practitioners in the field who want to effectively foster resiliency in children and youth. Her message is even more relevant today than when she shared it in Albuquerque.—N.H.

I want to offer a few observations in the light of my experience with a longitudinal study that I have been associated with over the past 30 years. Let me hasten to say I also have worked with other children in "at risk" situations. I spent a lot of time working for UNICEF in Southeast Asia, both during the Vietnamese war, then during the Indian Pakistani War. I've worked in Israel, Egypt, and in East Africa. So my concern with issues of resiliency really has cut across different cultures and ethnic groups, but also different contexts. I want to emphasize today which of those constellation of factors that we first found in our Kauai study we can now say seem to be universal, whether you apply it to children of African American heritage, Asian American heritage, Hispanic heritage, or Native American heritage here in this country, or [to] children in developing countries. Which of these buffers seem to help them even under extraordinarily trying circumstances?

> *"We've got to be really careful whenever we talk about fostering resiliency in our own particular neck of the woods [to] say what it is really that we want to do."*

Before I summarize these factors, I want to say something about the concept of "resilience." As evidenced by this and many other conferences and workshops—and I have to tell you I'm called upon to attend workshops on resilience in the learning disabled, resilience in Alzheimer patients, resilience in children of teen-age mothers—the concept has probably become too popular for it's own sake. Because if something becomes very, very popular, it loses its meaning. I'm not a politician; I'm trying to be a scientist.

We've got to be really careful whenever we talk about fostering resiliency in our own particular neck of the woods [to] say what it is really that we want to do: specifically in this school system, in the primary grades, in Albuquerque [for example], for children from these kinds of backgrounds.

I think the reason why the concept took off was it is so quintessentially American. I see in spite of all the dire newspaper headlines this wonderful optimism of this country that forever and ever and ever is hoping to live up to the Horatio Algiers stories. Maybe some of you have heard of them. Way back in the nineteenth century the theme was: "Go West young man, and you'll make it." I'm not saying that we shouldn't help children make it, whatever that "it" is. But we need to be specific about objectives. It bears remembering that the research base that undergirds your attempts at doing something for these children is based mostly on studies of children who did it themselves, with some informal help by kith and kin.

A Caution About Putting Children "in Boxes"

There are actually relatively few long-term longitudinal studies of "resilient" individuals. Most studies of resiliency focus on a couple of years, mostly in middle childhood or in adolescence. We need to look and see what researchers found in the first place. They found that there was an interplay of individual, environmental, and situational factors. It wasn't just that the children behavioral scientists studied were empty boxes into which someone poured "resiliency." First we used the term—and we still do—"at risk" or "high risk" children to describe youngsters with the odds against them. I always [got] this uncomfortable feeling that a child who was considered "at risk" was a nice little box in our diagnostic manuals or in our behavioral evaluations. Then, once we had him or her classified, we knew what we knew. Then we could check him or her up and that was it. Right? Some of you must have had that experience.

My sense has been that certainly all of you who are concerned with "at risk" children have hoped to get these kids out of those boxes and to look at their strengths instead. But in that process—I just want to put in a little warning—make sure that you don't get boxed in again and say "if they attend this workshop or if they've been in the system for three years in a program called 'Fostering Resiliency' we automatically shift them from 'at risk' to 'resilient'." They attended the program or their trainers went for so many hours learning how to teach life skills, so they must be resilient now, by definition.

We tend to get into this new box maybe too frequently, with our enthusiasm now about this concept. Because certainly if we look at studies, and especially in our study [done] over a long time, we find that "resiliency" is not something fixed, concrete. The very definition, which comes from engineering, has to do with bouncing back, right? If it was fixed, a bridge would collapse in an earthquake or hurricane. It's the going back and forth from vulnerability to resiliency that's actually the essence of the phenomenon. Look it up in Webster's dictionary! So, just a little note of warning: Let's not get boxed in again and suddenly call everyone "resilient" when they may be today as a child in a certain context, and they may not be ten years later, and then they may become again resilient in adulthood. But my words of caution should not dampen your enthusiasm!

> *"Let's not get boxed in again and suddenly call everyone 'resilient' when they may be today as a child in a certain context, and they may not be ten years later, and then they may become again resilient in adulthood."*

The Kauai Longitudinal Study

So what we have learned—you may want to look at the last one of the four books [we have written] on the children of Kauai, *Overcoming the Odds: High Risk Children from Birth to Adulthood*—is based on a group of children that represent a great number of different ethnic groups. Some certainly would be considered offspring of what you here in the Southwest or the Canadians call "First Nations" because the Hawaiians really were there in the first place, just like the Navajo and the Pueblo Indians were here in the first place before other immigrants came to settle. We have a fairly large proportion of [these] children and also children whose parents intermarried with the newcomers like the Japanese, Chinese, Filipino, and Portuguese. And we have

a fairly wide range of socioeconomic classes in our study. But more than half of the children have grown up in very restricted circumstances, if you just judge by where they came from: They were born and [were] reared in chronic poverty. They had parents who did not graduate from high school. Many parents had less than eight grades of education. Many had parents who had either physical handicaps or signs of psychopathology, including substance abuse. And the children themselves that were "high risk" oftentimes also had birth complications and suffered from perinatal stress. The presence of four or more such risk factors made us judge these children to be at especially "high risk" when we started our study at birth.

We looked at about 700 people over time for more than three decades; about one-third had grown up in this "high risk" context. When we first reported these findings, I thought there was something unusual with our findings because we were working in an exotic island. [It] may look good to you when you come to visit and you stay in hotels; [it] does not look good when you live there. Even today, the average income on Kauai is somewhere [around] $11,000, which I think, in California at least, qualifies for poverty level.

After we reported our findings, pretty soon other researchers who looked at cohorts (cohort means a whole group of people all born together at a certain time, [no one] selected out) of children in many communities in the United States [found] much the same—that about one-third or so, mostly in urban areas, but also in rural areas, were "at risk" because of those background factors [of] chronic poverty, poor parental educational level, and other issues, especially parental substance abuse and psychopathology.

Limits to "Fostering Resiliency"

I spent a quarter at the Kavolinska Institute in Stockholm this fall. I thought the Swedes who do everything for their children would have a much lower proportion of what we call "at risk" children. Then, I was interviewed by someone from the major Swedish newspaper and he asked right at the beginning, "What should we Swedes do about the one-third of our Swedes that we have written off?" And I said, "What? You've written them off? You who provide prenatal care free, postnatal care free, free housing, free subsidized day care, two years paid parental leave for both parents. You've written off one-third of all the Swedes?"

This is something we need to ponder, folks. Countries that have tried very hard to commit themselves to caring for their children from birth on by tremendous expenditures of taxpayers' money as the Swedes and the Danes do, when you look over time you still find that one out of three in a given community in these countries today is considered as "high risk"—mostly because of antisocial behavior, substance abuse, or mental illness. It means there may just be certain limits to what we can accomplish to foster resiliency against such odds. That doesn't mean we should stop trying. The Swedes and the Danes have much lower infant mortality rates than we have. They have much lower prematurity and low birth weight rates than we do. They have much less morbidity and mortality among preschool children. So in consequence they must have cut down on the number of children who might be hyperactive or might have a learning disability, right? They succeeded there. They have a longer life span than we have. So they must be doing something right about health. But even these countries, after two generations

> **"There may just be certain limits to what we can accomplish to foster resiliency …. That doesn't mean we should stop trying."**

of solid commitment to supporting their children and their grown-ups too—from the cradle to the grave—we find that there is a residue in their community of people whom they consider "at risk."

Believing that we can push everyone into being the "perfect" person, that may just be a little bit too much. The Navajo in your state I am told weave one little error in the rugs they make because they do not want to be considered gods. Only gods are perfect. We have to watch that our attempt at fostering resiliency isn't becoming an enterprise that might later just disappoint us a little bit because we're putting our promises so high up without quite knowing whether we really will be able to deliver down the whole long road. You may get down a little bit [of] the road but maybe not the whole road. And that's fine. Each step counts.

Protective Factors Transcend Ethnicity

What we know from research (and I ask you to look at Benard's paper) is that protective buffers—the ones I'm going to talk about—appear to transcend ethnic, social class, and geographical boundaries. We can agree that they seem to be helpful to us [as] members of the human race,

no matter what our ethnic background is. We also know that these protective factors appear to make a more profound impact on the life course of individuals who grow up and overcome adversity than do specific risk factors. There are some buffers within the individual, in the extended family, in the community that really do seem to cut across us as humankind, regardless of the stress and strains that we are individually exposed to. So those are the ones that we need to nurture most of all.

> **"Protective factors appear to make a more profound impact on the life course of individuals who grow up and overcome adversity than do specific risk factors."**

One of the first things we learned from studying children quite early—and ours is probably the only study that really started with "children who became resilient in spite of high risks at birth"—is it is easier for children who have an easy temperament and the ability to actively recruit competent adult caregivers to attract support from the extended family, the school, and the community at large. I'm not trying to say shy children or withdrawn children won't ever be successful candidates for any program to foster resiliency. I'm trying to say, and I think we forget this sometimes, that fostering resiliency isn't just putting stuff into an empty box by the teacher, or elder, or whatever else. It's based on countless interactions between the individual child or adolescent or adult and the opportunities [in their] world and the challenges they face.

Individual Differences

People do seem to differ—there's just no if, but, when about it—in their ability to make lemonade out of lemons. I think we sometimes forget this when we talk about programs for fostering resiliency for everyone. Of course, we can do something for everyone. But maybe for some we can do more things faster and in more areas of competency than for others. And that's just something we need to accept. I think we need to keep individual variability in mind all along when we talk about fostering resiliency. The whole concept came really from the idea that there are individual differences in response to risk factors. By the same token, there will be individual differences in response to programs that try to introduce protective factors into their lives. Not [just] our study but others [have shown] that the "at risk" children who seem to come through unscathed by the trouble in their background and are competent, caring, and confident, at a minimum have some skills in communication and problemsolving. We know that. [The children] on Kauai were not especially gifted. But on the average they had at least the sort of skills that didn't make them problem readers, for instance. Most all of the resilient children that have ever been studied had at least competence in reading skills, basic reading skills.

Reading is Essential

You might say, "Well this doesn't sound very dramatic, and this is sort of dreary. Why does she talk about reading? We want resiliency." Right? "We want something that really grabs us. [We] can preach about it." But reading is a skill that is essential to survive and in a sense essential to fostering resiliency in a society like ours that does depend on that written word.

> "Fostering resiliency isn't just putting stuff into an empty box by the teacher... It's based on countless interactions between the individual child ...or adult and the opportunities [in their] world..."

In my home state of California right now, one out of three—this is the magic number again—of children by the fourth grade are already behind in reading. One out of three. So, of course, those are the kids that are the first ones to never say no to experiments with drugs. Those are the ones that slowly but surely by the time they get to be in the fifth or sixth grade are the first to be truant and to do a couple of delinquent acts that may eventually set them on the road to disaster. Those are the ones that may eventually be teenage parents—the few who actually stay on the welfare roles because they don't have that skill. (The majority get off, by the way [as] I will mention in a moment.) We need to keep in mind that cognitive competence is one of the hallmarks of resiliency. So if we want to do something about fostering resiliency, let's remember that reading skills are all-important.

We do find, indeed, that most resilient children over time develop a positive self-confidence. But that comes from some competence. It comes from competence in reading and problem-solving skills. It comes from having a special hobby. It comes from some talent or gift that they can be proud of, that they can [use to] be accepted by their peers, and that can also provide them [with] solace when things fall apart in their home. That is certainly a very important buffer found in many, many studies, including ours.

A lot of emphasis [is placed] on high expectations in trying to foster resiliency. I want to sound a word of caution about high expectations. I would say what the research on resiliency shows is realistically high expectations. There is a difference. We've got to have realistically high expectations. It's like saying, "Black is beautiful. White is beautiful. Native American is beautiful." Yes, it's beautiful to be a human being no matter what your color or creed, but you've got to learn how to read.

> "Reading is a skill that is essential to survive and in a sense essential to fostering resiliency in a society like ours that does depend on that written word."

A Close Bond is Critical

Other buffers that we do know seem to cut across different cultures, creeds, and races: There's no doubt about it, a close bond with a competent, emotionally stable caregiver seems to be essential in the lives of children who overcome great adversities. As we know from studies of resilient children a lot of this nurturing can come from substitute parents, such as grandparents, aunts, uncles, older siblings. I'm sure that this is nothing new to the Native Americans in this group. We, as lonesome Caucasians, have to learn that lesson over again, that really a family and parents need not be just your biological father or mother. There are other folk who can step in, but one of them at least needs to be available and stable. A change of nannies in the most affluent families doesn't help, necessarily, if you have to relearn their names every two weeks or so. A stable, competent person needs to be around at the beginning of your life.

> "Cognitive competence is one of the hallmarks of resiliency."

The other thing that we found in our study that has been replicated (and the reason why scientists are so eager to at least say we need to repeat it once is to see if it was really so) in the Berkeley studies of ego-resilient children is a particular kind of childrearing orientation that appears to promote resiliency a little bit different in boys than girls. I haven't noticed reference to that much in talks and workshops on resiliency. What we found with our mostly Pacific Asian children, and what the people in Berkeley found with mostly Caucasian and African American children, is that resilient boys who overcome great adversities tend to come from households where there [are] structure and rules [and] a male who serves as a model of identification. But, again, it need not be the father. It could be a grandfather. It could be an older brother. It could be an uncle. There is also some encouragement of emotional expressiveness. For the girls, it's almost the flip-flop. The resilient girls tend to come from households that combine an emphasis on risk-taking and independence, with reliable support from the female caregiver. If it's not the mother [then] a grandmother, an aunt, an older sister.

Getting Away from Sex Role Typing

So, what you see at work here is a process of getting away from sex role typing in childrearing. The ones who held up the best over time in great adversities were boys and girls who could be assertive but also nurturant, emotionally expressive, but also willing to take a risk. It is apparently easier to overcome great odds if you have learned early that you don't have to fit into a prescribed role of the dependent female who cries or the macho male who can't cry. It helps to have both of these characteristics. That's something that we continue to observe in our study as we look at these resilient children in adulthood. Now as parents in mid-life, they very much take those same roles. They are nurturant fathers but also assertive fathers. And they are certainly caring mothers, but they're also mothers who want independence and autonomy in their children.

> *"A close bond with a competent, emotionally stable caregiver seems to be essential in the lives of children who overcome great adversities."*

One of the characteristics that we find in our own and a number of other studies that you need to think about when you look at children you want to work with, is how good are they at actively recruiting substitute parents. It really is amazing what individual differences you find among children even in the worst situations. It's amazing the difference you see among [some] young children's ability to reach out and make friends with everyone around the room versus others who shy back and cling only to their mothers. This ability is something I think really needs to be fostered because it was something these children actively practiced not only as toddlers but also in middle childhood and adolescence. In other words, they looked for the people who could give them the help they needed. They didn't passively wait until someone came and said, "I'm going to enroll you in a program that fosters resiliency."

"Giving Something Back" as Children and Adults

The interesting thing we found and they're beginning to find in other studies is that these children, by the time they got to middle childhood, also gave something back. They had learned to give something back to their family or neighborhood. Psychologists, who are good at inventing words, call this "required helpfulness." What they mean is these children really were part of a household, whether an extended family or even just a single parent family, where their input mattered, where they contributed to caring for another sibling, or taking over the household when a mother was incapacitated, or doing something for an elder, a grandparent, an older aunt, to make her life a bit easier. This sort of required helpfulness again seems to be a characteristic that in turn carries over into the adult lives of these children. As adults, no matter how poor they still may be and how busy they may be with the world of work and their own children, they do contribute something to their community as volunteers in church, in school, in their children's sports activities, as Big Brothers and Sisters—you name it.

As you may have seen, we're beginning to incorporate "required helpfulness" into service learning programs. I don't know if they do it here but in California slowly we're teaching kindergartners and first and second and third graders not to always say, "I, I, I," but to do something for other folks. You can do this even if you're five, six, seven years old.

> *"The ones who held up the best over time in great adversities were boys and girls who could be assertive but also nurturant, emotionally expressive, but also willing to take a risk."*

I have a student in my classroom from Ethiopia who at age seven during the civil war took care of four other brothers and sisters and fled with them at night across the Sahara desert to safety, the youngest being one year old. She is now a person who is going to go back to Erithrea, the part that's split from Ethiopia, as a medical doctor. It's people like her who learn this required helpfulness early who usually practice it later on. You don't have to tell them to do it, they [just] do it.

The Importance of Faith

One of the major themes we found [that] has sometimes been shortchanged in scientific studies is that these children had some faith that gave meaning to their lives. When I speak of faith, I don't mean necessarily a narrow denominational faith. We found in our study that regardless of whether you were Catholic, or Lutheran, or mainstream Protestant, or belonged to Jehovah's Witnesses, or were a Latter Day Saint, or practiced the old original Hawaiian religion, or whether you were Buddhist because Buddhism is the major religion in Kauai—the ones who were able to use this faith to overcome adversity were the ones that saw meaning in their lives, even in pain and suffering. It wasn't church attendance but it was a belief that life, despite everything, made sense and that even the pain they experienced could ultimately be transformed. Very young children—children of age ten—could actually verbalize that. That helped them not to be bitter later on when they confronted parents that may have gone astray, who constantly were in and out of hospitals, and were alcoholic and suicidal or were physically and emotionally abusive.

We do know, and you know now, that there are other sources in the community that also are buffers for children in adversity. All of the children in our study—and [this] comes through in other studies in North America—were good at making and keeping a few good friends. They didn't have to be popular or "in with the crowd" or admired by lots of boyfriends. [It was] just that as they were good at picking substitute parents, they were good at picking a couple of

> **"These children really remember one or two teachers who made the difference."**

friends that were with them and stayed with them, from kindergarten to middle age. Often in Kauai, they would pick these friends from neighbors' families where they might go to get some sense of stability. Many eventually got married to the sons and daughters of their neighbors. They now have a very good relationship with their in-laws because they first started recruiting them as their substitute parents in the neighborhood.

How Schools Make a Difference

We also know that school can make a difference. But it's not the trappings of the school—the building, the bricks, the resource rooms. It seems to be the model of adults that they find within the schools. That comes right back to you, whether you are a teacher, or a counselor, or a school nurse, or whatever. One of the wonderful things we see now in adulthood is that these children really remember one or two teachers who made the difference. And they mourn these teachers when they die. They mourn some of those teachers more than they do their own family members

because what went out of their life was a person who looked beyond outward experience, their behavior, their unkempt—oftentimes—appearance and saw the promise. That could happen anywhere along the way. It could happen in Headstart. It could happen in kindergarten. It happened a lot in the first three grades. It also happened in high school and even in community college for those who dropped out and went back later on.

> **"The ones who were able to use this faith to overcome adversity were the ones that saw meaning in their lives, even in pain and suffering."**

Participation in meaningful community activities that foster cooperation was [also] a very important protective buffer in the lives of these children. I don't mean "make believe" activities. It didn't need to be a costly enterprise like the theater, the ballet, or whatever. It included activities where you join a cooperative enterprise. On Kauai, it was mostly 4H or the Y or being a Big Brother or Big Sister to someone else, or being active in a youth group in church. But whatever it was, it was an activity where you were not just a passive recipient, but where you were called upon to help someone else and you grew up in the process.

The Long Term Perspective

These are certainly some of the protective factors that we know cut across many different studies and that we can hope to foster in whatever setting we're in. I want to also say something about the fact that resiliency or being "at risk" doesn't stop by the time you get through high school. One of the wonderful things we found as we're looking at these people now in adulthood is that there is a great deal of potential for recovering among "at risk" kids who have problems in childhood and adolescence. Among the group [of "high risk" children—one-third of the study's total cohort] in our study, two-thirds actually did develop problems in the first two decades of life. They did have problems in school, and they had behavior problems in adolescence. They [became] teenage parents. They [became] delinquents. They [had] mental health problems. But when we looked at them in their 30s and now at 40 we found that even out of this group, the majority staged a recovery.

I think right now teenage parents and the delinquents are among the most misunderstood. [They] are the object of a lot of vindictiveness in our society. When I speak of vindictiveness, I mean vindictiveness on the state and federal level including the press. Most magazine articles and newspapers talk about teenage parents as being a permanent welfare dependent, right? That's the image they portray but it does not jibe with reality.

> **"There is a great deal of potential for recovering among 'at risk' kids who have problems in childhood and adolescence."**

Most Teenage Mothers Do Get Off Welfare

The fact is that most teenage mothers do not end up permanently taking Aid For Families of Dependent Children. Very few people have bothered to study them over time. They make good headlines when they just had their second child, maybe the first at 14 and the other at 16. They've dropped out of high school, and they are on AFDC. But there are only three studies right now that have looked at these teenage mothers in later life. One is our study with Asian American children, one is a study in Baltimore with African American children, and one is a study in New Orleans with Caucasian and African Americans. There's three studies in three very different contexts—one in the Pacific West, one in the inner city ghetto of Baltimore, and another in the Deep South. All show the same trends—over time, teenage mothers do work themselves out of the dependency on AFDC, given two things: one, access to continued education, and the other, access to child care.

Of the teenage mothers in our sample only two with preschool children—that was less than five percent—were still on some kind of government support, when we saw them in their mid 30s. All the others had finished the equivalent of high school. If they didn't go back, then they got the GED or they went to community colleges. They then moved up the socioeconomic ladder as they got more education and more vocational skills, and were in their mid-thirties people who had pretty decent and well-paying jobs. The key was

> **"Over time, teenage mothers do work themselves out of the dependency on AFDC, given two things: one, access to continued education, and the other, access to child care."**

access to education and child care. I think that's the message you have to give everywhere at every level [and] to every governor. They're not lost causes at all, but they do need that kind of assistance.

Most Delinquents Don't Become Adult Criminals

Also, most delinquents in our study and in other longitudinal studies, both with African American and with Caucasian youngsters, actually do not turn out to become hardened criminals. In my state we now have the "three strikes against you and you are out" law. We no longer practice prevention but containment. We will spend much more money on prisons than we will in education. The money spent on prisons might save the UC system of higher education, once the pride of the nation. But we're building prison after prison after prison instead!

Three out of four of the delinquent males in our study and nine out of ten delinquent females, did not go on to become adult criminals. The difference between those who desisted and those who did go on depended on the people who saw to it that these youngsters got help—again, with reading skills because many of those kids were way below the third grade level in reading when they became delinquent. It lay in the presence of a foster grandparent, mother, or father who sat down and helped them in remedial work. It lay with probation officers who really cared and with a case load that was low enough so they could do something for the youth, not just check off a box. And it lay with the concern of other family members—if the father was absent then with other elders—who saw to it that someone helped this youngster go straight. We really need to look at the differences between the lives of young people who are only passing through a delinquent phase because of peer pressure and the really hardened criminal for whom we do need more serious measures. Those two groups do get confused in our attempts at so-called "violence prevention."

The Help of Good Friends

> **"The message you have to give everywhere at every level [and] to every governor... they're not lost causes at all."**

Finally, let me say something about the people who had serious mental health problems in our group. Again, we find that just with the help of good friends, I guess it was a Beatles' song, "I Get By With A Little Help From My Friends," two out of three in that group got by—because no one [else] helped them. They were diagnosed and filed away. What did help many was the presence of a strong church community. A number of youngsters in this group who [had] mental health problems in adolescence converted to a community that gave them structure and stability.

Jehovah's Witnesses are a remarkably disciplined group that has helped many of the kids who had serious mental health problems on the island. So did the Latter Day Saints. Those groups that attracted teenagers who had mental health problems did something for them that often takes many years of psychotherapy and $100,000 to accomplish. They gave them a sense of self. They gave them a sense of community. And [the church organizations] gave them some sense of a mission. I think the presence of a concerned church group should certainly not be underrated.

> "Most delinquents in our study and in other longitudinal studies ... actually do not turn out to become hardened criminals."

The Shifting Balance Between Vulnerability and Resiliency

I started out [by saying] we should not look at resiliency as something that's clad in concrete. Certainly, one of the trends we saw over time is that with each passing decade one gender was a bit more vulnerable than the other. In the first decade, we found more boys who were "at risk," who had problems. In the second decade, especially toward the end of adolescence, it was the girls. In the third decade, the pendulum swung back again. I think a lot of that has to do with the expectations we have for each gender at each of these stages. We need to think about programs with these expectations in mind. Protective factors did not always have the same impact at each stage of life.

What mattered in early childhood were protective factors that had to do with a caring, stable adult, that had to do with good health, with helping a child who had health problems, and that had to do with allowing him or her the opportunity to reach out to others, not just his own small family. Protective factors that worked well in middle childhood were building competency, problem-solving skills, concerned teachers, and responsible friends. Protective factors in adolescence had more to do with the building of self-esteem, an internal locus of control, and providing a sense of meaning for a youngster's life. As you look at the literature on resiliency you must look a little closer to see whether some of the things you are doing could possibly be focused a bit more on the needs of children at different stages of their lives and be tailored more toward those processes that are most effective at each particular stage. In adulthood what seemed to matter was the support of a close friend or mate, personal competence, and finally—again—faith that their world/life mattered.

"Where's the Beef?"—The Need to Evaluate

Let me say something about [what] was addressed admirably this morning, [the need for research]. Some of you may remember a commercial that was on television when Walter Mondale ran for the presidency against Ronald Reagan. It pictured a little old lady looking at a gaping hole in a hamburger. Remember that? She ask plaintively, "Where's the beef?" I haven't seen her lately, but I thought that was a wonderful commercial. I ask the same question really [in regards] to all the programs that have been discussed at the workshops at this conference.

I do not doubt the sincerity in commitment of the individuals [here]. But as a scientist I must ask, like the little old lady, for the hard evidence that these programs actually effect lasting positive changes in the behaviors of the individuals, not just in your hearts. You'll feel good after two and a half days of this [conference focused on resiliency]. But when you go back and do whatever you do, please try and find a way to see if it does make a difference in the lives of people you are trying to help that's beyond saying, "I feel good." We need to move from what I would consider almost an evangelistic fervor about resilience to evaluation because in Washington and the state houses, they [say not only,] "Where's the beef?" but they say, "Let's do away with the pork." Right?

> "Protective factors did not always have the same impact at each stage of life."

All of you may need outside money or seed money to start your programs. But those who are in charge of grants are going to ask much more now from you—not just how many people attended workshops, the thing that's called "bean counting," or how many processes you actually covered in your handouts in your program. You've got to show that it did make some measurable difference in the lives of youngsters you worked with. And they and the nation as a whole have a right to ask this question. [See Part Two, chapter three, for more information about program evaluation.]

I was thinking of the "fostering resiliency" program in Albuquerque, which is wonderful, inspirational—according to the video you prepared and showed at this conference. It stops now, as of today. This is the end now, right? Now we've got to find out how many principals are going to continue this program without money from the "Feds." Programs that foster resiliency as far as I'm concerned will not actually really foster resiliency unless they function without outside money. It's got to come from the community. UNICEF does a much better thing. They go into communities where they know that whatever problems they start [solving], their programs will be taken over by the community. They have only ten cents to spend for each of the two billion children in the world.

> *"When you go back and do whatever you do, please try and find a way to see if it does make a difference in the lives of people you are trying to help that's beyond saying, 'I feel good'."*

Even in this program in Albuquerque, if it could be shown that reading scores increased or fewer people had reading problems at grade four after they participated, or there was less absenteeism, or in the best of all possible worlds there was a lower drop-out rate, or fewer teenage pregnancies. Or did it make any difference at all? You've got to—in the end—present these hard data, not just a videotape. Because [otherwise] I would predict by the end of the millennium resiliency will be a concept that will be long forgotten. If you [just] use it as a buzzword to get grants or as a kind of power—oxygen at the end of a conference—it won't be enough.

You Can Foster Resiliency Wherever You Are

Having said this doesn't mean that we should despair. It is important to evaluate the effectiveness of your programs. That's absolutely necessary no matter how big or little your program is—preferably little, one step at a time, as kids grow up. But this doesn't mean that you personally wherever you are cannot foster resiliency in an individual child. It doesn't take any money from anywhere. It needs time for care and caring.

One of the most useful things [is what we have learned from] the life stories of the resilient youngsters we have studied, who are now adults. We've learned from them that competence and confidence and caring can flourish, even under adverse circumstances. If children encounter persons who provide them with a secure basis for the development of trust, autonomy, initiative, and competence they can successfully overcome the odds. That success brings hope, realistic hope. And that is a gift each of us can share. You can share that gift with a child at home, in a classroom, on the playground, or in the neighborhood. The rediscovery of the healing powers of hope may be the most precious harvest you can glean in the work you do—for yourself and for the youngsters whose lives you touch.

CHAPTER 4

The Faces Of Resiliency

by Nan Henderson, M.S.W.

After extensively reading research about youth resiliency, I decided to go into my community and find young people whose lives demonstrate "resiliency in action." I found that resilient kids are everywhere, that secondary teachers, college and university professors, youth agency workers, community and church youth workers, even my friends and neighbors all knew young people whose lives put faces on the concept of resiliency. I am passionate about sharing these "faces," documenting the specific stories and words of resilient young people. I hope readers will do the same— identify and publicize the many young people in their communities who are resilient—as one way to challenge the prevalent but inaccurate stereotypes of kids from "risk" environments.

Two such young people are profiled below. Though I interviewed and wrote about them for the first edition of this book, the themes and answers they shared are indicative of the hundreds of youth I have talked with in the past decade about how adults can foster kids' resiliency. When doing such interviews, I ask open-ended questions about their lives and their overcoming of adversity and about advice they want to share with others. The themes that emerge are right out of—and totally confirming of—the resiliency research, as well as the research on drop-out prevention and gang prevention.

Leslie Krug's story documents the critical need for caring and high expectations in schools, as well as the power of one person—in her case, her mother—who will not give up on a child. She also testifies as to the powerful influence of friends who themselves have bounced back and are doing well.

Phil Canamar's story shows the importance of caring adults outside the family. As he lists all the people who have contributed to his resiliency, we see the power of these other "surrogates" in a young person's community to make a difference. This validates the research of Gina O'Connell Higgins (1994) reported in her book, Resilient Adults: Overcoming a Cruel Past, *and others. His message confirms much of what is known about why young people get into gangs and offers inspiration about how they can leave. He also comments on the crucial components of effective schools that so many kids—those who drop out and those who don't—note as missing in traditional high schools. Finally, he demonstrates, as Emmy Werner so beautifully describes in the previous article, the importance of spiritual faith for many of those who are resilient.*

Leslie Krug: "I've Been In So Much Trouble and I'm Still Here"

Leslie Krug went through ninth grade in a traditional high school three times. A lot of her problems, she said, began in sixth grade when her dad died, which "hurt a lot." Though she was sent to counseling, seventh through ninth grade were years of skipping school, drinking, and using drugs.

Her message now: "I've been in so much trouble and I'm still here." At age 16, Leslie is back in school and doing well. She was one of two students selected, in fact, by the school staff of the alternative school she attends to be featured as a "face of resiliency." She is no longer using drugs, and is contemplating a future as a small business owner.

When asked who helped her bounce back Leslie credited her mom, her friends, her boyfriend's parents, and the school she now attends. She gave most of the credit to her mom. "She just kept making me go to school. She wouldn't let me drop out," Leslie said. She reports that during her years of skipping school and "hanging out" her mom got mad at her for her behavior, but she never gave up on her. No matter what, Leslie said, her mom "was just always there."

Leslie's advice to adults trying to help kids succeed is, "Show that they care. They've got to care." An absence of caring was a main reason Leslie struggled in traditional school. One teacher, she said, told her friends that one day they would be driving Mercedes and BMWs and Leslie would be working the window at McDonald's.

And, she reported, "there is so many drugs" around traditional schools. If a student is doing drugs, she added, "you're not going to do them at school." So that is another reason she skipped.

Leslie stopped doing drugs because of the influence of her friends, especially one, who stopped. Seeing him stop, she said, made her realize that it could be done. And seeing other friends going to school and doing well provided motivation for her to do the same.

She also gives credit to her Albuquerque Public Schools alternative school, School on Wheels. Leslie said she feels that the teachers at this school really care. "They're not here because it's their job. They want to teach." She added, "They treat you like things aren't just going to happen for you. You've got to work."

"They make you responsible and the teachers care," are two main reasons Leslie said she is doing well in school now. She also learns things "useful for my life." One example is discussions about racism in school curriculum. "All you learn about is George Washington" in traditional classrooms, Leslie said. "Here they teach you more about Hispanic heroes"— information about her culture she didn't get in school before. She said classrooms work as teams, with cooperation emphasized. And she gets a chance to pursue one of her main interests—art.

Leslie looks forward to finishing her high school credits at the local community college (TVI), through an arrangement between her alternative school and the college. "When we are 17 we can go to TVI and get our credits," she said. Through attending TVI, she hopes to pursue her goal of one day owning a small business.

Phil Canamar: "I Feel the Pain and Anger in Everybody's Heart that Joins a Gang"

Phil Canamar at 18 wrote a grant proposal to Honeywell asking the company for $80,000 to help "ten multicultural youth, to train them in the logistics of making videos." Besides attending school, he works in a local organization dedicated to getting youth involved in their own businesses. He is looking forward to graduating from high school, and pursuing his passion of video production.

Phil has come a long way since he began using drugs in middle school, robbed houses with his friends in ninth grade, joined a gang at age 16, dropped out of school, and ran away from home.

Phil said he has never known his father, whom his mother divorced when he was three. He lived until he was seven with his mother and grandfather. Then, his grandfather died. His mother had two other children, too, and had to work full-time. He remembers a childhood of being "treated like an adult... cooking for myself, cleaning for myself... and trying to be the father" for his brother and sister.

Eventually, about the time he was in middle school, "I started hanging out with the wrong friends and got into trouble." At first, Phil reported, it was telling teachers off and smoking. Then he began using drugs, partially because he was hanging out with his older sister's friends. He drank a lot, and used marijuana and other drugs. Then he began the house robberies with his friends. Getting caught, Phil said, taught him a lesson—"never do that again."

Phil dropped out of school in tenth grade. He said a lot of teachers had the attitude when he left of, "Well...see you later, bye." "Some of them did care," Phil said. But "many of them didn't want to help." They thought, "Well, he deserved it." After he dropped out, he hung around the house for about a year, "a bum, just doing nothing. I was looking for a job but no one would hire me. I was only 16 and I had dropped out of school."

He and his mom eventually got into an argument, during which she said, "'Go ahead. Go on. Go out on your own.' So I packed my stuff. I left." At age 16, Phil walked 40 miles into Albuquerque. Phil moved in with a friend he had met years before whose mom told him he could always come there if he ever had problems. For awhile he and his friend hung around, "smoking weed, drinking beer." Then his friend's mom started pressuring the boys to get jobs, but "no one would hire us because we weren't in school.

"Finally, I said, 'I'm going to go try School on Wheels'," Phil said. He had heard about the alternative school from his sister years before. He and his friend both decided to give it a try. From his first encounter with the school principal, Phil said his life began to change. "He said, 'Hey I remember you. You used to go to my church. We'll see what we can do about getting you in here because I know you are a good kid.'" The principal told Phil to call every day until there was an opening at the school. "I called for three or four weeks before I got in," Phil remembered.

Phil began attending the school and moved in with a man who had been a friend for years. "My mom met him when I was nine at the State Fair. She was always looking for a father image for me and my brother. She said to him, 'Can you help me with my kids...take them here or there or something?' and he said sure, 'I love kids, especially boys. I always wished I had a boy.'" This man, whom Phil calls Joe, has been an important part of Phil's life since that time.

He joined a gang, in fact, during a time when his mom wouldn't let him see Joe anymore, due to a misunderstanding. "It was at that point in time when I said, 'No one is here for me, you know. I'm sick of it.' And I turned toward the gang to find support.

"That's the pain and anger I feel in everybody's heart that joins a gang. They want to feel accepted, you know, because they don't have that going on in their home life. The mother or father isn't there."

Phil left the gang when he moved to Albuquerque. It was helpful, he said, that "that gang isn't here" though "everyone here in Albuquerque says 'Oh, you're Chicano, you must be in a gang.' Now," Phil said, "I just look at them. I have a lot of love." And, he tells them, "I'm here in peace."

In addition to Joe and Joe's parents, whom Phil calls "his elders" that give him care and support, he credits School on Wheels for his resiliency. "It was the structure there, then the environment, then third, but not least, Kathryn, my teacher. She always gave me encouragement to take it one day at a time."

Phil likes the team work, cooperation, the fact he has just one teacher, the experiential activities, and the caring he feels at School on Wheels. His advice to traditional schools: "Interview teachers to see if they do care about the students. And hire one principal. Most schools have four principals and they all have their own opinion of how to run the school. All they're doing is making chaos."

> "Phil has come a long way since he began using drugs in middle school, robbed houses with his friends in ninth grade, joined a gang at age 16, dropped out of school, and ran away from home."

Finally, Phil credits his Christian faith with helping him through his difficulties. He said that while many people have helped him along the way, "God told me, 'Take something of them. Don't take the bad part. Take the good part you like in them...take them with you.'" Phil added, "They've all given me a little piece, something that makes me grow. The major one is Joe, then my teacher, Kathy and my other teachers, Ron and Ed. The school helped a lot. And where I'm working. We're trying to get "at risk" youth involved in their own businesses."

Phil said he wrote the grant to Honeywell so he can offer something to other kids like himself. His goal is his own video production staff. He wants to give other kids this invitation: "Hey are you guys bored? Are you guys tired of gangs? Come over here. I'll teach you about video, let's make a video or a movie...let's make a music video." The purpose of the organization, Phil said, is "to give them meaningful stuff to do."

Phil's advice to other kids like himself is, "Don't drop out of school. Find an alternative." And his advice to adults trying to help kids is, "Take time out to see what they need. Try to provide what they need. I'm not sure if there is anything else to do."

CHAPTER 5

Tapping Innate Resilience in Children Exposed to Family Violence

by Zulema Ruby White

This article is reprinted with permission from the Fall, 2003 issue of Synergy: The Newsletter
of the Resource Center on Domestic Violence: Child Protection and Custody. *This newsletter
is published by The National Council of Juvenile and Family Court Judges.*

More than a decade of research demonstrates that exposure to domestic violence may have serious implications for the well-being of children. Numerous studies document the prevalence of and impact on children who witness domestic violence and provide evidence of the psychological, emotional, cognitive functioning, and longer term developmental problems associated with children's exposure to the assaults of one parent by another (Edleson, 1999).

However, the research also shows that most children exposed to domestic violence do not demonstrate adverse impact (Lang, 2000); that some show even higher competence (Jaffe, Wolfe, & Wilson, 1990); that each child's experiences, perceptions, and responses to domestic violence are unique and many variables need to be considered when assessing the impact (Edleson, 1999); and that interventions should provide children with protection against the risks they face in ways that recognize there is not a "one-size-fits-all" approach.

What is less clear is how to appreciate the composition, drama, and prose of each child's experience in order to design effective interventions, recognizing that many factors in a child's life remain supportive even in the face of violence. This article provides an overview of what current research and practice identify as specific elements of a child's environment that can serve as supportive factors and that should be used to inform appropriate interventions by professionals in the field.

Capturing the Complete Story

Identifying the factors that may facilitate success for children exposed to domestic violence requires that professionals capture the child's complete story. To do so involves assessing each child's unique experiences, needs, strengths, challenges, wishes, and life context. In addition, it is important that prevention and intervention systems examine their own values, conceptions, perspectives, and ability to listen and exchange ideas in order to support children by sending positive messages and providing relief in ways that

contribute to their safety, physiological, social, esteem, and self-actualization needs (see Maslow, 1987).

Moreover, meeting the needs of children exposed to domestic violence requires an acceptance of the principle that there is a great deal of variability in children's exposure to and experiences associated with domestic violence, as well as the impact of those experiences. It cannot be assumed that all children exposed to stress, trauma, or violence will show negative results; and it must also be recognized that some will. Longitudinal studies reveal time and again that 50 to 75 percent of children growing up in families suffering from domestic violence, as well as exposed to other risks defeat the odds and turn a life destined for further hardship into one that illustrates resilience and triumph (Benard, 1995).

Environmental Factors as Building Blocks

To determine what children from violent homes need requires us to examine thoroughly the environmental factors that have been found to be a source of strength and a source of risk for children. These factors include:

- the level of violence;
- the causes, nature, and extent of risk;
- whether or not the child is or has also been a victim of abuse;
- how much time has passed since the exposure, because the impact of immediate turmoil may temporarily escalate a child's problems and appears to have a greater effect;
- the child's characteristics, such as age and gender, since boys and girls are found to exhibit different problems, and developmental levels which contribute to the impact, and coping abilities; and
- environmental factors unique to that child such as individual coping skills, relationships, and social support (Spears, 2000).

When environmental factors are labeled as protective factors there is a tendency to assess which children possess such characteristics, rather than recognizing that all individuals have an innate capacity for growth in the presence of such environmental factors (Spears, 2000). What is more helpful to children is to conceptualize environmental factors as potential building blocks, or as basic elements or components of development, that can be nurtured in a way that will lead to positive outcomes. Some of these potential building blocks are discussed in detail below:

1. **A secure attachment to a non-violent parent, caregiver, or other significant adult.**

   The most important protective resource to enable a child to cope with exposure to domestic violence is a strong relationship with a competent, caring, positive adult— most often [but not always] a parent (Osofsky, 1999). A 1997 study (Evangelista, 1999) examined the life histories of women who had achieved professional and personal success and who were all adult daughters of battered women. Each woman described a life filled with frequent tension, unhappiness, and fear; but the common factor in all of the women "was a supportive adult—oftentimes the battered woman herself—who was able to mediate the damaging effects of a violent home." A close bond with an effective parent is related to better outcomes among children with ordinary lives as well as those who face domestic violence, child maltreatment, or multifaceted high risk. It is therefore vital to ensure children are not re-victimized by the removal of critical resources.

2. **Children's belief about their own success** (Henderson & Dweck, 1990).

   Children's beliefs are influenced by other's perceptions about their ability to succeed. Only recently, experts are coming to understand that children may be better served by interventions that incorporate a "challenge" model of resilience, which recognizes that children are impacted by family dynamics in ways that are both positive and negative (Biscoe, 1999). In families where there is abuse or multiple problems, professionals can work with children in a way that helps them to identify and capitalize on their strengths instead of highlighting why they are destined to fail or be "at risk." While society may prefer to label "high risk" children, such labeling is extremely problematic because it may negatively affect children's perceptions of their ability.

3. **High achievement in one or more areas** (Masten & Coatsworth, 1998).

   It is important to identify and nurture unique individual abilities. Good problem-solving skills, outstanding school performance and involvement, above average intelligence, and exceptional athletic ability and involvement in sports are examples of some of the ways children express their talents and abilities, and can be tapped into in order to create a fertile environment for successful development.

4. **Peers** (Hartup, 1996).

   Peers can provide motivation for increasing one's involvement in positive programs, activities, and leadership opportunities; serve as protective or pro-social models; and provide emotional support. Programs and interventions should work with children's peers, who can be allies in education, prevention, and solutions. However, programs and interventions must recognize that grouping deviant peers together may be counterproductive (Dishion, McCord, & Poulin, 1998).

5. **Access to health, education, housing, social services, and employment for the family** (Grotberg, 1995).

   Families often "fail" as a result of the way systems conduct business. One of the principal reasons for the lack of success can be attributed to the lack of comprehensive assessments of what families need. When a problem is identified and addressed independent of other problems family members may have, it is often determined that all members need the same services. Furthermore, families that may have divergent needs are referred to undifferentiated services because those are the only options available. Families are then often referred to multiple systems and organizations, with the hope that the interventions will somehow all come together. However, the issues many families face are not fragmented; they come together as a whole and should be addressed as such. Assessing families' needs includes recognizing multiple issues, such as poverty, environmental quality, and overcrowded and sub-standard schools and housing—all of which can be affected by direct or indirect discrimination. Access to health, education, housing, social services, and employment for the family can help lead to positive outcomes.

6. **Social support.**

   One study (Shpungin, 1999) examined the impact of social support in the lives of 80 children between the age of seven and 11 years old, whose mothers had experienced partner violence in the last four months.

Study results revealed that social support, specifically the number of people in the children's lives who cared about, listened to, and could be counted on by the children, was positively correlated to children's adjustment and self-esteem and also positively moderated the correlation between the violence witnessed and the children's behavioral adjustment.

Moreover, families may have unique social supports, particularly in communities of color that help to protect family members. These include involved extended family, participation in church or religious activities, strong identification with their racial group, and close attachments within their ethnic community. When developing interventions it is, therefore, critical to create environments with the flexibility to meet the unique social and cultural dynamics, as well as the mix of risk conditions and strengths, of each child.

7. **A strong cultural identity and ethnic pride** (Simmons, 1999).

It is vitally important that children have a sense of pride in every distinction that goes into making them the individuals they are. Children of color are exposed to stresses that can affect any child, but also experience other sources of stress related to racism, discrimination, and possible dislocated family background (Dwivedi, 1997). Programs and interventions should contribute to their development by highlighting the way their people, values, traditions, and social supports include important cultural contributions, positive gender roles, and an enriched or responsive social environment. Such services should also incorporate an understanding that different children and families in a given community or culture may have different values and expectations for success and competence. Interventions should acknowledge, respect, and include diversity in a way that does not ignore differences in life context for communities of color.

In particular, the life context of communities of color introduces many unique factors that need to be considered in domestic violence interventions. These may include:

- biases in delivery of services by the criminal justice systems;
- mistrust of mainstream formal systems;
- under-representation of people of color among service providers and in positions of leadership;
- formal systems that do not include relevant or alternative resources;

- the balance between disproving stereo-typical beliefs that only poor, minority women are battered and pushing them aside to focus on victims for whom the dominant culture will be more likely to express concern; and
- other possible personal and cultural barriers, present outside of communities of color as well, which may include elements such as intense loyalty to the extended family, deference to individual needs for family unity and strength, religious beliefs or spirituality, social unacceptability of separation or divorce, concentration in low paying jobs, language barriers and immigration issues, privacy and self-blame seen as virtues to maintain family honor, unfamiliar and uncomfortable surroundings, and tremendous within-group diversity (Valazquez, McPhatter, & Yang, 2003).

Applying the Lessons Learned from Children

The experiences of children demonstrating resiliency in the face of domestic violence require further exploration to observe, discover, and learn more about all of the nuances that combine to create positive rather than negative outcomes. Looking for the factors described above in assessments of children's and families' needs will advance a strengths-based approach to interventions with children exposed to domestic violence, rather than one that looks for factors which automatically label children "high risk." In order to create a nurturing environment for children that will allow them to flourish, we must believe in their capacity and enhance, not minimize, the critical building blocks in each child's life through careful, creative, and differential solutions.

References

Benard, B. (1995). Fostering resilience in children. *ERIC Digest, 1.* Retrieved from http://www.eric.edu.gov.

Dishion, T.J., McCord, J., & Poulin. F. (1999). When interventions harm: Peer groups and problem behavior. *American Psychologist, 54 (9),* 755-764.

Dwivedi, K.N. (1997). *Enhancing parenting skills.* Chichester, West Sussex, UK: Wiley Publications.

Dwivedi, K.N. (1999). *Meeting the needs of ethnic minority children* (2nd ed.). London, UK: Jessica Kingsley.

Edleson, J.L.(1999a). Children's witnessing of adult domestic violence. *Journal of Interpersonal Violence, 14 (8),* 839-870.

Edleson, J.L. (1999b). *Problems associated with children's witnessing of domestic violence.* Harrisburg, PA: National Resource Center on Domestic Violence.

Evangelista, A. (1999). Shedding childhood scars of violence. *The Science of Caring.* Retrieved from http://www.ucsf/edu/day-break/1999/07/09_violence.html.

Grotberg, E.H. (1995). *A guide to promoting resilience in children: Strengthening the human spirit.* The Hague, The Netherlands: Bernard Van Leer Foundation.

Hartup, W.W. (1996). The company they keep: Friendships and their developmental significance.*Child Development, 67,* 1 - 13.

Henderson, V.L. & Dweck, C.S. (1990). Motivation and achievement. In S.S. Feldman & G.R. Elliot (Eds.), *At the threshold: The developing adolescent* (pp.308-329). Cambridge, MA: Harvard University Press.

Jaffe, P., Wolfe, D., & Wilson, S. (1990). *Children of battered women.* Newbury Park, CA: Sage Publications.

Laing, L. (2000). *Children, young people, and domestic violence.* Sydney, NSW, Australia: Australian Domestic and Family Violence Clearinghouse.

Maslow, A.H. (1987). *Motivation and personality* (3rd ed.). New York: Harper and Row.

Masten, A.S. & Coatsworth, J.D. (1998). The development of competence in favorable and unfavorable environments: Lessons from research on successful children. *American Psychologist, 53,* 205-220.

National Resource Center on Domestic Violence. (2002). *Children exposed to intimate partner violence.* Harrisburg, PA: National Resource Center on Domestic Violence.

Neighbors, B., Forehand, R., & McVicar, D. (1993). Resilient adolescents and interpersonal conflict. *American Journal of Orthopsychiatry, 63,* 462-471.

Osofsky, J.D. (1999). The impact of violence on children. *The Future of Children: Domestic Violence and Children, 9* (3), 38.

Sen, R. (1999). Between a rock and a hard place: Domestic violence in communities of color. *ColorLines, 2* (1).

Shpungin, E. (1999). *Social Support as a protective factor in the lives of children exposed to domestic violence.* Master's thesis, Michigan State University, East Lansing, MI.

Simmons, K. (1999). *Pathways to prevention: Developmental and early intervention approaches to crime in Australia.* National Crime Prevention, Attorney-Generals Department, 13.

Skinner, E.A. (1995). *Perceived control, motivation, and coping.* Thousand Oaks, CA: Sage Publications.

Spears, L. (2000). *Building bridges between domestic violence organizations and child protective services* (revised ed.). Violence Against Women Online Resources, 22.

Valazquez, J., McPhatter, A.R., & Yang, K. (Eds.). (2003). Special issue: Perspective on cultural competence. *Child Welfare, LXXXII (2).*

Wolin, S. & Wolin, S. (1993). *The resilient self: How survivors of troubled families rise above adversity.* New York: Villard Books.

Zulema (Ruby) White Starr is the Program Manager, Children's Program's in the Family Violence Department of the National Council of Juvenile and Family Court Judges (NCJFCJ). Her areas of interest include children exposed to domestic violence, resilience, and cultural competence. She shares her professional experience and personal experience as a child witness and child and adult victim of domestic violence with the media and to various groups throughout the country in hopes that her experiences will lead to better practices and outcomes for both battered women and their children. She can be contacted at RWhite@ncifcj.org.

CHAPTER 6

A Resiliency Resource Primer:

Foundations of Resiliency

by Nan Henderson, M.S.W., and Bonnie Benard, M.S.W.

Benard, Bonnie. (1991). *Fostering Resiliency in Kids: Protective Factors in the Family, School, and Community.* Portland, OR: Western Regional Center for Drug-Free Schools and Communities. 1991. *This seminal publication on resiliency synthesizes more than 100 resiliency-related studies, books, and articles. Though the Western Regional Center no longer exists, the entire article is available at no cost from WestEd, a nonprofit research, development, and service agency headquartered in San Francisco. Download the article by going to www.wested.org/cs/we/view/rs/93.*

Benard, Bonnie. (1994). *Turning the Corner: From Risk to Resiliency.* Portland, OR: Western Regional Center for Drug-Free Schools and Communities. *This publication is a compilation of several shorter articles published between 1991 and 1993, which provide an update to Benard's 1991 work and address resiliency in several contexts. It is also available at no cost from Educational Resources Information Center (ERIC). Download the article by going to www.eric.ed.gov.*

Benard, Bonnie. (2004). *Resiliency: What We Have Learned.* San Francisco, CA: WestEd. *This is the most recent update to Benard's 1991 paper, a 150-page book with 500 resiliency-related references. It includes a crucial integration of research on "the resilient brain."*

Benson, Peter, Galbraith, Judy, and Espeland, Pamela. (1998). *What Kids Need to Succeed.* Minneapolis: Free Spirit. *In this updated version of the original book, the authors offer dozens of practical suggestions about how families, communities, and schools can build assets in youth. They include an informal asset assessment which parents can fill out and give to their children.*

Benson, Peter, Galbraith, Judy, and Espeland, Pamela. (1998). *What Teens Need to Succeed.* Minneapolis: Free Spirit. *The authors base both their books on surveys of over 350,000 U.S. teens, and include detailed information about the "positive assets" (another word for "protective factors") that contribute to an individual's success in life. Quotations, charts, graphs, quizzes, checklists, facts and statistics, anecdotes, and myriad resources are included.*

Botvin, Gilbert J. *Life Skills Training (an elementary, middle school, and high school curriculum).* White Plains, NY: Princeton Health Press. *This is the most thoroughly evaluated "skills curriculum" available, endorsed by the US Department of Education, the National Institute on Drug Abuse, the American Medical Association, the Center for Disease Control, the American Psychological Association, and the US Department of Justice. It is backed by more than 20 scientific studies that have shown significant long-term reductions in alcohol and other drug use and violent behaviors among youth who received this training as it is designed. Documented positive outcomes include development of positive self-image; development of decision-making, problem-solving, resistance, stress management skills; and fostering of effective communication, healthy relationships, and social self-confidence.*

Brendtro, Larry, Brokenleg, Martin, and Van Bockern, Steve. (1990). *Reclaiming Youth at Risk: Our Hope for the Future.* Bloomington, IN: National Educational Services. *Though not based on resiliency research per se, this book presents useful arguments and general approaches for "reclaiming" youth from risk to resilience.*

Brendtro, Larry, Ness, Arlen, and Mitchell, Martin. (2004). *No Disposable Kids.* Bloomington, IN: National Educational Service. *The authors challenge the notion of any child being "too far gone" to be helped. They share strategies drawn from the best resiliency models, and frame youth rebellious acts as signs of resilience. They also offer strategies for uncovering natural self-righting tendencies.*

Brendtro, Larry. (2006). *The Resilience Revolution: Discovering Strengths in Challenging Kids.* Bloomington, IN: Solution Tree. *The emphasis of this book is giving distressed youth the most important factor in their success: a positive adult connection. Based on resiliency research, the authors reframe "challenging behavior" as "pain-based behavior" and describe practical strategies adults can use to help young people overcome their pain and emerge resilient.*

Brooks, Robert, and Goldstein, Sam. (2001). *Raising Resilient Children : Fostering Strength, Hope, and Optimism in Your Child.* Chicago: Contemporary Books. *The authors ask, why do many parents insist on pointing out their child's weaknesses and try to mend them when harnessing the child's strengths is far more effective? And how can parents change their parenting to help kids become thoughtful, confident adults? They offer 10 essential parenting behaviors for nurturing resilience in kids.*

Brooks, Robert, and Goldstein, Sam. (2002). *Nurturing Resilience in Our Children : Answers to the Most Important Parenting Questions.* New York: McGraw-Hill. *Based on real queries put forth by parents, educators, and professionals, this book explains how parents can best help their children cope with specific adversities, offering a useful supplement to the authors' original book. It provides answers from a resilience perspective to the most challenging issues parents face.*

Desetta, Al, and Wolin, Sybil (Eds.). (2000). *The Struggle to Be Strong: True Stories by Teens.* Minneapolis: Free Spirit. *This book is a powerful collection of teen-written stories demonstrating individual "resiliencies"—characteristics that could also be termed "individual protective factors" identified by Wolin that help young people be resilient. The teens have been trained well as writers, and their stories contain gripping details of their individual journeys of overcoming abuse, abandonment, racial prejudice, parental addiction, the death of friends, and other "teen troubles."*

Desetta, Al, and Wolin, Sybil (Eds.). (2000). *A Leader's Guide to The Struggle to be Strong: True Stories by Teens.* Minneapolis: Free Spirit. *This guide offers educatorss, counselors, and other youth workers an easy-to-implement (and much-needed) way to teach students about the concept of resiliency and how to become resilient. It is filled with practical, user-friendly activities that help kids discover and strengthen their personal resiliency.*

Haggerty, Robert, Sherrod, Lonnie, Garmezy, Norman, and Rutter, Michael (Eds.). (1996). *Stress, Risk, and Resilience in Children and Adolescents.* Rochester, NY: Cambridge University Press. *This book is a series of articles by major researchers which furthers the study of the phenomenon of resiliency. It was developed as a follow-up to the seminal volume, Stress, Coping, and Development in Childhood edited by Garmezy and Rutter in 1983.*

Henderson, Nan, and Milstein, Mike. (2003). *Resiliency in Schools: Making It Happen for Students and Educators.* Thousand Oaks, CA: Corwin Press. *In this updated edition, the authors provide an overview of resiliency research and theory, detail how schools build resiliency in students, extend the findings to educators, and provide a step-by-step plan for changing schools into more effective resiliency-building organizations. All the information included can be adapted to other organizations and settings.*

Henderson, Nan, Benard, Bonnie, and Sharp-Light, Nancy. (2000). *Mentoring for Resiliency: Setting Up Programs for Moving Youth from "Stressed to Success."* Ojai, CA: *Resiliency In Action. Adult-youth mentoring is a programmatic approach to fostering resiliency that has extensive documented success--IF it is implemented correctly.   This book offers the research-based guidelines for setting up the most effective mentoring and other resiliency-building programs.*

Higgins, Gina O'Connell. (1994). *Resilient Adults: Overcoming a Cruel Past.* San Francisco: Jossey-Bass. *This book is based on the author's research on 40 adults who survived horrendous childhoods, winding up resilient in adulthood by their own report and by several psychological tests. Their stories provide specific information on how resiliency develops in people of all ages and "advice from the resilient."*

Jessor, Richard. (1993). *"Successful adolescent development among youth in high-risk settings." In American Psychologist, 48, 117.* *This article describes an ideal model of comprehensive research based on a resiliency (positive developmental) paradigm. The "Successful Adolescent Development in High Risk Settings" consortium examines from a multidisciplinary perspective the nature of environmental contexts that promote resiliency despite risks.*

Jones, Jami. (2003). *Helping Teens Cope: Resources for School Library Media Specialists and Other Youth Workers.* Worthington, Ohio: Linworth Publishing. *The author is on a mission to help librarians and media specialists understand their crucial role in fostering resiliency in children and youth. This book, however, is a wealth of resources for all who work with kids. The book introduces resiliency, and the concept of building resiliency through bibliotherapy. It includes a list of resiliency-building books for middle school and high school student pertinent to overcoming every major teen problem.*

Lifton, Robert J. (1999). *The Protean Self: Human Resilience in an Age of Fragmentation.* Chicago: University of Chicago Press. *In this updated version of the 1993 original, the author draws on interviews with several disparate groups (social activists, civic leaders, poor African Americans, and Christian fundamentalists) to document the incredible power of humans to transform "discontinuity and pain."* Lifton challenges readers to use this capacity to transform this market-driven, greed-oriented society to the *"more humane global values of a civil society."*

Muller, Wayne. (1992). ***Legacy of the Heart: The Spiritual Advantages of a Painful Childhood.*** New York: Simon and Schuster. *This beautiful book written by a counselor and theologian invites anyone who experienced a hurtful childhood—or anyone who works with children growing up in troubled families—to look at the strengths, i.e., resilience, their suffering fostered. The author provides a guided path "to awaken what is already wise and strong, to claim what is deep and true...to find inner balance and to reaffirm [one's] intrinsic wholeness."*

Muller, Wayne. (1996). ***How, Then, Shall We Live? Four Simple Questions that Reveal the Beauty and Meaning of Our Lives.*** New York: Bantam Books. *Muller is one of our very favorite spiritual/philosophical writers, incorporating wisdom from numerous spiritual traditions into his writing. This book is especially powerful in inspiring readers to excavate and honor "the resilient spirit that remains whole and true" despite all labeling and diagnoses.*

Richardson, Glenn E., et al., (1990). ***"The resiliency model."*** In ***Health Education, 21 (6), 33.*** *This article is another seminal work on resiliency, synthesizing a number of perspectives into an excellent model of how resiliency develops in individuals.*

Saleeby, Dennis (Ed.). (2005). ***The Strengths Perspective in Social Work Practice*** (4th ed.). Boston: Allyn Bacon. *First published in 1996, this book was "ahead of the curve." Written primarily for mental health practitioners, it is also a valuable resource for educators who want to put "a strengths perspective" into practice. Filled with practical chapters, including a detailed discussion of "strengths-based assessment," this book is both a forerunner and a classic in the area of "strengths-based practice."*

Sanford, Linda. (2005). ***Strong in the Broken Places: Building Resiliency in Survivors of Trauma.*** Holyoke, MA: NEARI Press. *NEARI Press has reprinted this pioneering book that was first published in 1990. It contains the stories of 20 survivors who prevail over a childhood of sexual and physical abuse, neglect, parental substance abuse, and other trauma. Therapist Linda Sanford asks them to look back and help us all understand how they fared so well. A valuable resource for every survivor, friend, family member, mentor, or helping professional.*

Seligman, Martin. (2006). ***Learned Optimism: How to Change Your Mind and Your Life. New York: Vintage.*** *A precursor to* **The Optimistic Child** *, this foundational work documents not only the power of optimism as a protective factor, but also how to work personally, with other adults and with youth, to transform negative, hopeless, explanatory styles to positive, optimistic ones. For readers wanting a skills-focused approach to resiliency, this book is a must.*

Seligman, Martin. (1996). ***The Optimistic Child: Proven Program to Safeguard Children from Depression & Build Lifelong Resilience.*** New York: Harper. *According to the author, 30% of American children suffer from depression. The purpose of this book is to teach parents and other concerned adults how to instill in children a sense of optimism and personal mastery. Seligman explains that authentic self-esteem comes from mastering challenges, overcoming frustration, and experiencing individual achievement. He offers a concrete plan of action based on techniques of self-evaluation and social interaction.*

Snyder, C.R., and Lopez, Shane. (2001). ***Handbook of Positive Psychology.*** New York: Oxford University Press. *Positive psychology is being called "a scientific revolution" and is based on, in part, and very connected to, the research on resiliency. With this publication "the landscape of our discipline may have changed forever," according to the review by* The Psychologist. *"Human strengths, happiness, positive emotions, wisdom, creativity, love, forgiveness, optimism, personal growth, humor (to name but a few) were traditionally...far from central to psychological endeavors, if not viewed through the lens of psychopathology. However, with the advent of the Handbook, they have found themselves a new home. [T]he Handbook should be considered essential reading for all those interested in positive psychology."*

Werner, Emmy, and Smith, Ruth. (1982, 1989). ***Vulnerable but Invincible: A Longitudinal Study of Resilient Children and Youth.*** New York: Adams, Bannister, and Cox. *The authors detail lessons from children born with several significant risk factors who developed no observable problems as they moved from infancy to childhood, and through adolescence to adulthood.*

Werner, Emmy, and Smith, Ruth. (1992). ***Overcoming the Odds: High Risk Children from Birth to Adulthood.*** New York: Cornell University Press. *This book documents in reader-friendly detail the results of the authors' 40-year longitudinal study. It includes chapters on how teen mothers, delinquents, and children and youth with mental health problems bounced back, and ties the research findings to similar studies in the US and elsewhere.*

Werner, Emmy, and Smith, Ruth. (2001). ***Journeys from Childhood to the Midlife: Risk, Resilience, and Recovery.*** New York: Cornell University Press. *In this eagerly-awaited sequel to the authors' previous books documenting their seminal 50-year "Kauai Study," the researchers explain additional resiliency-building factors that emerge as individuals enter mid-life. These protective factors include both those similar to what most helps children and youth, as well as some additional factors that emerge as powerful resiliency builders in adulthood.*

Wolin, Steven, and Wolin, Sybil. (1993). ***The Resilient Self: How Survivors of Troubled Families Rise Above Adversity.*** New York: Villard. *The Wolins challenge the popular culture's emphasis on victimization, describe seven "resiliencies" they have found in "survivors" of adversity, and emphasize the importance of moving from a "Damage Model" to a "Challenge Model" of viewing adversity.*

Wolin, Steven, and Wolin, Sybil. (1994). ***Survivor's Pride: Building Resilience in Youth At Risk (video).*** Vernona, Wisconsin: Attainment Co., Inc. *The Wolins' describe the "seven resiliencies" in the first part of this video, as well as the difference between the "Damage Model" and the "Challenge Model." Most of the tape, however, is in-depth interviews with resilient young people, documenting the Wolins' findings.*

PART TWO
RESILIENCY AND SCHOOLS

CHAPTER 1

Resiliency-Building "Hidden" Predictors of Academic Success

by Nan Henderson, M.S.W.

A growing chorus of prominent researchers and experts on effective education are documenting three "hidden" predictors of academic success. The evidence of the power of these three predictors is emerging as a result of an increase in research to discover why, in this era of "No Child Left Behind" many children are, in fact, left behind. Not surprisingly, these three predictors are intimately connected with fostering resiliency; fostering resiliency is, after all, another way of describing healthy, successful human development. And such development includes becoming a successful learner.

School Climate, Social and Emotional Learning, and Arts Education

In the last decade, and increasingly in the past five years, study after study is showing the impact of school climate, social and emotional learning (SEL), and arts education on student achievement. These three powerful connectors to academic success can be termed "hidden" only because they are so often overlooked. Potent and proliferating research, however, is showing the crucial impact of a positive school climate. In a very broad sense social-emotional learning and arts education can be viewed as contributors to an overall positive school climate, though each of these have their own growing data base documenting their connection to academic success as well.

> **"Potent and proliferating research, however, is showing the crucial impact of a positive school climate."**

Key components of positive school climate vary slightly study by study. Generally, however, they can be summarized as:

- Feelings of safety among staff and students;
- Supportive relationships within school;
- Engagement and empowerment of students as valued members and resources in the school community;
- Clear rules and boundaries that are understood by all students and staff;
- High expectations for academic achievement and appropriate behavior (Elfstrom, et al., 2006); and
- "Trust, respect, and ethos of caring" (Perkins, 2006).

It is interesting to compare these descriptors of positive school climate to the six primary environmental resiliency builders identified in The Resiliency Wheel (see Part One, chapter two) a decade ago. These six protective factors of caring and support, high expectations for success, opportunities for meaningful participation, pro-social bonding, clear and consistent boundaries, and life skills training, based on a synthesis of the body of research on fostering resiliency, formed the basis of a model of effective school reform (Henderson & Milstein, 1996, 2003). In the ensuing decade, the importance of addressing these six factors, under the rubric of improving school climate, providing social-emotional learning, and/or building student resiliency has been extensively validated.

A compelling case for addressing the inclusion of these general school climate/resiliency-building factors is now being made by those who are reviewing the growing weight of scientific evidence about the power of school climate to foster academic success for all. An article in the December, 2005, *American School Board Journal*, is indicative of the clarion call to schools to address school climate:

> Urban school leaders who want to reform low-performing schools usually embark on a series of…strategies…[that often] overlook an important piece of the puzzle:…Good climate. [It is] the key to success of urban schools, according to researchers who've spent years studying the subtle and interpersonal dynamics that take place [in schools]. "A school's climate is probably the best predictor of whether a school will have high achievement—more so than the socioeconomic status of students or the school's past levels of achievement," says Clete Bulach, associate professor emeritus of educational leadership at the University of West Georgia and a long-time researcher in the field. (Stover, 2005, p. 1)

The Most Comprehensive School Climate Research

Perhaps the most comprehensive and powerful research to date on the importance of school climate was just published (October, 2006). Researcher Brian Perkins studied the impact of school climate in 108 urban schools from 15 school districts across the country. Thirteen states were represented in this study, and the students, ages six to 20, included "self-identified 110 ethnicities or national origins; 32 % identified as African American, 26% as white, 29.6% as Hispanic, 6.8 % as Asian, 2.5% as Native American, and 2.2 % as another ethnicity." Perkins' research, "the CUBE Survey," was sponsored by the Council of Urban Boards of Education (CUBE) and the National School Boards Association (NSBA). The results revealed improved school climate contributes to:

- Higher student achievement;
- Higher morale among students and teachers;
- More reflective practice among teachers;
- Fewer student dropouts;
- Reduced violence;
- Better community relations; and
- Increased institutional pride (Bryant & Kelley, 2006, p. ii).

This research was a project of the Urban Students Achievement Task Force, which is sponsored by CUBE and NSBA. In his Foreword to the CUBE Survey research report, *Where We Learn: The CUBE Survey of Urban School Climate*, Yale University School of Medicine Associate Dean James Comer, writes:

> Students cannot learn well and are not likely to behave well in difficult school environments.... Good student development and academic learning are inextricably linked. Indeed, research-based evidence continues to demonstrate this critical connection....Unfortunately, however, the recent increased pressure to improve student test scores has led many to feel that they do not have time to address anything but academic instruction...But because relationships are so important to learning, strengthening instruction in a difficult school climate generally does not improve academic outcomes. (2006, p. 1)

Perkins concludes,

> School climate is the learning environment created through the interaction of human relationships, physical setting, and psychological

atmosphere. Researchers and educators agree that school climate affects student achievement. Yet many school improvement initiatives primarily address school structure and virtually ignore school climate. (2006, p. 1)

> *"The affective dimension of the school day—that is, how students feel about their experiences at school—is just as important as the academic dimension."*

His report offers six recommendations for schools, based on the findings that "The affective dimension of the school day—that is, how students feel about their experiences at school—is just as important as the academic dimension" (p.7). These are:

1. Districts should include a school climate assessment in their annual evaluation processe.
2. Schools should identify one or more key areas on the basis of these assessment findings...and implement strategies to improve these conditions and students' perceptions of them.
3. Parents should be encouraged to participate in the discussion, development, and implementation of strategies to improve school climate.
4. Students should engage with their peers, teachers, and administrators to address school climate issues, and [should themselves] contribute to a healthy school climate.
5. School officials should engage members of the community about the ways they can participate in and support the creation and development of healthy school climate.
6. Boards of education should establish clear policies to create a positive school climate and clarify expectations for teachers and administrators around their responsibilities to carry out these policies.

Two other related studies confirm the importance of positive school climate characteristics for preventing "all youth risk behaviors" and for promoting life success. Commissioned by Congress, the largest survey ever conducted of adolescents in this country confirmed that the number one condition in schools (and families) that protect kids from "all risk behaviors" is "feeling connected." At school, that means students feel teachers treat students fairly, that students feel "close to people at school," and students feel they are "a part of the school" (Resnick, 1997, et al.). In addition, the Gallup organization has been researching what leads to human success for several decades, surveying hundreds of thousands of people around the world, and conducting millions of interviews with "the best of the worlds' professions." Based on the organization's conclusion that

> **"Both students and teachers feel better about being at school and are more positively motivated when the school focuses on identifying and building student and educator strengths."**

the key to life success is identifying and building on one's strengths, Gallup has initiated building "Strengths-Based Schools" through its "Summit on Strengths-Based Schools" and related publications. One key finding: Both students and teachers feel better about being at school and are more positively motivated when the school focuses on identifying and building student and educator strengths (Buckingham & Clifton, 2001; Gordon, 2006).

Social and Emotional Learning as a Route to Improving Climate

That social and emotional learning connects to a positive school climate also comes as no surprise. School climate improvement recommendations include increasing an "ethos of caring and respect" between all members of a school community, including supportive relationships, and creating environments of safety and trust, including setting and maintaining clear rules and boundaries. Social and emotional learning is defined as "the process through which we learn to recognize and manage emotions, care about others, make good decisions, behave…responsibly, develop positive relationships, and avoid negative behaviors" (Zins, et al., 2004, p. 3). It is one thing to suggest school climate improvements; social and emotional learning interventions provide the strategies that can actually achieve the goal of creating a positive school climate.

A 2006 article in the American Association of School Administrators publication, *The School Administrator*, connects social and emotional learning, school climate, and academic success. Author Jose Torres concludes,

> [That] a strong relationship exists between social-emotional development and academic achievement cannot be denied. Caring relationships between adults and children in schools foster a desire to learn and a connection to school. When students' barriers to learning are removed, students do better, learn more,

and are more engaged…Social and emotional learning programs improve students' behaviors and academic learning. They do not focus on behavior at the expense of academics. The reverse is true. If we ignore students' social-emotional learning, we shortchange students' academic performance. (2006, p. 1)

> **"It is one thing to suggest school climate improvements; social and emotional learning interventions provide the strategies that can actually achieve the goal of creating a positive school climate."**

Torres bases his conclusions on a new comprehensive research-based discussion of the power of social-emotional learning, *Building Academic Success on Social and Emotional Learning: What Does the Research say?* This comprehensive book, edited by Zins, Weissberg, Wang, and Walbert, documents decades of research on the positive impact of social-emotional learning in schools. The "essential characteristics of effective social-emotional learning programs," documented in the book, include:

- Careful planning, based on theory and research;
- Teaching SEL skills that are relevant to "daily life" (such as recognizing and managing emotions, respecting others, positive goal-setting, making responsible decisions, and "handling interpersonal relationships effectively");
- Addressing affective and social dimensions of learning by actively building positive attachment to school, strengthening relationships in school, providing opportunities for meaningful participation in school, using "diverse, engaging teaching methods," nurturing safety and belonging in school, and emphasizing respect for diversity;
- Linking to academic outcomes through integrating with professional development on academic success, and coordinating with student support efforts (health, nutrition, service learning, physical education, counseling, nursing, etc.);
- Addressing key implementation factors, such as policies, staff development, supervision, adequate resources, and evaluation issues;
- Involving family and community partnerships; and
- Including continuous improvement, outcome evaluation, and dissemination components (Zins, et al., 2004, p. 10).

The book notes that many of the above characteristics are inherent in school-wide "risk behavior prevention" programs, violence (bully) reduction programs, and character education programs and directs readers to the 2002 US Department of Health and Human Services, Substance Abuse and Mental Health Services Administration publication, *SAMHSA Model Programs: Model Prevention Supporting Academic Achievement*. The editors conclude that "The research findings [on the powerful positive impact of social and emotional learning] are "so solid that they emboldened us to introduce a new term, 'social, emotional, and academic learning or SEAL'" (Zins, et al. 2004, p. 19).

> **"The research findings are so solid that they emboldened us to introduce a new term, 'social, emotional, and academic learning or SEAL'."**

Arts Education, Academic Achievement, and the Pursuit of Happiness

Similar powerful data is emerging about the contribution of arts education (visual arts, music, drama, and dance) to academic success. The data includes evidence that part of the positive impact of the arts is an improvement in school characteristics that comprise a positive school climate.

The Arts Education Partnership (AEP) is a coalition of more than 100 education, arts, philanthropic, and government organizations, funded by a cooperative grant from the US Department of Education and the National Endowment for the Arts. AEP published a report in 2002, *Critical Links: Learning in the Arts and Student Academic and Social Development*, a review of 62 "outstanding arts education studies." The *Critical Links* report concludes that learning in the arts positively impacts six important aspects of schooling:

1. Improvement of basic reading and writing skills and comprehension, through "forms of arts instruction [that] help children 'break the phonetic code' by associating letters, words, and phrases with sounds, sentences, and meanings"; and through engaging in dramatic enactments of stories (which is linked to increased comprehension, more effective writing, and the ability to read new material);
2. Improvement in mathematics, through music instruction (especially training in keyboard skills);
3. Improvement in fundamental cognitive skills and capacities, through individual art projects and "multi-arts experiences" that "engage and strengthen...fundamental cognitive capacities;"
4. Improvement in the motivation to learn, through the impact of engagement in the arts on self-confidence, self-efficacy, school attendance, educational aspirations, and "ownership of learning;"
5. Improvement in social behavior, which occurs through student experiences in drama, dance, and multi-arts activities that result in "growth in self-control, conflict resolution, collaboration, empathy, and social tolerance;" and
6. Improvement in "school environment," through the arts' contribution to teacher innovation, a "positive professional culture, community engagement, increased student attention and retention, effective instructional practice, and school identity."

> **"Similar powerful data is emerging about the contribution of arts education to academic success."**

James Catterall, a UCLA professor of education and a researcher on the *Critical Links* study, noted that the impact of the arts is especially potent "for economically disadvantaged children." However, he added,

> The beneficial effects of the arts...are reported for *all* children learning in the visual and performing arts....*Critical Links* identifies no fewer than 84 separately distinguishable, valid effects of the arts when we differentiate among groups of children who benefit.... Notions that the arts are frivolous add-ons to a serious curriculum couldn't be further from the truth. (2002, p. 6)

The idea of the benefits of creating educational and work environments that actually make people (students, educators) happy has recently entered the cultural dialogue about how schools can more effectively foster "what really matters in life." In *Happiness and Education* (2003), educational philosopher and reformer, Nel Noddings, Lee L. Jacks Professor of Child Education, Emerita, at Stanford University, comments that whenever parents are asked what they hope for the future of their children, the answer is they want their children to "be happy." Noddings goes on, "Happiness and education are, properly, intimately connected. Happiness should be an aim of education and a good education should contribute significantly to personal and collective happiness"(p.1). She rightly points out that beyond all the discussion in education about "aims talk" of standards and achievement should be a primary concern for human flourishing.

> **"Happiness and education are, properly, intimately connected."**

Happiness, as Noddings defines it, is not mere material gain or momentary pleasure. She notes that psychological research on "authentic happiness" concludes that beyond the poverty level, an increase in financial wealth does little to increase true happiness. Instead, Noddings discusses the authentic happiness that comes from caring relationships, feeling "connected," service to others, developing character, personal growth, experiencing delight, and finding work that one loves.

The best homes and schools are happy places. The adults in these happy places recognize that one aim of education (and of life itself) is happiness. They also recognize that happiness serves as both means and end. Happy children, growing in their understanding of what happiness is, will seize their educational opportunities with delight, and they will contribute to the happiness of others. Clearly, if children are to be happy in schools, their teachers should also be happy. Too often we forget this obvious connection. Finally, basically happy people… will contribute to a happier world. (p.261)

Research is documenting the power of positive school climate, social and emotional learning, and involvement in the arts to improve academic achievement. Though difficult to measure, it makes sense that people in schools (or other environments) filled with these—positive, caring, respectful climate, social-emotional support and training, the beauty and exhilaration of the arts--are *happier*. Any human endeavor is easier, more motivating, and enjoyable when we are happy. Discussing and researching what creates authentic happiness, flourishing, and deep life satisfaction in schools is another emerging and important perspective on academic achievement, resiliency, and life success.

References

Arts Education Partnership. (2002). *Critical links: Learning in the arts and student and academic and social development.* Washington, D.C.: Arts Education Partnership.

Bryant, A.L. & Kelley, K. (2006). Preface. In Perkins, B.K., *Where we learn: The CUBE survey of urban school climate* (p.ii). Alexandria, VA: National School Boards Association.

Buckingham, M. & Clifton, D. (2001). *Now, discover your strengths.* New York: The Free Press.

Catterall, J. (2002). *Critical links: Learning in the arts and student social and academic development.* Comments to the National Press Club in Washington, D.C., May 16.

Comer, J. (2006). Foreword. In Perkins, B.K., *Where we learn: The CUBE survey of urban school climate* (p.i). Alexandria, VA: National School Boards Association.

Elfstrom, J., Vanderzee, K., Cuellar, R., Sink, H., & Volz, A. (2006). *The case for programs that address school climate.* Oxford, OH: Miami University Department of Psychology Center for School-Based Mental Health Programs.

Gordon, G. (2006). *Building engaged schools: Getting the most out of america's classrooms.* New York: Gallup Publishing.

Henderson, N. & Milstein, M. (1996, 2003). *Resiliency in schools: Making it happen for students and educators.* Thousand Oaks, CA: Corwin Press.

Noddings, Nel. (2003). *Happiness in education.* Cambridge, MA: Cambridge University Press.

Perkins, B. K. (2006). *Where we learn: The CUBE survey of urban school Climate.* Alexandria, VA: National School Boards Association.

Resnick, M., Bearman, P., Blum, R., Bauman, K., Harris, K., Jones, J., Tabor, J., Beuring, T., Sieving, R., Shew, M., Ireland, M., Bearinger, L., & Udry, J. (1997). Protecting adolescents from harm: Findings from the National Longitudinal Study on Adolescent Health. *Journal of the American Medical Association, 278,* 823-832.

Stover, D. (2005). Climate and culture: Why your board should pay attention to the attitudes of students and staff. *American School Board Journal, December, 2005.* Retrieved from http://www.asbj.com.

Torres, J. (2006). Building academic success on social and emotional learning. In *The School Administrator, April, 2006.* Arlington, VA: American Association of School Administrators. Retrieved from http://www.aaa.org/publications.

Zins, J. E., Weissberg, R.P., Wang, M.C., & Walbert, H.J. (Eds.). (2004). *Building academic success on social and emotional learning: What does the research say?* New York: Teachers College Press.

Nan Henderson, M.S.W., is an international speaker, writer, and president of Resiliency In Action, a publishing and training company in Southern CA. She has authored several articles and coauthored four books on fostering resiliency, including Resiliency In Action: Practical Ideas for Overcoming Risks and Building Strengths in Youth, Families, and Communities *and* Resiliency In Schools: Making It Happen for Students and Educators. *She can be contacted at nhenderson@resiliency.com or at by calling 800-440-5171. More information is available at www.resiliency.com.*

CHAPTER 2

Fostering Resiliency and Positive Youth Development in Schools:
If Only Schools Were Like Baseball Teams!

by Kate Thomsen

Editor's Note: Teachers and other school staff are overwhelmed with myriad concerns. As a result, many view "fostering resiliency" or "positive youth development" as just "one more thing" to add to an already full plate. (Both terms are used to refer to similar attitudes, approaches, and strategies. See Part Five of this book, "Resiliency and Youth Development.") In this chapter, Kate Thomsen assists educators in understanding how positive youth development is inherent in good educational practice, and does not have to be one more thing. Using the metaphor of a baseball team, the author describes the core skills that educators need in order to develop students both academically and personally.

The basic tenets of fostering resiliency and positive youth development (connection, confidence, competence, compassion, and character) are inherent in good educational pedagogy, but many educators are unaware that they good things that they do every day are actually promoting positive youth development. If they knew, they might even be more deliberate about their efforts.

Think of how much more effective school and classroom environments would be if schools worked like baseball teams. Baseball teams bring highly skilled people together under the leadership of a person who has a vision for winning. Members train together, practice together, and celebrate together. They are very aware of what they have to do to win, and they give it their all. Schools could be like baseball teams, too, if their staffs stayed focused on playing the game.

Teachers often work on teams and plan together, but in practice, teachers' techniques are uniquely their own. Some utilize cooperative learning strategies; others on the same team do not. Some routinely integrate multiple intelligences strategies into their lessons, others do not. Some teachers are comfortable integrating service-learning into their curricula, others are not. If a school-wide plan for promoting positive youth development existed, all teachers would be regularly utilizing the approaches that are known to promote both academic excellence and personal/social development.

PYD Challenges Schools

School-based positive youth development (PYD) challenges school personnel to think very differently about young people. In the positive youth development approach, youths are no longer "vessels to be filled," "problems to be solved," "risks to be mitigated," or subjects to be tested (Astroth, Brown, Poore & Timm, 2002). Rather, they are partners in their own development with voices to be heard. They are resources to be tapped rather than liabilities to be managed. They are people to be empowered rather than to be made compliant. Youths are perceived as potential leaders, workers, parents, and neighbors. They are understood to be in the process of becoming adults, allowed to experiment with their ideas and to resolve any errors that might occur in the process. They are hopeful people who know that their voices matter, that they can depend upon caring adults to create safe environments where they will learn according to their unique styles, and that they will receive support and guidance when they need it.

The concept of positive youth development may be more familiar to those working with youth in community settings rather than in school settings. Principals and teachers who wish to see what positive youth development actually looks like in a school setting may find agency settings are not useful as models. School-based PYD will be very different from community-based PYD for a variety of reasons. For starters, community-based programs have flexible hours, are not required to test youths on standards, offer a relaxed, casual atmosphere, engage youths according to their interests, and are places where youths voluntarily congregate.

Schools, on the other hand, face state and federal mandates and are held accountable for the achievement of standards and outcomes. They answer to the governments, parents, and the community businesses for which they are preparing students to work. Schools' workforces are often under contract and flexibility is not always possible. Schools face great challenges in integrating positive youth development into their rather inflexible systems and into teachers' existing pedagogy. Even so, schools ought to be heartened by the fact that they are already in the ballpark, and caring educators have been helping their students "run the bases" of our educational system for quite some time.

Educational theorists like Goleman (1995) and Gardner (1983) have made significant contributions to the field of positive youth development within school settings while never using the term. Indeed, many of the current educational trends such as cooperative learning and learning styles theory have aspects of PYD at their core. Educators will feel more confident about meeting the challenges of integrating positive youth development into their culture when they see that many of the programs and strategies that they are already using have aspects of positive youth development within them.

Schools can be ideal settings for PYD because the adults who work with students within these settings have immense power to stifle or enhance a young person's development. Educators who view youths as having potential, who focus on strengths rather than only on problems, and who move from regarding youths as being "at risk" to being "at promise" can make the difference between success and failure for their young students.

Schools Are Already in the Ballpark

In order to integrate positive youth development into their schools, effective principals, like baseball managers, need many successful techniques. One technique is to make sure that staff within their buildings shares the same vision. A school that promotes positive youth development envisions youths engaged in their own development, making lasting relationships with staff and students, participating in challenging learning experiences, and interacting within environments where they feel bonded to the school.

Continuing the baseball metaphor, players must have core skills, such as throwing, catching, and batting. In the same way, school personnel who are focused on positive youth development must have a solid core of knowledge from which to develop practical applications. The following three trends lay a solid core of knowledge for school-based PYD teams.

Brain-based Emotional Intelligence

An understanding of how emotions promote, as well as hinder, learning is as essential to a school team as the ability to throw a ball is to a baseball team. This theory recognizes that emotions play as big a part in a child's learning as do intellectual ability or access to fine teachers. Goleman (1995) made the connection between emotions and the ability to learn in his book, *Emotional Intelligence*. Other educators who have researched the brain and learning have elaborated on the topic, leaving little doubt that students who are struggling with emotional issues are less likely to be able to learn (Wolfe, 2001, Jensen, 1998, Sprenger, 2001).

Students are individuals with emotional histories that accompany them into their classrooms, and teachers need to be adept at recognizing emotions and managing these histories. School personnel who understand this principle and take measures to assist students in managing emotions are incorporating aspects of positive youth development. Teachers who understand the impact of emotions on learning can incorporate strategies on a daily basis that give students of all ages opportunities to cope effectively with their emotions and free up the "working memory" (Thomsen, 2002). As a result, students will take these strategies into their adult lives and be able to navigate life's challenges better. These are a few simple strategies that help staff develop relationships with students and communicates to them that they are more to us than their test scores:

- Start out class by simply asking students to rate their day so far on a scale of 1 – 10.
- Teach kids how to identify stress in their bodies so they can be aware of their own responses and work toward self-calming.
- Find out when your kids are having birthdays and acknowledge them--in high school too!
- Help kids develop empathy for others by discussing diversity and challenges people face.

Multiple Intelligences and Learning Styles

Multiple intelligences theory is another key element of an effective team, as important as an outfielder's ability to catch a fly ball. Recognizing that students are capable of being "smart" in at least eight ways, educators who utilize multiple intelligences theory "pitch" their content to students in ways that ensure that they can really "catch it." These intelligences are: logical/mathematical, linguistic, musical, spatial, interpersonal, intrapersonal, naturalist, and bodily/kinesthetic. Gardner (1997) postulates that schools often overlook the many ways in which a child is intelligent, especially if the child in question is not thriving (testing well) mathematically or linguistically.

Unfortunately for many students, they are not given standardized tests in the areas in which they excel. Many students who struggle in school come to the conclusion that they are not "smart," when that is not the case. To avoid this, Gardner (1997) advises that the best way to teach a child something new is to utilize his or her strongest intelligence. For example, musically intelligent children would likely learn the times tables easier if they were put to music. Kinesthetically intelligent children would do better if they were allowed to physically move about or handle things as they learn.

- Help your students discover their strongest intelligence and their preference for learning and interacting with others. There are many surveys already available.
- Have students think of famous people and ask them to decide what their strongest intelligence is and what their learning style might be.
- Allow students to do a project in any way they wish (musically, artfully, danced, written, etc.).
- Offer students opportunities to contribute in the way that best suits their personalities. Outgoing students might give tours and greet visitors, others might care for plants.

Just like a pitcher must be adept at both throwing a fastball and reading the catcher's signals, school personnel must understand both multiple intelligences and the signals of students' learning styles. The skill of addressing learning styles cannot be separated from the ability to integrate multiple intelligences into classroom lessons. Silver, Strong, and Perini (2000) integrate Gardner's theories with their studies of learning styles. Each style has a strong preference for learning and interacting with others. By utilizing multiple intelligences and learning style theories in their teaching, educators are better able to engage students in their learning. Here are a few simple ways to start:

Building Character

Just as baseball players must be capable of taking their turns at bat, school personnel must "step up to the plate" when it comes to building character by first modeling the character traits they expect their students to acquire, and then reinforcing them when students demonstrate them. In schools, character education is often perceived as an activity when it is actually a process. Schools that engage their students in the process of building character are participating in positive youth development. Character education programs often focus entirely on the students, neglecting to hold staffs responsible for their actions and interactions.

Building character, on the other hand, is a process and a joint effort between both adults and students. These character-building strategies that promote bonding and connection to school may be incorporated into daily routines:

- Make sure that new students never eat alone. Pair them with other students to ease their transition. Be sure to prepare the "welcoming" students for the importance of their role.
- Show the respect to students that you wish to receive from them. Never assume they know how to be respectful.
- Teach them first by your example and expect that they will eventually be comfortable with the behavior.
- Create opportunities for students to contribute to others in some way.
- Ask for students' ideas and suggestions when creating classroom rules and procedures.

Baseball players enter a game equipped with their core skills of throwing, catching, and batting, but they also need additional tricks up their sleeves to help them win games. The same is true for educators. School personnel may rely on the three core elements we just mentioned to form the foundation for a great team effort, but additional strategies need to be developed if the team expects to connect kids to school and engage them in their own development.

Service-learning and Peer leadership

In the game of baseball, players work together, know each other's quirks and personalities, and encourage one another to be successful. They cheer from the dugouts and bolster those who may have become disheartened. Teamwork in a baseball game can be like service-learning and peer leadership in schools. These are strategies that teachers can use to transform students' lives.

When students seem unmotivated, disruptive or lacking in self-esteem, service-learning or peer leadership ought to be part of the game strategy. (See pp.81-88 for details of implementing effective service learning.) Students who are marginally connected to school become engaged when they can see, first, a value in what they are learning, and second, that they have something to offer to others. Too often, students sit in classrooms and absorb information year after year, rarely connecting the information to the real world. Only very rarely do they get to see how they can make a meaningful contribution to this process.

Service-learning or peer leadership are strategies that can get kids to show up at school because they know that someone, possibly a younger student or maybe a nursing home resident, is eagerly awaiting their arrival. Once they see that what they do is valued and appreciated, students are eager to remain engaged, just like baseball players stay in the game when they believe they can contribute towards a winning effort.

Often, academic areas improve because of the confidence gained through the experience of service. Service-learning and peer leadership can take many forms, and can range from very simple to more complicated (Thomsen, 2002). While there is little cost involved, coordination of projects is often time-consuming, but well worth every minute invested. Whatever form they take, service-learning and peer leadership strategies engage students in meaningful work, increase bonding to school, and foster relationships between adults and students.

Mentoring

Where would players be without their coaches? Even the most talented baseball player needs a coach to help him to stay on track and reach his full potential. In schools, the coaching function is filled by mentoring programs that connect students to caring, committed adults (or older students) who can fill gaps often left open by disconnected families. This strategy is a powerful one to use when students throw us curve balls. A student who has not responded to our interventions may need a caring adult more than anything else we can offer.

None of us entered adulthood alone. If we think about it, we can remember people, places, or experiences that helped guide us on our path. Mentors become the allies that youths need when they are unsure of themselves. They listen without judgment, ask questions that teach, and give the most precious gift of all, their time. Youths need quantity and quality time with adults. They need to know that someone will be there for them no matter what.

When we wonder why some students seem to be so unmotivated to succeed in school, we must remember that it is hard to care about yourself when it appears that no one cares about you. Mentors prove that youths are worth caring about because they are willing to invest their time in them. Every positive youth development approach underscores relationship as its core because without relationship, nothing is possible, but with it, magic can happen.

Cooperative Learning

Once again, baseball teams can be living examples of cooperation. It would be impossible to win a game if teams played like nine individuals competing with one another. In schools, students learn the value of cooperation and team effort through cooperative learning. These are strategies that, when implemented properly and consistently, have immense powers to positively influence youths' development. Skillful teachers can utilize these strategies to help students interact with groups to improve social skills.

As students work together on tasks, they learn more about themselves and those with whom they are working. Cooperative learning makes it easier to understanding the concept of teamwork and the importance of each team member's contribution. Cooperative learning brings the interpersonal and intrapersonal intelligences to every group task. The skills associated with these intelligences are skills for life, and the earlier they are honed, the better.

Playing the Game!

Any coach knows that finding the right players is only half of the job. The other half is to get the players to work as a team to create the environments in which students can thrive. Principals must make sure that each member of their team knows the score at all times when it comes to individual students. Wise principals and their teams know that students are full of surprises. When you least expect it, they throw you a curve!

Educators ought to feel heartened that they have been in the PYD ballpark for quite some time. To hit a home run, however, schools will have to play the game. First, they will change long-standing attitudes about students. Youths will become partners, not just recipients, in their learning and development. Youths' voices will be invited into all decisions affecting them and their schools. All youth, not just a select few, will have regular opportunities for meaningful participation. Teachers will know their students' dreams and fears, their pain and their joys. They will be their mentors, allies, and their advocates.

Baseball players do not hit home runs by accident, and neither do educators. Like professional ball players, effective educators work hard, practice, and are managed by people who know how to spot talent and nurture it. They focus on shared goals and work as a team for the benefit of their students. As they face the challenges of integrating PYD, principals and school personnel must remember that they are already in the ballpark, and when schools play like baseball teams, our students are the winners.

References

Astroth, K. A., Brown, D., Poore, J., & Timm, D. (2002). Avenues to adulthood or avenue to civic anemia. *In Community youth development anthology.* Institute for Just Communities.

Gardner, H. (1983). *Frames of mind: The theory of multiple intelligences.* New York: Basic Books.

Gardner, H. (1997, September). Multiple intelligences as a partner in school improvement. *Educational Leadership*, 20-21.

Goleman, D. (1995). *Emotional intelligence.* New York: Bantam.

Jensen, E. (1998). *Teaching with the brain in mind.* Alexandria, VA.: Association for Supervision And Curriculum Development.

Silver, H., Strong, R., & Perini, M. (2000). *So each may learn: Integrating learning styles and multiple intelligences.* Alexandria, VA.: Association for Supervision and Curriculum Development.

Sprenger, M. (2001). *Becoming a wiz at brain-based teaching.* Thousand Oaks, CA.: Corwin Press.

Thomsen, K. (2002). *Building resilient students: Integrating resiliency into everything you already know and do.* Thousand Oaks, CA.: Corwin Press.

Wolfe, P. (2001). *Brain matters: Translating research into classroom practice.* Alexandria, VA.: Association for Supervision and Curriculum Development.

Kate Thomsen, an experienced speaker with a talent for practical application of theory, specializes in the affective side of education, recognizing that the quickest way to students' brains is through their hearts. She has written two books, Building Resilient Students: Integrating Resiliency Into Everything You Already Know and Do *(2002, Corwin Press) and* Service-Learning in Grades K-8: Experiential Learning That Builds Character and Motivation *(2006, Corwin Press). In addition to curriculum and instruction, she has expertise in drug and alcohol abuse prevention, positive youth development, bullying prevention, resiliency, asset development, brain-based teaching/parenting, and staff supervision. She can be reached at 315-446-1747 or at fnthom@aol.com.*

CHAPTER 3

An Introduction to Program Evaluation:
A Step-by-Step Guide to Getting Started

by Craig Noonan, M.S.W., Ph.D., and Nan Henderson, M.S.W.

*"The most savage controversies are about those matters as to which
there is no good evidence either way."* –Bertrand Russell

"It is not enough to aim, you must hit." –Italian proverb

There's an old joke about a drunk man who leaves a bar one evening and is followed outside by a friend who is concerned about him trying to drive home. He finds his drunken friend accross the street, under the street lamp, on hands and knees, searching for something and asks him what he is looking for. The inebriated friend answers: "Dropped m' keysh." His friend comes over to help look and asks him where he lost them. The drunk man says: "Over by the door." The friend is puzzled and asks: "If you lost them accross the street, why are you looking for them here?" The reply: "Becaush the light ish better."

This story reminds us of the attitude that is often taken towards program evaluation in school settings. Often a mandate from the administration or the funding source to evaluate a program initiates the evaluation process and something is thrown together to satisfy the requirement—but doesn't provide very useful information. Unfortunately, the time and energy necessary to produce a meaningless evaluation could just as easily be used to produce one that is useful to both the "powers that be" and the program being evaluated.

Educators and other helping professionals often experience resistance to program evaluation based on several fears and misconceptions. Some think they need to be trained researchers and/or statisticians to do a proper job, and feel inadequate. Others think it will take too much time to conduct an evaluation and fear becoming overwhelmed. Another fear is that the program and/or jobs may be terminated due to a negative evaluation. Finally, some have the mis-conception that evaluation is unnecessary because the program or curriculum being used has already been evaluated.

These fears and misconceptions are far from true. The essential ingredient for a good evaluation is familiarity with and knowledge of the program. Researchers and statisticians can be consulted to fine tune evaluation projects, often for little or no expense. Many well designed and useful evaluations are conducted every day by staff who have very little formal training in research design and statistics.

The time necessary for an evaluation is always a trade off between practical limitations and needed information. (A better evaluation is always possible if more time, money, and resources are available.) The true creativity of a good evaluation lies in answering the desired questions using the fewest resources. Many of the best evaluation projects use data that are already being collected.

It is important to evaluate every program, even if it has already been evaluated and found effective (and the reality is many most drug and violence prevention programs and curriculum have not been evaluated). A previously evaluated program does not guarantee effectiveness because it was not evaluated in a specific school with specific students and staff. Effective programs require a combination of factors such as the appropriate intervention, the right dose, the proper duration, and a high quality of service delivery to be successful. Any one of these components could be less than adequate in a specific setting for specific students. Evaluating various aspects of the program to improve and fine tune it for the best results in each school should be a regular ongoing endeavor.

Evaluation as an ongoing process for program improvement is consistent with the way people naturally (every day!) evaluate their environment and behavior to make adjustments for optimal functioning. They use the information from this evaluation to improve their lives. In the same way, the best and most appropriate use of program evaluation is not to terminate programs and jobs but to help school staff, students, and administrators simply do what is better for them in their specific environments. Teachers, other educational practitioners, and some university researchers are advocating that an ongoing spiral of evaluation become the norm for staff development in education (see Figure 1) for this very reason—the benefits of improved programs for students and the sense of self-efficacy and self-empowerment for the educators actively engaged in systematic problem solving (Anderson, Herr, Nihlen, 1994).

Reasons for Program Evaluation

There are other reasons for evaluating programs but we think two are most important. The first is an ethical responsibility. The programs put in place in schools may affect the lives of young people in profound and long lasting ways. The intention is that these programs will have positive effects but that may not always be the case. Drug education seemed like a good idea in the 1970s but some types of education have been shown to actually increase drug use by desensitizing young people to a previously unknown and scary behavior. Educators have a professional responsibility to do no harm. The only way to insure this is to evaluate even the most well-intentioned and well-thought-out programs.

Figure 1: The Action Research Cycle

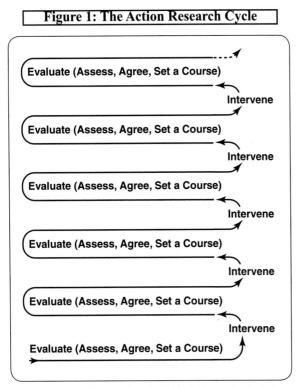

Reprinted from *Resiliency in Schools: Making It Happen For Students and Educators* (1996) by Nan Henderson and Mike Milstein, published by Corwin Press, Thousand Oaks, CA

The other important reason for program evaluation is to find out if programs and curriculums are making a difference. Why waste professional time and energy on programs that aren't accomplishing what needs to be done? There are also degrees of "making a difference." Educators all want to make the biggest difference with the least amount of effort. The time and resources that are saved can be put to other good uses. Program evaluation can indicate if programs are working, but more importantly, it can indicate how they can be improved. In other words, evaluation is the key to fine tuning any program to do the best job possible with specific students, at a specific school, and at a specific time.

Program Evaluation: Step by Step

Program evaluation can be as simple or as complicated as those doing the evaluation wish to make it. Some people drive VW Bugs and some drive Cadillacs. As with automobiles, the complexity of the evaluation model will depend upon specific needs and the kinds of questions that are being asked. Summative evaluation questions ask about outcome: Does a program "work?" Formative evaluation asks how well a program is working. It provides information about program consumers (how many, attitudes about program, demographics, etc.), resources expended for program delivery, whether the program is meeting the needs of the school community, and how efficiently the program is functioning. In other words, formative evaluation provides data to fine tune the outcome and efficiency of a program. It may even provide useful information about why a program is not working. It is often useful to combine both types of evaluation—formative information often provides the context necessary to understand summative data.

Nine steps for conducting a simple program evaluation are outlined below. Erudite volumes have been written on the topic and there are many excellent manuals that go through it, step by step (see bibliography). This brief guide is designed to get educators started in answering a few simple questions or to interest them in acquiring and using a manual. At several points, consultation with an evaluation design or statistics expert is recommended for those who don't have one already working with them. A second opinion is always helpful and can avoid a disaster when something is inadvertently overlooked. Most school districts, universities, or funding sources have such individuals either formally or informally available. Educators should find an evaluator who speaks their native language and have them review all evaluation plans. It is also useful if this consultant is willing to provide a practical education so the novice evaluator will eventually become an expert too. Before beginning, be aware of the old adage: "Be careful what you ask for." Once evaluators get answers to their initial questions, they will probably want to ask many more. Program evaluation is habit forming and contagious! It also is a natural fit into the vocation of education, which has as its central purpose finding ways to improve student learning, social development, and overall life success.

Step One: Identify Questions and Involve Others

The first step is to identify the questions that need answering and to involve as many others as possible in the process. What questions will provide the most useful information for making a program as effective as possible? What information would be useful to others (administrators, parents, teachers, students)? Worksheet 1 provides a series of questions that will help clarify important questions to ask. Enlist others in filling out this worksheet to get several perspectives. Use a brainstorming process for each of these questions, keeping in mind that the key to good brainstorming is to let the creative juices flow. Don't evaluate the importance or feasibility of answering specific questions, just get them all down on paper. It also is useful to brainstorm potential barriers (both personnel and systemic) to the project as well as possible remedies for these hindrances.

Include as many other school staff and students in the process of developing and choosing evaluation questions as feasible. This gives others some ownership of the project. If they don't decide to help, they will probably at least get out of the way. Get key people involved at an early stage and allay their fears about the project. Emphasize how the project will benefit them, the school, and the students. De-emphasize the evaluation of individual work and stress the evaluation of an entire program. Invite the biggest critic of the project to be part of the evaluation. He or she will help counteract biases. Also, try to include some staff who are knowledgeable about research design and statistics and some consumers of the program (especially students) on the evaluation team. They are worth their weight in gold for the mistakes they will prevent from happening.

Step Two: Prioritize Questions

The next step is to narrow the questions that have been identified down to a few that are most important. The more questions an evaluation tries to answer, the more complicated the project will get. Keep it simple is an important rule, especially for those just getting started with evaluation. Other questions can always be answered in the next evaluation project.

For summative evaluations, Worksheet 2 may be helpful in moving from the goals of the program to specific behaviors and the indicators that may measure those behaviors. Evaluating knowledge and attitudes can be useful, but don't stop there. Funding sources are interested in results and that means behavior change. Measure these outcomes as well.

Step Three: Define the Question(s)

Defining evaluation questions is one of the most important steps. This means translating general questions from Step Two into terms that can be measured. Filling out Worksheet 2 is a way to do some of this. "Is our program to increase

protective factors in the school environment working?" is a general question. "Did our new policy and student discipline program reduce behavioral incidents within the six months since it started?" is an evaluation question that can be measured. It is important to state each question in a way that clearly defines what it is that is being measured.

Worksheet 1: Clarifying Evaluation Questions

1. What reasons are there for program evaluation in our school? What purposes could it serve?
2. What are the goals of the program(s) that we might want to evaluate?
3. If we had unlimited resources, what would we like to know about our program?
4. What would we like to know about the population we serve?
5. What have we wondered about, or what questions would we like answered?
6. What are our biggest concerns and frustrations in our work? Do these suggest any evaluation questions?
7. In what ways would we like to see our services improved?
8. Is there anything we are considering adding or dropping from our program? Do these suggest any evaluation questions?
9. What is especially different about our program? Does this suggest any evaluation questions?
10. What is especially effective about our program? Does this suggest any evaluation questions?

Step Four: Choose the Measurement Tools

Choosing the right tool for the job will get it done quickly and properly. In general, the best measure is one that addresses the question being studied as directly as possible, or one that is already in place to gather some type of information relevant to the program evaluation now being conducted, and/ or a measurement instrument that is well established. Tools have already been developed for just about anything that might need measuring in a program evaluation. *The Mental Measurement Yearbook*, published yearly and available in the reference section of most university libraries, can be a useful source for finding measurement tools. Conducting a literature review on a specific program area will yield others.

Choose established instruments carefully and consider their relevance for the program being evaluated, whether they really measure what they are supposed to

Worksheet 2: Defining and Measuring Program Goals			
What are the goals of our program?	**What are the changes we expect to see for each of these goals in individuals or the community?**	**How would we know we have succeeded in effecting this change?**	**What could we measure that would indicate this change?**
#1. EXAMPLE: To increase caring and support in our school.	• Increased student involvement • Less conflict on campus	• Greater student attendance at school and classes • Fewer discipline referral to administration	• School attendance rates • Classroom attendance rates • Number of discipline referrals per week
#2. etc.			

(validity), and their ability to yield the same score or data on two separate occasions if no change occurred in between (reliability). Other important concerns are their comparability to other similar measures, their readability, their cultural appropriateness, and their ease of use in data collection and analysis. If it is necessary to design a measure for a specific evaluation, it is important to consult an expert so the instrument is designed correctly. Inexperience often results in a poorly designed instrument and a bad instrument can ruin an entire evaluation project.

Most variables that are measured in a program evaluation fall into one of the following categories: attitudes, knowledge, skills, behavior, or environmental factors. This data can be collected by self-reports, interviews, surveys, and from records in archival sources, observation, and/or current records. If the outcome being evaluated is actual behavior change, don't just measure attitude change. Figure out a way to actually measure behavior; better yet, measure both. Since attitudes are not always good predictors of behavior they cannot be used to provide the answer to the ultimate question: Did behaviors change as a result of this program? If a program does appear to change attitudes but not behaviors, based on looking at both, this may mean that a program is on the right track and simply needs some fine tuning for the attitude change to carry over to behavioral change. Prevention researchers have found, for example, that whereas several drug prevention curricula change knowledge and attitudes in the short-term, an adequate dosage (in terms of number of initial sessions), implementing the curriculum

exactly as it is designed (referred to as "imple-mentation fidelity"), and an adequate number of booster sessions for several years are necessary for attitude change to translate to behavior change in the long run (Botvin, 1992).

Finally, use a variety of measures whenever possible in finding the answers to the questions that are the focus of the evaluation. For example, for a program attempting to reduce school violence by teaching mediation skills to students, attitudes and knowledge about conflict resolution techniques could be measured using a student self-report instrument, mediation skills acquisition could be assessed using observers to objectively evaluate how well students picked up the skill, and mediation skill use in the real world could be determined by asking students in personal interviews and surveys, by using observers, and by surveying family, friends, and other collaterals. Furthermore, existing data already being gathered could be analyzed to assess the frequency of violence at school before and after the program was implemented, and the student body could be surveyed about their feelings of safety before and after the program. If all of these measures yield convergent results, this is strong evidence of a successful program. If they do not, the thoroughness of looking at the program from several different perspectives provides useful information about how the program can be improved.

Step Five: Design Your Evaluation

An evaluation design is simply a set of instructions or procedures about when, how, and from whom to collect data in order to answer the questions that have been posed. The design will largely be determined by the questions that need answering. Table 1 provides guidelines that can be used in designing the evaluation. Those inexperienced with evaluation design should consult an expert in research design and statistics for a final stamp of approval.

An important consideration in the design is the potential negative impact of the evaluation upon evaluation participants (e.g., poor performance on an outcome measure, violations of confidentiality or anonymity, membership in a no-program control group, etc.). Therefore it is also important to have the design reviewed by someone knowledgeable about this topic. Some school districts require formal approval for certain types or even all types of evaluation projects to ensure protection of those being evaluated.

Issues of anonymity and confidentiality are important concerns regarding the collection of data. Both generally result in more accurate data from individuals. Special data collection and storage steps may need to be taken to ensure anonymity and confidentiality. Also, in some school districts, confidentiality of sensitive information can be a politically sensitive issue. There may be policies against some types of confidentiality (e.g., if a student admits to regular cocaine use to school staff they may be required to report it). It is important to investigate district policies in this area to learn both the limitations to and requirements for confidentiality.

Another issue is who will be measured. Will the evaluation include every participant in the program or a smaller subset of this group? If a smaller subset of participants is selected, they must be randomly selected and representative of the larger group in order to generalize findings to this group. Random selection will usually insure a representative sample but measuring the sample on important characteristics (age, gender, culture, grade, etc.) after the sample is selected is a way to make sure the sample is close to the general population. If it is not, then results of measures on this sample cannot be generalized to the larger group. This is another area of the evaluation project that can benefit from research expertise. If in doubt, consult someone who has expertise in sampling. If this is not possible, be aware that the answers from an unrepresentative sample pertain to sample members only and cannot be used as representative evidence for the program as a whole.

Table 1: Evaluation Designs

Single Group Designs	Questions Answered	Limitations of Design
1 Deliver Program ⇒ Post Measure	Best for assessing feelings and attitudes of participants at any point in time	Cannot measure change because no pre-program measure
2 Pre-measure ⇒ Deliver Program ⇒ Post Measure	Best for assessing characteristics of program participants Good for assessing change in feelings, attitudes, knowledge, skills, or behavior	Cannot assess if change is due to program or another factor (maturation, time, school, etc.)
Two Group Comparison Designs (Matched or random assignment for best results)		
3 Deliver Program Group 1 ⇒ Post Measure Deliver Program Group 2 ⇒ Post Measure	Good for comparing program vs. no-program results if groups are equivalent before and subject to no other influence besides program	Cannot assess the extent of change or difference in results because no pre-program measure
4 Pre-measure ⇒ Deliver Program ⇒ Post Measure Pre-measure ⇒ Deliver No Program ⇒ Post Measure	Best for assessing extent of change as a result of the program	

Finally, lay out a time line for the tasks of the design, assigning responsibility for each of them, and outlining how they will be accomplished. Specifically, when will the data be collected (e.g., before, during, immediately after, and six months after the program)?, who will collect it?, how will they collect it?, and what will they do with it?. Include a plan for data management, organization, and analysis. Will results be tallied the "old fashioned way" or will the data be entered into a computer database? Selecting a project manager to oversee the overall process is a good idea. He or she can also deal with political and systems issues that may interfere with the project.

Step Six: Implement Your Plan

Implement the evaluation plan for a "pilot" or "trial" period of reasonable length. This may only mean pretesting all measurement tools and systems on individuals who are similar to those you will be using in your evaluation. Do not skip this process. Invaluable information about what has been overlooked that might cause problems or even invalidate the entire evaluation will be gained in this step of the process. Once this new information is incorporated into the evaluation design, it is time to launch the evaluation.

Step Seven: Organize and Analyze Your Data

This step should already have been anticipated in planning the evaluation design and should not pose a problem. Descriptive statistics are very straight-forward and provide a summary of characteristics of the evaluation participants and measurements. Most elementary statistics texts contain excellent chapters on how to describe data. Find the best way(s) to summarize the data for different audiences (e.g., those with different interests and knowledge levels). Make it user friendly.

Inferential statistics allows comparisons and an examination of relationships between different groups of participants. They also determine if any observed differences are meaningful or likely due to chance. They can be complicated and may only be applied to certain types of designs and data. Try a statistics text, use a statistician, or consult one for this step. There are many excellent and inexpensive statistical software packages on the market that also do most of the calculations. Again, there is most likely someone in the district who is knowledgeable about statistical processes who can be consulted for help.

Step Eight: Share the Results

This is an essential part of evaluation that is often neglected, or done poorly. It's the payoff! If results are positive, share them with everyone and anyone who has an interest. Design different reports for different audiences. Make the data live. Share what the numbers mean in terms of the difference one would see in the lives of real people. Use a variety of presentation techniques to maintain interest and an appropriate level of consciousness in the listener.

If the results are not positive, share them with those who need to know in the manner described above. Learn from the results. Some useful questions to ask include: Were the results caused by a poorly designed study, an ineffective program, or a poorly implemented program? Why isn't the program working? What is working and what is not working? The results can answer these questions and ultimately improve the program or provide the necessary information to develop a more effective one. When viewed this way, even negative results are worthwhile. If the ultimate goal is the implementation of programs and strategies that help students, "negative" results are just a stop on the road in designing approaches that make this goal a reality.

Significant results (either positive or negative) should be shared with the larger professional community. Professionals working with young people, and ultimately the young people themselves, will benefit from the creativity and the hard work that went into the evaluation. A variety of professional journals exist for just this purpose. Find one that relates to the area that has been evaluated, get a copy, and read the style and submission requirements before submitting a report.

Step Nine: Start All Over Again With New Questions

Once a first set of evaluation questions has been answered, and the results have been incorporated into an improved program, there is then something new to evaluate. New questions will almost always emerge that also need answers, and they form the basis of an ongoing evaluation process. Often, more staff are interested in helping with the new evaluation and may even want to consult on how they can do their own evaluation. Congratulations!

References and Bibliography

Anderson, G. L., Herr, K., & Nihlen, A.S. (1994). *Studying your own school*. Thousand Oaks, CA: Corwin Press.

The Burows Institute of Mental Measurements. (1995). *The mental measurement yearbook*. Lincoln, NE: The University of Nebraska Press.

Henderson, N. & Milstein, M.M. (1996). *Resiliency in schools: Making it happen for students and educators*. Thousand Oaks, CA: Corwin Press.

Linney, J. A. & Wandersman, A. (1991). *Prevention plus III: Assessing alcohol and other drug prevention programs at the school and community level*. DHHS Pub. No. (ADM)91-1817. Rockville, MD: Office for Substance Abuse Prevention.

National Institute on Drug Abuse. (1993). *How good is your drug abuse treatment program: A guide to evaluation*. NIH Publication No. 95-3609. Rockville, MD: National Institutes of Health.

National Organization of Student Assistance Programs and Partners. (1992). *Evaluation tools for student assistance programs*. Boulder, CO.

Wolfe, B. E. & Miller, W. R. (1995). *Program evaluation: A do-it-yourself manual for substance abuse programs*. Albuquerque, NM: University of New Mexico, Department of Psychology, Center on Alcoholism, Substance Abuse and Addiction (CASAA).

Craig Noonan, Ph.D., M.S.W., is a retired therapist, substance abuse treatment program supervisor, addictions researcher, and trainer. He can be reached at cnoonan@resiliency.com.

Nan Henderson, M.S.W., is an international speaker, writer, and president of Resiliency In Action, a publishing and training company in Southern CA. She has authored several articles and coauthored four books on fostering resiliency, including Resiliency In Action: Practical Ideas for Overcoming Risks and Building Strengths in Youth, Families, and Communities *and* Resiliency In Schools: Making It Happen for Students and Educators. *She can be contacted at nhenderson@resiliency.com or at by calling 800-440-5171. More information is available at www.resiliency.com.*

CHAPTER 4

Protective Beliefs Are a Key to Professionals' and Students' Resiliency

by Kerry Anne Ridley, L.C.D.D.

Recently I was conducting a support group for counselors from a large urban school district. The counselors were sharing concerns about their students that spanned a range of serious social problems, problems that have a tragic familiarity for educators throughout the country. They expressed con-cern for a boy who would soon be orphaned by the death of both parents to AIDS, a sixth grade girl who might be prostituting for family food money, and a prevalence of young people who have a parent or a sibling in the prison system.

Over the years, I've heard these counselors share stories of student abuse and neglect that are beyond the imagination of most ordinary adults. For counselors and teachers alike the face of neglect is not seen on the evening news or "made for T.V." movies, the face of neglect sits in their offices everyday. Coming in close personal contact with human situations that defy easy solutions can challenge the most buoyant person's mental health.

When a counselor becomes caught in a web of discouragement common patterns begin to emerge. The counselor may begin to doubt the potential success of the individual. How can this young person survive or thrive with such destructive circumstances surrounding him? In attempting to manage overwhelming numbers of young people in need, the counselor can develop mental categories which predict negative outcomes. Here is another student staying at home alone with her siblings. With no parental supervision they are up all hours of the night. How can she possibly learn in school? Finally, the counselor may begin to doubt his or her own abilities. Can I really help this person? I can't even imagine the horror of what she's endured.

These absolutely normal reactions to occupational stress can produce unintentional outcomes for the counselor and the young person. The problems presented all begin to sound the same, the young person becomes known for his or her problems rather than his or her unique humanity, and the solutions can become rote. Hope is diminished.

Yet time and time again, I have been dazzled by the ability of these counselors to manage stress. Counselors do wrestle with negative attitudes, but a tremendous degree of resiliency is the norm. I began to wonder: How were these individuals able to sustain a healthy perspective in spite of the tragic stories and consequences experienced by the students and their families? I asked the counselors attending the support group about their protective beliefs—beliefs which protect them from the effects of adversity. What beliefs did they have that helped them with feelings of responsibility and sometimes even inadequacy? How were they able to maintain enduring compassion and faith in the human spirit?

Four Categories of Protective Beliefs

The beliefs they expressed fall into four broad categories.

1 Belief One: Trust that human goodness and caring surpass human destruction. "During all the recent floods, earthquakes, and even hurricanes, for every person who looted or refused to help there were thousands who didn't commit a crime and worked tirelessly for the good of the community. Knowing this helps me when I'm preoccupied with worry about our students and all the potential dangers they face." The opinion of this counselor struck a chord of agreement with the others. Yes, violence and fear abound but human compassion is far more common and powerful.

2 Belief Two: View oneself as a helper amongst a community of helpers. A common theme was, "There have been many people before me who have helped this particular student and there will be many after me." Knowing the responsibility for the student's long term success does not solely depend on the current counseling relationship appeared to lighten the "psychic load" for many counselors.

3 Belief Three: Know that most people are capable survivors who possess appropriate solutions for their challenges. One counselor said, "I remind myself often about my students' smartness and common sense in creating

solutions; their solutions are like a seed breaking through concrete." Another counselor commented, "I remember the students who come back to visit. Five years ago it seemed like sone of those students wouldn't finish high school, and others wouldn't live much longer. Somehow they've made it and want to tell us about it!"

4 The final belief was focused on the ultimate mystery of life. Belief Four: Recognize that there are forces at work in all of our lives that are beyond human understanding. "Who grows up healthy, and who doesn't? Who experiences one trauma after another and who doesn't?" In posing these questions a counselor spoke of her helping philosophy. "I will always try to change the world's injustice so my students may have a fair shot at a good life, but I also know I am not in control. My influence and time are limited. I have to believe there is something bigger than me guiding a person's life." Different words were used in describing this belief–faith, collective wisdom, God, and even karma. These invisible forces were a source of comfort and reflection for many of the counselors.

The counselors who participated in this discussion had known they held a perspective or philosophy which allowed them to sustain compassion but they had never made them explicit. From this discussion they felt a new degree of clarity. They could now lead their students through a similar process.

Help Students To Identify Protective Beliefs

How can you begin an inquiry with your students about their protective beliefs? You can initiate a process of discovering with them their community of helpers, their experience with human goodness, and their own triumphs with "seed breaking through concrete" solutions. You can help make their own invisible protective beliefs more visible and potentially more useful.

In translating our own and others' protective beliefs into helping approaches we will be less likely to succumb to occupational hazards that weaken our mental health immune system. We are then better able to see possibilities and promise where before we saw predominantly limitations and despair.

Kerry Anne Ridley, L.C.D.D., is a consultant who assists schools and businesses in shifting from a predominantly "at risk" orientation to resiliency focused practices. She lives in Austin, Texas.

CHAPTER 5

Integrating Resiliency Building and Educational Reform:
Why Doing One Accomplishes the Other

by Nan Henderson, M.S.W.

"We just don't have time to do one more thing!" Those of us who have worked in prevention over the past two decades are used to hearing this lament from well-intentioned, caring, but overwhelmed classroom teachers as they are confronted with the prospect of implementing another program. Though they agree that students need prevention programming, in their frustration they often express the feeling: Why does this, too, have to be our job?

Several years ago, when I started a new job as a prevention program administrator with Albuquerque Public Schools (APS), I had an experience that helped me realize that the cutting edge of prevention— strategies for building resiliency in students—is not simply one more thing for schools to do.

Another person joined the APS prevention team when I did. She didn't have a background in prevention, per se, but had excellent training and practice in facilitating school reform—called restructuring in our district at that time—in dozens of schools throughout the district. When we began talking about our prospective backgrounds, I eagerly shared with her the emerging prevention paradigm of resiliency which was just making a splash in 1991. My new colleague listened carefully as I talked about the key concepts. Then she said, "I've never heard of this resiliency stuff, but I can tell you that everything you are talking about is the basis of school restructuring."

A wonderful collaboration was born. Together we reached the conclusion which many others familiar with the fields of prevention and school reform have also realized:

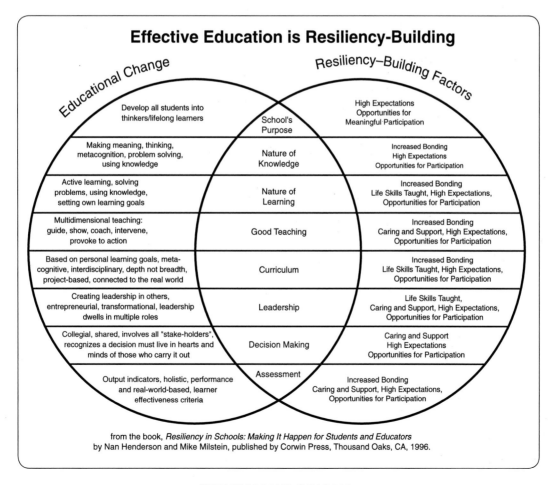

from the book, *Resiliency in Schools: Making It Happen for Students and Educators*
by Nan Henderson and Mike Milstein, published by Corwin Press, Thousand Oaks, CA, 1996.

Effective school restructuring produces a resiliency-building school. And resiliency building in schools is actually the foundation of effective education.

Deborah Meier, principal of Central Park East in East Harlem, New York, where 90 percent of the students graduate and 90 percent of those go on to college (in a school district where the average graduation rate is 50 percent) wrote in the July, 1995 issue of the *American School Board Journal* about her school's success: "There's a quality called 'hopefulness' that is a better predictor of success, even in college, than grade point average, class rank, or SAT score!" Reading about her school, it is clear that the all-important attitude of hope and optimism whatever the challenge, which I like to call "The Resiliency Attitude," permeates Central Park East. In addition, Meier reports the school integrates the trends in education documented in the diagram on the previous page. Report after report of schools that are successful beyond the norm, including the schools that have been mentioned by the students interviewed for the "Faces of Resiliency" featured in this book, characterize these schools similarly: Exceptional schools are imbued with that all-important attitude and are structured around resiliency principles—whether those involved realize it or not.

Helping educators understand this connection often brings a great relief and, in my experience, increased motivation to make the changes in their school that will both increase student academic success and foster greater life success in the form of less involvement in risky behaviors and increased resiliency. Helping preventionists realize this connection enables them to achieve what has been for us an historically elusive goal: Weaving the recommendations from prevention into the very fabric of schools.

Nan Henderson, M.S.W., is an international speaker, writer, and president of Resiliency In Action, a publishing and training company in Southern CA. She has authored several articles and coauthored four books on fostering resiliency, including Resiliency In Action: Practical Ideas for Overcoming Risks and Building Strengths in Youth, Families, and Communities *and* Resiliency In Schools: Making It Happen for Students and Educators. *She can be contacted at nhenderson@resiliency.com or at by calling 800-440-5171. More information is available at www.resiliency.com.*

CHAPTER 6

Resiliency-Building Approaches to School Discipline

Clear and consistently enforced boundaries and limits in the form of family rules, school discipline policies, and community laws and norms act as a protection for students, according to risk factor research. Several schools have also woven the resiliency-building concepts of providing caring and support, recognizing and reinforcing positive behavior, providing students with opportunities for meaningful participation, and teaching the social skills necessary to "stay out of trouble" into their approaches to school discipline. The following examples of resiliency-building school discipline policies are reprinted from Resiliency in Schools: Making It Happen for Students and Educators *by Nan Henderson and Mike Milstein. The elementary school policies are primarily the result of district-sponsored resiliency training conducted over a four year period in Albuquerque Public Schools (APS). This training was funded through a School Personnel Training Grant from the US Department of Education.*

Elementary School Approaches

The staff of Kit Carson Elementary School developed the following guidelines for "preventive discipline" after their participation in the APS project.

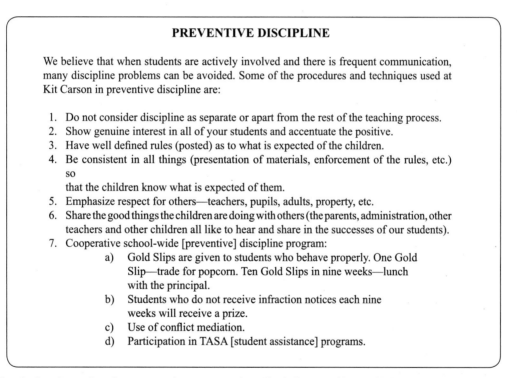

PREVENTIVE DISCIPLINE

We believe that when students are actively involved and there is frequent communication, many discipline problems can be avoided. Some of the procedures and techniques used at Kit Carson in preventive discipline are:

1. Do not consider discipline as separate or apart from the rest of the teaching process.
2. Show genuine interest in all of your students and accentuate the positive.
3. Have well defined rules (posted) as to what is expected of the children.
4. Be consistent in all things (presentation of materials, enforcement of the rules, etc.) so
   that the children know what is expected of them.
5. Emphasize respect for others—teachers, pupils, adults, property, etc.
6. Share the good things the children are doing with others (the parents, administration, other teachers and other children all like to hear and share in the successes of our students).
7. Cooperative school-wide [preventive] discipline program:
   a) Gold Slips are given to students who behave properly. One Gold Slip—trade for popcorn. Ten Gold Slips in nine weeks—lunch with the principal.
   b) Students who do not receive infraction notices each nine weeks will receive a prize.
   c) Use of conflict mediation.
   d) Participation in TASA [student assistance] programs.

The school also formulated an extensive "corrective discipline" policy, which clearly outlined eight key school rules and steps taken for each number of infractions. Its primary focus on "preventive discipline," however, is a resiliency-building approach—accentuate the positive to alleviate much of the need for "corrective discipline."

Another creative approach to discipline, designed to foster staff resiliency at Kit Carson, was the assignment of "buddy teachers"—individuals who could be called upon by other staff in the school in any "corrective discipline" situation. Through this approach, the staff built in caring and support for one another in what are often tense and stressful situations, and assured a greater likelihood of students being treated with caring and respect (through the intervention of a more neutral third party).

East San Jose Elementary School developed a discipline policy based on the idea that every student had certain rights, and formulated it as a list of rights for students.

EAST SAN JOSE
BILL OF RIGHTS

1. Everyone has a right to be safe and no one will be hurt.
　　_____ There will be no fighting, kicking, hitting, pinching, or pushing.
　　_____ There will be no weapons at school.
　　_____ Students will be at their assigned place at proper times.
　　_____ Students will use all equipment properly and safely.

CONSEQUENCES:

1st Offense: Time out with mediation and contract [see below]. Days in time out determined by completion of contract.
2nd Offense: Time out with mediation; parent contacted by classroom teacher.
3rd Offense: Time out with mediation; conference with parent and principal.

2. Everyone has the right to be respected.
　　_____ To dress appropriately.
　　_____ Foul language will not be tolerated.
　　_____ Destroying property will not be allowed.
　　_____ Defiance is unacceptable behavior.

CONSEQUENCES:

1st Offense: Time out with mediation and contract. Days in time out determined by completion of contract. Restitution for vandalism/graffiti.
2nd and 3rd Offense: Same as above with possible School Police involvement.

3. Everyone has the right to be drug-free.
　　_____ Alcohol, drugs, and tobacco will neither be used nor tolerated.

CONSEQUENCES:

1st Offense: School Police and parents will be called, counselor referral, in-house suspension.
2nd Offense: School suspension.

4. Everyone has the right to be happy and treated with compassion.
　　_____ We will not hurt each other's feelings.

CONSEQUENCES:

1st Offense: Time out with mediation. Days in time out determined by completion of contract.
2nd and 3rd Offense: Same as above.

Students violating this policy are sent to this school's "Responsibility Room" where they meet with a student mediator (a peer with training in conflict mediation) and fill out the following contract.

MY CONTRACT AND PLAN

1. Why are you here in time out?

2. What is wrong with that behavior?
3. What will you do to keep this from happening again?

_____ Student
_____ Mediator
_____ Parent
_____ Date

Resiliency-Building Intervention Strategies in Secondary Schools

How does a school intervention ("Care" or "Core") team handle students who are referred for serious or repeated violations of the school's discipline policy? Two approaches to supporting the resiliency building of students in these situations have been implemented by several schools. First, the intervention team focuses on the strengths of students as well as the problems. Referral forms that include equal space for identifying problems and strengths help assure that the students' strengths are looked at in equal proportion to the risks or problems. The team then poses this question in discussions about the student: "How can we use this person's strengths to facilitate solutions to the problems?"

The second approach involves making sure a student receives some help for his or her problem. Too often, schools send students out the door, assuming they will some how "be better" when they return to school days or weeks later. In reality, without increasing the web of protection diagramed by The Resiliency Wheel [shown in chapter two, Part One] in all likelihood the students' problems will get worse, and the overall health of the school community as well as that of the student will suffer. A resiliency-building approach adopted by many schools is to require an assessment for alcohol, other drugs, or other significant problems, administered by an in-school or outside agency trained professional, as a stipulation for returning to school. Without this approach, the resiliency of the student and the entire school community may decline.

The following "Statement of Philosophy" attached to the substance abuse prevention and intervention policy of Pojoaque Valley Schools in Pojoaque, New Mexico demonstrates a resiliency-building approach to student assistance.

The Pojoaque Valley School District recognizes that alcohol and other drug use/abuse is a treatable health problem. Health problems of youth are primarily the responsibility of the home and community; however, the schools share that responsibility because use, misuse, abuse, and dependency problems often interfere with school behavior, student learning, and the maximum development of each student. The schools shall intervene with students manifesting a sign of use, misuse or abuse, and make a concerted and consistent effort to educate and assist them in obtaining appropriate services.

[The consequences of violating the substance abuse policy are a two-day suspension and] the student cannot be reinstated until a meeting is held with the principal, parent/guardian, student, and others as deemed necessary by the Care Team. A no-use drug contract will be signed by the student and witnessed by the parent/guardian. As a part of the reinstatement, the parent must abide by the Care Team recommendation. This may include community service, professional drug use/abuse evaluation, counseling, etc. The parent/guardian and student will present a plan of action that is acceptable.

These are a few of the approaches schools are taking to integrate resiliency building into what has been until recently a deficit-focused arena—school policy. Further involvement of students in the discipline process, including initiation of student courts and tribunals, can be utilized to integrate even more resiliency building into schools.

CHAPTER 7

How We Revised Our School Policy to Foster Student Resiliency

by Georgia Stevens, L.P.C.C.

In the narrative below, school counselor Georgia Stevens details the changes in policy initiated in Rio Rancho Elementary School in Rio Rancho, New Mexico based on staff desire to increase student resiliency. She also offers some results of her initial evaluation as to how the policy revision has changed student attitudes and behaviors.

Bonding with students while making expectations clear is a challenge we've met at our school, using a revitalized discipline program that refers students with repeated problems into social skills development.

Staff training in resiliency concepts and funding through a grant (which paid for the necessary planning time) supported the revision of our entire discipline program. Teachers wanted a program that provided more immediate incentives and consequences as well as the development of intrinsic valuing of appropriate behavior. A team of primary and intermediate teachers, along with our principal and myself, met twice for several hours during the summer three years ago to create a new approach to discipline.

Responsibility was the concept we chose for focus. We wanted students to develop responsibility for themselves, their behavior, and their school. The revised rules, developed by our team, were first discussed with staff, who then discussed them with students in individual classes. They focused on disrespect toward staff and/or school property, foul language, fighting, and unsafe behavior—offenses for which discipline notices called "pink slips" are written. Pink slips can also be issued for serious harmful behavior in the classroom.

Recognition of responsible behavior is given in the revised policy to all students in classrooms where no student has received a pink slip during the previous week. The principal and myself cover playground duty at free recesses, so teachers get a break as well. Five weeks free of pink slips earn new pencils for the entire class, resulting in cheers from the students that can be heard down the school hallways! One additional incentive, carried over from our earlier policy, is also provided: A "Student of the Week" is selected by each classroom teacher, resulting in about 30 names read weekly over the intercom and awards of certificates at local fast-food restaurants presented to the students. The discipline phase of the program hinges on our "Responsibility Room," where students go during a recess soon after receiving a pink slip. We have chosen to use the long recess of 30 minutes after lunch for the "Responsibility Room." Teachers volunteer to staff this room in place of playground duty, and use the time helping students understand what led up to the infraction and what would have been more appropriate behavior. Sometimes an apology is written or a plan is developed for better behavior.

The "Skill Builders" Program

Any student who receives a third pink slip is referred to Skill Builders. Occasionally, a serious infraction will result in a referral when a student has just one or two pink slips. Five consecutive lunch recesses are spent in Skill Builders, followed by four weekly "booster sessions." Middle school students and/or a role model from the referred student's classroom sometimes participate in the skills training to provide positive models and/or inter-environmental reminders of the skills. Letters to parents, signed by the teacher, counselor, and principal, describe the reasons for a student referral to the program, the skills that will be developed, and the ways parents can support the training.

The Skill Builders training is based on cognitive behavioral approaches to behavior change, engaging the students' input, using behavioral rehearsal of covert self-statements, and "body anchors."

Step One   Initially, I discuss with students what they enjoy about school and the reasons they want to avoid trouble. They generate a list of consequences they want to avoid and another list of the privileges they seek.

Step Two   Next, a list of STOP words is generated—words that students can use to tell themselves to stop long enough to think a situation through. "Relax, it's not worth a pink slip" and "settle down" are covert self-commands that students have suggested for the list. A bilingual student suggested "para" which means "stop." Another suggested "no estoy bien" which in Spanish means, "I'm not well"—a phrase that told him things are not going well and he needs to think about what to do next.

Step Three The next step in the instruction is in consequential thinking, the THINK words. Students complete the sentence, "If I do that...." with short phrases.

Step Four Finally the DO list is introduced, with students generating ideas about ways to handle interpersonal problems. "Walk away," "talk it out," or "tell a teacher" are typical student suggestions. Another popular idea: "get a conflict mediator"—a validation of the credibility of our school-wide mediation program.

A practice phase follows. Students usually work in pairs to generate skits demonstrating use of the skills. The student demonstrating the skill is asked to include the following "body anchors" as he or she practices:

- hold a hand up to cue the STOP step;
- put a finger on the temple to cue the THINK step;
- give a "thumbs up" sign to cue the DO step.

On Fridays students currently in the Skill Builders group meet with students from previous groups for booster sessions. During these Friday sessions, mentors from a neighboring middle school, usually seventh graders, participate by acting in the skits, joining the discussion, giving advice, and occasionally pulling individual students aside to ask how they are doing. Fridays are the time for reflection on the question: "How have you used your STOP, THINK, and DO skills?"

Students graduate from Skill Builders after they have been in school four weeks without additional pink slips. If a Skill Builder does get into trouble, he or she continues to participate in Friday booster sessions until the achievement of four trouble-free weeks. Additional pink slips result in students going through a full Skill Builders program again, followed by four booster sessions. Some students have completed the training several times, and some of these have eventually become my assistants in training other students.

The graduation from Skill Builders consists of a simple party where student participants invite a friend for ice cream or pizza and games. Though these celebrations are uncomplicated, students love them. "This is a cool party" was written on my chalkboard by one student graduate and her friend—a sentiment often expressed by other graduates.

During the school year following graduation from Skill Builders students continue to receive recognition in increasing increments for the time they stay out of trouble. Incentives are offered at four weeks, five weeks, six weeks, etc. Last spring a local restaurant owner, whose son had completed the program, hosted a pizza party at the end of the school year only for students who had stayed out of trouble following their graduation from Skill Builders, as well as the seventh grade mentors. Parents and our school's DARE officer attended, and coupons for merchandize at local businesses were given out to the students at the party.

Results of the Program

Twenty-five students participated in the program during the first year it was implemented. Only 13 of those original program graduates attended our school the next year due to graduation to middle school and families moving out of the area. These 13 students received 25 percent of the pink slips issued in the first year of the program. The following year, this original group received only 12.5 percent of the pink slips issued during the year. Only five of the 13 repeated the program a second time during the second year. School-wide, the number of pink slips issued decreased by 14 percent during the second year of the program.

Further evaluation is needed to validate our anecdotal information and my personal observations that this program appears to increase students' help-seeking ability, use of a more appropriate repertoire of interpersonal skills, and the trust they have in the school staff.

Georgia Stevens lives and works in New Mexico.

CHAPTER 8

Publicizing the Positive about Kids May be the Best Prevention

by Nan Henderson, M.S.W.

This article is reprinted from the on-line newsletter, Resiliency In Action News To Use, *which can be accessed at www.resiliency.com.*

"The kids are all right," proclaimed the headline on the front page of the Life Section in the May 28, 2002 *USA Today*. "'Social norming' may be the strategy to keep them that way." The article went on to give this good news about kids:

- Nine out of every 10 college students have never damaged property because they were drunk or high.
- Three out of four have never blown an exam or school project because of alcohol or other drug use.
- Ninety-nine percent of college students who drink do not have unwanted sex.
- Each year, more students choose to abstain from alcohol, and fewer choose to smoke or do drugs.

In other words, "the widespread impression that the norm for today's young people is drunken debauchery simply isn't true." Reporting this type of good news is a growing movement on college campuses. Called "social norming," at least 30 college campuses around the nation have joined this movement and it is trickling down to high schools and middle schools. Initially aimed at curbing alcohol use, social norming is also expanding to curtail other risk behaviors.

The premise is that if most kids get the (accurate) impression that most of their peers don't drink or engage in other risk behaviors, then those who do will cut back and fewer will initiate those behaviors in the first place. "The key is to not over report the incidences of dangerous drinking that occur, and to broadly promote the general good health of students so that it is perceived as normal," the *USA Today* article explained.

Social Norming Reduces Drinking and Smoking for High School Students

The social norming approach works by simply refocusing the same data that traditionally emphasizes the minority of students who are engaged in alcohol, drug use, and other risk behaviors. When this refocusing happens, "most students are surprised," states Lydia Gerzel Short, who is behind the nation's first social norming program for high school students. Gerzel Short's three-year program in

two DeKalb County, IL high schools has results in drinking and smoking declines significantly greater than the national trends. Called the DCP/SAFE Social Norms Prevention Projects, the program has documented the following changes by comparing student survey results from 1999 (pre-social norming project) to 2001 (after project implementation):

- A 31% increase in NON-USE of alcohol during the past 30 days;
- A 34.4% increase in NON-USE of cigarettes during the past 30 days;
- A 28% decrease in smoking at parties;
- A 24% decrease in drinking at parties; and
- A 19% increase in NON-USE of marijuana during the past 30 days.

The DeKalb County approach involves a community-wide campaign, which has produced a "positive message" media campaign. Typically, without a focus on social norming by parents and teachers, many kids get messages from these adults that suggest drinking is the norm, especially at end-of-the-school-year events like the prom and graduation. "But everyone won't be drinking," notes Gerzel Short. "Most won't."

More information and resources on social norming are available at www.socialnorm.org.

Nan Henderson, M.S.W., is an international speaker, writer, and president of Resiliency In Action, a publishing and training company in Southern CA. She has authored several articles and coauthored four books on fostering resiliency, including Resiliency In Action: Practical Ideas for Overcoming Risks and Building Strengths in Youth, Families, and Communities *and* Resiliency In Schools: Making It Happen for Students and Educators. *She can be contacted at nhenderson@resiliency.com or at by calling 800-440-5171. More information is available at www.resiliency.com.*

Overview of the DeKalb County Social Norming
Prevention Project

Reprinted from the project website, www.dcpsafe.org.

The Social Norms Prevention Project is based on a model of identifying and reinforcing existing protective norms concerning alcohol, tobacco, other drugs, violence, traffic safety, and literacy issues [thereby] correcting misinterpretations about community behaviors and norms. The main method of this approach is social marketing, demonstrated by Northern Illinois University's Health Enhancement Program during 12 years of implementation and intervention. This model has been successfully replicated with the Communities Can! Project at DeKalb and Sycamore High Schools.

The major components of these projects target the youth, family, and school staff. Most of the expected outcomes focus on increasing pro-social, health positive behaviors, along with increasing more accurate perceptions of community norms. To accomplish this, however, this research-based approach to prevention moves out of the tradition "curriculum programs" and "scare tactics." This prevention model is research-proven, but the specifics of the strategy vary from population to population based on a market analysis of each of the population groups (i.e., high school students, parents, teachers, etc.).

Examples of social norming messages shared with students by teachers and parents are:

- "Most of the students at your school are not regular users of alcohol, even if they have tried it a couple of times."
- "More than half of the students at this school drink something other than alcohol at parties."

The project involves an extensive media campaign involving posters and flyers and radio spots that give similar information. Parents are also recruited as important partners through the media campaign, with messages such as, "Share the truth: Most students don't drink alcohol."

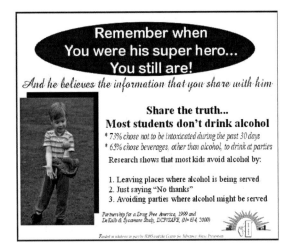

CHAPTER 9

A Resiliency Resource Primer
Resiliency and Schools

by Bonnie Benard, M.S.W., and Nan Henderson, M.S.W.

What follows are some of our favorites; however, this is far from an exhaustive list and many wonderful resources are not included. Some of these books and reports do not use the language of resilience but are about it nonetheless as they are focused on meeting the developmental needs of children, youth, and adults for belonging, respect, power, and meaning. Encouragingly, however, the specific language of "resilience in schools" has proliferated since the first edition of this book was published in 1999.

Arts Education Partnership. (2002). ***Critical Links: Learning in the Arts and Student and Academic and Social Development.*** Washington, D.C.: Arts Education Partnership. *This report reviews "62 outstanding arts education studies" and presents evidence of the positive impact of the arts on several measures of student success, including reading and writing skills, mathematics, "fundamental cognitive skills," learning motivation, and behavior management. Also presented is the positive impact of the arts on the overall "school environment." This is a "must-read" for educators as a guide to why and how to integrate arts education of all kinds (visual, dramatic, dance, and music) into schools.*

Benard, Bonnie. (2004). ***Resiliency: What We Have Learned.*** San Francisco, CA: WestEd. *This is the most recent update to Benard's 1991 paper,* ***Fostering Resiliency in Kids: Protective Factors in the Family, School, and Community,*** *her seminal publication on resiliency that synthesized more than 100 resiliency-related studies, books, and articles. This 150-page book, with 500 resiliency-related references, focuses much of its content on fostering resiliency in schools, including a crucial integration of research on "the resilient brain."*

Blum, Robert, and McNeely, Clea. (2002). ***Improving the Odds: The Untapped Power of Schools to Improve the Health of Teens.*** Minneapolis: University of Minnesota, Center for Adolescent Health. *An update on the comprehensive "Ad Health" study of more than 90,000 students, this publication documents the power of "school connectedness" to prevent all "risk behaviors" and contribute to adolescent health and success. What can schools do to promote this connectedness? This easy-to-read report includes practical strategies and recommendations.*

Boyd, Julie, and Dalton, Joan. (1992). ***I Teach: A Guide to Inspiring Classroom Leadership.*** Portsmouth, NH: Heinemann. *This is a "walk your talk" book grounded in the assumption that the key to learning and human development for students is the teacher's commitment to his or her own learning and growth. Through stories, vignettes, diagrams, charts, and activities, this book honors all learning styles and builds in active participation and reflection around its key themes of empowerment, relationship-building, modeling, and creating a community of learners.*

Brown, Joel, D'emidio-Caston, Marianne, and Benard, Bonnie. (2001). ***Resilience Education.*** Thousand Oaks, CA: Corwin Press. *This book also challenges the "at risk" label so liberally applied to students, by refocusing on the contribution to students' learning problems made by the pedagogical practices in schools. The book offers an alternative to a risk orientation: "resilience education," which emphasizes students' strengths. It then offers a PORT-able model for implementing resilience education: Participation, observation, reflection, and transformation.*

Curwin, Richard. (1992). ***Rediscovering Hope: Our Greatest Teaching Strategy.*** Bloomington, IN: National Educational Services. *This engaging book is premised on the belief that society's greatest risk factor is youth without hope. In compelling chapter after chapter this book offers educators the opportunity to reflect on how their school structures, policies, and practices either destroy or create hope—the key to learning and life success.*

Delpit, Lisa. (2006). ***Other People's Children: Cultural Conflict in the Classroom.*** New York: The New Press. *In this updated edition, this book of essays pierces to the heart of how schools must change if we are to successfully educate teachers to become successful educators of children of all ethnicities and cultures. Caring relationships, high expectations, and opportunities to be heard and to participate underlie the many stories in this volume of teachers who successfully are educating across cultural differences.*

Desetta, Al, and Wolin, Sybil (Eds.). (2000). ***The Struggle to be Strong: True Stories by Teens.*** Minneapolis, MN: Free Spirit. *This book is a powerful collection of teen-written stories demonstrating individual "resiliencies"--internal qualities identified by Wolin that help young people become resilient. The teen writers have been well trained and their stories contain gripping details of their individual journeys of overcoming abuse, abandonment, racial prejudice, parental addiction, the death of friends due to drug use and violence, and other "teen adversity."*

Desetta, Al, and Wolin, Sybil (Eds.). (2000). *A Leader's Guide to the Struggle to be Strong: How to Foster Resilience in Teens.* Minneapolis, MN: Free Spirit. *This leader's guide offers teachers, counselors, and other youth group leaders an easy-to-implement (and much-needed) way to teach students about the concept of resiliency, how young people become resilient, and how resiliency operates in students' own lives.*

Diero, Judith. (1996). *Teaching With Heart: Making Healthy Connections with Students.* Thousand Oaks, CA: Corwin Press. *This book reports the author's qualitative study of six teachers in six different high schools who are known for their positive relationships with students. Besides being rich in the voices of wonderful teachers and their students, this book identifies the nature of teacher-student relationships that make a difference; the traits, experiences, skills of these teachers; and the characteristics of schools that support nurturing.*

The Freedom Writers (with Erin Gruwell). (1999). *The Freedom Writers Diary: How a Teacher and 150 Teens Used Writing to Change Themselves and the World Around Them.* New York: Doubleday. *This book chronicles the amazing resiliency journey of 150 Long Beach, CA, high school students, once considered the lowest achievers and "least likely to succeed," who now are authors, speakers, and successful college students. Without the formal knowledge of the resiliency framework, teacher Erin Gruwell nonetheless drew upon her own innate resiliency to bring it out in her students. This book wonderfully documents the power of one teacher to dramatically change students' lives.*

Fullan, Michael. (1999). *Change Forces: The Sequel.* New York: Falmer Press. *This follow-up to Fullan's 1993 instant best-seller, Change Forces: Probing the Depths of Educational Reform, integrates the content of the 1993 book with more recent research and methodology. Drawing from theory and research of learning communities, this book clearly documents that educational change is inside-out change, beginning in the hearts and minds of individuals who share a vision and begin to build a critical mass that, indeed, can change the world.*

Gandara, Patricia. (1995). *Over the Ivy Walls: The Educational Mobility of Low-Income Chicanos.* Albany, NY: State University of New York Press. *This qualitative study of 50 high-achieving (doctoral level) Mexican Americans from low-income families (the only one specific to this cultural group that we know of) explores how these individuals succeeded academically despite the odds and makes several recommendations for educational reforms that challenge many current assumption. Not only is this a compelling read rich in the stories of these students, it validates the power of the school to make a difference, as well as the power of a bright future, "a culture of possibility," to motivate and sustain.*

Garbarino, James, et al. (2001). *Children in Danger: Coping with the Consequences of Community Violence.* Hoboken, NJ: John Wiley and Sons. *After documenting, through interviews with children and caregivers and supporting research, the realities of life for children growing up in "war zones" in the U.S., the authors document the critical importance the school plays (from pre-school through high school) as a safe haven, with the most important factor promoting children's mental health being a caring relationship between a teacher and his or her pupil.*

Gibbs, Jeanne. (2000). *Tribes: A New Way of Learning Together.* Santa Rosa, CA: CenterSource Systems. *Tribes is the best process for building communities in classrooms and schools that are rich in caring relationships, opportunities for participation, and high and positive expectations. This revision of Gibbs' earlier manual is grounded in resiliency and incorporates new research on cooperative learning, brain compatible learning, multiple intelligences, thematic instruction, human development, and social systems. For all the "hands-on people," about half this book consists of activities.*

Gordon, Gary. (2006). *Building Engaged Schools: Getting the Most Out of America's Classrooms.* New York: Gallup Publishing. *Building on the revolutionary book from the Gallup organization, Now, Discover Your Strengths, based on Gallup's decades of worldwide research on human productivity and life success, Gordon argues that schools, too, must identify and build on the strengths of teachers and students. He recommends forgetting about perfect curricula, increased testing, or tougher "standards"; instead he advocates paying closer attention to "the talent and the engagement levels of the people within an individual school." He challenges the mechanistic view of education now prevalent, arguing that knowing about the strengths of kids and caring about them must become the foundation of education.*

Henderson, Nan, and Milstein, Mike. (2003). *Resiliency in Schools: Making It Happen for Students and Educators.* Thousand Oaks, CA: Corwin Press. *A guide, par none, for schoolwide reform that incorporates the principles of resiliency. This book is rich with examples and tools to be used in creating resiliency-building schools. As Emmy Werner states in her Foreword, this book "should be read by all administrators, teachers, and parents concerned with the future of their children." This updated version includes extensive lists of resources for building resiliency in schools.*

Hooks, Bell. (1994). *Teaching to Transgress: Education as the Practice of Freedom.* New York: Routledge. *Creating learning communities wherein students are not only encouraged to challenge authority but taught to "transgress" against racial, sexual, and class boundaries in order to achieve the gift of freedom is the focus of this author's account of her life as a teacher and social justice activist. This book demonstrates critical pedagogy in action and how members of oppressed groups can move beyond blame to compassion and community activism.*

Kohl, Herb. (1994). *I Won't Learn from You*. New York: The New Press. *Titled after his powerful essay which documents the phenomenon of refusing to learn (i.e., resistance) when a student's intelligence, dignity, or integrity is compromised by a teacher, an institution, or a larger social mindset, this book of five essays takes on—in Kohl's passionate and compelling style—the Big Ones: Hope, Excellence, Equality, Equity, Democracy in Education. Especially great are his discussions of how caring teachers must "creatively maladjust" (requires all the resiliency traits!) to work in dysfunctional systems—and his passionate discourse on the at-risk label.*

Kohn, Alfie. (1992). *The Brighter Side of Human Nature: Altruism and Empathy in Everyday Life*. New York: Basic Books. *Kohn definitely makes the case—supported as always by tons of research —that schools that promote the development of caring offer the hope of personal and social transformation. All of Kohn's books support the resiliency perspective and provide research documentation extraordinaire (Also see his books: **No Contest: The Case Against Competition**; **Punished By Rewards: The Trouble with Gold Stars, Incentive Plans, A's, Praise, and Other Bribes**; and **The Case Against Standardized Testing: Raising the Scores, Ruining the Schools**.)*

Krovetz, Martin. (1999). *Fostering Resiliency: Expecting All Students to Use Their Minds and Hearts Well*. Thousand Oaks, CA: Corwin Press. *Krovetz includes detailed narrative examples in this book of how "resiliency," i.e., authentic learning that engages both the minds and hearts of students, is actually occurring in several schools. He offers several strategies for engaging students of all ages so they become excellent and motivated learners. He makes the case for fostering resiliency in everyone in schools as an essential ingredient for effective education.*

McCombs, Barbara, and Pope, James. (1994). *Motivating Hard to Reach Students*. Hyattsville, MD: American Psychology Association. *Operating from the assumption that all students are motivated to learn under the right conditions, this interactive book helps the teacher to create these conditions (i.e., protective factors) in the classroom. It also explains a process for helping students understand how their own conditioned thoughts interfere with accessing their innate resilience, motivation, and desire to learn.*

Meier, Deborah. (2002). *The Power of Their Ideas: Lessons for America from a Small School in Harlem*. Boston, MA: Beacon Press. *Meier, nationally known for "turning around" an inner-city, culturally diverse high school in Harlem (where 90% of the students now graduate and 90% of those go on to college), tells her remarkable story in this book. For any skeptics asking if resiliency-focused school reform works, give them this book. Also a critical pedagogist, Meier argues for education that is caring, built on community, based on questioning and critical thinking, grounded in high expectations for all in students, and participation by all—including parents and community.*

Meier, Deborah. (2003). *In Schools We Trust: Creating Communities of Learning in an Era of Testing and Standardization*. Boston, MA: Beacon Press. *Meier continues the themes of her previous books in this one: Schools must be smaller, more self-governed, and places of choice, so kids and their families feel they are truly part of these communities of learning. The book focuses on the crucial element of connectedness in schools: student-to-adult, families-to-schools, teacher-to-teacher. According to Meier, the current focus on standardized testing is, at best, irrelevant to academic excellence, and at worst, an actual deterrent, as teachers teach to the test and neglect anything that's not on it. She makes a compelling case that the emphasis on teaching test-taking techniques trains children to distrust their own intuition and turns off their creativity.*

Moffet, James. (1994). *The Universal Schoolhouse: Spiritual Awakening through Education*. San Francisco: Jossey-Bass. *Moffet challenges the school reform movement to reach beyond bureaucratic and corporate interests and to take on a more transformative mission by creating education that centers on personal growth, including growth of the spirit—education that enables students to adapt and thrive in spite of societal challenges and technological change. The structure for this visionary education is decentralized community-learning networks which, in essence, serve to rebuild community between young and old.*

Munson, Patricia. (1991). *Winning Teachers: Teaching Winners*. Santa Cruz, CA: ETR Associates. *This wonderful little book focuses on teacher's self-esteem (i.e., resiliency) as the key to successful school change. Filled with vignettes, pithy statements, and lots of passion, this book is a real boost to educators' self-esteem!*

National Commission on Service Learning. (2002). *Learning in Deed: The Power of Service-Learning for American Schools*. Battle Creek, MI: W.K. Kellogg Foundation. *This comprehensive study of the positive impact of service learning documents this strategy as an anecdote "to student disengagement" as well as a means to extend the standards' based school reform efforts, and a contributor to students' personal and career development. The report defines "quality" [i.e., effective] service learning, and gives suggestions, examples, and recommendations.*

Noddings, Nel. (1992). *The Challenge to Care in Schools: An Alternative Approach to Education*. New York: Teachers College Press. *An absolutely essential book and the "classic" on what a caring school looks like. Noddings creates a vision of a school system built on the central mission of caring (which in her model incorporates the other protective factors of high expectations and opportunities for participation) and which is organized around centers of care: care for self, for intimate others, for associates and friends, for distant others, for nonhuman animals, for plants and the physical environment, for the human-made world of objects and instruments, and for ideas.*

Noddings, Nel. (2003). ***Happiness in Education.*** Cambridge, MA: Cambridge University Press. *What might we teach if we were to take seriously every parent's number one goal for their children: happiness? Noddings challenges the current emphasis on economic well-being and pleasure as the very most important parts of life, and discusses the contributions to happiness of homemaking, parenting, cherishing a place, developing character, pursuing interpersonal growth, and finding work one loves. She also explores the importance of making schools and classrooms happy, cheerful places and discusses ways to do it.*

Perkins, Brian. (2006). ***Where We Learn: The CUBE Survey of Urban School Climate***. Alexandria, VA: National School Boards Association. *This is a fascinating report of the comprehensive "CUBE Survey" of urban school climate across the country, with detailed research results, compelling evidence of the connection between school climate and academic achievement, and practical recommendations for schools.*

Polakow, Valerie (1994). ***Lives on the Edge: Single Mothers and their Children in the Other America***. Chicago: University of Chicago Press. *Using the language of "at promise" (i.e., resilience), this powerful and eloquent book takes on not only the "at-risk" label but shows in classroom vignette after vignette how a teacher's high or low expectations either create possibility and hope or resignation and despair for poor children of color in inner-city schools. "An ethic of caring and a new way of seeing" the strengths of poor children and their families are the keys to successfully educating and empowering our children in these contexts and "for the unmaking of poverty and the Other America."*

Seligman, Martin, et al. (1996). ***The Optimistic Child: A Revolutionary Program that Safeguards Children Against Depression and Builds Lifelong Resilience***. New York, NY: Harper Paperbacks. *This book by a premier psychologist provides a step-by-step process for parents and teachers to teach children the skills of that powerful resilience trait, optimism—the metacognitive skills to change conditioned thinking and the social skills that will help children be connected to others. Seligman makes the convincing case that this approach can transform helplessness into mastery and reduce the risk of depression. It can also boost school performance, improve physical health, and provide children with the sense of autonomy they need to approach their teenage years.*

Sergiovanni, Thomas. (1999). ***Building Community in Schools***. San Francisco: Jossey-Bass. *This is the essential book for administrators on fostering resiliency in schools written by the premier authority on principalship. Sergiovanni challenges educators to change their basic metaphor for schooling to that of community-building, which means changing their basic thoughts and beliefs about students, teachers, and parents. "If we want to rewrite the script to enable good schools to flourish, we need to rebuild community." This book guides the way.*

Stewart, Darlene. (1991). ***Creating the Teachable Moment: An Innovative Approach to Teaching and Learning***. Blue Ridge Summit, PA: TAB Books. *Applying metacognitive psychology to working with students, this book helps teachers and counselors to understand the role their own thinking and moods make in creating a positive climate for learning. Illustrated through her personal story and the stories of students she's worked with, Stewart presents an approach grounded in the principles of caring relationships, high expectations, and reciprocity—and shows how easy and fun teaching can be from this perspective.*

Swadener, Beth Blue, and Lubeck, Sally (Eds.). (1995). ***Children and Families "at Promise": Deconstructing the Discourse of Risk.*** Albany, NY: State University of New York Press. *The 13 articles in this volume provide a powerful collection of both policy analysis and descriptive research studies capturing classroom "success stories" of survival, wisdom, courage, and strength in the face of apparent overwhelming odds. This book makes an eloquent plea for reframing the discourse that surrounds children and families who are poor, of color, and/or native speakers of languages other than English.*

Thomsen, Kate. (2002). ***Building Resilient Students: Integrating Resiliency into What You Already Know and Do.*** Thousand Oaks, CA: Corwin Press. *Thomsen builds on The Resiliency Wheel model developed by Henderson and Milstein (see above) to show how five existing major educational megatrends support and intersect with fostering resiliency. She discusses these megatrends—character education, multiple intelligences, emotional intelligence, service learning, and violence prevention—and shows their connection to the six primary protective conditions shown in The Resiliency Wheel. The best part of the book, however, is Thomsen's hands-on activities for all grade levels that can be used to simultaneously foster resiliency and promote the megatrends.*

US Department of Health and Human Services, Substance Abuse and Mental Services Administration. (2002). ***SAMHSA Model Programs: Model Prevention Programs Supporting Academic Achievement.*** Washington, D.C.: SAMHSA. *This is a guide to research-documented effective school prevention programs linked to increased academic achievement, recommended by the editors of **Building Academic Success on Social and Emotional Learning: What Does the Research Say?***

Wang, Margaret, and Gordon, Edmund (Eds.). (1994). *Educational Resilience in Inner-City America: Challenges and Prospects.* Hillsdale, NJ: Lawrence Erlbaum Associates. *This edited volume is a must for anyone studying resilience in schools and for anyone in a position to shape public policy or deliver educational and human services, especially to urban schools. It offers numerous suggestions for furthering a research agenda focused on the study of resilience in schools.*

Waxman, Henry, et. al. (Eds.). (2004). *Resiliency: Student, Teacher, and School Perspectives.* Charlotte, N.C.: Information Age Publishing. *This academic text includes three parts: Conceptual Issues and Reviews of Research; Studies of Students' Resiliency; and Schools, Programs, and Communities that Enhance Resiliency. A wide variety of resiliency-related issues, including "resiliency and the achievement gap," "teaching from a resiliency paradigm," and "future directions for resiliency educational research," are covered in this book.*

WestEd. (2001). *The Healthy Kids Resilience and Youth Development Module (RYDM).* San Francisco, CA: WestEd. *RYDM measures the protective factors/assets that researchers have consistently associated with resiliency/positive youth development, school success, and health-risk behavior protection. It assesses caring relationships, high expectations, and meaningful opportunities for participation in the school, community, home, and peer environments. The RYDM also measures six internal youth protective factors/ assets (achievement motivation, communication, empathy, problem-solving, self-efficacy, and self-awareness). Developed by a national panel of research experts, including Bonnie Benard, , the RYDM is theoretically anchored, developmentally and culturally appropriate, psychometrically reliable, and construct valid. Now widely used in California, the survey is also available to schools in other states. (More information available at www.WestEd.org.)*

Zins, Joseph, E., Weissberg, Roger, P., Wang, Margaret C., and Walbert, Herbert J. (Eds.). (2004). *Building Academic Success on Social and Emotional Learning: What Does the Research Say?* New York: Teachers College Press. *This book is a wealth of research on the positive academic outcomes associated with a variety of social and emotional "learning interventions" detailed here. It provides crucial ammunition for understanding and promoting the importance of "the affective side" of a students' life as inextricably linked to school success.*

PART THREE

RESILIENCY AND COMMUNITIES

CHAPTER 1

"Hard-Wired to Connect": A Report from the Commission on Children at Risk

by Nan Henderson, M.S.W.

This article is reprinted from the on-line newsletter, Resiliency In Action News To Use, *which can be accessed at www.resiliency.com.*

Children, according to recent scientific findings, are "hardwired for enduring attachments to other people and for moral and spiritual meaning," concludes the Commission on Children at Risk, a panel of leading children's doctors, research scientists, and youth service professionals. Meeting children's needs for enduring attachments and for moral and spiritual meaning is the best way to ensure their healthy development, according to the Commission's report, released in 2003.

The report is titled, *Hardwired to Connect: The New Scientific Case for Authoritative Communities.* "Authoritative communities" (as opposed to "authoritarian communities") are families, and all civic, educational, recreational, community service, business, culture, or religious groups serving children and youth that embody specific characteristics. These are:

- include children and youth;
- treat children and youth "as ends in themselves;"
- is warm and nurturing;
- establishes clear boundaries and limits;
- is defined and guided at least partly by "non-specialists;"
- is multi-generational;
- has a long-term focus;
- encourages spiritual and religious development;
- reflects and transmits a shared understanding of what it means to be a "good person;"
- is philosophically oriented to the equal dignity of all persons and to the principle of "love of neighbor."

"The basic conclusion of this report is that children are hardwired for closed connections to others and for moral and spiritual meaning," said Commission member Dr. Kenneth Gladish, National Director of the YMCA, at the time the report was released. The YMCA USA, Dartmouth Medical School, and the Institute for American Values all sponsor the Commission on Children at Risk.

According to the report, its publication "represents the first time neuroscientists have collaborated with social scientists" in drawing conclusions about what children need. It also "represents the first time that a diverse group of scientists and leading children's doctors are publicly recommending that our society pay considerably more attention to young people's moral and spiritual needs."

The Commission is made up of 33 leading scientists and doctors, including Peter Benson of the Search Institute; Elizabeth Berger of the American Academy of Child and Adolescent Psychiatry; T. Berry Brazelton of Harvard Medical School; Robert Coles of Harvard University; James P. Comer of Yale University; Kathleen Kovner Kline of Dartmouth Medical School (Principal Investigator); Alvin F. Poussaint of Harvard Medical School; Michael Resnick of the University of Minnesota; and Judith Wallerstein, of the Center for the Family in Transition.

Nan Henderson, M.S.W., is an international speaker, writer, and president of Resiliency In Action, a publishing and training company in Southern CA. She has authored several articles and coauthored four books on fostering resiliency, including Resiliency In Action: Practical Ideas for Overcoming Risks and Building Strengths in Youth, Families, and Communities *and* Resiliency In Schools: Making It Happen for Students and Educators. *She can be contacted at nhenderson@resiliency.com or at by calling 800-440-5171. More information is available at www.resiliency.com.*

What Research Suggests...

from Hardwired to Connect *by the Commission on Children at Risk, available from www.americanvalues.org*

1. Nurturing environments or the lack of them influence the development of brain circuitry and the ways genes affect behavior.

2. Rather than debating the impact of "nature vs. nurture" new scientific findings are teaching us to marvel at how nature and nurture interact.

3. These findings suggest that strong nurturing can reduce or eliminate the harmful effects of genes associated with aggression, anxiety, depression, or substance abuse.

4. Spiritual development can influence us biologically in the same ways that primary nurturing relationships do, including lowering stress, increasing optimism, and creating a commitment to helping others.

5. Religiosity and Spirituality significantly influence well-being.

6. The human brain appears to be organized to ask ultimate questions and seek ultimate answers.

CHAPTER 2

KIDS Consortium: A Model Service Learning Program

Editor's Note: Service Learning is a programmatic approach to fostering resiliency, including academic and life success. However, like mentoring programs or any positive youth development programs, it only works well if it is done well. No program demonstrates the power of "service learning done well" better than KIDS (KIDS Involved Doing Service) Consortium located in Lewiston, Maine. Below is a description of the program from the KIDS website. Bonnie Benard's review of the program, as well as her report on evaluation results for service learning in general, follows.—N.H.

Now in its second decade, the KIDS (Kids Involved Doing Service) Consortium is a 501(c)(3) organization that works with teachers, administrators, and community partners to involve K-12 students in addressing real challenges faced by their communities. Together they identify, research, and work to solve problems and meet needs. With guidance from KIDS, teachers match projects to school curricula and state standards, providing a powerful "hands on" learning experience that improves the community and brings academics to life.

The KIDS award winning service learning model has three essential components:

1. **Academic Integrity.** The KIDS model is an instructional strategy that provides a method for teachers and community organizations to link service-learning projects with clear learning objectives, including multiple state learning standards, and local curriculum and assessment requirements.
2. **Apprentice Citizenship.** KIDS views students as vital community members in training to become active participants in democracy. Students partner with people in the community doing real work that meets a local need.
3. **Student Ownership.** Using the KIDS approach, students are continually given decision-making opportunities, within groups, within the classroom, and with adults in the larger community. Adults share in the learning, as partners and coaches not just as "experts."

KIDS Consortium is currently working in partnership with over 40 school districts around Maine and neighboring New England states. Since 1992, KIDS has supported over 200,000 K-12 students in service-learning projects, involving thousands of teachers and community partner volunteers. KIDS Consortium has received national recognition, including:

American Planning Association Education Award (1996); Renew America Environmental Sustainability in Education Award (1998); Robert Rodale Environmental Achievement Award (2000); Renew America "Best of the Best" Award (2000); and Harris Wofford Award (2006).

KIDS in Action: Service Learning that is "Apprentice Citizenship"

by Bonnie Benard, M.S.W.

KIDS is not only service learning but, according to founder Marvin Rosenblum is "apprentice citizenship." Frances Moore Lappe, Co-Director of the Center for Living Democracy, cited the KIDS program as an example of "living democracy" in her book, *The Quickening of America*. She writes in her foreword to the KIDS Consortium publication, *Reform, Resiliency, and Renewal: KIDS in Action*:

If our democracy is to grow in its capacity to solve its weighty environmental, economic, and social problems, it will be because young people are learning to participate effectively in public life. It is because young people are discovering that involvement in public life is not what we leave to a public officicial to do for or two us. (1998, p.iii)

The Power of One

Like most stories of successful change—in families, schools, community-based organizations, or programs—KIDS demonstrates "the power of one." KIDS began in the heart and mind of one person, Marvin Rosenblum, who adamantly believed in young people's innate capacities and the critical need to provide them with opportunities to give their gifts back to their schools and communities. Lappe described her reaction to Rosenblum's approach:

What so impressed us was that Marvin's philosophy neither paternalized young people nor pandered to them. He simply turned traditional educational assumptions upside down and treated young people as contributing members of the larger community. His program realized that young people, like all of us, grow when they themselves have ownership of their work. (1998, p. iii)

KIDS success over almost 20 years compels adults to adapt Margaret Mead's now famous words to include the young and their imagination: "Never doubt that a small group of thoughtful, committed [young and imaginative] citizens can change the world: indeed, it is the only thing that ever has." Creating a walking tour of downtown Bath, Maine; building a nature trail in Moretown, Vermont; starting a Kids Korner Store in Wells, Maine; or planting a community garden in Oqunquit, Maine are testimonies to this statement. For those new to service learning, KIDS publications document how this community problem-solving process works, from discovery phase (see box on p.84) through the phases of research, goal setting, alternatives, action, and stewardship.

Lessons Learned from the Story of KIDS

Several important lessons in initiating positive individual, school, and community change are evident in the story of KIDS. The absolute need for *infrastructure* that not only trains but provides ongoing guidance and support of the KIDS coordinators is clear. *Integrating* KIDS into current school efforts so it does not become another added-on thing is also critical to KIDS' success. An emphasis on *building relationships*—not only youth-to-youth but teacher-to-teacher, school-to-family, community-to-school, intergenerationally, across sectors, and every which way—is essential. Probably the most important change in the KIDS' communities is the invisible one: the rebuilding of a sense of community from all these cross- and intergenerational relationships that link all people together.

Another big impact of change efforts like the KIDS model: They are intentionally guided by the principles of resiliency—caring relationships, high expectations, and opportunities for participation and contribution. When there is a focus at the community level on providing these developmental supports and opportunities, the positive outcomes hoped for are achieved in a fun, respectful, and mutually transforming way.

KIDS Gets Results

The University of Southern Maine did an initial evaluation of the KIDSNET project, finding positive effects on school attendance, grades, problem solving, and stewardship. Loren Coleman, Project Leaders of the KIDS evaluation, notes:

The University of Southern Maine's evaluative findings demonstrated the value of the KIDS model as a teaching tool and as a methodology for promoting resiliency in youth. Attempts to measure such outcomes have not occurred in the past, and we were pleased with the initial results. The implications of the KIDS model are significant, and the more data collected about it the better.

An interim evaluation of Learn and Serve programs nationally (Brandeis University & Abt Associates, 1996) has shown the power of service learning to affect not only individual outcomes but also to positively impact cooperating schools and community organizations, as well as the larger community.

Service Learning Impacts Students

Service learning programs showed statistically significant, positive impacts on several measures of civic and educational development, including:

- engagement in school
- personal responsibility
- grades
- social responsibility
- core subject GPA
- acceptance of cultural diversity
- educational aspirations leadership

Service Learning Improves Community Organizations

During the 1995-96 school year, Learn and Serve students were involved in more than 300 district projects or activities in each semester, providing more than 154,000 hours of service over the year. Officials of community organizations consistently gave students high praise for the "valued additions" they provided to their organizations' mission and work.

Service Learning Impacts Communities

Community officials give service learning projects high ratings and would use Learn and Serve students again. On a 10-point scale (with 10 as "best possible"), ratings for the student participants averaged:

- 8.7 for their impact on clients
- 8.2 for their community impact

In addition, 96% of the officials polled said they would use the student volunteers again; 75% said that the volunteers had helped raise the skill levels, engagement, and self-esteem of their clients; and over 66% said that the volunteers had fostered a more *positive attitude toward working with the schools*, with over 50% stating that new relationships with the public schools had been produced.

The KIDS Model and Key Components of Effective Service Learning

In an earlier study of service learning commissioned by the Carnegie Foundation (Harrington & Schine, 1989), researchers identified the key components of successful service learning as:

1. Staff *believes* that youth are resources.
2. Students make real decisions and solve real problems.
3. Responsibilities and accountability are clear.
4. Classroom learning occurs in authentic ways.
5. Teachers and adults involved are nurturing (an essential component).
6. Time for processing, planning, and reflection on service is provided for both students *and* teachers.

It is clear that KIDS is a model that absolutely does all of these, and more.

References

Brandeis University & Abt Associates. (1996). *National evaluation of learn and serve america school and community-based programs: Interim report.* Washington, D.C.: Corporation for National Service.

Harrington, D., & Schine, J. (1989). *Connections: Service learning in the middle grades.* New York: Carnegie Corporation.

KIDS Consortium. (1998). *Reform, resiliency, and renewal: KIDS in action.* Lewiston, ME: KIDS Consortium.

Lappe, F.M. (1994). *The quickening of america.* San Francisco: Jossey-Bass.

Bonnie Benard, M.S.W., has written widely and conducted workshops and trainings on resiliency for nearly 20 years. She currently works in the Health and Human Development Program of WestEd 's Oakland, CA office, where she has helped develop a statewide survey of students' perceptions of the protective factors in their lives (www.wested.org/hks). She can be reached by email at bbenard@wested.org.

How do we get started?

From *Reform, Resiliency, and Renewal: KIDS in Action,* pp. 20 – 21, published by KIDS Consortium, Lewiston, ME. For more information, go to www.kidsconsortium.org.

There is no one "right" way. A problem or issue might be generated by a student, teacher, parent, planner, or another community member in a lot of different ways. Whether it is a new project or an "old" project, discovery is about involving students in generating ideas in meaningful ways from the very beginning. The strategies listed below are illustrative, but not exhaustive.

1. *A neighborhood walk.* Arm students with cameras and clipboards to document what is good and what needs improvement in your school, your community, or the vacant lot down the street.
2. *A classroom discussion or writing project.*
3. *A newspaper headline.* "Abandoned warehouse a blight along waterfront." "50 acres of land donated to conservation commission." Sound familiar? Find the people behind the scenes and talk with them.
4. *A crisis in the school or community.* Sometimes a source of pain in the school or community can inspire anger, hope–and action.
5. *A guest speaker or panel of presenters.* Professionals such as planners, historians, and biologists not only have their hands on the hot ticket issues, but the agencies they work for usually have a mandate to promote public awareness, outreach, or education.
6. *A needs assessment.* How do people feel about_____? A survey–written or interview-style–designed by students can build awareness while generating ideas.
7. *A visit with students from another school who are working on their own community project.* Did the students across town do a great project? Invite them to make a presentation. They will be flattered.
8. *A link with a public agenda, grant or initiative.* Maybe your city just received a grant to construct a rails-to-trails. Or your town is celebrating its 200th year anniversary. Often, the planning or the product associated with these activities is done for young people, not with them.

Getting started is not just about coming up with an idea. It is not as simple as going with whatever the students want to do, or what the teacher has always wanted to try, or what the community wants the schools to produce. The decision making process about what to take on should balance student, school, and community needs. For example:

• Students: *What are interests and concerns of students?*
• School: *What curriculum areas does the teacher need to deliver through the project?*
• Community: *How will the community benefit from the project?*

When the interests of students, schools, and communities are balanced, the idea is bound to be viable from the very beginning.

CHAPTER 3

Sharing the Power:
The ELF Woods Project Taps the Energy and Talents of Students as They Improve Their Community

The following profile of the KIDS Consortium ELF Woods Project is reprinted by permission from the Spring, 1995 issue of Voices of Change, *a publication of the Maine Center for Educational Services in Auburn, Maine. The journal was funded by a grant from the Pugh Charitable Trust.*

The "snake trail" was a winding, eroded tar path, east of Edward Little High School in Auburn, Maine, neglected, littered, and notorious as a hangout for truants and troublemakers. In the fall of 1992 Brian Flynn, an English teacher, challenged his students to a simple writing assignment: "What would you do to improve the snake trail?" At first, students dreamed up impossible ideas—a water slide, castle, chair lift, flame throwing lights—and then some practical ones—a gazebo, pond, campground, trail system.... As students grew excited about the possibilities, they began to insist, "Instead of just talking about fixing up the area, why don't we actually do something?"

Since that time, over 300 students have been involved in designing and implementing a 50-page master plan to transform 40 acres of wilderness into a place that is safe, aesthetically pleasing, environmentally sound, and enjoyable for students and community residents alike. The master plan outlines the purpose, benefit, necessary modifications, term for completion, cost, and required manpower for the following six recommendations:

- 400-yard walkway resurfaced with asphalt and accented with cobblestone;
- Lights to facilitate evening commutes;
- Landscaping including picnic tables, benches, trash receptacles, and signs;
- Mountain biking trail with switchbacks and berms;
- Cross country trail for competitive athletic use;
- Obstacle course, complete with walls, tire swings, ropes, cargo net, and rocks.

The Model

The ELF (Edward Little Franklin) Woods Project is one of dozens fostered by the KIDS (Kids Involved Doing Service) Consortium, a 501(c)(3) private, nonprofit organization. KIDS as Planners is an innovative educational process [facilitated by KIDS Consortium] which engages students in working to solve real-life problems in their communities as part of math, science, English, social studies, and other subjects. In addition to land-use planning, students of all ages in over 50 towns across New England are protecting wildlife, preserving cultural artifacts, documenting local history, assessing public health, cleaning up rivers and ponds, designing parks and playgrounds, and generally "getting involved" in making a difference, not as a "nice" activity, but as an integral part of comprehensive planning and educational reform efforts.

The process directly addresses academic failure and lack of social bonding, the risk factors most common to substance abuse, juvenile delinquency, teen pregnancy, suicide, school dropout, and other destructive behaviors. In fact, research has shown that opportunities for young people to participate in the life of the community enables them to develop problem solving abilities, social competence, autonomy, and a sense of hope and future—attributes that enable them to "bounce back" from "at risk" environments.

The Town as the Classroom

Auburn sits on the Androscoggin River which, 20 years ago, provided lifeblood to dozens of shoe and textile manufacturing companies. But today, unemployment stands at 9%. The changes within the community are leading to changes in its schools. Over the past two years, a design team comprised of school and community members has been developing a strategic plan to restructure education in the Auburn school system "so that all students learn and succeed in a changing world."

The ELF Woods Project is the manifestation of this bold new approach to education. While English classes are still responsible for reading literature, building vocabulary, and writing journals and book reports, the City of Auburn has become the "test" for learning and applying these skills in a real-world context. In addition to writing, revising, and editing the master plan, students are involved in the following activities:

- Research, from conducting a site analysis to plot topography, wildlife, vegetation, water flow, and other natural features to investigating present and desired uses of the property through interviews with students and community residents and an analysis of historical records;
- Public speaking, from debate and consensus-making with fellow students to negotiation with city officials and formal presentations to the student body, school board, city council, civic organizations, and national audiences;
- Using technology to design maps, illustrations, charts, and timelines to effectively communicate the desired vision;
- Teaching, from producing television and film clips to apprenticing younger students and facilitating groups of teachers to help them plan community projects.

> **"Through the ELF Woods Project, students have been able to develop and apply a variety of talents including linguistic, logical, spatial, artistic, interpersonal, and leadership abilities."**

In order to balance the demands of content and process, teachers must establish parameters within which students can share the power and take responsibility for their own learning. Ultimately, "sharing the power" works both ways. When a teacher empowers students to make decisions about their own learning, they, in turn, must be willing to share their talents with the group. Through the ELF Woods Project, students have been able to develop and apply a variety of talents including linguistic, logical, spatial, artistic, interpersonal, and leadership abilities. Greg Lavertu, class of '94, admits that he was classified as an "at risk" student, "which means I wasn't supposed to get this far." But the experience helped him grow, and now, as a student at Unity College and a member of the Maine Conservation Corps, he recognizes that "everybody has something to offer, and it's our duty as intellects and human beings to take what that person has to offer." Sharing the power is the process that values student abilities and demands student performance.

Apprentice Citizenship

"If we are to apprentice young people as citizens of a democratic society, educators must value the application of knowledge over the mere acquisition of knowledge," asserts Marvin Rosenblum, executive director of the KIDS

Consortium. "Every kid deserves the opportunity to make a difference." Indeed, what makes KIDS as Planners different from other "project-based," "hands-on," and experiential learning methodologies is that students take action. Josh Stevens, a junior, explains, "Without approval, the master plan would have been just a 50-page plan sitting on a shelf somewhere." Instead, the students set up a referendum and brought it to the student body at Edward Little. The outcome? Over 360 students voted in favor, with only 59 opposed—a resounding six to one ratio.

> **"If we are to apprentice young people as citizens of a democratic society, educators must value the application of knowledge over the mere acquisition of knowledge."**

From there, students presented the plan to the school board and then to the city council, finally negotiating a $15,000 Community Development Block Grant to implement the plan. To date, students have raised over $34,000 with help from 30 public and private agencies, including International Paper, Maine Community Foundation, Geiger Bros., General Electric, and Project SEED. Public officials and private citizens have also served as important resources. Lee Jay Feldman, Auburn city planner, helped students develop the master plan. John Footer, a local stone mason, helped students harvest cobblestones. Specialists from the Soil and Water Conservation District certified control measures. A professional surveyor assisted students in plotting the features of the obstacle course. Currently, students are negotiating with General Durgan of the Air Force National Guard to provide about $80,000 worth of cable for the lights.

This kind of personal achievement is both public and permanent. "When students accept challenges and act on them, their success is what really builds self esteem," reflects Alumni Allen Campbell. There is no substitute for cre-ating something with your own mind, writing something with your own pen, or building something with your own two hands. Ironically, students have said that it is not what other people do for them that gives them confidence and strength, but what they do for themselves and what they do for other people in their community. Most of the time you will find that they have just never been asked.

Critical Mass

Last year, the KIDS Concortium trained over 600 people in the KIDS model. By bringing together educators, preventionists, public officials, business leaders, and community members to explore their own town as a classroom, KIDS workshops serve as catalysts to help schools break free of the "special project" design that plagues so many educational innovations. They also help create a critical mass of people willing to work together to structure and sustain learning opportunities that empower young people.

> *"Ironically, students have said that it is not what other people do for them that gives them confidence and strength, but what they do for themselves and what they do for other people in their community."*

At Edward Little, for example, the ELF Woods Project has fostered interdisciplinary learning. Pam Buffington, a computer technology teacher, helped students generate professional reports and products for the project. With the help of science teacher Margaret Wilson, students created scientific extracts to document flora and fauna native to the woods. This year, as a spinoff to the ELF Woods project, students in Tina Vanasse's geometry classes are designing and building a greenhouse that will operate as a student-run business.

Students are not problems to be solved but priceless resources with talent and energy. Likewise, teachers are not repositories of information but guides and facilitators for student learning. "Mr. Flynn looked to us for answers as much, if not more, than we did to him," reflects Greg Lavertu. When, at last, schools, towns, businesses, and community-based organizations can share the power of their talents and expertise, we can create learning that empowers and education that matters.

KIDS Beautify Norwich's Heritage Walkway

by the Norwich Connecticut Schools' Third Grade Classes

One day we were studying social studies. We talked about our community and what was fun in Norwich. One of the places we mentioned was Heritage Walkway. It is a 1.4 mile walkway that starts at the marina and ends at the old powerhouse on the Yantic River. We noticed that the walk was very dirty. People treated it like a trash can. We wanted to clean it up. It is important to all of us that nature is clean.

We made a plan to pick up trash, to plant flowers, and to put up some birdhouses. We listed all the things we needed to do the job. Then we listed the materials and the equipment we would need. Then we asked ourselves what steps would be needed. Then we put the steps in order. We thought of possible problems. Once we were done doing that we thought of the solutions for all of them.

We wrote a letter to Ms. Bram-Mereen, the assistant city planner, and asked if the third grade classes and Mrs. Mercier's kindergarten class could help clean it up. She sent a letter back saying we could help out on the city's Earth Day Cleanup. We invited her to come to talk to us about it. She gave us maps and told us that after the cleanup we would all have pizza and soda. She also gave our school a banner for taking part in the cleanup.

On Saturday, April 20, parents helped us to clean up. Ms. Bram-Mereen took care of the garbage cans and bags. We took care of the gloves. We worked hard for two hours. Ms. Bram-Mereen gave us little rose patches to thank us for helping.

We chose to plant flowers at a place near the power house. So far we have tested the soil for its pH level, worked the soil to remove grass and weeds, and planted some day lilies. Pretty soon we will plant more flowers. Then we will put up some bird houses that our families have made and sent in.

We Learned a Few Things, Too

Many varied and unusual things that we've learned along the way during our Heritage Walkway Project are:

- letter writing
- telephone manners
- making graphs
- writing math story problems
- testing soil for the pH level
- what perennials and annuals are
- estimating how long it takes to walk a mile
- estimating area
- estimating perimeter
- measuring area & perimeter
- measuring distances
- dividing tools among groups
- planning projects
- making decisions
- drawing murals
- working in groups
- writing summaries
- adding details to paragraphs
- using the computer to write
- drawing on the computer
- making a computer report about our project
- talking to people who can help us learn about our community
- helping our community is fun
- planting seeds and watching them grow
- learning what plants need to grow
- how birds like their own space

Reprinted with pewrmission from the KIDS Consortium Newsletter

CHAPTER 4

The Faces Of Resiliency

by Nan Henderson, M.S.W.

The drop out prevention, resiliency, and treatment literature is filled with research evidence about the detrimental impact of negatively labeling young people, adults, families, and communities. This literature is also rich with reports of how a single person or opportunity can turn around the life of a person, family, or community so labeled. L.W. Schmick's story personalizes this research. His wisdom, shared below, reiterates how labels do the opposite of helping, and how, in Bonnie Benard's words, resiliency is often the result of "one person or one opportunity or one caring family member, teacher, or friend, who encouraged a child's success and welcomed his or her participation."

L.W. Schmick: Challenging the "At Risk" Label

When L.W. Schmick was in middle school, he realized he was in a class that "was different" from other kids. By his freshman year in high school, he knew that his classes were for "at risk" students. Though he says he "wasn't ever mad at teachers for seeing that and being aware of that," he thinks the label was detrimental to himself and his peers.

"Putting an 'at risk' student in a separate class just separates them more. And I think that's what a lot of "at risk" students are trying not to do [be more separate]. I think they should be blended in more so they are not put in their own little group," L.W. explained.

> **"One of the results of being labeled, he said, is that students feel since they've already been labeled, why even try."**

One of the results of being labeled, he said, is that students feel since they've already been labeled, why even try. He used to say to himself, "It doesn't matter. I'll be 'at risk.' No big deal." He added, "It just seemed like everyone was waiting, watching for us to fail." He and his peers felt that all their behaviors were "under a magnifying glass."

L.W. was labeled "at risk" after he got into "a lot" of trouble in fifth and sixth grade. He and his mother had just moved to Maine from New York State, and for him the move "was a big deal." He had to leave his entire family behind, including his father who had been divorced from his mother when L.W. was only six months old, but who was still an important person in his life. His reaction to the move: "I was big for my age, so I had older friends around. I got in a lot of fights. I got in trouble at school, and I didn't get along with teachers very well." L.W. got suspended from school in sixth grade.

He says that in looking back at that time, he realized one of the major reasons he got into so much trouble was "I just wanted to fit in... and it is pretty hard to fit in when you're a six foot red head. Blending into a crowd isn't the easiest thing to do." This is one reason he feels that being separated in middle school into a class for tough kids only made things worse. He was thrown off the middle school basketball team "for being mean," he received a lot of detention, and he started drinking.

L.W. credits his parents with providing him with some of what helped turn his life around. He said he always felt unconditional love and support from both of them. His mom stopped working two jobs so she could be home when he got home from school. His dad encouraged him to find a vocation in life, which meant staying in school. And L.W. himself said he never seriously considered dropping out of school because he realized that would "be quitting and I don't like to quit."

His life began to change his freshman year in high school when he was forced to find new friends (who were more connected to school) because "all my other friends dropped out." In fact, only 2 of the 15 students in his "at risk" middle school class—the class "no one really wanted to mess with, the class for 'the bad kids'"—graduated from high school. L.W. was one of the two. And he graduated with the respect of his teachers, his peers, and his community thanks to a KIDS Consortium-trained teacher to whom L.W. gives most of the credit. L.W. said it is because of this teacher and the opportunity this teacher offered to become involved in a KIDS Consortium Project that he is headed this fall to college to become a teacher himself.

"In my sophomore year, I had an English class with Brian Flynn," who started the ELF Woods Project (see previous chapter). "A lot of teachers when they see an 'at risk' student, they automatically distrust and they

L.W. Schmick: "Just another person: Not an 'at risk' student."

don't give them some of the responsibilities they would give other students... because they're 'at risk' supposedly," L.W. said. But Brian Flynn "showed me respect and trust. He gave me a lot of power to take responsibility. He said, 'If you want an inch, take an inch. If you want a mile, take a mile.'" And, he added, in Brian's class, "I wasn't set apart as different. I was able to mix in. He saw me as just another person, not as an 'at risk' student."

> **"A lot of teachers when they see an 'at risk' student, they automatically distrust and they don't give them some of the responsibilities they would give other students... because they're 'at risk' supposedly."**

When asked what else about Brian Flynn was so different than other teachers he had previously had, L.W. added: "[Most] teachers see students as students and they're above you when they're teaching you and you listen to what they say because that's what is right. But Brian took a lot of what the students had to say, and that's how we did a lot of the things in the class. Someone would say 'it would be better like this,' so we'd try it like that. He shared his power with us."

After his experience in Brian's class, and working on the ELF Woods Project, L.W. said he became more involved with his community. And he gained more respect for community, "for all the hard work that it takes to do some things." The experience of having some of his work in the ELF Woods Project vandalized also taught L.W. "how people hurt when you destroy their things."

After his sophomore year L.W. stayed involved. He worked with the local National Guard to put lights along a trail behind his school. He worked with General Electric to get all the equipment and with the city of Auburn to get the permits.

After his work with the Elf Woods Project, and his continuing service in his junior and senior years, L.W. said, "That 'at risk' label had been erased. I liked school more." Other people saw him differently, he said, and when this happened, "then I changed."

His advice to teachers dealing with difficult students: "I can see how teachers would be a little weary of an 'at risk' student. But it doesn't necessarily mean that we're dumb or that 'at risk' [students] are less able to do things, it just means that sometimes for circumstances beyond their control they're 'at risk.' Which was my case, I think. So try to treat us like you treat everyone else."

Nan Henderson, M.S.W., is an international speaker, writer, and president of Resiliency In Action, a publishing and training company in Southern CA. She has authored several articles and coauthored four books on fostering resiliency, including Resiliency In Action: Practical Ideas for Overcoming Risks and Building Strengths in Youth, Families, and Communities *and* Resiliency In Schools: Making It Happen for Students and Educators. *She can be contacted at nhenderson@resiliency.com or at by calling 800-440-5171. More information is available at www.resiliency.com.*

CHAPTER 5

Hidden Treasures: Examples of "Building Communities from the Inside Out"

by Susan A. Rans

Editor's Note: The following is an excerpt from a community building workbook, Hidden Treasures: Building Community Connections by Engaging the Gifts of …People on Welfare, People with Disabilities, People with Mental Illness, Older Adults, and Youth People. *It is reprinted with permission from its publishers, the Asset Based Community Development Institute (created by John Kretzmann and John McKnight) at Northwestern University in Evanston, IL. The entire document, itself a treasure of resiliency-based community-building wisdom, strategies, and tools, is available to download at no charge from www.northwestern.edu/ipr/abcd/hiddentreausres.html.*

Introduction: Connecting Everybody

At core, a deeply connected community—a community in which every member is valued and challenged to contribute—is a strong and healthy community. But a collection of powerful forces stand in the way of connected community. Many members of any community are moved to its edges by a series of disconnecting labels—too old, too young, too poor, mentally or physically disabled, mentally ill. Not only do these labels serve to separate those labeled from the center of community life, but systems of service professing to "help" tend instead to further isolate them.

The Walls

The process of marginalization begins early, often with a diagnosis that carries a label. Once a person is labeled autistic, or bipolar, or "at risk," they are surrounded with professional services to help, protect, or fix them. Although well-meaning, these services and the professionals who provide them build walls that disconnect the labeled people from community life. Sometimes, those walls are physical—group homes and halfway houses. In other cases, the walls are walls of perception, but no less real—police targeting young people, poor people shunned by wealthier neighbors. Still other walls are walls of mobility—lack of transportation for seniors or people with disabilities that keep them from participating in community life.

When people are kept behind the walls of service, perception, or mobility, they become invisible to their neighbors. They become strangers in the midst of community. Too often, people of good will find themselves at a loss when they think about these strangers. Too often, the service providers in a community strengthen the walls and raise barriers to participation for those they purport to serve.

Too often, lack of knowledge on the part of well-intentioned neighbors leads to further isolation for those outside the center of community.

Keeping "labeled people" behind walls of service, perception, or mobility never allows them to contribute to community, to bring the gifts they have into the center of community life. And community suffers as a result. So, the challenge to those who care about community is to find ways to reconnect the disconnected. This undertaking is not about "helping" the disconnected.

Instead, it is about building strong communities that draw from the gifts and talents of every member.

> *"The challenge to those who care about community is to find ways to reconnect the disconnected."*

Why Build Community?

Much has been made of the threats to community life in today's busy, impersonal world. We have been warned about the increasing isolation, disconnection and passivity of civic life. We have also been bombarded with images and stereotypes of failed communities, impoverished places, dangerous places, places without hope. If these two jeremiads are combined, it would seem the future looks awfully bleak for our communities. But the overwhelming evidence of the hundreds of community efforts we have encountered since 1993 is that strong communities exist everywhere. They come in all shapes and sizes, all economic levels, urban and rural—but they share in common one important understanding: they are possessed of many assets, which, once mobilized and connected, can make great contributions.

Asset-based community development begins with the assumption that successful community building involves rediscovering and mobilizing resources already present in any community:

- The skills and resources of its individuals;
- The power of voluntary associations, achieved through building relationships;
- The assets present in the array of local institutions, the physical infrastructure of the community, and the local economy.

Another way of saying this is: Successful community development is asset-based, internally-focused, and relationship-driven. Although some resources from outside the community are often needed, the key to lasting solutions comes from within. The gifts and skills of residents and the assets of the physical community are always the starting place. No plan, solution, or organization from outside the community can duplicate what is already there. Over time, some simple but powerful tools have been developed to aid this rediscovery and mobilization, tools that have emerged from practical experience.

All communities are first composed of individuals, each of which has gifts she or he brings to the group. The best and most creative communities are aware of these gifts and provide opportunities for them to be given. But simply discovering and inventorying individual gifts is not enough. Asset-based community development is about finding ways in which to create connections between gifted individuals. Making these connections, building relationships, is the heart and soul of community building and the subject covered here.

> **"All communities are first composed of individuals, each of which has gifts she or he brings to the group."**

Individuals who share common interests and goals form associations. Garden clubs, fraternal organizations, bowling leagues, book clubs, church groups: Each brings individuals into association. Connecting individuals who have formerly been isolated to others who share their interests through community associations is the way to build long lasting, multi-faceted relationships where none previously existed.

All communities, no matter how poor, have within them a series of institutions that can support the gifted individuals and powerful associations found there. Asset-based community development involves local institutions in the process of community-building. Parks, schools, libraries, churches, businesses—all have a role to play. They can be involved with the local community as property owners, gathering centers, economic entities and incubators for community leadership.

Other assets include the physical environment of a community, its green spaces, transportation centers, and gathering places. And the local economy is an asset to be harnessed to build wealth and distribute benefits. Taken together, all of the assets listed provide strong bedrock upon which any community can build.

Dudley Street Neighborhood Initiative (DSNI), Boston, MA: A Story Within A Story

One of the most inspiring and well-documented stories of neighborhood empowerment is that of the Dudley Street Neighborhood Initiative. You find the DSNI story well-told in the book, *Streets of Hope: The Fall and Rise of an Urban Neighborhood* by Peter Medoff and Holly Sklar (South End Press, 1994)). An award winning video, *Holding Ground*, was also produced documenting DSNI. Anyone who has seen this video is familiar with the individuals who have played a significant role in the rebuilding of the Dudley community over the last 20 years. And the struggles and successes of DSNI have not only provided a framework for other communities around the world, but they have given rise to a whole new category of funding— "the comprehensive community initiative."

> **"Young people are seldom regarded as gifted members of community."**

The DSNI story will not be retold here; the sources cited above have done an excellent job already. Throughout the DSNI story, one theme ran in the background: that of the conscious and on-going effort to include young people at all levels of participation in the "rebirth of Dudley Street." Because connecting young people is sometimes overlooked or considered too difficult an undertaking for neighborhood groups, it is important to revisit that aspect of the DSNI story.

Youth and Stereotypes

Young people are seldom regarded as gifted members of community. They are described by the platitude, "leaders of tomorrow," but are often forgotten as "contributors of today." Left unchecked, the marginalizing of youth reaches its logical conclusion with many young people entering the juvenile justice system.

This trend is intensified in low-income communities of color. The automatic assumption of the media is that all young men of color are gang bangers, that all young girls of color are soon to be welfare moms, and that they are both dangerous by definition. These images of youth can also affect their closest neighbors. Coupled with the sometimes mysterious nature of all teenagers, these stereotypes can cause well-intentioned neighborhood groups to "target the problems" of young people instead of inviting them into the center of community. In this way, youth are "labeled people" just as surely as a person with disabilities or those living with mental illness.

Youth Organizing

That being said, some neighborhood organizations across the country have become involved in an effort to organize youth. Many have hired youth organizers, to work with young people to identify their own action agendas. Others have started youth advisory boards. In a few places, youth have come together to start organizations of their own.

Youth organizing does encounter challenges that differ from those of other organizing campaigns. The membership and leadership of youth organizations change rapidly. The endless meetings and slow base-building work required of organizers can be hard on young attention spans. Funding is hard to come by.

But the benefits are many, both for neighborhoods and for organizations. Young people bring new energy and creativity to the search for solutions to problems. They can hold particular institutions—the juvenile justice system, schools and child welfare agencies come to mind—accountable to the constituency those institutions are designed to serve. And youth organizing builds democratic, civic participation. Communities benefit as new leaders emerge.

DSNI has been part of this larger movement for its twenty years. And during that time, something inevitable has happened: Young people have grown up.

"Half My Life"

In the video *Holding Ground*, there is a scene in which the first young people's group introduces itself to the Board of Directors of DSNI. A young man identifies himself: "My name is Jason Webb, and I am 14 years old. I have been involved in DSNI for half my life."

Everyone laughs at this moment, both on screen and off. But for Jason Webb, being involved in his community since he can remember has had a profound affect on his life. He grew up always wanting to become a DSNI organizer.

By the time he was 14, he'd already been given an award by his neighbors for Community Service. DSNI helped him go to college.

Similarly, the Barros family plays a central role in the DSNI story. From the first marches to close the illegal dumping stations that were poisoning the community, to the election of 17 year-old John Barros as the first young person on the DSNI Board in 1991, the family is deeply involved in the community. The last we know of John Barros in both versions of the story is that he is accepted to and leaves to attend Dartmouth College. Today, John Barros is the Executive Director of the Dudley Street Neighborhood Initiative and Jason Webb is the Community Development Organizer.

> **"Are young people involved? If they aren't, then there is something wrong."**

"Are Young People Involved?"

Recent conversations with John Barros and Ros Everdell, a longtime DSNI organizer, filled in the details of twenty years. Although no one model of youth involvement has dominated in DSNI, valuing youth involvement has always been central to every activity. "That's one of the ways we evaluate effectiveness of anything we do," says Ros. "Are young people involved? If they aren't, then there is something wrong."

As young people have changed over the years, so have the ways in which they are connected to DSNI. Some times the DSNI youth have wanted a peer group within the larger organization, one that conceives of its own actions and agendas and carries them out. Other times, young people have been integrated into all of the activities of DSNI, taking leadership roles in the various committees and working groups. According to John, there is no one way, or best way, to involve youth: "We don't include youth; we include all. This is the core of what we do, not just a program." Every DSNI activity or group values highly youth engagement. It is in the water.

Similarly, there was never a conscious "program" to include young people. DSNI, as an organization, is very mindful of the "clash of two models" about youth development--services to clients vs. organizing community members. The earliest youth-oriented activity of DSNI brought young people right into the community planning process. The Young Architects and Planners activity recounted in

Streets of Hope provided local young people with a chance to design their own community center, with the help of some local architects. As Ros said then, "The young people in the neighborhood are really the ones who are going to live this revitalization much more than the adults who are currently planning it….From one generation to another you have a sense that 'this is my community, I can make a difference and we have power.'" (p. 221).

Today, a DSNI goal is to create "successors" who will lead the organization and the community. "Young people grow older," Ros Everdell said, "So youth development is always 'a pipeline of activists,' young people connecting to other young people." DSNI has established some programs to create and maintain this pipeline. Every summer there is a youth leadership camp; college graduates are mentors to high

Many DSNI members say that having youth organizers only working with youth can narrow the opportunity for relationships with youth and makes youth involvement unnatural. There are natural times for youth programs--like college mentoring or summer leadership or summer jobs. But at these times, adults and youth work together in a way appropriate to address the issue.

In a very organic yet self-conscious way, DSNI has continually brought young people into the center of the project of rebuilding and claiming their neighborhood over the course of twenty years. And, also in an organic way, those young people have grown into adults. These new adults are also committed to their neighborhood and to bringing young people into the center of its life.

In a Nutshell: Three Important Things for DSNI

Gifts and Dreams: DSNI focuses on the dreams of Dudley Street residents and the gifts they can bring to community building in every aspect of its work. No action on an immediate issue takes place without launching a "visioning" session, asking participants what they see in five or ten years now that the particular issue has been won. The focus on youth connected to everything is an extension of this commitment.

Citizens (Residents) Space: Again, control of planning and community building by citizens is at the heart of everything DSNI does. A place, a space, for residents to dream, plan, organize, and make decisions together.

Connectors: Moving back and forth between youth organizing and intergenerational organizing has served DSNI and the Dudley Street community well. Including young people is not a programmatic effort so much as a reality realized everyday. DSNI sees the connection of young people as an aspect of doing what it takes to build a strong community.

---

school students who want to go to college; recent college grads from the neighborhood are linked to high school kids from the neighborhood to guide them towards college.

In addition, DSNI has been thinking recently about how to work with kids who are not identified by the system as being in crisis. "We want to connect to less visible kids who are in danger of drifting out of community life," says Ros.

Everybody's Job

It is the job of all DSNI organizers, staff and members to be concerned with youth participation. "Every issue is an opportunity to involve young people," says Ros. So, there are no youth organizers at DSNI. In a sense every organizer is a youth organizer, as one test for any issue campaign is youth involvement.

Additional Lessons Learned from DSNI

• Young people need to be included in community planning efforts at every level. It will become their community.
• The key to engaging young people is talking and listening.
• Relationships are best built when the scale of the group or projects are doable (small); larger projects can become too focused on results rather than "a pipeline for participation."
• Peer-to-peer groups are sometimes useful for young people. However, they should not be the only way youth are involved in neighborhood efforts. Youth benefit from developing their own opportunities and voices but they need to be integrated in the broader neighborhood effort.
• There needs to be structured youth leadership. For

example, DSNI added youth seats on the Board of Directors and lowered the voting age to 15.

- Youth participation cannot grow unless the neighborhood effort is rooted in the empowerment of all residents.
- Opening the door to youth and creating an atmosphere of respect, safety, and caring will bring in youth.
- Youth should be the ones to mobilize and speak on their own behalf with the support of caring and committed adults.
- Youth development and community building are not quick fixes but an ongoing process that spans the generations.

From Hundreds of Community Efforts: "The Most Important Stuff"

The hundreds of successful community efforts we've seen stress three common lessons. These lessons are the most important stuff.

1. Connections should center on gifts.

Each person finds her or his place in community life through contribution. The framework for community building firmly rests on the identification and mobilization of people's gifts. A community that is growing strong does not waste people--everyone is needed; everyone has something to contribute.

Every person has gifts, talents, interests to contribute. So a first step toward community contribution is to listen for and identify gifts a person has that she wants to offer or dreams she wants to realize. All of the preceding stories had some mechanism or special time that allowed isolated people to talk about their gifts and dreams while others listened and gave support.

Gifts and dreams are best fulfilled in places where they make sense. You would sing in the choir but not in the library. A person needs to participate in places where it makes sense to contribute. Out of this participation and contribution come new relationships and opportunities that lead to friends, meaning, and resources.

A person must be able to be present in community life to participate. A lack of accessibility or a lack of available transportation can make it impossible for a person to be a contributor to community life. The key to moving from the edge to the center is to discover an opportunity where an isolated person can be a contributor. Three questions lead you to the "right place":

- What are the gifts and dreams?
- Where are places for participation where these gifts and dreams make sense?
- What people and resources are needed to make this connection of the person to the right place?

2. Community "connectors" understand the nature of "citizen space."

A connector is a special kind of community leader who opens doors for other people. A connector is a person who is trusted, is influential, and has a wide circle of relationships. A connector believes that all people have gifts to offer. A connector believes her or his community is a good place where residents truly care about each other. A connector is always developing other people's opportunities to contribute, connecting people to new possibilities.

The bridge to community is built of relationships. The every day life of citizens in communities is where the relationships exist that can build this bridge for isolated people. Services from helping agencies cannot build this bridge. "People not programs" do this work. Always connect an isolated person to "citizen space" that is rich in relationships with opportunities for contribution: associations, congregations, local small business, some government and non-profit agencies all can offer opportunities for relationships. The challenge is getting an isolated person (who is often a human service client) outside of the world of clients and services.

The process of relationship building can be made most effective by following a few simple rules:

- The less the person is identified as a client with a service agency the more likely that the person will be recognized as a person with gifts to offer rather than a needy person.
- People are best connected on the basis of mutuality rather than on the basis of neediness. I should join the choir because I love singing not because I am lonely. Going to an event like a movie or simply being present at the swimming pool will not lead you into relationships and towards community. Working at the movie theatre or being on the swimming team will build relationships. The person must be an active contributor in order to build relationships.
- A person will likely participate and contribute best where he or she joins the purpose of the group out of shared interest.

- Connections to groups offer more possibilities than connections to individuals. Associations, congregations, and local businesses all offer a connection to a group of people where friendships, opportunities, and possibilities can arise.

The key is to find a place for participation outside services where an isolated person can be present, participate, and contribute on the basis of shared interest. DSNI and other community "success stories" show groups going to great lengths to keep community connections in citizen space.

Another characteristic of citizen space is that it is rather small and always local. By that we don't mean that there isn't much citizen space, but that each particular group is not so large that it blurs the importance of real relationships. "Dare to Think Small!" is a good slogan for this concept. Thinking small enough to keep relationships at the center of the enterprise, or local enough to make it possible for mobility—this thinking is key to creating or locating the space for community connections.

It is like fishing: Where you fish has everything to do with whether you catch a fish. If your goal is to help a person enter into community, the right place to be is where local people in small groups are actively doing things together.

3. Connectors should be valued.

Building connections successfully is about connectors using their relationships effectively much more than it is about ideas, concepts, or methods. A connector can lead a person to the right group and open the door. Another connector within the group can pave the way for a person's participation to be successful. Groups of connected people who are willing to use their relationships for the purposes of building community are very valuable people in any community's life.

In many cases, a citizen-led connection initiative raises money and hires one of its own to serve as a kind of administrator. After all, a project focused on individual gifts and dreams takes time and effort, and can become overwhelming for volunteers alone. A paid or volunteer connector:

- Recruits other connectors and enroll connection places.
- Carefully listens for gifts and dreams of people to be connected.
- Supports connections, which may involve visiting connection places, talking with the person connected about how things are going, helping

solve problems that arise, or developing needed resources for the connected person like child care or transportation.
- Handles administrative tasks, engage in fundraising and train other participating citizens.
- Is constantly involved in building relationships for the betterment of the community.

This work requires a seasoned experienced person. It is not the work for a person right out of school, new to the community, or new to community building work. Connectors are the key to successfully building community.

> *"Communities growing in power naturally or intentionally identify the capacities of all their members and ensure that they are contributed."*

Connecting everybody is important stuff. This information is offered as a roadmap, as a route across the bridge into community life. Connectors are the guides. Traveling this road will result in stronger, engaged communities where everyone has value and all gifts are given.

References

Lipman, M. & Mahen, L. (1997). *Holding ground.* Harriman, NY: New Day Films.

Medoff, P. & Sklar, H. (1994). *Streets of hope: The fall and rise of an urban neighborhood.* Cambridge, MA: South End Press.

Susan Rans is a researcher at the Asset Based Community Development Institute at the School of Education and Social Policy at Northwestern University. She can be contacted at the Institute, abcd@northwesern.edu. 847-491-8711.

How to Use a Capacity Inventory

Reprinted with permission of John P. Kretzmann and John L. McKnight from Building Communities from the Inside Out: A Path Toward Finding and Mobilizing a Community's Assets,*(pp. 19-25), Evanston, IL: Institute for Policy Research (1993).*

In many communities, the natural ways of the local people and their associations and institutions constantly connect local capacities. For example:

- Neighbors have a tradition of helping each other by trading their skills. Mary repairs a dress while Sue watches her children.
- A local association of religious men combines their construction skills and builds a community center.
- A neighborhood school involves the local students in using the environmental knowledge they've gained to do a study for city council of whether a local pond is polluted.
  In addition to these natural developments, other communities have intentionally used tools like the Capacity Inventory to identify local citizen talents. Then these groups have become active in making the necessary connections to mobilize the capacities. Some examples:
- A neighborhood organization interviewed over 100 local residents and found many women who had worked in hospitals, hotels or cared for sick and elderly people. Many of these women had families and were unemployed. They wanted to work part-time. The association brought them together and they formed a "company" to sell their services as home health care providers. There was great demand for their services and over 80 women were connected to neighbors needing community care. This connection met a community need and increased the income of the women.
- A group of residents of a public housing project organized and became powerful enough to gain control of their buildings. Their association took over the management and finances of the project. As a result they were able to employ residents to carry out the maintenance functions such as painting rooms, fixing broken windows, running a laundromat, etc. In order to exercise their new-found power, they needed to know which residents had the necessary skills to do the work of maintenance and management. They used a Capacity Inventory to gather this information and their association connected residents to the new job opportunities that improved the quality of the local buildings.

It is significant to note two common characteristics of these efforts. First, a local group acted as a connecter. Second, the local group took people as they were and mobilized their existing capacities. They did not start with the idea that the local people needed to be trained, educated or treated. Instead, they started with the idea that capacities were there and that the community-building task was to identify capacities, and to connect them to people, groups and places that can use the capacities.

Does Everyone Have Capacities?

There are some people who seem to be without any gifts or capacities. They may appear to be like an empty glass. And so they get called names like mentally retarded, ex-convict, frail elderly, mentally ill, illiterate, and gang member. These are names for the emptiness some people see in other people. They are labels that focus attention on needs.

One effect of these labels is that they keep many community people from seeing the gifts of people who have been labeled. The label often blinds us to the capacity of the people who are named. They appear to be useless. Therefore, these labeled people often get pushed to the edge of the community, or they are sometimes sent outside the community to an institution to be rehabilitated or receive services.

Nonetheless, every living person has some gift or capacity of value to others. A strong community is a place that recognizes those gifts and ensures that they are given. A weak community is a place where lots of people can't give their gifts and express their capacities.

In weak communities there are lots of people who have been pushed to the edge or exiled to institutions. Often, we say these people need help. They are needy. They have nothing to contribute. The label tells us so.

For example, "She is a pregnant teenager. She needs counseling, therapy, residential services, special education." But also, "She is Mary Smith. She has a miraculously beautiful voice. We need her in the choir. She needs a record producer."

Her label, pregnant teenager, tells of emptiness and calls forth rejection, isolation and treatment. Her name, Mary Smith, tells of her gifts and evokes community and contributions. Communities growing in power naturally or intentionally identify the capacities of all their members and ensure that they are contributed. However, the most powerful communities are those that can identify the gifts of those people at the margins and pull them into community life.

There are many other kinds of people with community contributions to make. The task of community builders is to expand the list of potential gift givers and create methods to connect those gifts to other individuals, local associations and institutions.

To download a free copy of the Kretzmann/McKnight Community Capacity Inventory, go to www.northwestern. edu/ipr/abcd/abcdci.html.

The Resiliency Postcard Project: An Innovative Way to Recognize, Reward, and Recruit Mentors

from the Alberta Alcohol and Drug Abuse Commission

Editor's Note: A creative, inexpensive, and effective way to promote and strengthen "naturally occurring" positive adult-youth connections is the Resiliency Postcard Project developed by the Alberta, Canada Alcohol and Drug Abuse Commission (AADAC). The Project is used extensively across Alberta in all types of schools, organizations, and communities. An inexpensive kit with posters, postcards, and detailed instructions is available from AADAC (www.aadac.com). What follows is a description of the Project from the ADDAC kit as well as comments about how the program has worked and how it is being expanded.—N.H.

Research shows that every child, no matter what their life circumstances, has the potential to lead a successful and balanced life. The likelihood of a positive outcome is greatly increased when one or more adults, inside or outside the family, take an active role in the life of the child. Having a supportive and caring adult in one's life while young is a powerful predictor of success later in life. Children who do are able to build on inner strengths and develop their own sense of "resiliency."

Adults can contribute to a child's life in both big and small ways. Helping them to learn a new skill, going for walks, providing a helping hand or being there to talk are all ways to promote resiliency in a young person. A caring adult can provide support in difficult circumstances; help a child feel good about himself or herself; and provide guidance and friendship.

How to Use the Resiliency Postcard Project

The Resiliency Postcard Project is designed to help participants identify those adults who have made a difference in their lies. For kids, describing such relationships will help them to have a clearer understanding of what healthy relationships should be. Ideally, they will then seek out such positive interactions elsewhere in their lives. For adults, thinking about the role models in their lives may inspire them to spend time with a child.

You may use this exercise in a variety of settings to help participants identify supportive relationships in their lives. From classrooms to youth groups, seniors groups and more, this tool is an excellent way of building the concept of resiliency.

If you are a teacher or facilitator who would like to implement a school-wide or group initiative, we suggest that you train a "postcard team." This group could consist of five to ten youth volunteers who are interested in delivering the campaign to rest of their school or group. Once your postcard team has been selected, set up a training session with them. Discuss resiliency and the role mentors can play in young people's lives.

Encourage the group to share their own experiences of positive relationships with an adult or adult in their lives. You may wish to share the following example of a completed postcard with them, submitted by a seventh grade student. "There is a neighbor down the road who is elderly. Almost every night he walks down to our house just to talk. Sometimes he will just listen to me when I take my dog for a walk down to his house. Once I was sick and he came down just to check that I was fine. This was very special to me, not only because he cares, but because he is my friend. He is also the protector of our lane and a friend to all."

After reviewing the concept of resiliency, discuss with your postcard team what resiliency means to them. Ask them each to fill out a postcard about a caring adult in their life. Some team members may want to share what they have written. This will provide further examples for the team and ensure that they are grasping the concept.

Help your team come up with a plan to implement the postcard project in their school or group. Ideas might include:

- having the team staff a table to promote participation in the project;
- selecting team members to give short classroom presentations;
- interviewing students in the halls [or at other places kids gather]; or
- promote the contest during school announcements.

The team will need to explain resiliency to their classes or groups. They then hand out the postcards to the group and invite their peers to take part. The activity should be voluntary. You may want to reward the participants with a randomly drawn prize. A local business might sponsor this.

Posters [included in the AADAC kit] can be displayed in hallways or rooms in order to remind students to take part and to let them know where to drop off their completed postcard. Some of the best cards can be featured in your local or school newspaper. Be creative and have fun!

Results of the Postcard Project

Pamela Bragg, AADAC Addictions Counselor in the Athabasca area office, notes on the AADAC website that the postcard project can be used with youth as well as with adults. "For children and youth, describing such relationships may help them have a clearer understanding of what healthy relationships look like," she said. "Ideally, children will then seek out such positive interactions elsewhere in their lives. For adults, thinking about the role models in their lives may inspire them to spend time with a child."

Bragg says that when the postcards are filled out, they can then be:

- mailed to the adults involved ;
- published in the local newspaper to build awareness in the community; and/or
- used to encourage people to think about mentoring children and youth .

She said, "The comments of the youth who participated in our postcard campaign affirm that it was the small moments shared indirectly with an adult that changed participants' sense of self-worth and values. It was the awareness of being important in the lives of others that made the difference for youth. In the hundreds of postcards that were generated, many of the youth spoke about the direct actions of parents, teachers, coaches, neighbors, siblings, work-experience supervisors, and adult friends. They spoke about how those informal contacts assisted them in gaining new perspectives.

"One youth explained, 'It wasn't really anything he did, but it was an attitude he had towards me--complete love no matter what I did. I always knew that would never change. ... [That person] was my grandfather.' Another youth shared, 'Once when I was really sick, my best friend's mom brought me over some chicken soup.' Yet another youth shared, 'My Grade 4 teacher was always there to give me a hug and encourage good advice. Because of her, I got over a huge identity crisis and I love her for that.'"

Bragg also notes that the Athabasca Mentorship Program and the Athabasca Teen Centre Society have recently launched a pin project connected to the Resiliency Postcard Project, called "Who I Am Makes a Difference." The purpose of this project is to recognize and honor informal mentors. The campaign includes several components:

- A unique stylized pin with the words "Who I Am Makes a Difference" is mounted on a gift card. The gift card states, "Today you received a pin from someone who believes you have made a difference in his or her life. What you said or did is the role that mentors play-in making small moments matter."
- One section of the card has a detachable portion that converts into a tent card for office or home. It says, "I MAKE a difference."
- The recipient is also invited to fill in a postcard about his or her experience as a mentor and return the comments to the committee.

The purpose of the campaign is to encourage the positive daily interactions that individuals have with others and to underscore how meaningful these interactions can be.

"Both the Resiliency Postcard Project and the Pin Project underline how adults and youth alike have had their lives changed for the better by casual and informal mentors," Bragg said.

Front of postcard

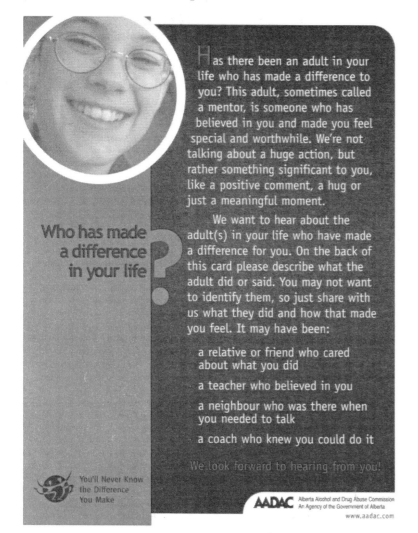

Who has made a difference in your life?

You'll Never Know the Difference You Make

AADAC Alberta Alcohol and Drug Abuse Commission
An Agency of the Government of Alberta
www.aadac.com

Has there been an adult in your life who has made a difference to you? This adult, sometimes called a mentor, is someone who has believed in you and made you feel special and worthwhile. We're not talking about a huge action, but rather something significant to you, like a positive comment, a hug or just a meaningful moment.

We want to hear about the adult(s) in your life who have made a difference for you. On the back of this card please describe what the adult did or said. You may not want to identify them, so just share with us what they did and how that made you feel. It may have been:

a relative or friend who cared about what you did

a teacher who believed in you

a neighbour who was there when you needed to talk

a coach who knew you could do it

We look forward to hearing from you!

Back of postcard

An adult who made a difference in my life...

Name _____ Age _____

Resiliency Postcard Project

This project is designed to help individuals identify those people who have made a difference in their lives. It can also motivate adults to spend time with a child. The Postcard Project Kit contains 100 specially designed postcards and two posters. Available free of charge to Albertans in limited quantities. Outside Alberta, kit is $20 plus GST, shipping. and handling. To order, contact:

AADAC Resource Development
#200, 10909 Jasper Avenue
Edmonton, AB, Canada T5J 3M9
Toll free 1 (800) 280-9616
Fax (780) 422-5237
E-mail rdm@aadac.gov.ab.ca

RESILIENCY AND COMMUNITIES

CHAPTER 7

Libraries as Resiliency Havens for Children and Youth

by Jami Jones, Ph.D.

"How do you make a difference that changes people's lives for the better?" This is a question that is rarely discussed in university training for librarians. Instead, the educational focus is typically proficiency in collection development, reference, cataloging, and management. In addition, children's and school librarians focus on literature and programming. Only recently have librarians considered their role in making a difference by strengthening and building resiliency in children and teens. Yet libraries serve as havens of safety and resiliency-building protective conditions for countless children and teens.

A model for more consciously incorporating the tenets of fostering resiliency into librarianship is the "Library Ladder of Resiliency," which is based on the research of Werner and Smith in their Kauai Longitudinal study (See Part One). Werner supports this model of resiliency building and its integration into librarians' professional practice (Werner, 2006). Libraries most in need of implementing this model are those whose youth population is most vulnerable because of factors such as poverty, minority status, parental abuse and neglect, divorce, teen pregnancy, substance abuse, and educational failure.

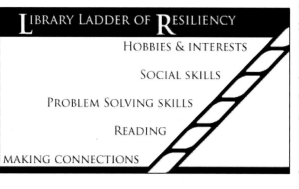

The first rung of the Library Ladder of Resiliency—the most important rung of all—is mentoring and making connections. In the Kauai Study, resilient children often reported remembering a teacher who listened, helped, and supported them. Likewise, librarians need to think of themselves as potential mentors for children and youth. It is common knowledge that many teens have been turned-off to libraries because some staff members are not welcoming and programs and services are not developmentally appropriate. The American Library Association is rectifying this situation through its "Serving the Underserved" project, and librarians can also contribute to solving this problem by carefully considering how to make a meaningful connection with children and teens.

Very simple yet effective ways to connect are greeting children and teens with a smile and a courteous and welcoming demeanor. It is important to understand the developmental stage of adolescence because many behaviors that adults find annoying are actually normal for teens during these years. Another simple strategy librarians can utilize is organizing a teen advisory board to plan programs and services and offer advice about collection development and other issues. Librarians should always ask for teen input before making policy changes that impact them. When Sheppard Memorial Library in Greenville, North Carolina, developed a summer teen program, librarians were surprised to learn that activities were not important to the kids; it was relationships that were paramount. "The teens just wanted to be here to talk and be together. It didn't matter whether an activity was planned or not. They still wanted to meet," reported Tami Fulcher, head of public services at the library.

The second rung of the Library Ladder of Resiliency is reading. Reading is a resiliency-promoting protective factor for two reasons. One, "effective reading skills by grade four were one of the most potent predictors of successful adult adaptation among the high risk children in our study" (Werner & Smith, 205). The single greatest predictor of school dropout is reading below grade level. Two, reading can be a bright spot for troubled teens that need to momentarily forget their difficulties. When life is a challenge, books provide solace. "I've never known any trouble that an hour's reading didn't assuage," wrote Montesquieu, the famous French political thinker who lived during the Enlightenment. Books open doors and provide new experiences. Strategies for encouraging teens to read include: Developing a collection of books and resources they want to read; holding interest- and gender-based book clubs; providing a variety of high-interest magazines; making available books and resources that help teens solve real-life problems they are experiencing; and creating interesting displays that entice teens to read.

When Deborah Svec, a media specialist at Palm Beach Gardens, FL, High School, was asked by the football staff to coach two football players who were unable to pass the state-mandated reading test required for graduation, she leapt into action and developed an intervention that included reading *Friday Night Lights*, a popular book about a high school football team in Odessa, Texas. Several other football players joined their teammates simply because they wanted to read the book too. The message for adults is never to underestimate the value of building on a teen's interest. The two football players Svec tutored did graduate and are attending college.

The third rung is promoting decision-making and problem-solving skills. These skills are not inherited, but must be developed and perfected with the help of caring adults. Children and teens have little experience in this area even though they face significant challenges and problems. Hersch in *A Tribe Apart: A Journey into the Heart of American Adolescence* (1998), reported today's teens "spend virtually all of their discretionary time without companionship or supervision by responsible adults." Without adult involvement, teens may have a difficult time developing skills in problem-solving, decision-making, and goal-setting. To teach social skills, librarians can be role models for youth by being good problem-solvers themselves. They can verbalize each step taken so teens know how the problem was solved. They can also help youth use information skills such as "Big6" and "Flip It!" to solve problems. In addition, librarians can use characters in stories and books to demonstrate how problems are solved. An important outcome of having a teen advisory board is teens practicing these skills.

The fourth rung is social skills. Children and teens that have friends have a strong support network to help when the going gets tough. They are also more likely to enlist the help of adults to become mentors. Libraries need to provide opportunities for youth to come together to socialize, read, plan, and have fun. An example is a program called "The Lunch Bunch," developed at Cardinal Newman High School in West Palm Beach, Florida. When media specialist Nelle Martin noticed the same students coming into the media center every day during lunch without ever interacting with others, she became proactive with a plan to rectify the situation. Martin talked to these students and discovered that they were "outsiders" who were "unable to face the terrors of the cafeteria." In the application form for the Amanda Award, an award sponsored by the Florida Association of Media in Education that recognizes media specialists who develop programs that promote resiliency and self-esteem, she wrote: "It became my mission to create a welcoming environment where they could truly belong. By the end of the year, we had created the 'Lunch Bunch.' Suddenly, friendships were forged and the media center became the place to be." Martin won the 2002 Amanda Award for her Lunch Bunch program.

The fifth rung is developing hobbies and interests. Libraries are logical places to develop hobbies and interests for several reasons. Libraries house many books and resources that promote hobbies and interests. One entire section of the collection–the Dewey 700s–is arts and recreation. Knowing that this material can potentially strengthen youth may provide the impetus for libraries to increase the budget in this area. Furthermore, libraries are often community meeting places where people come together to share their talents and it is within the mission of most libraries to support the recreational interests of community members. This can be done is by organizing a hobby fest to bring adults and youth together to talk about shared interests. Librarians can also support hobbies and interests by creating a website with links to this information.

An example of an interest-promoting public library program is the Philip S. Miller Library in Castle Rock, CO, where the Young Writers Guild meets regularly to help teens ages 12 to 18 hone their writing skills. Over time, these teens have become a supportive network for one another. When a teen in the community committed suicide, they helped each other cope with this death. To commemorate the opening of a new facility, members of the group researched the county's history in order to write a collection of short stories about the library's past and present.

The future of librarianship may depend on how successfully librarians are able to embrace this crucial role of strengthening youth and creating libraries that truly meet their needs. The Library Ladder of Resiliency is a helpful model and blueprint to ensure that teens get the libraries they need and deserve. Whenever I am asked what I do for a living, I respond, "I am a librarian and I build resiliency!"

References

Hersch, P. (1998). A tribe apart: A *journey into the heart of american adolescence.* New York: Ballantine Books.

Werner, E., & Smith, R. (1992). *Overcoming the odds: High risk children from birth to adulthood.* Ithica, NY: Cornell University Press.

Werner, E. (2006, July). Telephone interview.

Jami L. Jones, Ph.D., is assistant professor in the Department of Library Science and Instructional Technology at East Carolina University in Greenville, NC. After the death of her son's girlfriend, Dr. Jones became interested in studying the response of adults within her profession to strengthen and promote resiliency within youth. She is the author of Bouncing Back: Dealing with the Stuff Life Throws at You, *a book for teens published in 2006. She also authored* Helping Teens Cope: Resources for School Library Media Specialists and Other Youth Workers *and can be contacted through her web site at www.askdrjami.org or by e-mailing jonesj@ecu.edu*

CHAPTER 8

A Resiliency Resource Primer:

Resiliency and Communities

by Bonnie Benard, M.S.W., and Nan Henderson, M.S.W.

The field of community development contains many fine theoretical books and pragmatic manuals for mobilizing communities, which are not emphasized here. Rather, the following is a list of resources that speak to building and reinventing community as we move into post-industrial society. Most of these books address the critical question: Can youth and families be provided with the supports that facilitate healthy development in light of the technological forces that have been gradually breaking the natural intergenerational bonds that have sustained the human family during its existence?

Bellah, Robert, Madsen, Richard, Sullivan, William, Swidler, Ann, and Tipton, Steven. (1992). ***The Good Society***. New York: Vintage Books. *By the same authors as Habits of the Heart, this book looks critically and with historical perspective at our political, economic, educational, and religious institutions, which have grown out of control and even beyond an ability to understand them. It makes the case that a compassionate and caring society is only possible through active citizen participation*

Bellah, Robert, Madsen, Richard, Sullivan, William, Swidler, Ann, and Tipton, Steven. (1996). ***Habits of the Heart: Individualism and Commitment in American Life***. New York: Perennial Library. *This landmark book is based on the authors' massive five-year cultural study of hundreds of individuals and various American communities. Central to their study were the questions: "How ought we to live? How do we think about how to live? Who are we, as Americans? What is our character?" Central to their findings was the conclusion that Americans, largely confined to an identity of individualism, have lost a sense of being in community with others and, concomitantly, a sense of moral purpose and coherence in their lives.*

Benson, Peter. (2006). ***All Kids are Our Kids: What Communities Must do to Raise Caring and Responsible Children and Adolescents*** (2nd ed.). San Francisco: Jossey-Bass. *This second edition updates the ways that communities of all sizes can promote healthy development for their children and teens. Benson, president of the nonprofit Search Institute, argues that social norms must shift so that all community residents understand their responsibilities to the young, a reiteration of the African proverb "It takes a village to raise a child." The book explains the Search Institute's research on "developmental assets" needed for optimum healthy development of children and youth and offers numerous useful examples of community groups that have effected positive change for their kids.*

Blyth, Dale. (1993). ***Healthy Communities, Healthy Youth: How Communities Contribute to Positive Youth Development***. Minneapolis, MN: Search Institute. *Using data from 112 communities that initially surveyed 9th-12th grade students with the Search Institute's student profiles, this report examines the way youth experience their community's strengths and how these factors contribute to youth development. Among other conclusions, their data, presented in the Institute's great and compelling graphs, demonstrate that while caring and supportive families make a major difference in the lives of their own youth, family factors do not differ very much between the healthiest and least healthy communities.*

Commission on Children at Risk. (2003). ***Hardwired to Connect: The New Scientific Case for Authoritative Communities.*** New York: Institute for American Values. *This ground-breaking report represents the "first time a diverse group of scientists and leading children's doctors are publicly recommending that our society pay considerably more attention to young people's moral and spiritual needs." The 33-menber panel included such leading authorities as T.Berry Brazelton, James Comer, Robert Coles, Judith Wallerstein, and Peter Benson and concluded that meeting children's needs for enduring attachments and spiritual meaning is the best way to ensure their healthy development. "The basic conclusion of this report is that children are hardwired for close connections to others and for moral and spiritual meaning," said Dr. Kenneth L. Gladish, National Director of the YMCA, USA, which along with Dartmouth Medical School, sponsors the Commission. The report is packed with specific recommendations for all types of groups and organization wanting to create the type of communities children and youth need.*

Coontz, Stephanie. (2000). ***The Way We Never Were: American Families and the Nostalgia Trap.*** New York: Basic Books. *A brilliant examination of the history of the family which clearly makes the case—and illustrates it with lots of data— that stable communities and economies are the bedrock of stable families, not the reverse!*

Eccles, Jacquelynn., and Gootman, Jennifer. (Eds.). (2002). ***Community Programs to Promote Youth Development***. Washington, D.C.: National Academic Press. *This academic publication is an overview of research on community programs that can, due to their effectiveness, service as "models" of positive youth development. It examines what is known about the design, implementation, and evaluation of these model programs. Communities, as defined by this report, include "neighborhoods, block groups, towns, and cities, as well as nongeographically defined communities based on family connections and shared interests or values." The findings on "what kids need to do well," as well as the recommendations offered to communities about how to programmatically meet these needs, totally align with resiliency research on "how to move kids from 'risk' to resilient."*

Forsey, Helen, (Ed.). (1993). *Circles of Strength: Community Alternatives to Alienation.* Philadelphia, PA: New Society Publishers. *A fine collection of essays on community-building experiences—all focused on creating ecologically sustainable communities. The various stories illustrate that there is no one right way, yet the bottom line principle must be the respect for all of life.*

Gambone, Michelle, and Arbreton, Amy. (1997). *Safe Havens: The Contributions of Youth Organizations to Healthy Adolescent Development.* Philadelphia: Public/Private Ventures. *This study examines the affiliates of three national youth organizations-Boys & Girls Clubs of America, Girls Incorporated, and YMCA of the USA. It is "a first step toward defining the activities and experiences that contribute to youth development in such settings." The assessment found "that in six of seven developmental areas (safety, challenging and interesting activities, sense of belonging, supportive relationships with adults, involvement in decision-making, and opportunities for leadership), the majority of [all] youth at each organization are deriving positive developmental experiences" from their participation in these programs.*

Gardner, John. (1991). *Building Community. Paper prepared for the Leadership Studies Program.* Washington, D.C.: Independent Sector, September. *A wonderful treatise on community and its place in protecting democratic freedom along with responsibility. Gardner describes the essential characteristics and elements of effective communities and welcomes the reinvention of community—in whatever form it may manifest—in our swiftly changing world.*

Graham, John. (2005). *Stick Your Neck Out: A Street-Smart Guide to Creating Change in Your Community and Beyond.* San Francisco: Berrett-Koehler. *The author is president of the Giraffe Heroes Project, an organization dedicated to identifying and encouraging individuals who "stick their necks out" for positive social change. This book is filled with practical advice and useful suggestions for getting involved. Topics covered include how to recruit like-minded volunteers, formulate action plans, negotiate with opponents, raise funds, and work with the media. The book also includes inspiring profiles of ordinary people who are accomplishing extraordinary things in their communities and is a superb source of encouragement for people considering getting involved for the very first time. The theme of this book is every person has something valuable to offer.*

Henderson, Nan, Benard, Bonnie, and Sharp-Light, Nancy (Eds.). (2000). *Mentoring for Resiliency: Setting up Programs for Moving Youth "from Stressed to Success."* Ojai, CA: Resiliency In Action. *Adult-youth mentoring is a programmatic approach to fostering resiliency that has extensive scientific documentation of its success—IF it is implemented correctly. This book offers the research-based guidelines for setting up successful youth mentoring and other resiliency-building programs. With an introduction by Emmy Werner, it includes information on which programs are most effective, the necessary elements of creating effective programs, how educators can be "turn around" mentors for their students, and the connection between self-esteem and mentoring.*

Herrera, Carla, Sipe, Cynthia, and McClanahan, Wendy. (2000). *Mentoring School-Age Children: Relationship Development in Community-Based and School-Based Programs.* Philadelphia: Public/Private Ventures. *This report is based on interviews with over 600 volunteer mentors. It compares their experiences and the development of their relationships with youth in community- and school-based settings. The authors conclude that "both types of programs have the potential to create positive mentoring relationships," and they highlight factors associated with the closest, most supportive, and effective mentoring relationships.*

Horton, Myles with Kohl, Judith, and Kohl, Herbert. (1997). *The Long Haul: An Autobiography.* New York: Teachers College Press. *An inspiring story—filled with stories!—of the life of Myles Horton who for more than 50 years trained leaders, including Martin Luther King, in community organizing for social justice. His empowerment philosophy, like that of Paolo Freire's in Brazil, was based on developing local, indigenous leadership.*

Ianni, Francis. (1998). *The Search for Structure: A Report on American Youth Today.* New York: Free Press. *Ianni provides rich, in-depth research support (over a decade of observations and interviews with thousands of adolescents in families, schools, peer groups/gangs, youth programs, street corners, and even jails in ten diverse communities) for the roles community support, resources, and opportunities play in promoting positive youth development. His findings challenge the prevailing notion that "youth culture" is a separate social system immune from the community context.*

KIDS Consortium. (2005). *KIDS As Planners: A Guide to Strengthening Students, Schools and Communities Through Service Learning* (2nd ed.). Lewiston, ME: KIDS Consortium. *KIDS (Kids Involved Doing Service) Consortium is an award-winning, research-evaluated service-learning organization in Maine, and has developed our favorite service learning model. The organization describes this book as "a comprehensive guidebook that provides teachers, school administrators, students, and community partners with a step-by-step process for designing, implementing, and evaluating a quality KIDS service-learning project. It demonstrates how service-learning can effectively meet many educational reform objectives: standards-based learning, character education, and school-to-career initiatives." The book is filled with reader-friendly reproducible examples, tools, and strategies, and is an excellent resource to help schools advance educational goals while deepening the relationship between students and their communities.*

Kretzmann, John, and McKnight, John. (1997). *Building Communities from the Inside Out.* Skokie, IL: ACTA Publications. *A user-friendly and inexpensive guide to capacity-driven community development, complete with "Capacity Inventories" for mapping individual, organizational, institutional, and economic strengths.*

Lerner, Michael. (1997). *The Politics of Meaning: Restoring Hope and Possibility in An Age of Cynicism.* Reading, MA: Addison-Wesley. *While really a policy framework for creating a resilient society based on caring and meaningfulness rather than on the current ethos of selfishness and cynicism, the agenda and strategies Lerner lays out are commonsensical, human, and doable. If only Americans can create the political will by—you guessed it!—building community through the creation of grassroots mobilizing.*

Lofquist, William. (1983). *Discovering the Meaning of Prevention: A Practical Approach to Positive Change.* Tucson, AZ: AYD Publications. *This is the classic prevention text by the "guru" of prevention and positive youth development. Lofquist's concept of prevention is grounded firmly in the community development process and in building on people (including youth) as resource models. If only this developmental model had become the modus operandi of the prevention field.*

Louv, Richard. (2006). *Last Child in the Woods: Saving Our Children from Nature-Deficit Disorder.* Chapel Hill, NC: Algonquin Books. *The author makes a compelling case that replacing meadows, woods, and wetlands with manicured lawns, golf courses, and housing developments has a disastrous effect on our children. What little time children now spend outdoors is mainly on cement foundationed playgrounds or in fenced yards. Drawing on personal experience and the opinions of urban planners, educators, naturalists, and psychologists, Louv links children's alienation from nature to attention-deficit hyperactivity disorder, stress, depression, anxiety, and childhood obesity. He recommends reacquainting our children and ourselves with the richness of the natural world and argues convincingly that by so doing, we can reduce the frequency and severity of emotional and mental ailments and more fully recognize the importance of preserving nature.*

McKnight, John. (1996). *The Careless Society: Community and Its Counterfeits.* New York: Basic Books. *In his compelling story-telling way McKnight takes on four community "counterfeiting" systems: human service systems, professionalism, medicine, and the criminal justice system. He shows how the institutionalization (i.e., the growth of bureaucracy) of caring roles have worked to undermine community. McKnight calls for "opposing those interests of governmental, corporate, professional, and managerial America that thrive on the dependency" of people, that have turned citizens into clients. This book should be required reading for all helping professionals.*

Mills, Roger. (1993). *The Health Realization Model: A Community Empowerment Primer.* Alhambra, CA: California School of Professional Psychology. *This short "primer" concisely and clearly summarizes the health realization approach to planned change, an inside-out process that illustrates the systemic nature of resiliency. Based on teaching people the simple truths about their innate resilience and mental health and about how their thinking affects their feelings and behaviors, this simple but deeply systemic approach has demonstrated miraculous results at the community level.*

Public/Private Ventures. (2000). *Making a Difference: An Impact Study of Big Brothers/Big Sisters.* Philadelphia: Public/Private Ventures. *This is a re-issue of P/PV's 1995 impact study of Big Brothers/Big Sisters, which "proved that high-quality mentoring can have tangible and significant effects on the lives of youth," This study documented that weekly meetings with a mentor for (on average) a year reduced first-time drug use by almost half and first-time alcohol use by a third, cut school absenteeism by half, improved parental and peer relationships, and gave the youth confidence in doing their school work, as well as improved grades.*

Rans, Susan. (2005). *Hidden Treasures: Building Community Connections by Engaging the Gifts of…People on Welfare, People with Disabilities, People with Mental Illness, Older Adults, and Young People.* Evanston, IL: Northwestern University, ABCD Institute. *Based entirely on the community asset model of John Kretzmann and John McKnight, this practical and inspiring report documents several success stories of "building communities from the inside out." In clear, reader-friendly language, the author shares the guiding themes of the Kretzmann/McKnight model, the details of the successful community approaches, and "lessons learned."*

Rifkin, Jeremy. (2004). *The End of Work: The Decline of the Global Labor Force and the Dawn of the Post-Market Era.* New York: Jeremy Tarcher. *Daring to discuss the unspeakable, Rifkin boldly—backed with more data than you wish he had!—documents the alarming move to a 21st century society devoid of employment opportunities for a majority of people. However, this visionary also proposes a viable solution which includes the voluntary sector and the rebuilding of local working communities.*

Schor, Juliet. (1993). *The Overworked American: The Unexpected Decline of Leisure.* New York: Basic Books. *For those people with jobs, Harvard economist Schor documents the trend toward "overwork" and asks the question, "Why are we—unlike every other industrialized Western nation—repeatedly choosing money over time?" And, "What can we do to get off the treadmill?" She, like Rifkin, forces us to examine the deep, systemic questions about who Americans are, what we're doing, and why we're doing it.*

Shaffer, Carolyn, and Anundsen, Kristin. (1993). *Creating Community Anywhere: Finding Support and Connection in a Fragmented World.* New York: Jeremy Tarcher. *This book focuses on exploring the wide variety of community forms in late 20th century America—from support groups, workplace teams, new forms of residence sharing, and neighborhood associations to electronic networks, intellectual salons, and spiritual communities. Besides discussing the personal stories of individuals in search of community, it profiles successful communities in the US. It also serves as a self-reflective guide for readers to assess what types of support and belonging they want and need in their lives as well as a practical guide for developing community-building skills, i.e., effective communication, conducting productive meetings, working through conflicts, etc.*

Thomas, Marvin. (2004). ***Personal Village: How to Have People in Your Life by Choice, Not Chance.*** Seattle, WA: Milestone Books. *Based on the "hard evidence that we thrive when we are with one another" and the historical propensity of all peoples to cluster in clans and tribes, the author validates a growing chorus of voices asserting, "community is at the very core of what it is to be human" and "without it...our overall satisfaction is lower and we do not live as long." He offers 12 "essential ingredients of a healthy community" as well as a "community effectiveness checklist" and numerous strategies for building a personal community wherever you are.*

Whitmyer, Claude, (Ed.). (1993). ***In the Company of Others: Making Community in the Modern World.*** New York: Jeremy Tarcher. *As Eric Utne says in the introduction, Whitmyer has "assembled a veritable pantheon of some of the best thinkers and visionaries of our time." This makes for a rich exploration of the concept of community and the many forms community can manifest. Like the Shaffer and Anundsen book, it also offers practical tips for building and sustaining community.*

RESILIENCY AND COMMUNITIES

PART FOUR

Resiliency Connections: Mentoring, Counseling, and Support

CHAPTER 1

Mentoring: Study Shows the Power of Relationship to Make a Difference

by Bonnie Benard, M.S.W.

The assumption of the resiliency approach in working with youth is that by meeting youth's developmental needs for safety, belonging, respect, accomplishment, power, and meaning, adults are promoting positive youth development *and*, thereby, preventing problems like alcohol and other drug abuse, teen pregnancy, violence, delinquency, and school failure. This perspective is supported not only by the strongest possible research base—longitudinal prospective studies on human development—but also by research on healthy families, effective schools, competent communities, successful change, learning organizations, and positive program evaluations. What these distinct bodies of research have documented is that successful development in *any* human system is dependent on these needs being met through the relationships, beliefs, and opportunities within the respective system. Caring relationships that convey high expectations—including a deep belief in a youth's innate resilience—and that provide opportunities for ongoing participation and contribution have been found *in natural settings* to be the key to successful development in any human system, and for positive youth development. However, what the resiliency approach to prevention has not had until now is an *evaluated planned preventive intervention* focused on creating this protective relationship.

> *"The most notable results are the deterrent effect on initiation of drug and alcohol use, and the overall positive effects on academic performance that the mentoring experience produced."*

A decade ago, Public/Private Ventures (P/PV), a national not-for-profit research corporation based in Philadelphia, published the fourth and final volume of its three-year, $2 million evaluation of Big Brothers/Big Sisters of America (BB/BS)—an *impact study* of the oldest and most carefully structured mentoring effort in the US According to the authors of the study, titled *Making A Difference*, "Our research presents clear and encouraging evidence that caring relationships between adults and youth can be created and supported by programs, and can yield a wide range of tangible benefits" (p. iv). Furthermore, *"The most notable results are the deterrent effect on initiation of drug and alcohol use, and the overall positive effects on academic*

performance that the mentoring experience produced" (p. iv). In essence, the resiliency/youth development approach to healthy development and successful learning are validated in this scientifically reliable impact evaluation.

Study Overview

Briefly, P/PV, using a classical experimental research methodology with random assignment, conducted a comparative study of 959 10- to 16-year-olds who applied to BB/BS programs in eight geographically diverse cities in 1992 and 1993. Half of these youth were randomly assigned to a treatment group for which BB/BS matches were made or attempted; the other half were assigned to waiting lists. After 18 months the two groups were compared. Participants in a BB/BS program were less likely to start using drugs and alcohol: 46% less likely to start using illegal drugs; 27% less likely to start drinking. However, the effect was even stronger for minority Little Brothers and Sisters who were 70% less likely to initiate drug use than other similar minority youth! Little Brothers and Sisters were about one third less likely than controls to hit someone. They skipped half as many days of school as did control youth, felt more competent about doing schoolwork, skipped fewer classes, and showed "modest gains in their grade point averages"—with the strongest gains among minority Little Sisters (p. iii). Lastly, they improved their relationships with both their parents and their peers relative to their control counterparts.

Of particular note is that probably all of these youth—both treatment and control groups—would be considered "high risk" youth:

- 90% lived with only one of their parents;
- over 80% came from impoverished homes;
- over 40% received either food stamps and/or cash public assistance;
- 40% came from homes with a history of alcohol and drug abuse;
- nearly 30% came from families with a record of domestic violence; and
- nearly 30% were victims of emotional, physical, or sexual abuse.

Conversely, the Big Brothers/Big Sisters were generally well-educated young professionals. About 60% were college graduates; nearly two-thirds had a total household income over $25,000 (with 40% over $40,000). Also of note, about three fourths of the volunteers were white. In essence, despite this enormous social distance between the youth and the volunteers, they were able to establish successful relationships—across their class and race differences. To what, then, does P/PV credit this accomplishment?

The three earlier studies in P/PV's four-part evaluation of BB/BS answer this question. These earlier studies looked respectively at (1) program practices (implementation of the program model), (2) volunteer recruitment and screening, and (3) the nature of the relationships between volunteers and youth (how they form, are sustained, and end). From these earlier examinations the researchers attribute the successful outcomes to two overall characteristics: the *one-to-one relationship and the program's supportive infrastructure.*

Characteristics of Effective One-to-One Relationships

First of all, the relationship was of sufficient *intensity*. From my 15 years of reviewing prevention evaluation research, the *lack* of intensity is continually identified as a barrier to positive results. However, in the 400 matches studied here, more than 70% of the matches met three times a month for an average of 3-4 hours per meeting and 50% met one time a week. This comes to around 144 hours of direct contact a year, not counting telephone interaction.

> **"Sustained relationships were those in which the mentor saw him/herself as a friend, not as a teacher or preacher."**

Secondly, even though this outcome study did not examine the nature of the relationship between the adult and youth, the third companion study (*Building Relationships With Youth in Program Settings,* 1995, May) illuminated the nature of the relationships that were of sufficient intensity and duration to produce these effects. Certainly coming as no surprise, but presenting powerful validation of the resiliency perspective, is the finding of this third study that sustained relationships were those in which the mentor saw him/herself *as a friend, not as a teacher or preacher* (Part Four, p. 51). These "developmental" relationships were grounded in the mentor's belief that he or she was there to meet the developmental needs of youth—to provide supports and opportunities the youth did not currently have.

While most developmental volunteers ultimately hoped to help their youth improve in school and be more responsible, they centered their involvement and expectations on developing a reliable, trusting relationship, and expanded the scope of their efforts only as the relationship strengthened. (III, p. ii)

These volunteers placed top priority on having the relationship enjoyable and fun to both partners. Furthermore, they were "there" for the young person, listened nonjudgmentally, looked for the youth's interests and strengths, and incorporated the youth into the decision-making process (gave them "voice and choice") around their activities. From a resiliency perspective, they provided the protective factors of a *caring relationship* that conveys *positive expectations and respect,* and that *provides ongoing opportunities for participation and contribution*—and saw risks existing in the *environment,* not in the youth.

In contrast to these developmental relationships (fortunately, two thirds of the 82 relationships examined were developmental!), were the "prescriptive" relationships in which the adult volunteers believed their primary purpose was guiding the youth toward the values, attitudes, and behaviors *the adult* deemed positive. "Adults in these relationships set the goals, the pace, and/or the ground rules for the relationship. These volunteers were reluctant to adjust their expectations of the youth or their expectation of how quickly the youth's behavior could change" (III, p. iii). A majority of these prescriptive volunteers were basically there to fix kids—typically to improve school performance—and most of their shared time was spent in conversation—not fun activities—around grades and classroom behavior. For these volunteers, risk lay within the youth:

> What seemed to stand out for these prescriptive volunteers was less the deficiencies present in the youth's environment, and more, particularly in terms of morals and values, those present in the youth themselves—deficiencies prescriptive volunteers frequently sought to rectify. (III, p. 40)

Not surprisingly, the adults and youths in these matches found the relationship frustrating and nonsupportive. Of these prescriptive relationships, only 29% met consistently (compared to 93% of the developmental) and at the 18-month follow-up, only 32% were ongoing (compared to 91% of the developmental) (III, p. 18). What is particularly frightening in reading some of the interviews with the youth and the prescriptive volunteers is the fact that these relationships are probably doing more harm than good—are becoming themselves another risk factor in an already stressed young life as illustrated by the following poignant statements:

Youth: When I went out with my Big Brother he... said okay, let's go get the library card and let's go to the library and check out a book. But I stayed at the library all day and he kept coming back, and telling me I didn't have the right information. So I studied there until closing time in the library. I was sitting there doing a report on toads and frogs, and when he came back, I had my report done, but I didn't have a rough draft. So like I wrote word for word out of the book; he said that's cheatin'.

Interviewer: He said that's cheating?

Youth: I just sat there and dropped in tears.

Interviewer: You started crying?

Youth: I mean it's something that I just can't hold them in...

Interviewer: What upset you about that?

Youth: I don't know. I didn't wanna stay there, I felt like I was supposed to write the report in my own words. Like some of it I got out of the book and some of it came out of my own head... I had to do it over.

Interviewer: You had to do it over?

Youth: Yeah, and he picked me up from the library and it was raining. (III, p. 63)

In contrast, this is the voice of a developmental volunteer:

[When he told me about a bad grade] I kind of focused on his other grades first; he said that he had done a good job with the other ones. And then I asked him if he wanted to do better in it, and then I kind of asked him how he could do better. And it was a pretty simple thing because he just didn't do a couple reports. So we decided that, you know, the next ones he got I would help him with them if he wanted. And we did that twice. You know, so it's like what can we do together to do this... When I came home with even a B or even an A-, sometimes it would be well, why did you get a minus here. It wasn't like, oh you did great. So I was sensitive to that. (III, p. 59)

The youth-centered approach—asking the youth what he needed and wanted—and then offering help as a shared activity, as well as the strengths-focus, sensitivity, and empathy displayed by this volunteer stands in sharp con-

trast to the earlier volunteer who didn't ask what the youth wanted, who left the youth alone and on his own with no assistance, who clearly had decided the youth should spend time at the library, and who displayed only insensitivity and lack of empathy. According to the researchers,

That participation in BB/BS was able to achieve transformative goals [outcomes like reduced alcohol use] while taking a general developmental approach lends strong support to the emerging consensus that [ironically!] youth programs are most effective in achieving their goals when they take a more supportive, holistic approach to youth." (III, p. 51)

Certainly, this study proves the deep truth of Nel Noddings' (1988) statement: "It is obvious that children will work harder and do things—even odd things like adding fractions—for people they love and trust."

> **"Serving the needs of mentors is as important as serving the needs of youth."**

Program Infrastructure: "Prerequisites for an Effective Mentoring Program"

From the studies of BB/BS' program practices and recruitment and screening as well as earlier Public/Private Ventures' research on mentoring, the researchers conclude that "the following program irreducibles are prerequisites for an effective mentoring program:"

- Thorough volunteer *screening* that weeds out adults who are unlikely to keep their time commitment or might pose a safety risk to the youth;

- Mentor training that includes *communication and limit-setting* skills, tips on *relationship-building* and recommendations on the *best way to interact with a young person;*

- Matching procedures that take into account the preferences of the youth, their family and the volunteer, and that use a professional case manager to analyze which volunteer would work best with which youth; and

- *intensive supervision and support of each match by a case manager* who has frequent contact with the parent/guardian, volunteer and youth, and provides assistance when requested or as difficulties arise. (IV, p. 52)

Supervision is a hallmark of the BB/BS approach to mentoring... [and] the program practice most associated with positive match outcomes" (I, p. 61). The earlier study found that those sites following the BB/BS procedures for regular supervision had matches that met at the highest rates; those agencies that reduced this function had problems. As several studies of mentoring have discovered, serving the needs of mentors is as important as serving the needs of youth; you can't have one without the other! According to Ron Ferguson's (1990) earlier study,

Most programs expect to use volunteer mentors to supplement the love and attention that their paid staffs provide to children, but those that have tried have experienced only limited success at finding mentors and keeping them active. *They have discovered that fulfilling mentors' needs is as important for sustaining their involvement as fulfilling youths' needs is to sustaining theirs.* (p. 15)

This is a finding directly paralleling what educational researchers have found about meeting the needs of *teachers* as a fundamental prerequisite to engaging students!

Another critical benefit of having paid staff is the stability and continuity they provide. Case managers ensure that youth are not left on their own if their mentor leaves. In fact, several investigators have found that even in programs that employ volunteer mentors, it is the case managers/youth workers that are often the real mentors to youth (Freedman, 1993; Higgins et al., 1991; Ferguson, 1990).

> *"The development of a caring, trusting, respectful, reciprocal relationship is the key to reducing risks, enhancing protection, and promoting positive youth development in any system."*

Implications for Prevention, Education, and Youth Development

The youth development/resiliency approach is key to successful learning and social development.

Perhaps the finding with the greatest implication for prevention and education is the power of a non-problem-focused intervention to produce positive—and superior—results compared to the targeted problem-focused interventions that dominate the prevention field, from substance abuse to dropout, to teen pregnancy, to violence prevention.

Participation in a BB/BS program reduced illegal drug and alcohol use, began to improve academic performance, behavior and attitudes, and improved peer and family relationships. *Yet the BB/BS approach does not target those aspects of life, nor directly address them.* It simply provides a caring, adult friend. Thus, the findings in this report speak to the effectiveness of an approach to youth policy that is very different from the problem-oriented approach that is prevalent in youth programming. This more developmental approach does not target specific problems, but rather interacts flexibly with youth in a supportive manner. (IV, p. 1)

I would extend this conclusion to the whole youth-serving arena, including families and schools. The development of a caring, trusting, respectful, reci-procal relationship is the key to reducing risks, enhancing protection, and promoting positive youth development in *any* system.

Creating "mentor-rich" environments must be a major focus.

As I stated in an earlier work on mentoring, an approach to mentoring especially compelling to me is the concept of infusing mentoring—as a way of being with youth—into social institutions: families, schools, and communities. Creating what Marc Freedman (1993) refers to as "mentor-rich environments"—environments that create lots of opportunities for young people to interact with an array of caring adults must be the focus.

Creating mentor-rich settings—schools, social programs, youth organizations—is one way of moving beyond the chimera of super-mentoring, in which a single charismatic adult is called on to be a dramatic influence, providing all the young person's needs in one relationship. In reality, young people need more than one relationship to develop into healthy adults. (p. 111)

He states,

Our aspiration should be to create planned environments conducive to the kind of informal interaction that leads to mentoring. Indeed, such an approach is rooted in the historic strength and traditional practice of extended and fictive kin structures in many low-income communities—particularly African-American neighborhoods. (p. 112)

What this means is expansion of the world of adult contacts for all youth in their natural environments. This means supporting families in their efforts to parent via family-centered social policies that promote flexible work policies, parental leave, time off to work in schools, decent wages, family healthcare benefits, and quality child care. Communities must also create opportunities for youth to be directly involved with more adults through community

> "[To] expand the world of adult contacts for all youth in their natural environments... means supporting families in their efforts to parent via family-centered social policies that promote flexible work policies, parental leave, time off to work in schools, decent wages, family healthcare benefits, and quality childcare."

service, work apprenticeships, more involvement in local government, and so on. Young people need more opportunities to interact and form relationships with the older generation—the generation that currently is abdicating its responsibilities to the young.

Creating mentor-rich environments means relationships must be the central focus of reform efforts.

Creating mentor-rich environments in schools, community-based organizations, and communities as a whole means relationships must be the top priority in any prevention effort or educational reform. As this study so eloquently proves, a focus on outcomes alone inevitably leads to youth-fixing, control strategies in our institutions—and often deleterious ones. For example, an outcome of reduced alcohol and drug use often leads schools to zero tolerance strategies which expel youth from school and push them onto the streets. At its extreme, this prescriptive approach leads to the imprisoning of more and more young people.

The BB/BS study, along with all the research on resiliency and positive youth development, shows clearly the path for youth policy and educational reform. Unless there is a focus on the mediating variables of relationships, beliefs, and opportunities for participation, the desired outcomes of reduced alcohol and other drug abuse, school success, and compassionate and responsible citizens will

never be achieved. This is the key message of resiliency research and the BB/BS evaluation; this is the message to sell to preventionists, educators, youth and educational policy makers, and adult society. All these constituencies must see that (1) What works is known!, (2) It's never too late to transform young lives, (3) Caring is not a "touchy-feely" add-on luxury but a critical necessity to educational and social change and perhaps the most important, and (4) Adult society has a civic and moral responsibility to the next generation—to "other people's children."

Other People's Children

The last point remains the ultimate challenge. While mentoring programs, as the BB/BS evaluation shows, have demonstrated their power to promote healthy development and prevent problem behaviors, they ultimately serve only a few of the millions of children who could benefit and have

> "Relationships must be the top priority in any prevention effort or educational reform."

a hefty price tag of $1,000 a match. Moreover, they are a limited intervention in the realm of systemic social change. Just as disadvantaged children have been and continue to be socially created by policies that systematically deny them opportunities to succeed in society, to change this situation requires new social policies. These policies must address the most powerful risk factor a growing number of children and youth, and their families, face: poverty. Many policy experts agree with Stanley Eitzen's (1992) vision of just what these changes must look like:

> Since the problems of today's young people are largely structural, solving them requires structural changes. The government [and the government is all of us, folks!] must create jobs and supply job training... as well as exert more control over the private sector. In particular, corporations must pay decent wages and provide adequate benefits to their employees.... There must be an adequate system for delivering health care, rather than our current system that rations care according to ability to pay. There must be massive expenditures on education to equalize opportunities from state to state and from community to community. There must be equity in pay scales for women. And finally, there must be an unwavering commitment to eradicating institutional sexism and racism. (p. 590)

That these systemic changes will be costly there is no disputing; however, far more costly will be society's refusal to pay what it costs to provide the developmental opportunities and supports all young people need. As Mike Males (1996) states in *The Scapegoat Generation*, his compelling investigation of America's War on Adolescence, "The deterioration in public support for families with children [is] a direct result of declining tax revenue and school funding [and] reverberates across generations" (p. 285). He claims, "America's level of adult selfishness is found in no other Western country," citing a 1995 National Science Foundation-funded study that found the US ranking first in per-person affluence, "producing a higher gross domestic product with 250 million people than the other 17 nations, population 400 million, combined!" Furthermore, "The US, by an even larger margin, also ranks first in child poverty." (p. 7)

> *"What [mentoring] offers besides a transformational experience to the young people involved, is the opportunity to reconnect the young and old, to reweave the intergenerational threads that are essential to a healthy society."*

While mentoring is a limited intervention, what it offers besides a transformational experience to the young people involved, is the opportunity to reconnect the young and old, to reweave the intergenerational threads that are essential to a healthy society. While Males acknowledges that "the path to intergenerational cooperation [is] difficult at this advanced state of deterioration..., it lies in inviting adolescents into adult society." Furthermore,

What is needed is not a revolution of fiscal policy or remedial plan, but one of fundamental attitude. Nothing good will happen until elder America gazes down from our hillside and condominium perch and identifies the young—darker in shade as a rule; feisty; lustful as we were; violent, as we raised them to be; no different from us in any major respect—as our children. (pp. 291-292)

According to Freedman (1996), mentoring offers just this opportunity to identify and realize our shared humanity.

Mentoring amounts to the "elementary school of caring" for other people's children, the children of the poor. It is a specific context in which to initiate the process of reconstructing empathy.... Mentoring brings us together—across generation, class, and often race—in a manner that forces us to acknowledge our inter-dependence, to appreciate, in Martin Luther King, Jr.'s words, that "we are caught in an inescapable network of mutuality, tied to a single garmet of destiny." (pp. 134, 141)

References

Note: The Big Brother/Big Sisters evaluation was published in four volumes available through Public/Private Ventures, 2005 Market Street, Suite 900, Philadelphia, PA 19103; 215-557-4400 ; www.ppv.org.

I.   *Big Brothers/Big Sisters: A study of program practices* (1993, Winter).
II. *Big Brothers/Big Sisters: A study of volunteer recruitment and screening* (1994, Fall).
III. *Building relationships with youth in program settings* (1995, May).
IV. *Making a difference: An impact study of Big Brothers/Big Sisters* (1995, November).

Benard, Bonnie. (1992). *Mentoring programs for urban youth: Handle with care.* San Francisco, CA: WestEd. (June).

Eitzen, D. Stanley. (1988). Problem students: The sociocultural roots. *Phi Delta Kappan, December,* 296-298.

Ferguson, Ronald. (1990). *The case for community-based programs that inform and motivate black male youth.* Washington, DC: The Urban Institute.

Freedman, Marc. (1993). *The kindness of strangers: Adult mentors, urban youth, and the new voluntarism..* San Francisco, CA: Jossey-Bass.

Higgins, Catherine, et al. (1991). *I have a dream in Washington, D.C.:* Initial report, Winter. Philadelphia, PA: Public/Private Ventures.

Males, Mike. (1996). *The scapegoat generation: America's war on adolescents.* Monroe, ME: Common Courage Press.

Noddings, Nel. (1988). Schools face crisis in caring. *Education Week, December 7,* 32.

Bonnie Benard, M.S.W., has written widely and conducted workshops and trainings on resiliency for nearly 20 years. She currently works in the Health and Human Development Program of WestEd 's Oakland, CA office, where she has helped develop a statewide survey of students' perceptions of the protective factors in their lives (www.wested.org/hks). She can be reached by email at bbenard@ wested.org.

CHAPTER 2

Putting the Strengths-Based Approach Into Practice:
An Interview with Dennis Saleebey, D.S.W.

by Bonnie Benard, M.S.W.

Dennis Saleebey is a Professor of Social Welfare at the University of Kansas in Lawrence. The forth edition of his book, The Strengths Perspective In Social Work Practice, *is now available. I highly recommend this edited book for all helping professionals in terms of both policy and practice. I also "recommend" Dennis as a caring person with a warm heart and a sense of humor. —B.B.*

BB: You've just published another edition of *The Strengths Perspective In Social Work Practice.* I assume the first one must have been a success, or they wouldn't ask you to do others!

DS: It was a surprising success to me. Many people in schools of social work around the country are apparently using it as a supplemental text. I've even heard that some people are using it in England.

BB: Wonderful!

DS: I actually was very surprised. I didn't think there would be that kind of interest in the idea of a "strengths" perspective.

BB: What do you see as constituting a strengths perspective?

DS: To me the essence of the strengths perspective is that you actually believe that everybody—every community, every family, every individual—has a fund of knowledge, of capacities and skills, of personal traits and resources that exists within them and around them that are tools to be used in helping people move towards a better quality of life or move in a different direction. Most importantly, it's helping people move toward what they want, what they see as possible in their lives, their visions and dreams.

BB: You say that operating from a strengths perspective is really good basic social work. I have always found that true. I remember in my social work program we were trained to have that sense of honoring and respecting the resources that people bring. Why do you think, then, that the deficit view seems to be so powerful when social workers and other helping professionals go out into the world? What is it that becomes so compelling about a deficit view?

DS: Some of it is mystifying to me, too. I think there are a lot of factors and I'll just respond with what pops into my head. One is that, for some reason, the dominant culture we live in, that we see in the market place and the media, is just obsessed with problems and psychopathologies, with moral

and relational aberrations and difficulties, and with trauma and catastrophe. They're celebrated on the news. They're celebrated on talk shows. We see people confessing to the world about terrible things that they think they've done or others have done to them or confronting their abusers in public. It's an amazing array of entertainments that are based on problems and difficulties and the worst side of human nature and the human condition.

And you add to that the recovery and the victimization movements. These have been really important in the lives of many people—especially in that people who have been hurt are no longer silenced. But now it's extended way, way beyond its original intent. I mean we have people who feel that they're victims because their parents yelled at them a lot, and they can't get over it. Worse than that, if you're defined as a victim or in recovery, it never is over. It continues. These words become, in some ways, designations, imagery, symbols that people carry in their heads; they become part of their identity.

BB: It's really the idea that we must name the problem so that a person isn't either silenced or in denial, but that we must not get stuck defining ourselves only by the problems we've experienced, i.e., as victim. It can be kind of a fine line.

When I interviewed Steve Wolin for a past issue of *Resiliency In Action*, Steve said something about it being human nature to get stuck in the damage. That's part of it. On the other hand several writers, including you in your book, talk about the importance of telling the stories. When you look at different cultures you realize how storytelling has been part of every culture. And the stories are ones of strength and courage in the face of great barriers and adversity. Maybe the strengths or resilience perspective (I see them as one and the same) is a way to put these important stories into the culture of helping.

DS: I think it is. The root to me in discovering people's resiliency and their strengths is to have them tell their stories. I mean to really listen to their stories—not force them into a story that you like. They are often tales of failure but rebounding; triumph and tragedy. They're well-rounded stories. In our culture, for some reason, we seem to only celebrate the falls from grace or the difficulties that people have and how enormous they are. I mean we celebrate the plane crashes, but not all the planes that make it. That's really stupid.

There are also other things that play into the predominance of the damage perspective. This may be too strong, but I don't think so: The insurance companies, the pharmaceutical companies, and the medical profession have become an enormously powerful cartel in our culture and probably throughout the Western world. What they thrive on is illness and pathology and its recognition.

BB: This brings up a question I was going to ask you a little later. Do you think there's much hope for a strengths perspective in a managed care?

DS: Oddly enough I do. Using a strengths perspective is very efficient; it's very powerful; and it doesn't take forever. At least in my experience, once people are on the road to expressing and employing their strengths and continuing to discover other strengths not only in themselves but in their environment, they're going to continue to move. There'll be setbacks for many people, but basically, once they take the first step, the second step is much more likely. The third step is even more likely after they take the second. You can start talking about strengths in the first five minutes that you see somebody. As we discused, it doesn't mean you have to ignore pain or their difficulty or sickness. However, as soon as I see somebody, the first question I usually ask is, "Well, how have you survived so far? How have you made it to this point?" (I mean [whether they are] talking to me here in my office, my car, or standing on the street corner). So, the work begins immediately.

BB: We know from anecdotes and from longitudinal research in resiliency that this perspective works. Do you see that there is a need to start doing more evaluation or something else in order to help sell this perspective to managed care companies as they dominate more and more of the health care field?

DS: Yes. The people here at the University of Kansas School of Social Welfare have been very important in developing the basis for the strengths perspective and actually using it with people who have chronic and persistent illness. We have done evaluation research and much more of it needs to be done. As a matter of fact, several of our faculty were very instrumental in helping the State of Kansas revise its approach to mental health policy by including the ideas of community-based strengths-oriented practice for people with chronic mental illness. I also had a project in public housing, and although we do some traditional things, we also do some community development activities based on the idea that everybody there has assets and strengths that they can contribute their own life and also to the life of other residents.

BB: The community development approach is really grounded in strengths and grows out of the old social work tradition of community based, multi-service settlement houses.

DS: I'd say in the late '60s to mid '70s almost every social work school had a community track, and now most don't. However, the resilience research seems clear to me: The resilience research obliges you to always look at individuals in terms of their families and their communities. You can't get away from it. You've got to do that.

BB: It certainly gives us some strong, powerful studies to support strengths-based practice. We're starting to see more and more people writing about resilience and strengths-based practice. Do you think this deeper paradigm of personal and cultural strength and triumph is trying to rear its head and catch on throughout the helping field?

DS: Clearly something is happening, and I think it's very exciting. It would be amazing to think that we survived as a species all these thousands of years with nothing but sickness and deficits as our stuff. Clearly, as organisms and as collectives of organisms, there have got to be processes that allow us to continue to meet the continually changing demands of the environment.

BB: I would even make the bold statement that we're genetically programmed—hard wired—with all of the traits that resilience research has documented help people survive: social competence or relational skills, problem-solving and planning skills, a sense of self and autonomy, and a sense of purpose and hope.

DS: An analogy to me is the health and wellness literature. It's clear that our bodies have an enormous capacity for transformation and regeneration or rebounding from illnesses. Sometimes we're compromised by the enormity of the disease or the stress, but we do often get better. We can even improve that capacity by doing many obvious and often simple things in our relationships, in our personal practices and, very important to me again, in the community.

BB: Moving from the big picture to practice, what would you see as constituting good strengths-based practice? What would a social worker, community organizer, teacher, or family advocate have to do to be working from a strengths-based perspective?

DS: The first thing that everyone must do is to look at their own particular theories, whatever they're using, and to ask to what extent those define who they see. To what extent are those definitions in some way negative attributions? To what extent do they think people are damaged goods—damaged by their past or damaged by their current stress? You have to do a gut check first to see where you are.

The second thing is to really understand that for many people this is a change in the lens that they're used to looking through. It often requires that the scales have to drop from their eyes, because the power of the problem or the deficit-based approach is enormous. There is also a fear that somehow they'll be regarded as too idealistic or as a Pollyanna—that they don't see the real problems people have.

BB: I'm always accused of that!

DS: After this critical preliminary "lens" check, the strengths-based approach consists of three components. One is that people have to acknowledge and talk about and maybe even catalyze their pain. We're not just going to pretend that it didn't happen. We have to be extremely vigilant to let the person or the family, whoever it is, let them name it; let their theory prevail about not only what it is but what they want to do about it. Too often we assume because of our theories, "Oh, yeah, we know what that is. We know what abuse does to kids; we know that you're probably going to have disassociative identity disorder." Acknowledging and really respecting what the individual says about their problem and saying, "That is the theory that I must attend to, at least in part." However, when they talk about their pain, they're also going to be talking about their strengths and their hopes as well.

The second part is really beginning to discover and talk about and make an accounting of the assets, the capacities that people really have. They can be cultural. They can be familial. They can be in the neighborhood. They can be personal virtues like loyalty people have learned. They can be talents like tap dancing. I don't care what it is. Too often people don't honor those. They don't think of them as strengths or they don't think of what they learned in their troubles as strengths. So this step is about finding them,

discovering them, and learning how they might be used. This takes a lot of work! It doesn't necessarily take a long time, but it takes a lot of work to be vigilant about this.

BB: It's sounds simple, but it's not easy. It's funny that something as simple as listening and mirroring back the story of strength, which usually isn't acknowledged by the person, has such power.

DS: People say, "Well what else do I do? Don't I explore the subconscious?" Also, it really isn't reframing their misery. For example, if someone had schizophrenia then you wouldn't just say, "I think that you're just exquisitely sensitive to stimuli in your environment." That isn't helpful. We're looking at real possibilities.

The third part is finding out what people think their possibilities are, what their hopes are, how they want life to be in terms of work, relationships, community involvement. I don't care what it is; it doesn't make any difference. In fact, it's probably several things. So what you do in your work is to align their capacities and external and internal resources with their hopes and visions. And you work together to define a doable goal. Then you or the individual or family or community develop a collaborative project about how to get there. We need to ask, "How can I help you? What do you want to do for yourself? What could be the first step we could take?" When you do these things, it just changes the quality of the work that you do.

BB: What do your students or practitioners say when they start working from this perspective? How do they feel?

DS: Number one, there is a lot of resistance to the whole idea—even among some students: "Oh, come on. I came here to find out what's wrong with people." And practitioners are often very skeptical, especially those who work with people who have been abused and their perpetrators—"perps." The first time I heard that term I was doing a workshop, and somebody said, "Well you know I work with perps." I didn't know what it was—people from a planet, Perpetron?

BB: That's a big word now. So is the term "predator"—especially youthful predators. Have you heard of "preds"?

DS: The power of a word. If you're called a predator, that's a thing you have to live up to. I am sure that you'll continue predation once that puts you in the slammer...

Anyway, there is initial resistance to working from this perspective. However, I say, "Play with this. You're not going to hurt anybody. There're a lot of ways you can ask people things. Like ask someone what they like about themselves. Ask somebody what they learned when they were struggling with this horribly abusive marriage. There're a lot of ways you can ask people to get talking about their strengths." It comes by conversation. Even though we do have some strengths assessment forms, I don't particular like them, but they can be useful.

BB: I guess if you have to have forms, you might as well have some of the good stuff on them.

DS: If it's a great conversation, then you can do the assessment yourself or together if you want. People do feel a sense and a change in the energy exchanged between them and those they are trying to help. Again, I'm not going to make this a miracle. It's a human endeavor. When people start thinking that they have power within them to change elements of their lives, and that they're going to do it without me saying, "Well you can't do that because you're schizophrenic, you know," then they feel differently about what's going on.

BB: Practitioners often describe working this way as a feeling of chemistry or like you've really made a deep connection, a sense of spiritual or human connectedness...that you feel like you're in the "flow" where even though there's work to do, there is also a sense of effortlessness about it because you're sort of engaging working from a part of them that's very healthy.

DS: You are tapping into something that may have been buried by a lot of very obnoxious relationships, definitions, experiences—often in the social service or mental health system!

BB: It was neat to see in your chapter on community empowerment that you mentioned the Health Realization approach of Roger Mills. A statement Roger made that describes your work in connecting people's strengths to their hopes and dreams is that, "People's lives become what they think is possible."

DS: Absolutely. Discovering possibilities in people's lives is really important collaborative work. People start thinking of the possible—what they would like, what they've hoped for years, even those hopes that have been lost, so that you're both in the process of rethinking and revisioning what could happen. There's a lot of terrific stories about people who said, "Well I really want to do this." And somebody said, "Well, how would we do it? I don't understand why you can't do that."

Here's the thing to me. It doesn't really make any difference if they actually get to the final step of the destination. It's the fact that they're taking trips there and to other points that they never thought they'd stop at. My favorite story, which I probably tell too much, is of the student who is interning in a community support program and screening—*from a strengths perspective*—a person who has had a diagnosis of chronic schizophrenia for over thirty years. Because she was a student—and not steeped in the language of damage yet—she just interviewed him in a very nonjudgmental way. Finally, after learning a lot of stuff about him that nobody else knew because she'd actually listened and talked to him, she asked him, "What do you want to do, Harry?" He said, "I want to be a pilot." The first response she gets, of course, "Come on now, somebody with schizophrenia a pilot? Maybe a politician, but a pilot?!" However, she worked with him on this. They developed a collaborative project that had steps toward it. He had been washing dishes in town. Then he went to the airport and did dishes. Next he got a job on the tarmac. I don't think he'll be a pilot. But I don't know. I don't know. She says, he loves it. The planes and the jet fuel and the excitement of all that. He loves it.

BB: Who are we to say what are realistic expectations; we all have to have dreams. And maybe even he knew that he wouldn't actually become a pilot...

DS: There's a part of him that had doubts but those doubts are less important than what he gathered about himself and discovered in the smaller steps.

BB: I think a lot of the readers of *Resiliency In Action* are people that are really doing this positive stuff. They're excited about this approach, but often find themselves working in organizations that are really into a deficit or pathology model of working with people. What advice would you give them?

DS: That's a great question because people say, "Well I would do it but I'm in an agency that thrives on psychopathology." My advice is you've got to keep thinking, reading, talking—use every opportunity—to learn about these perspectives (there's more than one obviously) so that you feel comfortable with the language, you feel comfortable with the point of view and standpoint that it brings. Also talk it up in your agency with people you feel comfortable with. You have colleagues. Not every colleague is going to say, "Well you can't talk that way." You might even find coalitions of people who are willing to bring it up at staffing or include it on their case reports. Sometimes I've told students that if you're working in a mental health agency and you're using the *DSM* [*Diagnostic and Statistical Manual* published by the American Psychiatric Association]—which you inevitably are these days—add "axis six." Axis six is an accounting of people's resources and their capacities and their dreams.

BB: Is that your term, "axis six"?

DS: Right. You don't have to add it in a chart if it would embarrass you. You've got it there in your desk and you can discuss it with the people. You would do axis six together with that person.

BB: That's great advice. My last question: What are your hopes and fears for the future of the strengths perspective?

DS: My hope is that all these various approaches toward respecting people's strengths, resilience, and capacities will continue to find each other and build momentum and that there will be cross talks. For example, finding the resilience approach was great for me because it gave me other ideas and allowed me to talk to more people. I even went to Steve and Sybil Wolin's workshop in Kansas City when I first heard about resilience. I hope these people form an increasingly large cadre. Also, I hope we don't all just do one thing. I probably can't do exactly what Roger Mills does, but it's great that that's going on, and I draw a lot of stuff from his work.

Another hope is that this perspective will get strong enough, so that it will be a counter voice to the voice of pathological doom, the *DSM*.

BB: Frankly, I can't quite imagine you teaching it! I bet you make it a funny class.

DS: I say this is the language you have to learn, but you have to learn how limited this language is and how it can really hurt people. Also, it's a stupid language because many of the things that we regard here as mental disorders are, in fact, physical disorders that haven't been diagnosed yet. I hope that there are other voices in the land that actually begin to be heard not just between themselves but by people who need to know like policy makers and agency heads and so forth. One of my fears is that this will become pop psych, you know, and we'll be doing infomercials on the strengths perspective!

BB: Emmy Werner certainly always cautions people that resilience is a hot term now but it's getting overused.

DS: I hope that we continue to be real about the complexity of people's lives. I don't know who, but somebody said, "It is as wrong to deny the possible as it is to deny the problem." To me that kind of sums it up. You've got to do both things and see how they interact.

BB: All of us involved in resilience and strength-based perspectives owe you a debt of gratitude for this wonderful book.

Bonnie Benard, M.S.W., has written widely and conducted workshops and trainings on resiliency for nearly 20 years. She currently works in the Health and Human Development Program of WestEd 's Oakland, CA office, where she has helped develop a statewide survey of students' perceptions of the protective factors in their lives (www.wested.org/hks). She can be reached by email at bbenard@ wested.org.

Using a Strengths-Based Model in Assessment and Intervention Planning

Suggestions adapted from *The Strengths Perspective in Social Work Practice* (1997)
Dennis Saleebey, editor

Philosophy: It is essential to remind yourself that the person in front of you possess assets, examples of resilient overcoming of life's challenges, resources, wisdom and other internal and external strengths you probably know nothing about.

People are "more motivated to change when their strengths are supported" (p.13). Instead of asking people what their problems are, ask about the strengths they possess. Then, help them to link utilizing these strengths in their current situation.

"If assessment focuses on deficits, it is likely deficits will remain the focus of both the worker and the client during remaining contacts....Strengths are all we have to work with" (p. 62).

What are Strengths?

1. What people have learned about themselves, others, and their world (including what lessons have been gleaned from problems, trauma, illness, confusion, etc.).

2. Personal qualities, traits, and virtues.

3. The talents and capabilities people have (such as athletics, performing arts, woodworking, writing poetry, speaking foreign languages, cooking, etc.).

4. Any ways that people contribute to helping/serving others (including caring for family members, babysitting, helping a neighbor, and more formal service programs).

5. Cultural and personal traditions/lore (including cultural traditions that increase bonding, family stories that inspire, other personal, family, cultural stories of "falls from grace and redemption") (p. 51).

6. Pride in overcoming or just coping with the day-to-day reality of life –often hidden "under the heap of blame, shame, labeling" (p.51).

7. Relationships with others–peers, family or extending or "adopted family, neighbors, teachers, a faith community, youth workers of any kind–that provide caring and support, empowerment, positive feedback, and optimism.

8. The larger community, including school and/or work, resources of a neighborhood (including parks, libraries, etc.), even an on-line community that provides a pro-social, uplifting connection of any kind.

Guidelines for a Strengths Assessment

1. Give preeminence to the client's understanding of the facts.
2. Believe the client.
3. Discover what the client wants.
4. Move the assessment toward personal and environmental strengths.
5. Make assessment of strengths multidimensional (see, "What are Strengths?").
6. Use the assessment to discover uniqueness.
7. Use language the client can understand.
8. Make assessment a joint activity between worker and client.
9. Reach a mutual agreement on the assessment.
10. Avoid blame and shaming.
11. Avoid cause-and-effect thinking (realizing "causal thinking represents only one of many possible perspectives of the problem situation, and can easily lead to blaming").
12. Assess, do not diagnose.

The Elements of Strength-Based Practice

1. Acknowledge/validate/normalize the pain (including grief, anger, frustration, confusion).

2. Stimulate a discussion of resilience and strength.

3. Link, Educate, Advocate (link clients to their own internal and other useful environmental resources, continue to educate about the capacities and resilience of the self, advocate for the client when needed with families, schools, organizations, etc.).

4. Move toward normalizing and capitalizing upon strengths. "Over time...often a short period of time...begin to consolidate the strengths that have emerged, reinforce the new vocabulary of strengths and resilience, and bolster the apacity to discover resources within and around" (p.56).

CHAPTER 3

Shifting the "At Risk" Paradigm

by Sybil Wolin, Ph.D., and Steven Wolin, M.D.

Editor's Note: This article offers invaluable insight for everyone wanting to know how to "get buy-in" to the resiliency approach. The Wolins offer unique insight to this challenge and suggestions about how it can be overcome.—N.H.

As ideas go, the concept of paradigm shift is "in." Educators, preventionists, clinicians, and policy makers everywhere are decrying the drawbacks of an "at-risk" paradigm for understanding, serving, and programming for children and youth. The alternative they advance is a resiliency model which breaks with a long tradition of research and practice emphasizing problems and vulnerabilities in children, families, communities, and institutions burdened by adversity. Instead, the resiliency model credits people with the strength and the potential to recover and bounce back from hardship. It honors their power to help themselves, and casts professionals as partners rather than as authorities, initiators, and directors of the change process.

We agree. An important part of our own work has been to develop a resilience paradigm and to advocate for a shift away from the risk paradigm. At the same time, we have learned from our experience training hundreds of teachers, school and agency administrators, counselors, therapists, youth workers, and others that paradigm shifts are much more easily talked about than accomplished. Resistance is both natural and expectable.

The Case of Anita

The case of Anita, a 14-year-old student in an inner city junior high school illustrates the nature of the task. Upon entering junior high school, Anita was immediately identified as an "at-risk" student. She was brought to the attention of the guidance office and the special education screening team by her teachers who supported their dim view of her with the following obsevations: Anita is disruptive in class, frequently calling out and making inappropriate remarks. All of her academic skills are two to three years below grade level. Her school record does not indicate a home address or the name of her father. Her mother, who was a teenager when Anita was born, is addicted to crack cocaine. Anita is frequently absent or late to school. Notes sent home about her absences, her behavior, and her poor academic work are unanswered.

This recitation of "facts" is the data usually marshalled to support the risk paradigm and from which its conclusions are typically drawn. By documenting one problem after the next, the paradigm gives the impression of Anita as a teenager who is well on the way to repeating her mother's life. It predicts that because Anita is academically deficient and behaviorally and emotionally impaired, she is more likely than not to drop out of school. With few skills and little idea of a work ethic or the rules of the marketplace, she will be pushed to the margins of society. According to the risk paradigm, little in her past gives a reason to be hopeful about her future.

Using a resiliency paradigm leads to an opposing conclusion, not by denying the facts cited by the risk paradigm but by looking at another part of the picture—her social and emotional intelligence. For instance, at home Anita takes care of both her mother and her brother. Because her mother resists treatment, Anita escorts her to the drug treatment center and often waits many hours for her to be seen. She also goes along to the supermarket to be sure that her mother buys food rather than getting sidetracked and spending her money on drugs.

Anita cooks and prepares meals for her brother. She insists that he attend school, even when she does not. Anita has woven a safety net for herself by cultivating a relationship with her Aunt Edith. It is to Edith's house that she goes with her brother whenever her mother disappears or brings home a man who is frightening.

Acknowledging these "facts" as well as Anita's school records and psychological and educational assessments, a resiliency paradigm holds out hope for her. It views Anita as someone with inherent strengths and the capacity to direct her future provided she is given the right support. Specifically, she is a mature individual—even wise beyond her years. She is moral and has a deep sense of obligation to her family. She is self-sufficient and has considerable common sense.

In the training we have conducted, we have tried to instill doubts about the risk paradigm by introducing this type of positive information. We have tried to convey a sense of hope to those who would see Anita exclusively in terms of her problems and who, on that basis, would write a scenario of doom for her. We have encouraged participants entrenched in the risk paradigm to broaden their perspective and to consider information that is normally omitted in risk assessments. We can't say that we have always been successful. On the contrary, we've had to learn and understand what we are up against.

Impediments to Change

Shifting one's paradigm requires personal change, and personal change requires hard work. Consider how difficult it is to make even small personal changes. How often have you vowed not to blow up at your teenager only to find yourself in that very act the next day or the next hour? Or to begin a diet, or to start exercising, or to put your credit card away, or to stop procrastinating?

Compared to the difficulty of changing behaviors such as these, shifting one's paradigm is a different order of magnitude. Paradigms are not overt behaviors such as eating too much, exercising too little, or flying off the handle. Paradigms are deeply embedded in the self. As Steven Covey (1989) explains, a paradigm is a map inlaid in the mind which determines the way you see the world. Paradigms are conditioned by inborn temperament, upbringing, family, friends, colleagues, schooling, and work environment. Deeply rooted as they are, paradigms are seldom scrutinized. Rather, they are accepted without question, driving the assumption that what you see is a correct representation of reality. One's paradigm precludes other people's realities. When contradictions arise in an encounter with someone else's paradigm, these are dismissed as inaccuracies, misperceptions, or mistakes. The whole process repeats itself again and again without notice. It is not easily interrupted.

New information does not change paradigms. Training in skills and techniques does not change paradigms. And telling others about a new paradigm in the hope that they will give up theirs and adopt yours does not often work either. As Bonnie Benard (1993) has noted, changing paradigms requires nothing less than changing people's hearts and minds. In our attempts to do that, we have identified three specific obstacles to the acceptance of the resiliency paradigm. We describe them below and make suggestions for overcoming each.

1. The distance between the resiliency and the at-risk paradigm, as each is typically described, is too great for people to cross comfortably.

The resiliency paradigm is often portrayed as the opposite of the risk paradigm. Therefore, acceptance of the resiliency paradigm requires the unlikely event that people will stop believing that the children and youth they see in their offices, classrooms, and agencies each day have been severely damaged by the hardships they face. Instead, they will begin thinking that the damage in these children and youth is not as significant as their strengths and resources that have previously been ignored.

We believe that presenting the resiliency paradigm as the opposite of the risk paradigm is a misrepresentation and oversimplification that stirs up resistance rather than paving the way to change. A more accurate representation is that the risk paradigm, which we have called the Damage Model, and the resiliency paradigm, which we have called the Challenge Model, complement rather than oppose one another.

The Damage Model portrays the harm that troubled and dysfunctional families, communities, and societies can inflict on children. It paints children as passive and without choices or the ability to help themselves. As a result, the best they can do is to cope with hardship; but, over time, coping takes its toll and gives way to pathology. As the process continues, pathologies are layered upon pathologies, and the child becomes an adult with serious and often irreversible problems.

The Challenge Model starts with the same sequence. It does not require demoting or overlooking the deleterious effects of hardship. It does, however, add another dimension to the risk story. In the Challenge Model, hardship is not only destructive but also is an opportunity. Children are wounded in the Challenge Model, as they are in the Damage Model, and they are left with scars as adults. But they are also challenged by troubles to experiment and to respond actively and creatively. Their preemptive responses, repeated over time, become incorporated into the self as lasting resiliencies.

Seen from the perspective of the Challenge Model, hardship has a paradoxical effect, causing strength and weakness simultaneously. In our workshops, we have found that this notion of paradox is more easily accepted than the idea of dropping the risk paradigm completely and working instead from a strengths angle only. We also believe that a paradoxical formulation, in contrast to the either/or alternative of risk vs. resiliency, is more clinically accurate and responsible.

2. Compared to the resiliency paradigm, the risk paradigm carries considerable authority which is difficult to question or deny.

The risk paradigm is based in a long and venerable tradition of research and practice. It stems from a medical model which seeks to identify and eradicate the cause of physical diseases. The fields of psychiatry and psychology extended this model from diseases of the body to disorders of the mind. Its medical roots leant particular authority to the innovation.

Since the 1940s, when Rene Spitz (1945) first investigated hospitalism in institutionalized infants, researchers have been studying the specific disorders of the mind associated with stress and hardship in early childhood. They have uncovered the myriad ways that children's psyches can be harmed by disruptions in their parent's, family's, and community's functioning. Their work has filled libraries with data on the maladies that beset children with schizophrenic mothers, divorcing parents, alcoholic fathers, handicapped siblings, premature separations, and other similar traumas. In conjunction with clinical observations of the ill, this work shapes the American Psychiatric Association's *Diagnostic and Statistical Manual (DSM-IV)*, which sets the standard and provides the vocabulary for diagnosing mental illness. It is hundreds of pages long and is replete with categories, subcategories, flow charts, and axes.

Worthy as the investigation and identification of pathology have been, we believe it is a one-sided endeavor, painting a distorted picture of human frailties and vulnerabilities and the insufficiencies of children to master their problems. On the other hand, the resiliency model which fills in the picture is a relative newcomer that is not yet fully enough developed to balance the distortions of the risk paradigm. Less than [three] decades old, it lacks the aura of legitimacy that history, research, and a medical background bestow upon the risk paradigm. Next to the risk lexicon, a resiliency vocabulary is scant and pallid. The paradigm itself is only just beginning to enter the clinical arena.

As a result, the resiliency paradigm is no match for the risk paradigm. Talking about the human capacity to repair from harm, inner strengths, and protective factors, professionals feel that they have entered alien territory. They grope for words and fear sounding unschooled and naive when they replace pathology terminology with the more mundane vocabulary of courage, resourcefulness, hope, creativity, competence, and the like. Putting it all together, many prefer the familiarity and safety of the risk paradigm to the struggle of adopting a new mode of thinking. We believe that the struggle can be tipped in the other direction by offering a systematic, developmental vocabulary of strengths that can stand up to pathology terminology that is standard in the field. Our own work has taken that direction. We have also found that some of the skepticism that is typically associated with the resiliency paradigm dissipates with information about the growing and promising field of resiliency research.

3. Talking about strengths in children who are suffering provokes moral hesitations.

As sentient beings, people are more apt to think in risk rather than resiliency terms. Professional adults as well as lay people feel a natural protectiveness toward children. Their small size, their weaknesses and dependencies, and their injuries stir people's deepest sympathies. Innocent children who are needlessly hurt ignite moral outrage. It is an appalling spectacle when they are homeless, hungry, abused, or uneducated. In the face of such suffering, talking about strengths in children of hardship seems all wrong. This sense of incorrectness stands in the way of widespread acceptance of a resiliency paradigm. Feeling on shaky moral ground, professionals tend to retreat to the safety of the risk paradigm and are reluctant to move out of its enclosure.

In our workshops, we have found that the most effective way of lowering this resistance is by discussing it directly. The interchange is usually thoughtful and sobering, encouraging participants to examine and question, some for the first time, the paradigm that governs their work.

We have approached the topic in several ways. One of the most successful has been to ask workshop participants to view *Salaam Bombay*, a movie about Krishna, a young Indian boy who has been abandoned on the streets of Bombay. His trials and pains are monumental. They can be discussed without inhibition. His strengths and integrity of character, which are equally compelling, cause internal conflict within the viewers. On the one hand, participants see the strengths and want to acknowledge them. On the other hand, they fear that mentioning the strengths of children like Krishna who suffer terribly will dampen the moral outcry the movie is meant to rouse.

We use this conflict as a jumping off point to discuss the basic underlying issue. Do individuals become party to the world's injustice by focusing on Krishna's strength rather than taking action or advocating for change on his behalf? In general, does an emphasis on strengths in children of hardship dilute society's obligation to disadvantaged populations?

Although we rarely reach clear answers, an open airing of these questions at least begins the process of opening people's minds and hearts. We have found that most of participants, in the course of this discussion, become curious about their own paradigms and the reasons that keep them in place. And more than a few reach the conclusion that while talking about resilience in children of extreme hardship can go against the grain, it can be done responsibly, and it can result in benefits to children.

Understanding Resistance to Change as a Starting Point

Traditionally, the fields of education, prevention, and therapy for children who struggle with hardship have been dominated by an at-risk paradigm. The results of this approach have been disappointing to professionals and the public alike. Hence, from all quarters, there are urgings for something new and better. The most talked about alternative is a resiliency paradigm which honors the strengths of youth and children and their capacity to recover from hardship. We join with those calling for this shift. At the same time, we have seen that the expectation that people can shift easily from one paradigm to another is naive. Therefore it behooves trainers and supervisors who wish to encourage change in the direction of the resiliency paradigm to understand the nature of the resistances and what is entailed in lowering them. We hope this article serves as an effective starting point.

References

Benard, B. (1993). *Turning the corner from risk to resiliency*. Portland OR: Northwest Regional Educational Laboratory.

Covey, S. (1989). *The seven habits of highly effective people: Powerful lessons in personal change.* New York: Simon and Schuster.

Spitz, R. (1945). Hospitalism. An inquiry into the genesis of psychiatric conditions in early childhood. *The Psychoanalytic Study of the Child, 1,* 57-74.

Sybl Wolin, Ph. D., and Steven Wolin, M.D., are co-directors of Project Resilience. They have co-authored The Resilient Self: How Surviores of Troubled Families Rise Above Adversity, *and are featured in the educational video,* Survivor's Pride: Building Resilience in Youth at Risk. *The Wolins conduct training across the United States and internationally. They can be reached at Project Resilience, 202-966-8171 or by email, info@projectresilience.com.*

CHAPTER 4

Confessions of a Counselor: What the Resiliency Literature has Shown Me

by Craig Noonan, Ph.D., M.S.W.

I have worked as a counselor and therapist in a variety of settings, including schools, community agencies, medical clinics, and hospitals. I have worked with adolescents, adults, and families experiencing a variety of problems, including alcohol and other drug use, mental health issues, relationship problems, HIV positive, and problems connected to behavioral medicine. I strongly believe that the resiliency perspective needs to be integrated into counseling and psychotherapy.

The resiliency literature offers an alternative and more positive paradigm for viewing and working with clients than I have observed in much of my practice. Unfortunately, most counselors and therapists are trained and taught to view clients primarily from a pathological or deficit perspective, focusing on assessment of problems. Rarely are counselors taught how to identify, appreciate, and utilize client strengths. As a result, all too often I have observed that counselors (including myself, at times) provide ineffective and even counterproductive services because of agendas, roles, and systems that restrain their humanity. These services too often are not research-based, and do not meet the needs of their clients.

I have seen clients blamed and labeled for their counselors' failures to provide effective counseling or to even establish a positive relationship. I have had clients tell me about being burdened and limited by counselors' low expectations regarding their ability to overcome the adversity in their lives or to succeed in specific activities. The really sad part of this situation is that most of these counselors are well-intentioned and only wish the best for their clients. I know that I have always been similarly well-intentioned and yet I, too, have fallen victim to some of the above practices at times.

The resiliency literature provides counselors with a more effective and personally satisfying way to work with and relate to their clients. I am specifically concerned with incorporating the six protective conditions associated with resiliency (caring and support, high expectations, meaningful opportunities for involvement, pro-social bonding, clear and consistent boundaries, and "life skills") into counseling relationships so as to encourage the growth of resiliency in clients (see The Resiliency Quiz, chapter 11, for more information on these six conditions, as well as The Resiliency Wheel in chapter eight). There is a robust body of research literature in the counseling and therapy fields supporting the importance of "therapist factors" (the therapist's level of empathy and view of client, for example) and the therapeutic relationship in promoting positive change. Although this literature does not often use the word "resiliency," the power of the protective conditions mentioned above is at its heart.

I am also committed to helping counselors view client problems as just that--a presently occurring scenario upon the landscape of an entire human being, not the sum total of who the person is or can be. I have learned my most important lessons about the power of protective conditions and the limitations of diagnostic labels from my clients.

I remember a client in one group that I ran who had a history of torturing and killing small animals as a child, who was very guarded and suspicious in all of his relationships, and who displayed no empathy for other group members. Shortly after becoming a group member, his behavior terrified the other members of the group so much that he had to be removed for a short period of individual counseling and stabilization. When he returned to the group he remained largely uninvolved and withdrawn until he began doing volunteer work for the Red Cross assisting people who were experiencing catastrophes access services. Within a month or two of beginning this work, he became an empathic and involved group member--often providing positive and empathic feedback to other group members. Other members of the group were astounded at the changes in him and became more hopeful regarding their own growth.

Sadly, when he lost his Red Cross position I saw him return to his former withdrawn and nonempathic behavior, though he did not again become threatening to the group. When I left the group, he and the new group leader were working hard at trying to reinvolve him in some new service-oriented volunteer work. My client had recognized its value for himself and was seeking a new position.

Counselors need to know about protective factors, and the power of a diagnostic approach that focuses on a more complete picture of the people they counsel. With this knowledge, they can look for individual strengths and environmental protective conditions, nurture them, and try to facilitate their growth in the lives of their clients. This will no doubt result in changes in how we do our work, and how we view the people who come to us. I agree with the wisdom of Saleebey, who writes in The Strengths Perspective in Social Work Practice (1997):

> To really practice from a strengths perspective demands a different way of seeing clients, their environments, and their current situation. Rather than focusing on problems, your eye turns toward possibility. In the thicket of trauma, pain, and trouble you can see blooms of hope and transformation. Clients come into view when you assume that they know something, have learned lessons from experience, have hopes, have interests, and can do some things masterfully. These may be obscured by the stresses of the moment, submerged under the weight of crisis, oppression, or illness, but, nonetheless, they abide. (p.3 & p.12)

References

Saleebey, D. (Ed.). (1997). *The strengths perspective in social work practice* (2nd ed.). New York: Longman.

Craig Noonan, Ph.D., M.S.W., is a retired therapist, substance abuse treatment program supervisor, addictions researcher, and trainer. He can be reached at cnoonan@resiliency.com.

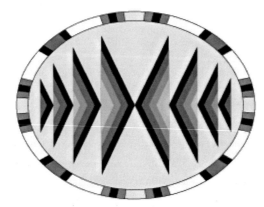

CHAPTER 5

The Connection Between Effective Brief Intervention and Fostering Resiliency

by Craig Noonan, Ph.D., M.S.W.

Brief intervention strategies identified in the substance abuse treatment literature embody the strengths-based approach using the protective factors that have emerged from resiliency research. Though many of the examples of brief intervention described below are connected to substance abuse treatment, the strategies included can be used to help children, teens, adults, and families make any needed behavioral change.

The effective "active ingredients" of brief intervention were described by Miller and Sanchez (1994) in their review of the brief therapy literature. They identified eight strategies, using the first eight letters of the alphabet as a mnemonic device, that could easily have been developed from the list of protective factors. The eight ingredients are:

1) Give **Advice**;
2) Remove **Barriers**;
3) Provide **Choices**;
4) Decrease **Desirability**;
5) Practice **Empathy**;
6) Provide **Feedback**;
7) Clarify **Goals**; and
8) Actively **Help**.

These "active ingredients" reveal in yet one more way how the resiliency framework can form the foundation of effective helping relationships. Henderson (1999) identified six broad protective factors in The Resiliency Wheel Model: 1) Caring and Support; 2) Prosocial Bonding; 3) Opportunities for Meaningful Participation; 4) High Expectations; 5) Clear and Consistent Boundaries; and 6) Life Skills Training (see The Resiliency Wheel in chapter eight). A brief description of each of the ingredients of brief intervention will clarify their strong connection to these protective factors.

Giving brief and non-coercive **advice** has proven effective in many studies, especially those where doctors advise patients to stop smoking or drinking. The most effective advice is offered in the spirit of heartfelt concern, and it is not repeated. It identifies the problem, explains why change is important, and advocates a specific change. In my

practice, I do not offer advice unless it is asked for or unless I am given permission to do so first. When I do, I offer it sparingly and with clear messages that it is the client's decision as to whether to take it or not. A reasonable guideline is that advice offered more than twice is nagging.

The process of advising is clearly connected to the first crucial protective factor of providing caring and support but can also be seen as a statement of high expectations that the client is capable of making the advised change.

Removing **barriers** means helping the client to problem solve some of the practical and subjective barriers to making a change. A client may be more than willing to make a change but may be discouraged from doing so by some specific practical (e.g. cost, transportation) or subjective barrier (e.g. fear of being alone, social anxiety). In traditional alcohol and other drug treatment, these barriers are often unexplored or left up to the client to solve with statements such as: "You managed to get to the liquor store or your dealer to get your alcohol and drugs so you should be able to get to an AA meeting." This is not very helpful or supportive of the client and does nothing to help solve the transportation difficulties. The statement is also punitive and blaming which does little to help the client to develop a more positive and efficacious self-image that will facilitate the change process. Research has demonstrated that assisting clients in overcoming this barrier can make the difference between no clients attending AA meetings and all clients attending (Sisson & Mallams, 1981).

Removing barriers is also a demonstration of caring and support and can be used to teach problem solving skills providing another protection--teaching life skills.

When a person feels that their freedom is being limited or threatened they often react reflexively and resist the threat. This may mean resisting a suggested change plan that is perceived as disagreeable or too limiting. Offering **choices** allows clients to feel in control, which is what they need to feel if they are to successfully change their behavior. It empowers them to be involved in and to take charge of their change process. They will generally be more intrinsically committed to change strategies that they have chosen than those chosen by others. Unfortunately, limited choices and treatment options are the rule in most alcohol and other drug treatment approaches. Such practices decrease client motivation and compliance and lead to treatment dropout.

Offering choices provides the client with a clear opportunity for meaningful participation in the counseling and change process. It also gives vote of confidence or statement of high expectations that the client will make the right choices.

Decreasing **desirability** is a strategy for clients in the contemplation stage of change (see chapter six). Their internal debate continually weighs the positive and negative incentives for engaging in the problem behavior. The positive incentives are usually the more powerful and immediate, supporting the continuation of the behavior. Counselors often fail to appreciate that clients have powerful reasons for continuing their problem behaviors and focus only upon the adverse consequences. It is important for the counselor to assist the client in identifying all of these positive incentives in a safe, non-judgmental arena. Once the counselor has a clear idea of these incentives, he or she can begin looking for effective ways of undermining them. There are many strategies for doing so but the most effective go beyond a mere rational consideration of the pros and cons of the behavior. The most successful strategies engage the client's value system (not the counselor's). They juxtapose the behavior and the positive and negative incentives with the client's values, hopes, dreams, and goals in a way that puts them at odds. Traditional treatment approaches often emphasize what the counselor or the program considers to be important for the client. This carries no "emotional weight" for the client. It is important that counselors fully explore the *client's* reasons for maintaining or changing the behavior. This juxtaposition creates an uncomfortable emotional response that increases motivation to change. When properly engaged in this collaborative process, the counselor provides the client with three of the protective factors: caring and support, high expectations, and meaningful opportunities for participation.

Empathy is one of the most researched therapist characteristics and studies have shown that it is associated with lower client resistance and greater long-term positive behavior change (Miller & Soveriegn, 1989; Miller, Taylor, & West, 1980; Patterson & Foghatch, 1985). Accurate empathy is a specific, learnable, and active skill that communicates understanding of a client's experience. I believe that it should be the foundation of every counselor's work and that it creates the "right circumstances" that allow clients to move from unhealthy to healthy behaviors.

Feedback can come in many ways and from many sources. Having difficulty getting into the jeans worn last summer is feedback and can have a significant effect upon the day's eating behavior. Expressions of concern from loved ones, comparing the extent of the problem behavior to various normative groups (e.g., the general public, people seeking treatment for alcohol problems), results from objective tests (especially medical tests that document the extent of harm from a behavior), can all be useful motivators. The important issue here is how this feedback is offered. Clients are often badgered and assaulted with this information and naturally they become resistant and defensive. Clients need feedback because they lack problem recognition, not because they are in denial. If this is kept in mind, the information can often be offered in an empathic and nonconfrontive manner that is more likely to be listened to and may then become an effective motivator.

Once again, the most obvious connection to the protective factors here is the caring and support that is demonstrated when giving appropriate feedback.

Clarifying **goals** goes hand in hand with providing feedback. Feedback helps clients to understand where they are and where they have been. Goal setting helps to clarify where they want to be and the importance that they attach to getting there. Comparing feedback and goals generally reveals discrepancies between the current behavior and the desired situation resulting in the emotional distress that can motivate change. It is important that the goals be seen as realistic and obtainable, otherwise this energy for change may be channeled into avoidance. As before, the client's values are being accessed to fuel the fires of change. It is client goals and perceptions of situations, not the counselor's, that will motivate positive change.

Once again, as with "desirability," the client is engaged in a collaborative process that demonstrates high expectations and provides a meaningful opportunity for participation.

The final "active ingredient" of effective brief counseling interventions is active **helping** by the counselor. I once worked at an alcohol treatment agency where the "cultural norms" were that the client must take responsibility for their counseling. Counselors did nothing if a client did not show up for a session or call to cancel. It was the client's responsibility to call and reschedule. The no-show and drop out rate for counselors at the agency was more than 50%. I subsequently worked as a clinician on a national multi-site research study where counselors were required to call their clients when they missed a session to express concern and encourage them to attend their next scheduled session. The no-show rate for counselors and two-year drop-out rate on the project was approximately five percent. That a simple phone call resulted in a ten-fold increase in counseling attendance is why active helping is so important! Active helping is also effective when making referrals. In one study where the counselor made a phone call for the client to set up a referral appointment the follow through rate by the clients more than doubled (Kogan, 1957).

Many counselors in the alcohol treatment field have call such behaviors "enabling" because they take responsibility for the client. I call them expressions of caring and support and good modeling for being actively engaged in the change process.

Most of the "active ingredients" of effective brief interventions that motivate people to change represent specific strategies that could have been developed to foster resiliency in the counseling relationship. All of the ingredients communicate caring and support to one degree or another and especially when they are grounded in the "resiliency attitude"-- a positive view of the client. Most of them also provide the client with meaningful opportunities for participation in a collaborative dialogue and communicate high expectations by putting the client clearly in charge of their behavior change efforts. Setting clear expectations and prosocial bonding are inherent in the counseling process with competent counselors and in therapeutic relationship.

The only protective factor that is not clearly represented in these "active ingredients" is skill building. Skill building is usually a longer-term strategy that is used when the motivation to change has been established. It is often one of the choices offered to clients to assist them in their behavior change efforts. It can also be incorporated into the "active helping" ingredient. Skills training also has excellent support in the research literature as one of the most effective methods for assisting clients in eliminating their problematic drinking (Miller et al., 1995).

The connection between the resiliency framework and effective brief intervention offers yet one more example of the connection between the findings of resiliency research and findings in other fields about how to effectively assist human change and development.

References

Bergin, A. E. & Garfield, S. L. (1994). *Handbook of psychotherapy and behavior change* (4th ed.). New York: John Wiley & Sons, Inc.

Blum, D. (1998). Finding strength: How to overcome anything. *Psychology Today*, May/June.

Henderson, N. (1999). Fostering resiliency in children and youth: Four basic steps for families, educators, and other caring adults. In N. Henderson, B. Benard, B., & N. Sharplight (Eds.), *Resiliency in action: Practical ideas for overcoming risks and building strengths in Youth, Families, and Communities* (pp. 161 - 167). Ojai, CA: Resiliency In Action.

Henderson, N. & Milstein, M. M. (1996). *Resiliency in schools: Making it happen for students and educators.* Thousand Oaks, CA: Corwin Press, Inc.

Holder, H., Lonabaugh, R., Miller, W. R., & Rubonis, A. V. (1991). The cost-effectiveness of treatment for alcoholism: A first approximation. *Journal of Studies on Alcohol, 52*, 517-540.

Kogan, L. S. (1957). The short-term case in a family agency: Part II. Results of study. *Social Casework, 38*, 296-302.

Leake, G. J. & King, A. S. (1977). Effect of counselor expectations on alcoholic recovery. *Alcohol Health and Research World, 11* (3), 16-22.

Marlatt, G. A. & Gordon, J. R. (1985). *Relapse prevention: Maintenance strategies in the treatment of addictive behaviors.* New York: Guilford Press.

Miller, W. R., Brown, J. M., Simpson, T. L., Handmaker, N. S., Bein, T. S., Luckie, L. F., Montgomery, H. A., Hester, R. K., & Tonigan, J. S. (1995). What works? A methodological analysis of the alcohol treatment outcome literature. In R. K. Hester & W. R. Miller (Eds.), *Handbook of alcohol reatment approaches: Effective alternatives*, (2nd ed.) (pp. 12-44). Boston: Allyn and Bacon.

Miller, W. R. & Rollnick, S. (1991). *Motivational interviewing: Preparing people to change addictive behavior.* New York: Guilford Press.

Miller, W. R. & Sanchez, V. C. (1994). Motivating young adults for treatment and lifestyle change. In G. Howard (Ed.), *Issues in alcohol use and misuse by young adults* (pp. 55-85). Notre Dame, IN: University of Notre Dame Press.

Miller, W. R. & Sovereign, R. G., (1989). The check-up: A model for early intervention in addictive behaviors. In T. Loberg, W. R. Miller, P. E. Nathan, & G. A. Marlatt (Eds.), *Addictive behaviors: Prevention and early intervention* (pp. 219-231). Amsterdam: Swets & Zeitlinger.

Miller, W. R., Sovereign, R. G., & Krege, B. (1988). Motivational interviewing with problem drinkers: II. The Drinkers Check-up as a preventive intervention. *Behavioral Psychotherapy, 16* (4), 251-268.

Miller, W. R., Taylor, C. A., & West, J. C. (1980). Focused versus broad-spectrum behavior therapy for problem drinkers. *Journal of Consulting and Clinical Psychology, 48*, 490-601.

Noonan, W. C. & Moyers, T. B. (1997). Motivational interviewing: A review. *Journal of Substance Misuse, 2,* 8-16.

Patterson, G. R. & Forghatch, M. S. (1985). Therapist behavior as a determinant for client noncompliance: A paradox for the behavior modifier. *Journal of Consulting and Clinical Psychology, 5,* 846-851.

Prochaska, J. O. & DiClemente, C. C. (1982). Transtheoretical therapy: Toward a more integrative model of change. *Psychotherapy: Theory, Research, and Practice, 19,* 276-288.

Prochaska, J. O. & DiClemente, C. C. (1984). *The transtheoretical approach: Crossing traditional boundaries of therapy.* Homewood, IL: Dow Jones/Irwin.

Prochaska, J. O. & DiClemente, C. C. (1985). Process and stages of change in smoking, weight control, and psychological distress. In S. Schiffman & T. Wills (Eds.), *Coping and substance abuse* (pp. 319-345). New York: Academic Press.

Prochaska, J. O. & DiClemente, C. C. (1986). Toward a comprehensive model of change. In W. R. Miller & N. Heather (Eds.), *Treating addictive behaviors: Processes of change* (pp. 3-27). New York: Plenum.

Saleebey, D. (Ed.). (1997). *The strengths perspective in social work practice* (2nd ed.). New York: Longman.

Sisson, R. W. & Mallams, J. H. (1981). The use of systematic encouragement and community access procedures to increase attendance at Alcoholics Anonymous and Al-Anon meetings. *American Journal of Drug and Alcohol Abuse, 8,* 371-376.

Werner, E. E. & Smith, R. S. (1992). *Overcoming the odds: High risk children from birth to adulthood.* New York: Cornell University Press.

Craig Noonan, Ph.D., M.S.W., is a retired therapist, substance abuse treatment program supervisor, addictions researcher, and trainer. He can be reached at cnoonan@resiliency.com.

CHAPTER 6

A More Humane and Effective Approach to Motivating Change

by Craig Noonan, Ph.D., M.S.W.

In substance abuse treatment, clients are regularly subjected to beliefs and practices that lack any scientific support for their effectiveness (Holder, Lonabaugh, Miller, & Rubonis, 1991). Often these practices are also abusive and potentially harmful. I have worked with numerous clients motivated to make positive changes in their problematic alcohol and other drug use who were discouraged and harmed by the beliefs and practices of treatment programs and counselors.

One client was labeled as "unmotivated" and "in denial" by staff and fellow clients because he would not accept the label of "alcoholic" or attend AA meetings that made him uncomfortable. He was terminated from treatment with no referral and told to go out and continue drinking until he "hit bottom" and was "ready" to work the "program." At the same time these counselors were telling clients that continued drinking is fatal.

Another client was kicked out of a recovery home because he would not share painful feelings in group therapy because he did not trust the group members. They had previously shared his "confidential" information with others outside of the group. When he shared his concern regarding confidentiality with staff they did nothing to address the groups behavior or to make him feel safer in the group. In a similar group therapy situation, one client was coerced by the group leader and members to share a painful child molestation experience. He attempted suicide that evening and had to be transferred to the psychiatric unit where I was working.

A fourth client was dropped from treatment because he got a job. The treatment program did not approve of clients getting jobs in early recovery because it might distract them from their recovery program. They also would not allow him to substitute an alternate AA meeting for one that his new job conflicted with. They labeled him as non-compliant and he left the program discouraged and confused about the successful recovery he had already established.

A teenage client was told by her group counselor, in front of the group, that she had to leave group because she had a bad attitude. He had asked her why she was in the group and she had answered honestly that the only reason she was attending the group was because she had to. Needless to say, this counselor's behavior did little to help this teenager engage in the group or to find other reasons to be there.

The endless list of these types of situations are a reflection of the institutionalized beliefs and practices in the addictions field. I have personal knowledge of these beliefs and practices because they were part of my training and practice during my early career. I was new to the field and unfamiliar with the clinical research literature. I accepted the "wisdom" of others with more experience in the field than I. Fortunately, with many years of study and experience, I have left most these beliefs behind, but they continue be too common in the field.

Evidence Supports Other Approaches to Changing People's Behavior

Common sense dictates that the kinds of treatment experiences mentioned above are not helpful for clients and may even be harmful. Fortunately, scientific evidence is emerging from several unrelated sources that supports this "common sense" notion of a more humane and effective approach to motivating positive behavior change. These common threads are emerging in the strength-based approaches of social work practice (Saleebey, 1997), similar strength-based trends in the field of psychology (Seligman, 1998), the protective factors of the resiliency movement (Henderson & Milstein, 2003), and the methods of motivational interviewing that grew from the work of addictions researchers and clinicians themselves (Miller & Rollnick, 1991; Noonan & Moyers, 1997).

The first common theme in these approaches has to do with basic positive assumptions about human beings that are not evident in the questionable clinical behavior described above. These positive beliefs characterize human beings as having inner strengths, skills, and goodness that allows them to resist the negative influences in their lives and to change problematic behaviors and lifestyles that have resulted from these negative influences. Henderson (1997) considers these beliefs to be the cornerstone of facilitating resiliency in others and has coined the term "resiliency attitude" to describe them. Miller (personal communication, April 23, 1995) demonstrated this attitude when he described the core belief about clients in motivational interviewing that every therapist should work to develop. He said that "given the right circumstances, people will inherently choose healthy behaviors over unhealthy ones." For counselors and prevention specialists, the most powerful intervention comes from holding these positive beliefs about clients. It is my belief that this attitude is what creates the "right circumstances" that facilitate resiliency and positive change.

That these beliefs alone can facilitate positive outcomes in counseling is illustrated in a classic study by Leake and King (1977). In this study, alcohol counselors were told that psychological testing had identified some of their clients as having an excellent prognosis for recovery. In truth, these clients were randomly selected from counselor caseloads and were no different from other clients. At the end of treatment, however, the clients with the "good prognosis" were seen as more compliant and involved in treatment and also had more positive outcomes in drinking behaviors than the clients who were given "no prognosis." The only difference between the two client groups were the beliefs that their counselor had in them. In some way, the positive beliefs were communicated to the clients with the "good prognosis" and became a self-fulfilling prophecy. Whenever I feel that I am not doing enough to help my clients, I remember this study and am comforted by the knowledge that if I am holding these positive beliefs about my clients, I am doing plenty.

The Stages of Change Model

Another common theme in these more positive and strength-based approaches has to do with beliefs about the change process itself. In traditional alcohol and other drug treatment, clients are often seen as motivated for treatment or "in denial." When they are "in denial" and initial efforts are unsuccessful at creating motivation, they are often sent packing. The research and thinking of Prochaska & DiClemente (1982, 1984, 1985,1986) offers an alternative and more hopeful perspective on motivation to change called the Stages of Change Model. This model describes six stages of change that have been identified in their research with smokers who were trying to quit smoking without professional help. The existence of these stages has subsequently been confirmed in other self-changers of addictive behaviors and in treatment settings as well. The stages, representing a developmental process of change, are: **1) Precotemplation; 2) Contemplation; 3) Determination; 4) Action; 5) Maintenance; and 6) Relapse.** These stages give counselors more positive alternatives for assessing client motivation and, more importantly, more therapeutic strategies and guidelines for working with clients at different stages that will move them along to the next (Miller & Rollnick, 1991).

A precontemplator is someone who is not even considering the possibility of change and would probably be surprised or even upset if you suggested it. These are the clients who are often seen as "in denial" but in fact they are more often just lacking in problem recognition. They lack the information that would allow them to evaluate their behavior and conclude that there possibly is a need for change. These clients need information and the counselors most effective role is that of an impartial non-judgemental educator. When these clients are provided with normative feedback (e.g., how their drinking compares to national norms) or objective assessment data about their behavior (e.g., liver function tests or how the negative consequences of their drinking compares to drinkers seeking treatment) they often become

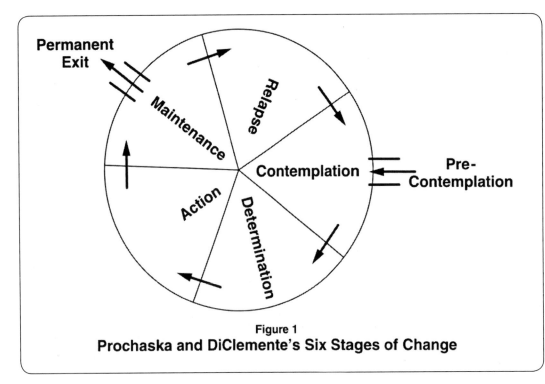

Figure 1
Prochaska and DiClemente's Six Stages of Change

more motivated to change and their behavior and become contemplators or move even further along in the change process (Miller & Soveriegn, 1989; Miller, Sovereign & Krege, 1988).

Contemplators are ambivalent about change. They see that a behavior change might be necessary but they are not sure or are having mixed feelings about it. They often engage in an internal debate and alternately take both sides of the argument. They may also be seen as "in denial" but are viewed as more workable because they are unsure. Contemplators need to process their ambivalence and they can only do so in a safe and non-judgemental arena. If a counselor takes one side of the ambivalence argument (arguing for change), the client will often take the opposite side of the debate and argue against it because that is what they do internally. The counselor has then created a situation where the client is talking himself or herself out of change rather than into it. The point here is that the confrontive methods that are often used in traditional alcohol and other drug treatment are likely to be counterproductive and create resistance to change in the contemplator. Research has verified that confrontive techniques create client resistance and that empathic methods are more effective in creating a situation where clients can talk themselves into change (Miller & Rollnick, 1991). When this occurs they are then more intrinsically motivated.

Someone in the **determination** stage has made the decision and commitment to change and is looking for ways to do so. He or she may find these ways personally or seek the assistance of a counselor. Counselors can share their expertise on the ways that have proven most effective for others making similar changes and assist clients in choosing what they think will work best for them. Traditional addictions treatment often falls short here because it generally provide only one or very limited treatment options. Unfortunately, traditional treatment centers stay in business because most of them offer the same type of treatment and have little competition offering other alternatives.

An individual in the **action** stage is engaging in change behaviors. Providing support is the key idea at this stage of the change process. This support should be client centered and may come from a variety of sources such as a professional counselor, self-help organizations, or family and friends. The nature of the support will vary from individual to individual and may range from mild encouragement to assistance in problem solving major roadblocks or setbacks.

The **maintenance** stage is very much like the action stage except the changes being made are broader life-style changes that will support the specific behavior changed during the action stage. These changes might be a new social support system, new health care behaviors, a change in employment, and so on. Such changes also may require assistance with accessing resources, problem solving, and general emotional support. The idea is that they will create a life rich in rewards and low in stress so that the chances of a return to the old behavior (such as alcohol or other drug use) are minimized.

The Importance of Dealing with Relapse

The last stage of change is that of **relapse**. It is part of the change process; approximately two-thirds of people trying to change addictive behaviors have a relapse within the first 90 days. Prochaska and DiClemente (1982, 1984, 1985, 1986) found that people making changes often must go through the stages of change several times before they successfully complete the change process. During each cycle they generally do a little better. This fact is very important because it normalizes and destigmatizes relapse.

One of the most difficult parts of making a change is how to think about and deal with a relapse to the old behavior. When someone on a diet eats a piece of cake that is not part of his or her diet plan, the person often feels like a failure, that they have "blown" the diet. When someone feels like a failure it is difficult to continue with a change plan and it is often abandoned. In fact, the dieter has not "blown" the diet, he or she has just had a piece of cake. In the same way, someone who is trying to stop drinking has not failed in their sobriety when they have had a relapse, they have had a drink (or two, or six, or 12). The most important job of a counselor is to help the client focus on the success that they have had, to problem solve what caused the relapse and how to deal with it in the future, and to get back to working the change program they have designed.

In traditional treatment programs, relapse is typically seen as a failure and the counter of clean and sober days is reset to zero. This negates the success the client has had up to that point and contributes little to continued motivation to change.

A third theme in these emerging beliefs and practices are the remarkable similarities between the recommendations of divergent fields for what is effective in promoting positive change. The resiliency literature has identified factors in the lives of individuals that appear to protect them from the development and persistence of negative behaviors. The negative behaviors either never develop or they are changed to more positive ones more rapidly than with individuals whose lives lack these factors (Werner & Smith, 1992). Henderson and Milstein (2003) summarized these protective factors into six general categories that can be used as guidelines for the development of specific strategies to foster the development of resiliency. These six factors are: 1) Caring and Support; 2) Pro-social Bonding; 3) Opportunities for Meaningful Participation; 4) High Expectations; 5) Clear and Consistent Boundaries; and 6) Life Skills Training. (See The Resiliency Wheel in chapter eight.)

The protective factors identified in the resiliency research and what really works in helping people make positive life changes overlap. In fact, the resiliency framework forms the foundation of effective helping relationships.

References

Blum, D. (1998). Finding strength: How to overcome anything. *Psychology Today*, May/June, 36-38, 66-72.

Bergin, A. E. & Garfield, S. L. (1994). *Handbook of psychotherapy and behavior change* (4th ed.). New York: John Wiley & Sons, Inc.

Henderson, N. (1997). Fostering resiliency in children and youth: Four basic steps for families, educators, and other caring adults. *Resiliency in Action*, Spring.

Henderson, N. & Milstein, M. M. (2003). *Resiliency in schools: Making it happen for students and educators* (2nd ed.). Thousand Oaks, CA: Corwin Press.

Holder, H., Lonabaugh, R., Miller, W. R., & Rubonis, A. V. (1991). The cost-effectiveness of treatment for alcoholism: A first approximation. *Journal of Studies on Alcohol, 52*, 517-540.

Kogan, L. S. (1957). The short-term case in a family agency: Part II. Results of study. *Social Casework, 38*, 296-302.

Leake, G. J. & King, A. S. (1977). Effect of counselor expectations on alcoholic recovery. *Alcohol Health and Research World, 11* (3), 16-22.

Marlatt, G. A. & Gordon, J. R. (1985). *Relapse prevention: Maintenance strategies in the treatment of addictive behaviors.* New York: Guilford Press.

Miller, W. R., Brown, J. M., Simpson, T. L., Handmaker, N. S., Bein, T. S., Luckie, L. F., Montgomery, H. A., Hester, R. K., & Tonigan, J. S. (1995). What works? A methodological analysis of the alcohol treatment outcome literature. In R. K. Hester & W. R. Miller (Eds.), *Handbook of alcohol treatment approaches: Effective alternatives*, (2nd ed.) (pp. 12-44). Boston: Allyn and Bacon.

Miller, W. R. & Rollnick, S. (1991). *Motivational interviewing: Preparing people to change addictive behavior.* New York: Guilford Press.

Miller, W. R. & Sanchez, V. C. (1994). Motivating young adults for treatment and lifestyle change. In G. Howard (Ed.), *Issues in alcohol use and misuse by young adults* (pp. 55-85). Notre Dame, IN: University of Notre Dame Press.

Miller, W. R. & Sovereign, R. G., (1989). The check-up: A model for early intervention in addictive behaviors. In T. Loberg, W. R. Miller, P. E. Nathan, & G. A. Marlatt (Eds.), *Addictive behaviors: Prevention and early intervention* (pp. 219-231). Amsterdam: Swets & Zeitlinger.

Miller, W. R., Sovereign, R. G., & Krege, B. (1988). Motivational interviewing with problem drinkers: II. The Drinkers Check-up as a preventive intervention. *Behavioural Psychotherapy, 16* (4), 251-268.

Miller, W. R., Taylor, C. A., & West, J. C. (1980). Focused versus broad-spectrum behavior therapy for problem drinkers. *Journal of Consulting and Clinical Psychology, 48*, 490-601.

Noonan, W. C. & Moyers, T. B. (1997). Motivational interviewing: A review. *Journal of Substance Misuse, 2*, 8-16.

Patterson, G. R. & Forghatch, M. S. (1985). Therapist behavior as a determinant for client noncompliance: A paradox for the behavior modifier. *Journal of Consulting and Clinical Psychology, 5*, 846-851.

Prochaska, J. O. & DiClemente, C. C. (1982). Transtheoretical therapy: Toward a more integrative model of change. *Psychotherapy: Theory, Research, and Practice, 19*, 276-288.

Prochaska, J. O. & DiClemente, C. C. (1984). *The transtheoretical approach: Crossing traditional boundaries of therapy.* Homewood, IL: Dow Jones/Irwin.

Prochaska, J. O. & DiClemente, C. C. (1985). Process and stages of change in smoking, weight control, and psychological distress. In S. Schiffman & T. Wills (Eds.), *Coping and substance abuse* (pp. 319-345). New York: Academic Press.

Prochaska, J. O. & DiClemente, C. C. (1986). Toward a comprehensive model of change. In W. R. Miller & N. Heather (Eds.), *Treating addictive behaviors: Processes of change* (pp. 3-27). New York: Plenum.

Saleebey, D. (Ed.). (1997). *The strengths perspective in social work practice* (2nd ed.). New York: Longman.

Werner, E. E., & Smith, R. S. (1992). *Overcoming the odds: High risk children from birth to adulthood.* New York: Cornell University Press.

Craig Noonan, Ph.D., M.S.W., is a retired therapist, substance abuse treatment program supervisor, addictions researcher, and trainer. He can be reached at cnoonan@resiliency.com.

CHAPTER 7

Building Resilience Through Student Assistance Programming

by Tim Duffey, M.Ed.

The Maine Department of Education Student Assistance Team Unit has trained over 320 building-based student assistance teams in past years. The Unit has received national recognition for the strength of its programming and high quality support materials. The program has been highlighted at the National Student Assistance Conference and the National Conference for Coordinators of Homeless Children and Youth. Denver, Colorado schools received training in the Maine Model as a prototype of service delivery for their system. The 250-page training manual utilized to train teams is regularly mailed to all state Safe and Drug-Free Schools and Communities Coordinators. This dissemination has resulted in frequent citation of the manual's quality and comprehensive nature by student assistance professionals around the country.

The process utilized by the teams trained in the Maine model is outlined below.

1. **An Identification Process:**
   School personnel or other concerned persons initiate referral to student assistance team. Student self-referral also is possible. Referrals are based on observable behavior.

2. **An Intervention Process:**
   Trained student assistance team members discuss referral information and develop short term action plan outlining steps to be taken, timelines, and account-ability for completion.

3. **A Referral Process:**
   Action plans indicate appropriate referrals for assistance to resources within and outside the school setting.

4. **An Implementation Process:**
   Individual team members or designated referral sources carry out recommendations. Designated team member serves as "case manager" to monitor plan implementation.

5. **A Follow-up Process:**
   Team evaluates success of intervention strategies on a regular basis. Adjustments are made as necessary.

Though the membership of Maine student assistance teams is determined by individual schools, emphasis is placed on team com-position reflecting the diverse training, experience, and professional expertise available within Maine schools. Administrators, classroom teachers, nurses, school counselors, special educators, and/or migrant educators, chemical health coordinators, and school social workers are all roles likely to be represented on local student assistance teams (SATs). In many instances, cooperative agreements (emphasizing confidentiality) with local law enforcement and social service providers allow community professionals to add their unique backgrounds to the teams.

This multi-disciplinary approach, built upon effective team development, provides a means of operation rarely found within existing school structures. The process builds a sense of "our students" rather than "your students." This approach differs from the prevalant paradigm of student assistance, where students are identified by who is seen to have primary responsibility for them and their behavior (classroom teacher, special education, school counselor, etc.) and as a result, school staff feel isolated and overwhelmed with the nature of issues they are left to deal with... seemingly on their own.

In addition to emphasizing a multi-disciplinary approach, the Maine project's focus has evolved over time from one targeting the "at risk" population to one that emphasizes the strength and power of addressing resiliency and asset development for ALL children and youth. This change in focus reflects recent shifts in the field of prevention recognizing the potential for increased harm by labeling a child "at risk" (Benard, 1993, 1995) and the tendency to describe children "by the problems they face rather than by the strengths they possess" (Benard, 1989). The result has been a stronger alignment with resiliency and asset development research.

History of the Maine
Student Assistance Project

The student assistance effort in Maine grew from a variety of sources during the 1980s. A grassroots demand by school staff to address increasing needs for alcohol and other drug services within schools led to high level dialogue by Department of Education staff. This discussion led to a state-wide Task Force Report on Affected Children (Department of Education, 1988). Among the findings of this report was the fact that many children affected by the alcohol or other drug use, abuse, or dependency of another person in their lives were being referred to special education. Behavioral patterns of these affected children often mimicked those of learning disabled students. Such patterns often led teachers to refer these youngsters for a special education screening.

The report stated that when these students did not qualify for special education services, they often fell in the proverbial "crack" between programs. They were not succeeding in the regular education setting as currently constructed, yet they did not meet special education criteria enabling them to receive assistance from learning specialists. The Task Force recommended that a better system be developed to ensure all Maine school children receive appropriate assistance to achieve success. It was also clear that alcohol and other drug issues were not the only concern facing Maine students, families, and educators. From its earliest stages, this project was designed to be flexible enough to address the wide range of concerns facing Maine youth. To meet the needs evident within schools, this process would have to provide staff a more effective intake and referral mechanism for students regardless of the underlying issues.

Sharon Rice, Special Education Director in Auburn, Maine, served as a member of the development and implementation team that brought the program to reality. "In addition to the physiological and neurological difficulties many children face, we must also recognize that our youth are mirrors of societal trends," she says. "They reflect the fragmentation of our culture. Our challenge is to move beyond the fragmentation into more wholeness within our entire society, of which our schools are but a single part." The program was designed to bring together key players in the educational system to meet this student need.

Department staff began to explore the potential for student assistance programs in use by other states as a means to address the varied needs of Maine students. In addition, the efforts of business and industry to improve problem solving and product delivery through the use of interdisciplinary teams was explored as a means of improved service delivery. A model began to take shape incorporating these two fields of education intervention and industrial teaming. In the process, a wide range of constituents were consulted to formulate these supportive services for Maine's children and youth. School counselors, nurses, social workers, teachers, and administrators were among those contacted for input into the model.

A hallmark of the Maine model is an emphasis on essential team skills. Skills critical for the successful formation and operation of any team-based program over an extended period of time were seen as critical tools. Meeting skills also received attention, ensuring teams access to the skills and resources needed to conduct efficient meetings. Such attention to honoring the time investment various professionals provide such an effort was a unique feature of the Maine approach to student assistance.

The resulting model was submitted to the US Department of Education (USDE) "Personnel Training Grant" process for funding consideration. In 1990, the Maine Department of Education received its first allocation of funds from the USDE to begin disseminating the model to Maine schools. The formation of the "Student Assistance Team Unit" within the Department ensured that consistency in training, technical assistance, and follow-up services were in place for schools adopting the student assistance philosophy and Maine's model for delivery.

Measures of Success

The program has utilized a variety of evaluation methods to measure the success of the project. One indicator of success is the finding that nearly 80% of trained teams continue to function beyond the first year following initial training. With the multitude of demands facing educators today, longevity of a project often reflects an investment of time and resources that provide a measure of reasonable "return on investment." In follow-up contacts, student assistance team members frequently cited a sense of accomplishment in working in these teams that they said they feel lacking in much of their work. They said they know their time will be well spent in the meetings attended and they will be among peers of a common mind working to improve conditions for all students. Also, members reported they appreciate the team focus on developing action plans that address specific, observable behaviors which enhance student performance, as well as identifying systemic issues impacting all students and staff.

The annual SAT project evaluations have uncovered other interesting results. Over half the schools surveyed indicated that referrals to special education are "more appropriate" as a result of utilizing this process. Comparison of student assistance team sites and non-SAT sites indicate that those schools having teams are more likely to have an effective referral process in place for alcohol and other drug issues. The SAT process was described as "beneficial" by 100% of those surveyed in trained sites, and "effective" by 73%. In addition, 68% of respondents indicated that a written follow-up procedure was used in the team's strategy planning (Medical Care Development, 1995). Such consistent follow-up is often lacking in student referral and intervention processes.

Resiliency Integration

Over the past three years, the Student Assistance Team Unit staff have made a concerted effort to provide local teams with a foundation in resiliency principles. This information has been viewed as essential to keep the work of this project at the forefront of effective prevention and intervention programming. Initial team training now contains a segment outlining the research on resiliency and positive youth development. References utilized focus on the work of Bonnie Benard, Peter Benson, Emmy Werner and Ruth Smith, Steve and Sybil Wolin, and Nan Henderson and Mike Milstein, among others. Regional networking meetings of existing teams have highlighted resiliency research and philosophy as well.

Unit staff are frequently called upon for resiliency-based presentations in conferences and training sessions conducted by other Department of Education staff. Their involvement has led to inclusion of resiliency principles as central tenets within several Department publications. *Fostering Hope: A Prevention Process*, developed by the Department's Prevention Team (Maine Department of Education, 1996) and the state's Improving America's Schools Act (IASA) application, are two examples of documents now reflecting the resiliency paradigm. Such inclusion is reflective of Department staff members' belief that school reform and resiliency building are simul-taneously achieved.

In November 1994, an historical event resulted from the resiliency foundation being built by Department of Education personnel. A day-long resiliency training was held with representatives from ALL departments of state government impacting families and youth. The memo announcing the event was a piece of history in itself. This document was the first to invite staff from these departments with signatures from each of the departments' Commissioners. The workshop facilitated development of common language for all in at-

tendance, regardless of their work unit. While bureaucracies are notoriously slow to change, the initial effort of this event is still having ripple effects. Various departments continue to converse intra-departmentally regarding the im-plications of resiliency research on their activities.

Sample forms provided to local teams have also undergone change to reflect the resilience-building paradigm. Student referral forms have been drastically altered from the deficit-focused forms used in the 1980s to forms balancing statements of concern (based on observable behaviors) with statements of student strengths and assets.

The sample form on the following page is one example. Developed by SAT Unit staff, it is designed to assist local SATs in building student intervention plans that align with resiliency principles. Such additions ensure that asset and resiliency development are considered in balance with behavioral concerns and are consistent with current thinking on this topic (Henderson and Milstein, 1996; Henderson, 1996). Other excamples are two forms published in *Student Assistance Journal* (Henderson, 1996). [These are included here as well.]

Student assistance team members are being encouraged to consider how they can effectively inform students of resiliency characteristics and assist them with identifying and describing those present in their lives. This emphasis on identification of strengths and assets versus a problem focus will impact ways of thinking for both students and staff. Protective factors identified by Hawkins and Catalano (1992), resiliency factors described by Benard (1993), [both reflected in sample action planning form], and the resiliency elements of insight, independence, relationships, initiative, humor, creativity, and morality described by the Wolins (1993) are outlined for team integration to existing efforts.

SAMPLE
Resiliency-Based Action Planning Form

Student: _____   Grade: _____

Referred by: _____

Statement of presenting problem(s):

To enhance the quality of interventions, identify how each of the six elements of building resiliency will be addressed for this student.

Pro-Social Bonds
Identify positive connections this student currently has with people (peers & adults), programs, or activities, clubs and organizations:

Positive bonds will be fostered for this student as follows, based upon identified interests and strengths:

Social Skills
Describe strengths observed in this student's social skill development. Identify life skills training they have received/are receiving:

The social skill development of this student will be enhanced in these ways:

Clear and Consistent Boundaries
The following efforts are in place to provide clear and consistent boundaries for this student school-wide:

Clarity and consistency of boundaries school-wide will be enhanced for this student in the following ways:

Care and Support
This student is provided clear messages of care and support in the following ways:

Messages of care and support for this student will be strengthened in the following ways:

High Expectations for Success
Clear messages of high expectations for behavior and performance are provided this student in the following ways:

High expectations will be strengthened for this student by:

Meaningful Participation
This student is currently involved in the following ways that provide meaningful participation within and outside the school setting:

Meaningful participation for this student will be enhanced by:

References

Benard, B. (1993). *Turning the corner from risk to resiliency*. Portland, OR: Western Regional Center for Drug-Free Schools and Communities, Northwest Educational Laboratory.

Benard, B. (1995). How schools can foster resiliency in children. In *Western Center News. September*. Portland, OR: Western Regional Center for Drug-Free Schools and Communities, Northwest Educational Laboratory.

Hawkins, J.D., Catalano, R.F., Jr., et al. (1992). *Communities that care*. San Francisco, CA: Jossey-Bass.

Henderson, N. (1996). SAPs that build student resiliency. In S*tudent Assistance Journal, March/April*. Troy, MI: Performance Resource Press.

Henderson, N., & Milstein, M. (1996). *Resiliency in schools: Making it happen for students and educators*. Thousand Oaks, CA: Corwin Press.

Maine Department of Education. (1988). *Task force report on affected children*. Augusta, ME.

Maine Department of Education. (1994). *Student assistance team training manual*. Augusta, ME.

Maine Department of Education. (1996). *Fostering hope: A prevention process*. Augusta, ME.

Medical Care Development. (1995). *Maine student assistance team process evaluation, 1994*. Augusta, ME.

Office of Substance Abuse. (1996). *Report of the Governor's Task Force on adolescent suicide & self-destructive behaviors*. Augusta, ME.

Wolin, S. J., & S. (1993). *The resilient self: How survivors of troubled families rise above adversity*. New York, NY: Villard Books.

Tim Duffey, M.Ed., is Past President of the National Association of Leadership for Student Assistance Programs, and is currently a senior trainer for Search Institute. He can be reached by calling Search Institute Training, 800-294-4322.

The following forms, adapted from "SAPs that Build Student Resiliency" by Nan Henderson, which appeared in the March, 1996 Student Assistance Journal, *provide additional examples of student assistance paperwork reflecting the process of integration of resiliency principles into student assistance programs.*

Assessment of Environmental Resiliency-Builders

NAME OF STUDENT_____

1. *Positive bond's in this student's life:*
   People _____
   Interests/Activities _____
   Describe your connection to this student: _____
2. *Situations where the student experiences structure/clear boundaries:*
   _____
   _____

3. *The student has learned these life skills (as evidenced by their use):*
   _____
   The student is currently receiving life skills training (describe):
   _____
4. *Individuals/organizations/settings that provide this student with caring and support:*
   _____
   _____

5. *Individuals/environmental situations that communicate high expectations for success to this student:*
   _____
6. *This student is involved in helping others/making positive contributions in the following ways:*
   _____
   How can these environmental resiliency-builders be used in intervening with this student?
   _____

Assessment of Internal Characteristics of Resiliency

NAME OF STUDENT_____

Check the following personal resiliency-builders you have observed in this student (in addition to problems). (Source: *Resiliency in Schools: Making It Happen for Students and Educators* by Nan Henderson and Mike Milstein, published in 2003 by Corwin Press). These are ways that individuals cope with stress and adversity in their lives, and research indicates one or more of these can be identified in every student (and in every adult).

❏ Relationships - Sociability/ability to be a friend/ability to form positive relationships
❏ Service - Gives of self in service to others and/or a cause
❏ Life Skills - Uses life skills, including good decision-making, assertiveness, and impulse control
❏ Humor - Has a good sense of humor
❏ Inner Direction - Bases choices/decisions on internal evaluation (internal locus of control)
❏ Perceptiveness - Insightful understanding of people and situations
❏ Independence - "Adaptive" distancing from unhealthy people and situations/autonomy
❏ Positive View of Personal Future - Expects a positive future
❏ Flexibility - Can adjust to change; can bend as necessary to positively cope with situations
❏ Love of Learning - Capacity for and connection to learning
❏ Self-motivation - Internal initiative and positive motivation from within
❏ Competence - Is "good at something"/personal competence
❏ Self-Worth - Feelings of self-worth and self-confidence
❏ Spirituality - Personal faith in something greater
❏ Perseverance - Keeps on despite difficulty; doesn't give up
❏ Creativity - Expresses self through artistic endeavor and/or other creativity.

(From research by Richardson, et al., 1990; Werner and Smith, 1992; Hawkins, et al., 1992; and Wolin and Wolin, 1993)

How can we further nurture/build upon these resiliency builders in this student's life?

How can they be used in intervening with this student?

Chapter 8

Using the Resiliency Wheel in Crisis Counseling/ Intervention

adapted by Nan Henderson from The Tucson Resiliency Initiative

Editor's Note: After 9/11, The Tucson Resiliency Initiative, a model for communitywide commitment to fostering resiliency, developed brief, easily implemented suggestions for using the six elements of The Resiliency Wheel in crisis counseling. The suggestions below were adapted from TRI's initial list.

TRI mobilizes all aspects of the community, particularly schools, to build resiliency in youth. TRI is a broad coalition with committee members representing six southern Arizona school districts, the University of Arizona, social service agencies, and law enforcement, and currently works with 17 partner schools in four districts. For more information on the Tucson Resiliency Initiative, go to www.tusonresiliency.org.—N.H.

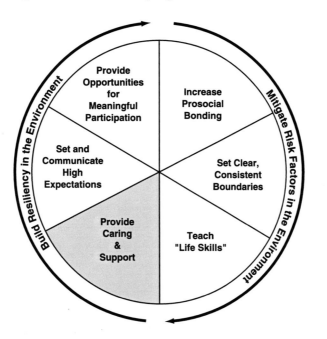

Caring and support:

Listen to the concerns of students or those you are trying to help (about the crisis or stressful situation) and answer their questions in direct, factual, and age-appropriate ways. (Be careful not to give too much information to children.)

High Expectations:

Express your certainty that whomever you are talking with can cope with the situation, and your faith in their strength and inner resources.

Opportunities for Participation:

Help students or those you are helping come up with ways they can address the crisis by taking action themselves: Raising money to help, sending e-mails to those involved, forming a Peace Club or Tolerance Club, and/or writing to elected officials are some ways to do this.

Pro-Social Bonding:

Organize activities that students or others can do as a group that give a sense of purpose. Encourage people to take time to participate in groups, social activities, and pleasurable hobbies that they have enjoyed in the past.

Clear, Consistent Boundaries:

Strike a balance between listening to and addressing concerns and getting on with a "normal schedule." Familiar rules and routines provide a sense of safety and security for people of all ages.

Life skills:

Model, coach, and provide activities for people to communicate thoughts and feelings. Sometimes a structured group activity in which everyone shares the answer to a question, or draws a "feelings picture" or writes a poem is the best way to draw the feelings out. (However, balance is also important, especially with children and youth. Don't let the group activities escalate to a place where everyone feels overwhelmed.)

CHAPTER 9

Rest and Resiliency, A Spiritual Perspective:
Mary NurrieStearns interviews Wayne Muller

from *Personal Transformation*

Wayne Muller is a therapist, author, ordained minister, and founder of Bread for the Journey, an innovative organization serving families in need. When his book, Sabbath (2000), crossed my desk I savored it, for this treasure of a book is medicine for our harried lives. In it, Muller shows us how to create a special time of rest, delight, and renewal—a refuge for our souls. He also makes clear how constant striving causes exhaustion, deprivation, and longing for rest and time with loved ones.

Sabbath is a time of sacred rest that restores us, pleasures us, and eases the suffering caused by the maddening lifestyle of our modern society. Wanting readers to discover how Sabbath can reduce suffering and bring joy, I contacted him for an interview at his home in northern California, where he lives with his family.

Personal Transformation: In your book *Sabbath,* you refer to the mainstream American lifestyle as the road of progress, one that pursues accomplishment, materialism, and productivity. What is the suffering caused by this lifestyle?

Wayne Muller: The sufferings are of different kinds, some obvious, others delicate and not so obvious. On the obvious level, as we become busier, we move quickly and hold many responsibilities in our hands, so that even when we try to do good, we do good badly. We don't have the wisdom required to hear what is truly necessary—to hear right action, right understanding, right livelihood. We inadvertently break things even as we try to fix them. Our busy-ness becomes a kind of violence because it destroys the root of inner wisdom that makes work fruitful. On one level, suffering comes because we inadvertently bring harm to the world that we're trying to help—whether we're raising money to pay the bills, serving the homeless, or feeding the hungry. Having been in non-profit worlds for 25 years, I can say that the faster we go, the more we unintentionally mishandle the ones we love. They become an object of our ambition rather than the subject of our heart's attention, which requires a certain amount of time and company as well as money.

On more delicate levels, suffering comes because we don't allow time for the ache in our soul to be healed or for us to be shown the way. In spiritual practice we invite forces larger than us…to work on us in some way. Some amount of time is required for us to be worked on. Healing doesn't always require us to work; sometimes we need to be worked on. Sabbath allows us to compost in a way that the quiet seeds planted in the soils of our bodies, hearts and minds can germinate. If the seeds that we so diligently plant with our spiritual practice aren't given a period of dormancy, then like iris bulbs planted in the fall, without dormancy, they will not flower in the spring. We lose the harvest of our practice if we don't have time to take our hands off the plow and rest in the hammock of delight provided for us by the Sabbath precepts of many spiritual traditions.

PT: Are you saying that suffering isn't caused as much by the pursuit of accomplishment as by our sped-up relationship with time?

Muller: The problem is imbalance. Clearly both time and action are necessary. Things need to be done in the world. Homes need to be built, children need to be raised, food needs to be grown, medicines need to be discovered. Because we're incarnated in human bodies, there are things in the world that require our attention in order for us to be healthy and to grow as a family of beings on the earth. The problem is not necessarily working hard, the problem is working so hard and long without rest that we begin to imagine that we're the ones making everything happen. We begin to feel a growing, gnawing sense of responsibility and grandiosity about how important our work is and how we can't stop because everything is on our shoulders. We forget that forces much larger than we are, in fact, do most of the work. When we don't stop, we don't remember that. One thing I love about the Sabbath practice in most spiritual traditions is that it starts at a particular time, like the sun going down in the Jewish tradition or the sun coming up on Easter Sunday morning. The onset of Sabbath is usually tied to the sun or the moon—something that you can't mess with. You can't negotiate away the time to stop working. You can't say, "I'll stop as soon as I finish this report." Sabbath time is the time when we get stopped.

PT: In our society, we think of rest as useless. You describe rest as joyful as well as useful.

Muller: We need to listen to the spiritual traditions. Jesus said, "Behold, I bring you tidings of great joy," and "Come, that you might have life and have that abundantly." The Buddha spoke about joy being the fruit of spiritual practice. No spiritual tradition says that God wants us to be exhausted. No scripture says we're supposed to be totally burned out. Almost every scripture says that the fruit of life is joy—being happy in all that we have been given and all that arises in the course of human life. There are sorrows, but the more spacious we become, the more joyful we become in being able to embrace everything. The Sabbath has a joyful uselessness to it. We are not supposed to accomplish anything of any significance so that we can stop looking for what's not there and have the time to drink from what's already here. When we're on the wheel of constant work, our eye is on the next thing that has to be done, what hasn't been accomplished yet. Sabbath is a time to eat what you've cooked, to harvest what you've planted and to give thanks for what you've been given. It's a time to bless our loved ones and to eat, drink, and make love. The sensual delight associated with Sabbath reminds us that one of the fruits of spiritual practice is useless happiness.

PT: As I listen to you, I understand that the Sabbath is a gratitude for and a pleasuring in the abundance of our lives and loves rather than an external pursuit of abundance.

Muller: Right, and in fact, petitionary prayer is discouraged in the Hebrew tradition on the Sabbath. On the Sabbath, you don't ask for anything, you just give thanks. You can ask all you want on the other six days but the Sabbath is the day that you just give thanks. Sabbath also brings up a different definition of abundance. Abundance can be an image of more than we need rather than an image of sufficiency that means whatever we've been given is enough. The Sabbath invites us to consider that whatever we have is abundance and that we don't always need to accumulate. Sabbath is about feeling the desperate urge for some new acquisition fall away at the end of the day of walking, praying, napping, eating, and making love. You don't feel that desperate need to accumulate after a lovely day like that.

PT: I'm quoting you, "Sabbath; the time to stop, to refrain from being seduced by our desires." Talk about the difference between the pleasure and joyfulness of Sabbath and the seduction of desire.

Muller: Desire is a powerful force. The Buddhists describe desire as a thirsting and craving that is the ultimate source of human suffering. Desire is a fundamental dissatisfaction with what we have and a thirsting and craving for what we don't have. Pleasure and delight is feeling the blessing of what we already have. Our civilization canonizes desire as the engine that drives our monetary system, which is sad because desire, by definition, is based on dissatisfaction. When you're satisfied, your desires melt away. When you have a

nice meal, your desire to eat more disappears. When you have a relationship with someone you love, the desire to run off and meet somebody else naturally falls away. Whenever we're satisfied with what we have, desire dissolves of its own accord. We place desire on the altar of our civilization. Once you have one car, you're supposed to want two. Once you have a two-bedroom house, you're supposed to want a three-bedroom house. Once you make $25,000, you're supposed to want to make $50,000. Everything is supposed to grow. The ethos of the free marketplace is that there is always supposed to be more. The Sabbath is a revolutionary challenge to the presumption that that's what life is for.

PT: Let's talk about love. What happens to our innate ability to love when we rarely slow down?

Muller: Love is an enormous word that conveys many feelings and experiences and relationships. There's love of design, love of fragrance, love of our children, sexual love between partners, love of music, love of humanity. Regardless of how we define love or which aspect of love we talk about, love requires time in order to grow. Love experiences require the sweet soil of unstructured time in which we bring presence, resting our attention on the subject of our love…The currency that gives birth to love is time. All love grows in time. When we live without taking time for love to grow, there is only a thin veneer of what we really are looking for. The depth of the love we seek requires time to work in us. Most spiritual traditions counsel that Sabbath time isn't a lifestyle suggestion for your blood pressure, it's a commandment. Rest. You must stop your work and allow yourself to be worked on by time.

PT: What else grows in the soil of time?

Muller: Some people lament the fact that we've lost the traditional values in our civilization, and write books about honesty, courage, integrity, and responsibility. While I appreciate the question of where these values have gone in America, I think it's dishonest to question individuals in a civilization without looking at the civilization itself. Our civilization requires people to trade time for money. Honesty, courage, mindfulness, and integrity can't grow without time for thoughtful reflection on our behavior. These values require time to be together with one another, to teach each other how it is to be in the other's company. That's how we grow in relationship skills. When I see the impact that my tone of voice or actions have on my children, by taking the time to listen to what they have to say, then I, God willing, learn how to be a better parent. We can't purchase these things. They only grow in time.

PT: Discuss [the concept from the Christian tradition] the, Biblical scripture Mark 2:27, "You are not made for the Sabbath, the Sabbath is made for you."

Muller: Some of us associate Sabbath with dry, boring Sundays of our childhood, where Sabbath was the day you had to get dressed up and not have any fun. That's not what I'm invoking. I'm invoking what Abraham Hesholl, the Jewish scholar, calls the day of delight. The Sabbath precept in most religions is a vehicle for our delight.…The point is to take Sabbath in order to be as nourished, fed and delighted as we're meant to be.

PT: Does Sabbath require a certain intention or expectation as we undertake it?

Muller: .…The Sabbath is an instruction about how to feel the rhythm of time. Our heart and lungs are a rhythm. The tides of the earth and the seasons have a rhythm. Everything alive has a rhythm, and if we fall into Sabbath rhythm, we fall into rhythm with the heartbeat of the world. When we work twenty-four hours a day, seven days a week, we live like people who are at war, we live in war-time. What's the war about, whom are we fighting and how will we know if we've won? The Sabbath intentionality is to open up a space for listening to that which is most precious, nourishing and deeply true, and letting ourselves be worked on and delighted and fed

PT: Say more about letting ourselves be worked on.

Muller: There's a story about a nun who used to walk the fields where they kept cattle, near the convent. As she walked she looked for herbs. There were about a half dozen herbs growing naturally in the field. The herbs she stumbled upon helped her decide what she was going to cook that day. A visiting herbiculturist explained to the convent residents that rather than allowing the cattle to graze the whole field, it would be better to keep them in a small section of the field for a period of time and let the rest of the land lie fallow. The herbiculturist recommended a Sabbath for the land, something the Hebrews talked about 3,000 years ago. This Sabbath consisted of letting the animals graze and fertilize one section of the land, then moving them after a season from one section of the field to the other. One spring, after two or three years of this practice, the nun went looking for herbs and found about a dozen new herbs growing in the field that had never grown there before. Nobody planted them, nobody seeded herbs in the field. When the cattle roamed the field, the herbs tried to come up but they never made it. They were in the soil, but because of the constant activity of the cattle on the ground, they never had the time or the space to break through the ground. In a way, Sabbath time allows those plants that are ready to break through the crust of the soil of our life to do so. If we presume that we have to make everything happen, that the only way to get herbs in the field is to plant them, we never stop or rest, and we never know that the herbs come up by themselves.

PT: Let's move to a discussion about being Sabbath. You quote Mother Teresa as saying, "Let us remain as empty as possible so that God can fill us up." How do we become Sabbath

Muller: A couple of images come to mind. As a psychotherapist, I noticed over the years that I did less therapy and more holding the faithfulness present in the midst of whatever sorrows or aches people brought to me. Even on my good days, the best I could do was sit and patiently see where they were already the light of the world… My job was to sit there with no agenda and to simply be in their company as they poured their sorrows into this empty vessel that we became together. Then the grace, the courage, the inner light—whether you call it Buddha nature or kingdom of God—that refused to be extinguished, slowly arose of its own accord, without anyone doing anything to anybody. The quote, "to attain knowledge every day, something is added to it; to attain wisdom every day, something is subtracted," also speaks to us being the Sabbath. There is a way in which we empty ourselves of preconceptions and presumptions. Emptying ourselves of expectations, we can be filled by whatever winds blow through us, cultivating what Suzuki Roshi called the beginner's mind. You can cultivate emptiness through a Buddhist meditation practice where you follow the breath and allow the preoccupation with thought to soften and fall away. In the emptiness, new kinds of peace, equanimity and well-being become possible. Sabbath is an opportunity, every week, to have a new beginning, where all things become new, as it says in the Christian gospel.

PT: Talk about the relationship between Sabbath and healing.

Muller: …Like love, healing grows in the soil of time. Healing requires time for the body/soul/spirit to reorganize itself in a new way. Transformation is dependent on right effort, right understanding, right livelihood and right mindfulness, but it also requires a willingness to surrender into the arms of the divine. It requires a surrender into knowing that forces larger than us can have their way with us and do the work that they need to do on us without our being involved directly. Obviously, physical rest is important, but also, the rest of thinking that it's all up to us, one of the gifts of Sabbath, allows those things working on us to do their work so that we can be the recipient of their blessing. It's hard to be blessed if you don't stand still.

PT: This culture of progress focuses on individual pursuit and implies that we are alone. The Sabbath reminds us that we are connected to something greater than our individual selves.

Muller: In most Sabbath traditions, there is at least some time dedicated to gathering in community with other people. We gather with friends or with family. We put our hands on the heads of our children and offer them our blessing or we go to church or the synagogue. We have some kind of worship with other beings. We get isolated in ever-smaller cubicles into which we are being put in the marketplace. Sabbath time brings us back together.

PT: In the same way that marketplace activities separate us from people, busy-ness separates us from ourselves. If keeping busy is, at times, an attempt to cope with suffering inside, won't resting on the Sabbath bring all that forth?

Muller: Certainly, some of our busy-ness can be a mask for ache, sadness, or grief. A couple of doctors told me that living so close to people's illnesses and often deaths, they fear that if they stop and feel their deep sadness they would weep for a month. A lot of treatment speed is to avoid the invariable tenderness that would arise if they were open all of the time. Another physician made the same point from the opposite direction. In medical school, he learned to be exhausted, which is, as I understand, the primary curriculum of medical school. The more tired he got, the more tests he ordered on people. As he grew more exhausted, he could rely less on his intuition, his quiet voice that told him what was going on with a patient. When he got some rest and returned, he could hear what was going on with a patient and order one test to confirm the diagnosis. Even when the practice of speeding up to avoid suffering looks like a good idea it isn't necessarily ultimately a useful practice.

PT: Although pain that we have been avoiding may arise when we rest, the comfort that soothes the pain also emerges in rest.

Muller: A lot of people are afraid to stop because they're afraid that if they do, they will feel those aches or an emptiness inside that frightens them terribly. That's why I think very few Sabbath practices focus on self-introspection. Sabbath is not to go inside and find who you are or to root out all those demons, it's to stop and enjoy yourself. It's seductive for the mind to think that it always has to work on problems. If we presume that larger forces than us are already at work

on our problems, we can sing songs and have a good time while the forces work on them.

PT: Before we close, discuss…, "Where your treasure is, there will your heart be also."

Muller: …Whatever we give our time and attention to gets our love. If we give all our attention to our job, we'll be successful at work and other things will fall by the wayside. Whatever we give our attention to flourishes—it's going to end up on the altar of our life's story. If you want to know what you love, open your appointment book. Whatever you give your time and attention to is, in effect, what you really love. Sabbath practice invites us to be more intentional on a regular basis, making sure that we put on our altar things that are delicious and delightful so that when we taste, hold, and dance them, they bring us delight and help us remember that we're the light of the world and that God wants us to be happy and not exhausted. Sabbath is a time to treasure those things that are completely free and gratuitous—the smell of warm bread, making love with your lover, taking a walk in nature. When we make time for those things, we begin to remember that joy is one of the things that a human life is for.

There is little permission in our culture for Sabbath. In fact, the only permission we have is illness, so cancer becomes our sabbatical. When people get a life-threatening illness like cancer or AIDS, everyone agrees that it's all right for them to take time off. But to say, "I'm leaving now and I'm not going to work today," is looked upon as self-indulgent and people feel guilty. In reality, it's a commandment in most of the world's spiritual traditions. If we don't take this time, we will not do well in the world. It's hard to live ethically without rest, when we speed along trying to get projects done. It's easier to talk ourselves into lying about this or that because we know it'll help get the project done. The more we live without rest, the easier it is to live out of balance. It's strange, living in a world where no one feels permission to rest, while we simultaneously claim to ascribe to spiritual traditions that insist that we rest. I'm making a plea for Sabbath-keeping, reminding people that they already have permission to rest. Sabbath doesn't need to be justified with the promise of some great spiritual insight. Sabbath is a gift that we're supposed to drink from.

Personal Transformation *magazine was founded by Marie NurrieStearns and her husband Rick, and was published from 1996 to 2000. Back issues can be accessed and downloaded from the Personal Transformation website, www.personaltransformation. com. Marie NurrieStearns can be contacted at Info3@PersonalTransformation.com.*

A RESOURCE FOR TEENS: COPY AND USE

How to Become Resilient: You've Got the Power to Help Yourself Bounce Back...from Life!

by Jami Jones, Ph.D.

Justin was stressed. It seemed his life was falling apart. At home it was tense. Money was tight. His parents were fighting. He had failed a few tests. Friends were on his case. "All in all," thought Justin, "life these days is a real struggle."

Justin's not alone. Many teens face challenges stemming from problems with friends, school, teachers, parents, and work. Although life is difficult at times, the good news it doesn't mean you have to be overwhelmed by these struggles. You can bounce back from them and become stronger and wiser in the process.

The word for this is *resiliency*. At Dictionary.com, resiliency is defined as "an occurrence of rebounding or springing back." A growing field of psychological research is documenting that everyone has the power to spring back from difficulties. Resiliency is like a rubber band that gets stretched almost to the breaking point. Instead of snapping, it is able to spring back into shape. One teen-ager described resiliency as "bouncing back from problems and stuff with more power and more smarts."

There are many studies that document resiliency in children and teens. One of the most significant is called the Kauai Longitudinal Study, which looked at all the children born in 1955 on the island of Kauai in Hawaii. These children were studied from birth until 50 years of age. The authors of this study, psychologists Emmy Werner and Ruth Smith, identified children who were struggling with poverty, parental addictions and mental illness, divorce, health problems, and other significant issues. A lot of these children were doing well in spite of their difficulties. Most of them eventually bounced back from the negative impact of these problems.

Werner and Smith called these children resilient and they identified that resilient kids had *protective factors* that helped them handle their problems without becoming overwhelmed. These *protective factors* are available to you too.

What are these *protective factors* and how do you add them to your life?

1. **Making connections.** One of the most important *protective factors* is making connections with caring adults who will listen and help you put your problems into perspective. These important people are sometimes called mentors, and can be family members, teachers, coaches, counselors, ministers, neighbors—any adult you know who cares about kids.

   It will be up to you to find a mentor. Tell this special person that you need him to help you with the challenges in your life. Keep in mind that a mentor will never ask you to do anything that is illegal or makes you feel uncomfortable. If this ever happens, tell another adult immediately!

2. **Reading.** Some teens think that the only kind of reading that counts is what you do in class. Wrong! The most important benefit of reading is to learn about things that are important to you. Reading is a skill that improves with practice and reading will most certainly help you get ahead in life. Read anything—books, websites, and magazines!

3. **Problem-solving and goal setting skills**. Some research shows that one factor that separates the resilient teens from the not-so-resilient ones is the ability to solve problems and set goals. Dr. Gregory J. Williams, a professor at Pacific Lutheran University in Tacoma, Washington, developed a four-step technique called "I CAN" to help teens do this.

   - **I** Identify the problem. You need to understand the problem and its causes before a solution is possible. To determine the cause of the problem, ask "who, what, where, when, and how" questions. Ask your friends or mentor to help you.

   - **C** Can you name some solutions? Begin by brainstorming as many solutions as possible – no matter how far-fetched, silly, or wild they seem to you. At this step it is the number of solutions that counts, not quality!

- **A** Analyze the solutions. How will they work? Now is the time to analyze solutions and discard the ones you think will not work.

- **N** Now, pick one and use it! It if works, great! If not, try another one.

4. **Social skills.** When life seems to be falling apart it is important to have trusted friends to count on. Teens with good social skills are more likely to enlist the help of friends and adults during difficult times. To have friends, it is important to be a friend. Do you know the five most desirable qualities in a friend? Kids want to be friends with other kids who express a sense of humor, friendliness, helpfulness, frequent compliments, and offers to get together. Likewise, the qualities that are real turn-offs are verbal aggression, anger, dishonesty, being critical, and bossiness. Volunteering is one way to broaden your network of friends. The simple act of helping others lets you to put your problems into perspective, makes your community stronger, and is a great way to meet people and develop new interests. Go to the Do Something website at www.dosomething.org to learn more about volunteering.

5. **Hobbies and interests.** The research is clear that resilient teens have hobbies and interests they enjoy. It could be playing a sport or musical instrument, painting, reading, scrapbooking, or writing poetry. Perhaps the greatest benefit is that when the going gets tough, hobbies and interests can help you forget for a time your problems and stress.

Life can often be difficult. The good news is that you are able to control how you respond to difficulties adding *protective factors* today so you will be more resilient tomorrow. Start now by *putting together your resiliency plan that includes these protective factors.*

- Make connections and find at least one mentor. Know when to ask for help.
- Use "I CAN" to solve problems and set goals.
- Read so you can make good decisions.
- Be a friend. Help someone whose problems are more serious than yours.
- Enrich your life with a hobby or interest.

Researchers Werner and Smith developed a simple way to define a resilient person. They say that a resilient person *loves well, works well, plays well,* and *expects well.*

What they mean is that resilient people have some loving/caring relationships in their lives, are successfully working on a job or in school, have fun (play) utilizing hobbies and positive leisure-time interests, and expect a positive future for their lives. You can increase your resiliency by using the suggestions in this article. You can also learn more by going to www.resiliency.com

Jami L. Jones, Ph.D., is assistant professor in the Department of Library Science and Instructional Technology at East Carolina University in Greenville, NC. After the death of her son's girlfriend, Dr. Jones became interested in studying the response of adults within her profession to strengthen and promote resiliency within youth. She is the author of Bouncing Back: Dealing with the Stuff Life Throws at You, *a book for teens published in 2006. She also authored* Helping Teens Cope: Resources for School Library Media Specialists and Other Youth Workers *and can be contacted through her web site at www.askdrjami.org or by e-mailing jonesj@ecu.edu*

THE RESILIENCY QUIZ

by Nan Henderson, M.S.W. (reprinted from www.resiliency.com)
© Resiliency In Action, Inc. (Copies can be made for educational purposes only.)

I developed this quiz for anyone—teens, adults, elders—to assess and strengthen the resiliency building conditions in their lives. Use it for yourself or use it as a tool to help others you care about build their resiliency.

PART ONE
Do you have the conditions in your life that research shows help people to be resilient?

People bounce back from tragedy, trauma, risks, and stress by having the following "protective" conditions in their lives. The more times you answer yes (below), the greater the chances you can bounce back from your life's problems "with more power and more smarts." And doing that is a sure way to increase self-esteem.

Answer yes or no to the following. Celebrate your "yes" answers and decide how you can change your "no" answers to "yes." (You can also answer "sometimes" if that is more accurate than just "yes" or "no".)

1. Caring and Support

_____I have several people in my life who give me unconditional love, nonjudgmental listening, and who I know are "there for me."

_____I am involved in a school, work, faith, or other group where I feel cared for and valued.

_____I treat myself with kindness and compassion, and take time to nurture myself (including eating right and getting enough sleep and exercise).

2. High Expectations for Success

_____I have several people in my life who let me know they believe in my ability to succeed.

_____I get the message "You can succeed," at my work or school.

_____I believe in myself most of the time, and generally give myself positive messages about my ability to accomplish my goals–even when I encounter difficulties.

3. Opportunities for Meaningful Participation

_____My voice (opinion) and choice (what I want) is heard and valued in my close personal relationships.

_____My opinions and ideas are listened to and respected at my work or school.

_____I volunteer to help others or a cause in my community, faith organization, or school.

4. Positive Bonds

_____I am involved in one or more positive after-work or after-school hobbies or activities.

_____I participate in one or more groups (such as a club, faith community, or sports team) outside of work or school.

_____I feel "close to" most people at my work or school.

5. Clear and Consistent Boundaries

_____Most of my relationships with friends and family members have clear, healthy boundaries (which include mutual respect, personal autonomy, and each person in the relationship both giving and receiving).

_____I experience clear, consistent expectations and rules at my work or in my school.

_____I set and maintain healthy boundaries for myself by standing up for myself, not letting others take advantage of me, and saying "no" when I need to.

6. Life Skills

_____I have (and use) good listening, honest communication, and healthy conflict resolution skills.

_____I have the training and skills I need to do my job well, or all the skills I need to do well in school.

_____I know how to set a goal and take the steps to achieve it.

PART TWO

People also successfully overcome life difficulties by drawing upon internal qualities that research has shown are particularly helpful when encountering a crisis, major stressor, or trauma.

The following list can be thought of as a "personal resiliency builder" menu. No one has everything on this list. When "the going gets tough" you probably have three or four of these qualities that you use most naturally and most often.

It is helpful to know which are your primary resiliency builders; how have you used them in the past; and how can you use them to overcome the present challenges in your life.

You can also decide to add one or two of these to your "resiliency-builder" menu, if you think they would be useful for you.

PERSONAL RESILIENCY BUILDERS
Individual Qualities that Facilitate Resiliency

Put a + by the top three or four resiliency builders you use most often. Ask yourself how you have used these in the past or currently use them. Think of how you can best apply these resiliency builders to current life problems, crises, or stressors.

(Optional) You can then put a • •by one or two resiliency builders you think you should add to your personal repertoire.

☐ Relationships -- Sociability/ability to be a friend/ability to form positive relationships
☐ Service – Giving of yourself to help other people; animals; organizations; and/or social causes
☐ Humor -- Having and using a good sense of humor
☐ Inner Direction -- Basing choices/decisions on internal evaluation (internal locus of control)
☐ Perceptiveness -- Insightful understanding of people and situations
☐ Independence -- "Adaptive" distancing from unhealthy people and situations/autonomy
☐ Positive View of Personal Future – Optimism; expecting a positive future
☐ Flexibility -- Can adjust to change; can bend as necessary to positively cope with situations
☐ Love of Learning -- Capacity for and connection to learning
☐ Self-motivation -- Internal initiative and positive motivation from within
☐ Competence -- Being "good at something"/personal competence
☐ Self-Worth -- Feelings of self-worth and self-confidence
☐ Spirituality -- Personal faith in something greater
☐ Perseverance -- Keeping on despite difficulty; doesn't give up
☐ Creativity -- Expressing yourself through artistic endeavor, or through other means of creativity

You Can Best Help Yourself or Someone Else Be More Resilient by...

1. Communicating the Resiliency Attitude: "What is right with you is more powerful than anything wrong with you."

2. Focusing on the person's strengths more than problems and weaknesses, and asking,
   "How can these strengths be used to overcome problems?" One way to do this is to help yourself
   or another identify and best utilize top personal resiliency builders listed in The Resiliency Quiz Part Two.

3. Providing for yourself or another the conditions listed in The Resiliency Quiz Part One.

4. Having patience...successfully bouncing back from a significant trauma or crisis takes time.

Nan Henderson, M.S.W., is an international speaker, writer, and president of Resiliency In Action, a publishing and training company in Southern CA, which she cofounded in 1996 to "redirect the national obsession with risks and weakness to embracing the reality and power of human resiliency." She has authored several articles and coauthored four books on fostering resiliency, including Resiliency In Action: Practical Ideas for Overcoming Risks and Building Strengths in Youth, Families, and Communities *and* Resiliency In Schools: Making It Happen for Students and Educators*. She can be contacted at nhenderson@resiliency.com or at by calling 800-440-5171. More information is available at www.resiliency.com.*

Questions and Activities for Teaching about Resiliency

by Nan Henderson, M.S.W.

I am often asked, "When you speak to a group of students and have only an hour or two to explain/teach about resiliency, what do you say? What do you do?" The answer is that I most often use the questions listed below, or a variation of these questions, to teach kids about their innate resiliency. I also use the activities that follow this list (which can also be used with groups of adults).

These questions can be used in a large group discussion. However, depending on the characteristics of the group, often it is more effective for students to pair up or work in groups to answer each question and then come back for a larger group discussion.

1. If resiliency is defined as "the ability to bounce back from, and successfully overcome risks and adversity," why are you a "resilient" person?

2. What are some of the struggles, challenges, difficulties you have faced in the past (or currently face)? Go into as much detail as you feel like sharing.

3. Share how you overcame these difficulties...
   A. What did you DO?
   B. What BELIEFS about yourself and others guided you?
   C. WHO helped you?
   D. HOW did they help?
   E. WHAT else helped you?

4. How can you use these same things now or in the future in dealing with problems (or the current problem)?
   What can you do that worked in a similar situation in the past?
   Who can you go to for support or more information? Is there a way to maintain a greater access to these individuals?

   Is there a place or another kind of resource that would help? How can you access it?

5. Can you connect the personal ways you have overcome problems to the list of resiliency builders?
   (See the previous article, The Resiliency Quiz, for a list of environmental resiliency builders, part one, and individual resiliency builders, part two) that research studies have shown help people overcome problems?
   (Share both individual and environmental lists of resiliency builders.)

   Can you think of other times/ways you have used your resiliency builders?

6. What would you tell another kid who was going through your situation?
   What advice do you have for other kids going through some of the problems and difficulties you have gone through?

7. What advice do you have for adult trying to help kids to be "resilient"?

8. How well are adults providing the six environmental resiliency builders (refer to part one of The Resiliency Quiz) or to The Resiliency Wheel (in chapter eight)? What are adults doing well? What do adults need to do better?

9. What barriers do you think stand in the way of kids being more resilient (in your school, or family, or church, or community)? What ideas do you have about how to change these barriers?

Activities for Teaching, Celebrating, and Growing Personal Resiliency

Reprinted from The Resiliency Training Program Training of Trainers™
by Nan Henderson, M.S.W.

(The following activities can be used with youth and adults.)
Individuals need at least a basic understanding of the definition of resiliency and protective factors to do the following activities. Use a handout of "Personal Resiliency Builders" (taken from The Resiliency Quiz) for these activities.

1. WHAT'S IN MY WALLET

Have participants pair up with one person they do not know, and sit knee to knee. Instruct them to show their partner one thing they have in their purse or wallet that is connected in some way to their personal resiliency, and explain to their partner how it connects.

2. NAMING OTHERS' RESILIENCY BUILDERS

Have participants move to groups of four (pairs connect with other pairs who have done "What's In My Wallet" or this activity can stand alone with groups where everyone knows each other, such (as a staff or class). Each person must introduce his/her partner by identifying at least one personal resiliency builder he or she has identified in his/her partner (from the list of personal resiliency builders) and share how they have observed this resiliency builder in the partner.

3. WHO AND WHAT MADE ME RESILIENT?

In groups of four, have participants share answers to these questions: Who and what made me resilient? How did they do it? Who and what keeps me resilient now? How?

4. TOP RESILIENCY BUILDERS

Ask each participant to look down the list of personal resiliency builders, identifying the top three they use when they are facing stress or crisis. (Make the point that all of us lean towards a few of these based on our personality type and life experiences.) Tell the participants to raise their hands as you call out each of the resiliency builders. Using an overhead/slide of the list of personal resiliency builders, note the number for each.

5. USING PERSONAL RESILIENCY BUILDERS

Have participants move to groups of eight, and take turns introducing themselves to one another by sharing their top three resiliency builders and a time they used one of them.

6. ADDING TO YOUR RESILIENCY BUILDERS

Have participants, in groups of eight, share one personal resiliency builder (again referring to the list of personal resiliency builders) that they are working on, or think they should work on, and ideas about how to go about it.

7. RESILIENCY BLIZZARD

Have participants work as a large group, or stay in groups of eight: Instruct each person in the group to write down on a scrap of paper a sentence conveys a message they would like to receive more often that would help them feel more resilient. When they are finished, have participants throw their papers in the middle of the group.

Each person should then pick a paper not their own and read it aloud to their group (without comment). Groups should then discuss *any common theme* that emerged.

8. <u>REFLECTING UPON RESILIENCY</u>

At the conclusion of these activities (or at the end of a resiliency presentation), have participants silently reflect on the following:

1. Do you feel more resilient than you did at the beginning of these activities?
2. If so, how does this resiliency feel inside of you?
3. How did it happen?
4. Do you feel more able to successfully cope with a problem or make a change?
5. What does this mean for the work you do? For your life?

Participants can then share in their groups any realizations they want to make sure to remember.

9. <u>DRAWING RESILIENCY</u>

Have participants use crayons and paper that you provide to draw their representation of what resiliency looks like/feels like inside of them. Have them share these drawings in their groups of eight.

Display these drawings in a location where all training participants can view them.

Nan Henderson, M.S.W., is an international speaker, writer, and president of Resiliency In Action, a publishing and training company in Southern CA, which she cofounded in 1996 to "redirect the national obsession with risks and weakness to embracing the reality and power of human resiliency." She has authored several articles and coauthored four books on fostering resiliency, including Resiliency In Action: Practical Ideas for Overcoming Risks and Building Strengths in Youth, Families, and Communities *and* Resiliency In Schools: Making It Happen for Students and Educators. *She can be contacted at nhenderson@resiliency.com or at by calling 800-440-5171. More information is available at www.resiliency.com.*

PART FIVE

RESILIENCY AND YOUTH DEVELOPMENT

Connecting Resiliency, Youth Development, and Asset Development in a Positive-Focused Framework for Youth

by Peter Benson, Ph.D.

In efforts to increase the health, well-being, and life chances of America's youth, two paradigms coexist. Both are important, but they have different implications for policy and practice. The historically dominant paradigm focuses on naming, counting, and reducing the negative. The "negative" includes developmental risks (e.g., poverty, family dysfunction, unsafe schools and neighborhoods, negative peer pressure) and problem behaviors (e.g., teen pregnancy, substance use, school dropout, antisocial behavior, the violent resolution of conflict). For lack of a better descriptive term for this approach, let's call it a problem-focused paradigm. This approach—this way of thinking and conceptualizing—often dominates the way communities plan, organize, and implement youth-serving policy, program, and practice.

> *"Problem-free is not the same as health, a concept which demands the pursuit of the positive as much or more than reduction of the negative."*

The problem-focused paradigm is fueled by several cultural dynamics. Funding programs, particularly at the federal level, often create categorical initiatives attacking particular problem behaviors. These programs are housed in bureaucracies with problem-focused names. The Center for Substance Abuse Prevention and the Center for Disease Control come to mind. The language of problem and the language of risk are reinforced by a litany of research studies organized to track and monitor high-risk behaviors and by a media (television, radio, print) which, according to recent journalism studies, accents human mayhem. As much as two-thirds of all news rotates around conflict, destruction, violence, and disaster. Lesser emphasis is given to stories of connection, integration, harmony, unity, compassion, and justice.

> *"The two sides of the coin, reducing the negative and promoting the positive, are not opposites. There is a synergy, an interaction between these."*

The problem-focused approach is deeply entrenched. It both reflects and shapes a predilection to think, plan, and evaluate in terms of problems. It is dedicated to reducing or controlling negative developmental experiences or acts, through prevention, early intervention, social services, and/or treatment when problems escalate. It is an important and useful approach to healing what ails us as a culture. Indeed, health-compromising, future-jeopardizing, safety-threatening environments and actions must be tackled head on. But by itself, this approach is limited and incomplete. As one wise sage of youth development, Karen Pittman, puts it, problem-free is not the same as health, a concept which demands the pursuit of the positive as much or more than reduction of the negative.

Promoting the Positive: The Other Side of the Coin

In raising healthy and whole children and adolescents, like attention needs to be given to naming, counting, understanding, and promoting the positive. It is the other side of the coin. The two sides of the coin, reducing the negative and promoting the positive, are not opposites. There is a synergy, an interaction between these. For example, the strategy of promoting the positive (e.g., belonging, connection, engagement, empowerment) can reduce the negative. And reducing family dysfunction or economic inequality, for example, clears the way for belonging, connection, and empowerment to occur.

Three approaches to naming and promoting positive psychosocial development emerged in the 1990s. They travel under the names of "resiliency," "youth development," and "asset development." Each of these three is both a conceptual model naming core elements of positive human development and an area of practice seeking to alter policy, environments, and individual-level characteristics.

Of the three, resiliency has the deepest research tradition. Its scientific grounding is in studies of children and adults who overcome or transcend adversity. In essence, it discovers and names the strengths, experiences, and environmental conditions which bolster, inoculate, and protect. *Resiliency in Action* provides the best, ongoing synthesis of this field's research and practice.

Youth development is an emerging and somewhat eclectic conceptual framework seeking to define the skills and competencies youth need to be successful in a rapidly changing world. It is more a philosophy than an area of direct, integrated scientific inquiry. Youth development practitioners advocate paying attention to needs, skills, and competencies during the second decade of life, with an accent on organizing youth programs, schools, and community policy to be particularly responsive to engagement, belonging, connection, and empowerment.

> **"It has become normative for most youth in all communities to lack many of the developmental assets."**

Perhaps the strongest articulator of this model/philosophy/way-of-thinking is Karen Pittman. In 1991, Pittman and Michelle Cahill produced a seminal paper titled *A New Vision: Promoting Youth Development*. It provided a first attempt to name the critical components of youth development needed to promote "fully-prepared" adults. The model included both needs (safety, belonging, self-worth, independence, closeness, competence, self-awareness) and competencies (health, sociability, vocational competence, citizen-ship, knowledge, reasoning, and creativity).

Asset development is a relatively new conceptualization of healthy child and adolescent development, rooted in an ongoing national research and community change initiative at Search Institute in Minneapolis. The recent configuration of developmental assets synthesizes research on 30 initially identified environmental and individual dynamics (expanded to 40, see chart), which serve as protective factors inhibiting health-compromising behavior and/or as enhancement factors which promote academic achievement and parallel forms of success.

The 40 assets are grouped into eight categories: support, empowerment, boundaries and expectations, the constructive use of time, commitment to learning, values, social competencies, and positive identity. The national research, based on assessments of public school students—both middle school and high school—in hundreds of school districts, documents both that it has become normative for most youth in all communities to lack many of the developmental assets and that as the number of assets rises, multiple forms of "high risk" behavior decrease and multiple forms of thriving (school success, affirmation of diversity) increase (Benson, Galbraith, & Espeland, 1994, and Benson, 1997).

Resiliency, Youth Development, Asset Development: Unique, Yet Similar

These three approaches, each naming essential elements of psychosocial development, emanate from somewhat different sources. Resiliency researchers tend to identify developmental factors which distinguish individuals who cope successfully with adversity—versus those for whom adaptation is less effective. Youth development and its advocates and practitioners tend to focus on the competencies needed to help youth transition from adolescence into successful adulthood. Implied in this approach is a deep critique of how this society relates to adolescents, particularly those in urban or other settings in which systems and policy are too inattentive, unresponsive, or counterproductive. Asset development is a framework which articulates basic developmental necessities during the first two decades of life. Asset development theory extends the cultural critique, arguing that many of the core processes of healthy development, rooted ideally in norms and relationships within community, are ruptured or incomplete for most American youth.

Not surprisingly, the three models both share intellectual space and at the same time possess unique accents. The content similarities are pronounced. Each model highlights the importance of caring relationships, meaningful participation in decision-making, organizational life and community, problem-solving skills, social competencies, adult advocacy, and personal efficacy. The implication of this heavy overlap is that some of the "good stuff" plays multiple human development roles.

> **"Not surprisingly, the three models both share intellectual space and at the same time possess unique accents."**

Each of the three approaches to naming the characteristics of healthy human development have high face validity. And each has devotees developing strategies and tactics to build and promote the elements of healthy development. This is creative and exciting work, with evaluations underway or emerging to help refine models and understand best practices. The Kellogg Youth Initiative Partnerships initiative, designed to unleash youth development energies in Michigan communities, is grounded in an ongoing learning and reflection process. Project Competence at the University of Minnesota is an ongoing program development and research effort to "understand the development of competence and resilience in the presence of risk." And Search Institute's efforts to mobilize communities have been informed by a five-and-a-half year Colorado initiative to unite communities, systems, and citizens around the asset development model.

In promoting the characteristics of positive human development, multiple strategies are needed as shown in the chart above. Though all three "schools of thought" speak of all three strategies, resiliency has particular strength in shaping hands-on strategies, with particular applicability to vulnerable youth. Youth development practitioners have particular strength in awakening youth-serving programs and systems to systemic commitment to positive development. The asset-development model has its strength in unleashing community-wide efforts.

Again, the distinctions named above are about tendencies and instincts, not absolutes. Over time, it appears that the distinctions are becoming blurred. Resiliency is increasingly discussed as a general human competence that should be nurtured in all youth and adults; developmental assets are being appropriated by program developers in designing short-term interventions.

But this is not the kind of choice I'd advocate. Because the three models are highly complementary, and because all youth need greater systems of support in both the short-term and long-term, the integration and synthesis of the three models will take us further.

None of us—researchers, model developers, or practitioners—yet knows enough of the truth about promoting positive development in a child-unfriendly world to claim we know the way. Hence, this essay is, more than anything, an invitation to build bridges of dialogue across the three "schools of thought," to unleash the kind of research dollars needed to refine and integrate and encourage practitioners to experiment with synthesizing the approaches and then sharing their wisdom with all kindred spirits and soul mates. Ultimately, if this is to become a child-friendly culture, we will need the strength of cooperation, shared inquiry, friendly debate, and an openness to change.

Resiliency, youth development, and asset development are variations on a theme. And the theme is more important than the players.

	Resiliency	Youth Development	Asset Development
Key Strategies	Development of hands-on-programs and interventions	Transformation of youth-serving systems via training, planning, and policy	Uniting all sectors of community; unclashing and sustaining long-term movements of residents and systems
Target Populations	Vulnerable children and adolescents	Ages 12-21	All children and adolescents

Integrating and Synthesizing the Models

It is difficult—at this moment in history—to articulate which approach (resiliency, youth development, asset development) is the best for addressing a particular need. This ambiguity is fed by conceptual overlap and the infancy of evaluation studies. Until the science of promoting positive healthy development catches up to its practice, practitioners have to make difficult choices about how to proceed. If one must choose just one approach, then I would suggest tilting to the resiliency paradigm for shaping interventions and approaches needed now for vulnerable or troubled or "at risk" youth and to the asset-development paradigm for reclaiming the power and energy of intact, whole, and effective communities.

References

Benson, P.L., Galbraith, J., & Espeland, P. (1994). *What kids need to succeed.* Minneapolis, MN: Free Spirit Publishing, Inc.

Benson, P. (1997). *All kids are our kids.* San Francisco, CA: Jossey-Bass.

Masten, A.S., et al. (1995). The structure and coherence of competence from childhood through adolescence. *Child Development, 66,* 1535-1659.

Pittman, K.J. & Cahill, M. (1991). *A new vision: Promoting youth development.* Washington, DC: The Center for Youth Development and Policy Research.

Dr. Peter Benson is President of Search Institute, an organization of more than 20 social scientists and educators dedicated to "practice research benefiting children and youth" and creators of the "Healthy Communities • Healthy Youth™" initiative. He has authored several publications, including What Kids Need to Succeed.

RESILIENCY AND YOUTH DEVELOPMENT

Changing the Condition, Place, and View of Young People in Society: An Interview with Bill Lofquist

by Bonnie Benard, M.S.W.

BB: You've been a visionary in this whole field of youth development. Your work has been trying to put a whole human development/youth development perspective into all of youth services and youth-serving systems.

Would you define what "youth development" means to you?

BL: Youth development refers to the overall condition and place of young people in the community, how they are viewed and valued, opportunities of development available to them, resources available to them when they have problems, opportunities they have to contribute policies that effect them, the quality of their relationships with peers and adults.

> *"Youth development refers to the overall condition and place of young people in the community, how they are viewed and valued, opportunities of development available to them, resources available to them when they have problems, opportunities they have to contribute policies that effect them, the quality of their relationships with peers and adults."*

My definition really takes a fairly broad look at the circumstance and life experience of young persons—both internally as they develop as individuals and their external relationships as they interact with the people around them and the basic institutions of our society.

BB: It shouldn't be considered a radical perspective to have the kind of child-centered or youth-centered service system that you advocate and yet somehow it still seems to be the case. Would you share how you came to this perspective, just a little bit about who you are and what you've done?

BL: I guess it would go back to my own early experience. I was born in Mississippi and grew up in the South during the time of segregation. I became aware fairly early on that the culture of my family and the values that I got from my family were far and away stronger for me than the culture of the community in which I lived.

I moved from Mississippi to Virginia when I was nine years old for a few months and then to North Carolina, which I consider home. The strength of my family culture personally overpowered that strong southern segre-gationist culture. And that was a real issue just by virtue of where I lived.

It became a very personal thing both in regard to race as well as many, many other issues. I think the same values that inform our attitude about race inform other attitudes. My dad was a Presbyterian minister who worked for social agencies in a variety of things in Asheville, North Carolina. He would frequently bring home people that he was working with and sort of used our house as an informal foster home. That was a routine experience at our house in my later elementary years and junior high and senior high years. I think that had a lot of influence on me.

I went to seminary for three years and during that time became convinced that I wanted to work in child welfare. I attended the University of North Carolina School of Social Work after seminary. Another influence that I found important was volunteer work in the summers that was organized by the American Friends Service Committee, the Quakers. I worked in a "Native American Community" in Maine and one that was in Europe, and one that was in the Illinois State Training School for Boys, outside Chicago. After graduation, I went to work in a church-related children's home. So from the beginning, I was involved in youth-focused kinds of things.

I then went to work for the University of North Carolina School of Social Work as a faculty field instructor at a juvenile court and worked there for about six years. Then I got involved in the late '60s in the youth service movement. That's when I really got into prevention work.

I had a community or sociological bent probably more strongly than a psychological bent. I was an undergraduate major in sociology, and I was interested in institutions. By institutions, I mean the basic institutions of family and school, religious institutions, the economy, and government, and the impact those have on people, and the interaction we have with the institutions that we participate in.

Also, I've come over the years to have a stronger and stronger feeling that the way a community or society views and treats its young people, that's basically the way it views and treats all of its citizens. Young people serve as a metaphor for people of all ages. And the general belief we have about youth development can generally be applied to people of all ages.

BB: That's certainly what Margaret Mead said, too. You're in good company. I think Meister Eckhardt, a mystic in the Middle Ages, said something like, "God is like a river and is accessed by many different wells." No matter what language we use, we're talking about the same good stuff.

> *"The way a community or society views and treats its young people [is] basically the way it views and treats all of its citizens. Young people serve as a metaphor for people of all ages."*

BL: People all around the world are essentially looking at the same phenomenon, though we come at it from different angles. But there's an inherent consistency frequently found as people look at different philosophies, different theologies, different ways of politics—that we're all dealing with the same phenomenon wherever we are in the world.

BB: It seems that you're getting at that deep humanity that we all share. Obviously, your family and the loving and caring of your father in taking in other young people allowed you to see the humanity of marginalized groups.

BL: Yes, and especially being in the South at that time. The civil rights movement to me was a very exciting time. It represented a breaking out of that confining culture that really did violence to many, many people, both black and white.

BB: We need another one! Now, you've had this perspective for over 30 years. You started the wonderful publication, *New Designs for Youth Development,* in 1980. It's interesting to me that people are starting to rediscover youth development. I go a lot of places and hear people talking about Karen Pittman and the work that she did while she was at the Center for Youth Development and Policy Research in Washington, DC I think this organization brought a lot of new attention to youth development through Karen's leadership in getting a strong funding base and her focus on trying to develop a policy perspective that's very different from where we seem to have arrived in prevention.

This brings me to another issue of looking at the whole question of prevention and its relation to youth development.

When you wrote *Discovering the Meaning of Prevention* (1983), which is still one of the best books in the whole field, you very diplomatically discussed how prevention has typically been defined from a public health perspective in terms of primary, secondary, and tertiary, but that the whole medical model approach has kind of moved us towards approaches of fixing deficits—in kids especially—and fixing them with programs. It seems to me that this has been the federal policy approach channeling the moneys that have flowed to the prevention field.

Finally, my question: Do you think that this risk-focused approach, the idea that we can fix individuals and kids with programs, has maybe had a negative effect—what John McKnight calls an "iatrogenic" effect—that may be hurting youth development efforts?

BL: I've labeled it the "diagnose problem" model. One of the problems with it is that it's determined from the point of view of the person doing the diagnosis, who is usually a professional. While that's an important perspective, it's a very limited and limiting perspective. It's linear. It's from the perspective of the way the diagnoser is looking at it. And the shortcoming of the model is that when we ask, "Where does success lie?", that model really doesn't give a way back towards success.

I think that what's happened as a result is that we have terribly, terribly fragmented human service work by seeing some programs (which really are sets of activities) as being prevention and some as being treatment. And the context of intervention is a real muddy context anyway, so that any effort to change anything is really an intervention process. We need an alternative model to this "diagnose problem" perspective.

I've tried to develop and use for the past 18 to 20 years now an alternative model that I called the "Arenas of Human Service Activity." I now call it the "Arenas of Action" because I think it's much broader than just human service work. My approach makes a distinction between development and problem solving. I define development as an active process of creating conditions and fostering personal attributes that promote the well-being of people; problem solving is a reactive, corrective effort to bring about change where there is a recognized problem. Both of these are obviously very important. I think most of what we do falls pretty clearly and cleanly into one or the other.

What the "diagnose problem" model doesn't do is show the dynamic interplay between development and problem-solving work—and that success lies on the development side. Effective treatment is going to lead people towards a positive development mode or way of viewing life and relating to life. What we need is a model which might start with problems but points back in the other direction towards development.

BB: Towards developing people so that they can feel a sense of their own power and begin to solve their own problem—which is the only way they'll ever be solved to begin with! I've been reading a book called *No Enemy Within* by Dawna Markova, a Jungian psychologist, and she states that in our culture we have become experts at diagnosing problems and at putting all the problems inside ourselves and all the solutions outside ourselves—where only experts can solve them. They can do this with programs! I thought this was a good way to say it.

BL: On the other hand, in the alternative model, the nature of a specific action is determined by the purpose of the activity

> *"What the 'diagnose problem' model doesn't do is show the dynamic interplay between development and problem-solving work—and that success lies on the development side."*

and not by a diagnosis. In this more dynamic model, human service planning can move clearly and easily between development and problem solving depending upon the purpose. In this way success and problem solving can be described as moving toward development work, and development work can be seen as an alternative to problem-solving work. Treatment professionals can more clearly become involved in development work, thus enriching the concept of treatment in opening new opportunities for the professional and the beneficiary of the work. People in treatment can be participants in development work, both as resource people and as beneficiaries. And partnerships can be shaped that bring people together in new ways. I'm finding people's response to this alternative way of looking at things is one of excitement and hope.

BB: Oh, yes. Why, then, do you think this perspective is always—I called it radical earlier—a kind of "counter-cultural" perspective?

BL: It's radical in the best sense of that word in that it gets more deeply into the root of what we might be concerning ourselves with. Radical is not a dirty word. I think it's an important word—basic, fundamental questioning of the status

quo. I think that some of the methods we use don't lead to change at all. They're more related to the status quo. A lot of the methods we're using in human service work now—and I think that increasing numbers of people agree with this—is just not getting the work done. They're not effective. They're not getting the results that we need to be getting through the work that we do. So many of our resources in human service work are used carrying out human service activities and not getting very significant results. We need to look more deeply and fundamentally at what we're doing and question that deeply; this is the beginning of fundamental or transformational change. That's what we need to be more attentive to—and the word radical relates to this.

BB: It certainly says something about having human service work really be work in the community and not just carrying out bureaucratic mandates and federal policies. It's going to take some really deep commitment to community development.

BL: I think that community development is essentially a local responsibility and a local transaction that takes place where people work and live and learn and spend their time and spend their leisure. This gets into some really important policy considerations. The localness of the work that we do needs to be supported by policies and practices and understandings that occur at those levels in government that are removed from the local situation. People that work even at the county level or the state level or the national level need to be helped to become more attuned to what local realities are.

BB: In the book *The End of Work*, Jeremy Rifkin says our essential question is, how do we achieve our sense of social

> *"Radical is not a dirty word. I think it's an important word—basic, fundamental questioning of the status quo."*

identity in a world devoid of work? When he discusses solutions he says we aren't looking at the incredible power of the third sector, which is the volunteer sector, and small community-based organizations. If we can support those community-based organizations through giving our tax dollars back to these local community organizations, we would really see systems where communities truly would take care of their own.

BL: I think that what we value needs to be seen as legitimate work and there are all kinds of quality of life issues that the economy needs to be responsive to. We do need to reshape the economy. I think it's in as much need of radical transition as the other institutions. And the way those five basic institutions [family, school, church, economy, and government] interact with one another is so important to the quality of a society.

So we need to redefine the work to be done. The way I've tried to go about doing this and engaging other people in thinking about it is to think about the whole concept of a compassionate society. It seems to me that when we think about that, the alternative is an antagonistic society. A mirror that we can hold up to what we do and how we do it has to do with whether what we're doing is compassionate or whether it's antagonistic. Some of what we do even within human service work—that has the best of intentions—can become quite antagonistic, especially when the methods we use tend to view and treat people as objects or recipients rather than respect and engage them as resource people.

> *"Some of what we do even within human service work—that has the best of intentions—can become quite antagonistic, especially when the methods we use tend to view and treat people as objects or recipients rather than respect and engage them as resource people."*

BB: It's really that ultimate challenge of whether we develop compassion or whether we keep promoting a greed-based society based on consumerism. It's clearly a major challenge for the whole next century. It's kind of mind-boggling.

How do you see the concept of resiliency, and resiliency research, supporting community development in the work that you do?

BL: Resiliency research has certainly been deepening my belief that there's a powerful, powerful connection between looking at the way an individual grows and develops and the way that the community impacts us. The interaction between the person and the situation in which they find themselves is not an either/or situation at all. It's always a both/and. I think if we lean too much toward either the psychological or sociological, we get ourselves in trouble. In whatever we do, we must take both the person and the situation into consideration.

A number of years ago my wife and I went to one of Sid Simon's personal growth workshops. We went to two week-long ones. Those were both marvelous experiences. Because while Sid Simon works in the personal growth area, from the first minute of his workshop he begins to create a community context in the workshop for doing that, and everything he talks about has implications for the individual's relationship to the larger community through the relationships that they have and the quality of those relationships.

The whole process of resiliency is so integral to both personal development and to community development. And there is both a personal and a community side to the concept of resiliency. I'm finding that exploring this concept in new ways is adding a whole new dimension, even to the community development side of things. What we've been trying to do in these workshops is to relate the concept of resiliency not only to what comes from the inside out from the individual but also to look at those realities that impact us and to look at the way we relate to those realities and the inner strength that we need just to live.

BB: One thing so compelling to me about Emmy Werner's work is that she is one of the resiliency researchers that really understands that transactional process of the person and the environment—and that both of these are human systems. It's also fascinating that no matter whether you look at an individual or a small group or a classroom or a community—these are all human systems. It's the power of the relationships that we create and the beliefs that we have about people and their opportunities to contribute and participate that are the factors that promote success in any of those systems.

BL: Exactly. I remember back in college in a zoology course, "Ontogeny recapitulates phylogeny." What I understand that to mean is that the growth and development of the individual replicates what has happened over time in the growth of the whole species. It can even be seen in the development of the embryo. This is getting into evolution. However, the relationship of the individual is so incredibly phenomenal. Physiologically, there is a replication or a recapitulation of what the scientists believe may have happened over time. We have within each of us, individually, that relationship to the larger picture.

I think it's so astounding and mind boggling. It's awe-inspiring when we think about it. Then when we begin to look at the world around us and within us from a larger development perspective, we see the connectedness of things. It's not accidental that so many wonderful serendipitous kinds of things are constantly happening.

BB: I think the word "connectedness" is one of the key words in youth development. It is critical to our work that we help people see those connections. Connections to other people and to ideas and probably connections to a deeper spiritual essence is absolutely the critical essence of a developmental approach.

One last question: What is your hope for the future of the youth development movement in human services?

BL: That's a very good question. For me it's focused in one of our models that I call the "Spectrum of Attitudes." It really has to do with the nature and quality of relationships between and among people. It says, quite simply, that there are basically three ways that people view and treat other people...as objects, as recipients, and as resources. There

> *"There is both a personal and a community side to the concept of resiliency. I'm finding that exploring this concept in new ways is adding a whole new dimension, even to the community development side of things."*

are qualitative differences between and among those three things. One of the things that I've tried to do in my workshops and my writing is a consciousness-raising approach toward encouraging people to consider the qualitative differences towards those three attitudes and kinds of behavior.

What people tend to come to over and over again is that much of youth work in the past and present (because of cultural and other kinds of things) has tended to view and treat young people as either objects—of our good intentions at best, or we've actually been abusive of young people at worst—or we've seen them as recipients of our well-intended approaches to things, rather than respecting and engaging them as resources.

What I would like to see in the future of youth work is attention to what I see as a civil rights issue in our society: age discrimination, which is not unlike race discrimination and gender discrimination. We need a new kind of consciousness about young people as individuals and as people in their own right. Adults don't always know what's good for young people. We need—from the earliest ages—to begin engaging children and youth in making decisions that affect them. This starts best at very, very early ages—from birth really—in the family.

When we begin to show respect for young people as resources and our consciousness is raised in that direction, we're going to find increasingly that this is directly related to the kinds of symptomatic behaviors we see young people express. We continually find ourselves reacting to substance abuse, teen pregnancy, gang violence, delinquency, under achievement, you know all the rest. We can make a long list of them. Those symptoms are essentially related to the nature and quality of experience in relationships that young people have from the time that they're born.

I would like to see us reconceptualize youth work from a community development perspective that doesn't so much see young people as the objects of good intentions of adults, but sees young people as key actors and participants and partners with adults. Some of the best and most exciting breakthroughs I see happening in youth work is built around that idea. It's creating new partnerships between young people and adults as very respectful relationships.

BB: I think you've said it all right there: it is that whole idea of respect and somehow making those intergenerational linkages. While in the past, societies have seen young people as resources because their work was needed, we must reclaim that perspective once again. The work of young people is desperately needed now; it's just that adult society doesn't realize it! We need their energy, their enthusiasm, their creativity, their morality, their caring for the earth, and their work to repair all the damage adult society has done.

> *"We need a new kind of consciousness about young people as individuals and as people in their own right. Adults don't always know what's good for young people.*

I think your work is putting this message out there—a message we probably need now more than ever. There is certainly a lot of youth bashing going on, unfortunately, by a lot of federal agencies that a lot of us have worked for.

BL: We need to practice that in the localness of the things that we're doing. Yet it's so related to the larger issues we see in the world of human dignity, of human rights, of democracy.

BB: It's thinking globally and acting locally. You are certainly an inspiration to all of us in doing just this.

Bill Lofquist lives and works in, Tucson, AZ.

Bonnie Benard, M.S.W., has written widely and conducted workshops and trainings on resiliency for nearly 20 years. She currently works in the Health and Human Development Program of WestEd 's Oakland, CA office, where she has helped develop a statewide survey of students' perceptions of the protective factors in their lives (www.wested.org/hks). She can be reached by email at bbenard@ wested.org.

CHAPTER 3

Resiliency and Asset Development:
A Continuum for Youth Success

by Nan Henderson, M.S.W.

A New England school district I worked with was struggling with some important questions: How does the resiliency approach to working with young people connect to the asset-development approach promoted by the Search Institute (see related chapter five)? When should one approach be used and when another? Do they overlap? Do they involve doing different things for kids? How can we sort this out for all those in our school community who are interested in both fostering resiliency and asset development for students? Finally, given the reality of limited time and resources, which approach should our district concentrate on?

> *"Fostering resiliency and asset development are complimentary approaches to working with youth."*

When I was in the district, these questions were addressed to me. I am asked similar questions in communities around the country. Many of my colleagues report that they, too, have been asked for a clarification of the similarities and differences between the resiliency and asset-building approach to youth development.

As Benson suggests in his article on the same subject (see chapter one), fostering resiliency and asset development are complimentary approaches to working with youth. It is clear to me that the choice must be to do both, rather than one or the other, because each approach provides important contributions to the positive development of young people.

Why All Kids Need Both Resiliency and Asset Development

Fostering resiliency and increasing the developmental assets of young people comprise the continuum of a comprehensive approach to improving the lives of all kids.

Resiliency, as Benson points out, was initially aimed primarily at youth identified as "at risk," but it is increasingly recognized as a need of all children and youth. The evolution of the definition of resiliency to an ability to spring back, rebound, and/or successfully adapt in the face of adversity (Henderson & Milstein, 2003), including all the environmental risks, personal traumas and tragedies, or individual challenges such as physical, mental, or emotional disabilities, clarifies why every young person alive (indeed, every person of any age!) needs to develop this capacity. It is of course more critical, and often more difficult, for those faced with greater adversity and tragedy to be resilient than for those whose lives are "easier." But some resiliency researchers and theorists argue (persuasively, in my opinion) that the process of encountering and successfully meeting challenges, and becoming wiser and stronger in the process, is, in fact, the overall purpose of life for all (Richardson, et al., 1990). No one can deny the "high risk" and uncertain nature of the world children and youth encounter today (documented by the Search Institute research finding that only a small fraction of youth experience the optimum number of assets for adolescent development) that contributes to the requirement of resiliency for all kids.

Developing resiliency is first and foremost a person-to-person process. Resiliency is forged in the crucible of caring human relationships, as documented by the numerous studies and personal reports (see Seita, chapter six) that explore just how people do succeed in the face of often seemingly overwhelming obstacles. The crucial foundation of a resiliency-building relationship, however, is what I have labeled the resiliency attitude, which is characterized by the messages "I see what is right with you," "Your strengths are more powerful than your problems," "No matter what your past, you can be successful in the future," and "We will work together to find a way for your success."

> *"The crucial foundation of a resiliency-building relationship, however, is what I have labeled the resiliency attitude."*

While resiliency is built in relationships characterized by the resiliency attitude and unconditional caring and empowering interactions, asset development is more focused on rebuilding "the societal infrastructure" (Search, 1996) of support for children and youth, with an emphasis on organizational and community mobilization. Examples of this approach include increasing opportunities in the community for intergenerational interaction, engaging children and teenagers in community service, and the establishment by businesses of "family-friendly" policies. In the very broad sense, asset development also focuses on local, state, and national politics and policies that relate to youth. In a narrower sense, it gives much organizational and programmatic direction to the spheres that surround each child: families, neighborhoods, schools, churches, and other community groups.

This, then, is the resiliency/youth development/asset development continuum (see diagrammed):

1. Resiliency is at the heart, developed in caring and empowering daily interactions, which provide right now most of the environmental protective factors that mitigate the impact of stress in a young person's life.

2. Youth development (as Benson explains) approaches and asset development approaches are inherent in programs and organizational structures and strategies, which may take time to redesign.

3. Asset development is the long-term guiding force of communities—improving the environmental infrastructure in significant ways, a complex and often political process that can take years.

> *"The resiliency attitude can be summarized as a strength-based philosophy, and must be infused across this resiliency/youth development/asset development continuum."*

Infusing the "Resiliency Attitude" Across the Continuum

The resiliency attitude, which can be summarized as a strength-based philosophy, must be infused across this resiliency/youth development/asset development continuum. To create intergenerational interaction opportunities or service learning programs, for example, that are characterized by typical adult attitudes and behaviors towards "youth at risk"—labeling, condemning, lecturing, disempowering, and distancing—will doom this potential asset building to failure.

This critical issue of attitude is, in fact, one danger of the entire asset assessment approach that forms the basis of the Search Institute research. While resiliency research is primarily a body of life span studies, which show how

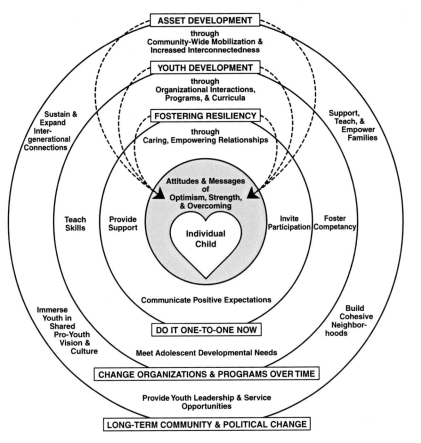

The Resiliency/Youth Development/Asset Development Continuum Needed By All Youth

individuals over the long run succeed in the face of great adversity (that certainly includes "too few developmental assets"), asset research (using the "Profiles of Student Life" developed by the Search Institute) is similar to most risk research that measures only "a snap shot" of a young person's life at any given time. Both risk research and asset assessment document that at a given moment in time (when the research is conducted) the absence of important environmental supports is correlated with the presence of "at risk" behaviors, including alcohol and other drug abuse, early/unsafe sexual activity, violence and gang involvement, and problems in school. Both of these types of research fail to document, however, what many resiliency researchers refer to as the innate human capacity to successfully overcome the environmental risks, i.e., asset deficits—the ability in the long run, with the help of both internal capacities and external environmental protective factors that mitigate the impact of risks, to become successful adults that "love well, work well, play well, and expect well."

In my work as a consultant and trainer in hundreds of communities and school districts around the country, I have heard about disturbing distortions of the asset assessment approach that fly in the face of the resiliency research documenting the need of young people to encounter "the resiliency attitude" in their environments. These include reports of school counselors and teachers using informal asset checklists (not even the scientifically validated instrument) to scare both parents and kids; classrooms of children filling out these informal checklists and comparing scores (and sometimes taunting peers who checked only a few of the assets on their questionnaire); and children who are "devastated" when their score on the checklist is only eight or 12. These examples of working with asset-building intention without "the resiliency attitude," result in turning a strength-based approach into a deficit-focused one, and in the process, hurting kids.

> **"Every child, no matter how few his or her assets, must get the message 'you can succeed' rather than the still-prevalent attitude of doom and gloom."**

Though I hope these are rare occurrences, such reports emphasize how critical it is for all who are engaged in youth development and asset development—even as we are painfully aware of the significant gaps in the "asset infrastructure" for children—to adopt the resiliency-based strength-affirming philosophy described above. Every child, no matter how few his or her assets, must get the message "you can succeed" rather than the still-prevalent attitude of doom and gloom.

I Had Only 16 Assets

One reason I believe this is true is because I had only 16 assets (out of the initial 30 identified by Search) when I was in junior high and high school, nine short of the 25 Search recommended as optimum for youth success. And yet, like Seita (see chapter six), I, too, have emerged as a resilient adult. Like many other resilient adults now involved in promoting resiliency, I question how my own resilient recovery from childhood adversity would have been impacted by an early label as an "at risk" child or an "asset-poor" one. What would my long-term reaction have been to a checklist that showed me I had only half of the "assets" deemed important to youth success (16 assets are described as "a start, but not enough" by Benson, Galbraith, & Espeland, 1994, p.6)? Fortunately, these labels (and such unscientific use of "checklists") were not being liberally applied to kids when I was in school in the 1960s. I did have along the way several adults who knew some of my struggles and yet conveyed to me that resiliency attitude of optimistic caring and empowerment, and numerous others—never having been exposed to the current stereotypes

about "youth at risk"—who conveyed success-promoting messages to all kids.

On the other hand, I would have benefited enormously—and would have no doubt rebounded with less pain and less potential for lifelong scars—from living in a community and/or attending schools consciously working to create asset-rich environments (without negatively stigmatizing or stereotyping anyone). Improving the developmental infrastructure for youth is a crucial goal for families, schools, churches, community organizations, and entire communities. But youth and asset development must happen on the foundation of resiliency research: with the "resiliency attitude" and with the certainty that most "asset-poor" kids will eventually succeed. Increasing the prevalence of assets in young people's lives in the long run will no doubt make this route easier, less painful, and less fraught with danger, than it is today.

A Message for All Youth: "You Are Resilient"

At a conference a few years ago, I heard a group of students share their incredible stories of overcoming sexual abuse, addicted and homeless parents and parents who kicked them out of their homes, being regularly beaten, and involvement with gangs and violence. Each of these young people had rebounded from great adversity and were now experiencing life success. True to the resiliency research, they each pointed out pivotal adults, most often outside of their immediate families, who had provided them with the

> **"What would my long-term reaction have been to a check-list that showed me I had only half of the 'assets' deemed important to youth success?"**

caring, optimistic, role-modeling relationships that helped them to do so. They were selected by a school counselor to tell their stories at a resiliency conference because of their resiliency. Yet, when I spoke to them about it, each of them dismissed the idea. "I'm not resilient; I just survived as best I could," was a typical comment. They all admitted they had never heard the term "resilient," but when they did hear it and learned its definition, they all insisted the word resilient didn't apply to them. How many times have they heard they were "at risk?" I wondered. I was sure that term was one that had been communicated to them frequently.

Those of us who work with and parent youth need to tell them that they have within them innate resilience, and help them to identify the internal and external characteristics of their lives that they can draw upon in times of adversity. With this realization, I have begun talking to groups of students about their resilience, using the list of questions boxed here. Often, I meet with peer mentors, natural helpers, and other groups of youth leaders. After I explain the concept of resiliency to them, I ask them what kinds of circumstances they have had to overcome, i.e., what in their lives has necessitated them drawing upon their resilience? Typical responses to this question include: parents divorced, friend died, pet died, worry about friends who are drinking, worry about friends using drugs, worry about friends engaging in unsafe sex, didn't make team or wasn't accepted to some other type of organization, just moved, parents are fighting, a parent has been layed off from work, struggling in school, illness or death of a family member. I then share with them characteristics of resiliency, and help them to identify the

> *"Youth and asset development must happen on the foundation of resiliency research: with 'the resiliency attitude' and with the certainty that most 'asset-poor' kids will eventually succeed."*

characteristics within themselves and the people and organizations within their environments that do—and can in times of stress—help them be resilient. I believe these problems are typical for all youth (and many face even greater difficulties) and that learning about resiliency can help make it a reality.

Recently, after an afternoon of such interaction with a group of students, a mother of one of the girls present approached me that evening at a community meeting. "What did you say to my daughter today?" she asked. She reported that the girl had come home with a completely changed attitude about a difficult problem she was dealing with in her life. "I know now I can get past this," the girl told her mother. "And I have some ideas about how to do it."

Messages of resiliency can be given anytime. They can have an immediate impact. They can be integrated into almost any curriculum by utilizing stories that show human resiliency and then discussing the inherent lessons. They can become a part of all of interactions with youth, by actions (as Seita so poignantly shares), and in conversation. ("You are a wise girl," I tell my niece. Listen to that wisdom in your heart. It will tell you what is right.") They are a crucial foundation of an integrated, comprehensive positive approach for children and youth, which starts with that message of strength and optimism in caring relationships, and includes all the programmatic and community change recommendations from the fields of youth and asset development.

---

for students...
QUESTIONS FOR DISCUSSION ABOUT YOUR RESILIENCY

1. If resiliency is defined as "the ability to bounce back from, and successfully overcome risks and adversity," why are you a "resilient" person?
   A. What are some of the struggles, challenges, difficulties you have faced in the past or currently face (go into only as much detail as you feel like sharing!) ?
   B. Share how you overcame these difficulties....
      • What did you do?
      • What beliefs about yourself and others guided you?
      • WHO helped you?
      • How did they help?
      • What else helped you?
2. How can you use these same things in the future when you are dealing with problems? What can you do that has worked in the past? Who can you go to that will give you support? Is there a way to maintain greater access to these individuals?
3. What advice do you have for other kids going through problems, risks, and difficulty?
4. What advice do you have for adults trying to help kids be resilient?
5. What barriers do you think stand in the way of kids being resilient? What ideas do you have about how we can change these barriers?

References

Benson, P., Galbraith, J., & Espeland, P. (1994). *What kids need to succeed.* Minneapolis, MN: Free Spirit Publishing, Inc.

Henderson, N. & Milstein, M. (2003). *Resiliency in schools: Making it happen for students and educators.* Thousand Oaks, CA: Corwin Press.

Richardson, G., Neiger, B., Jenson, S., & Kumpfer, K. (1990). The resiliency model. *Health Education, 21* (6), 33-39.

Search Institute. (1996). *Healthy communities, healthy youth: A national initiative of Search Institute to unite communities for children and adolescents.* Minneapolis, MN: Search Institute.

Nan Henderson, M.S.W. is an international speaker, writer, and president of Resiliency In Action, a publishing and training company in Southern CA. She has authored several articles and coauthored four books on fostering resiliency, including Resiliency In Action: Practical Ideas for Overcoming Risks and Building Strengths in Youth, Families, and Communities *and* Resiliency In Schools: Making It Happen for Students and Educators. *She can be contacted at nhenderson@resiliency.com or at by calling 800-440-5171. More information is available at www.resiliency.com.*

CHAPTER 4

Developmental Assets:
A Framework for All Youth

The following is reprinted with permission from the booklet, Healthy Communities, Healthy Youth: A National Initiative of Search Institute to Unite Communities for Children and Adolescents, *published by the Search Institute, 700 South Third, Suite 210, Minneapolis, MN 55415, 1-800-888-7828.*

Beneath the headlines about youth violence, crime, pregnancy, and other problems is an even more important and urgent story: In all towns and cities across America, the developmental infrastructure is crumbling. Too few young people grow up experiencing key ingredients for their healthy development. They do not experience support from adults, build relationships across generations, or hear consistent messages about boundaries and values. Most have too little to do that is positive and constructive. The result is that communities and the nation are overwhelmed with problems and needs in the lives of youth.

Thus the real challenge facing America is not to attack one problem at a time in a desperate attempt to stop the hemorrhaging. The real challenge is to shift our thinking to a new approach—one that addresses deeper causes and needs. The real challenge is to rebuild the developmental infrastructure for our children and adolescents.

Though professionals and the public sector have a role to play, much of the responsibility and capacity for the healthy development of youth is in the hands of the people. Search Institute has created a model for understanding the developmental needs of children and adolescents. Rooted in research on [hundreds of thousands of] American youth in grades six to 12, the framework identifies 40 building blocks, or "developmental assets," that all children and adolescents need to grow up healthy, competent, and caring (see next page). These assets provide a powerful paradigm for mobilizing communities, organizations, and individuals to take action for youth—action that can make a real difference.

The Power of Assets

When drawn together, these assets are powerful shapers of young people's behavior. The more assets young people experience, the more they engage in positive behaviors, such as volunteering and succeeding in school. The fewer they have, the more likely they are to engage in risk-taking behaviors, such as alcohol and other drug abuse, antisocial behavior, violence, and others (see graphs). Thus, while each asset must be understood and is important, the most powerful message of developmental assets comes in seeing them as a whole. These assets are cumulative or additive; the more the better.

In short, young people who experience more of these assets are more likely to grow up caring, competent, and responsible. This important relationship between developmental assets and choices made has been documented for all types of youth, regardless of age, gender, geographical region, town size, or race/ethnicity.

The Crumbling Infrastructure

Most people recognize that influences such as caring families, discipline, educational commitments, social skills, and other assets are important for healthy development. Yet society seems to have forgotten how to make sure young people experience and develop these things. Out of [all] sixth to twelfth graders who have been surveyed, the average young person experiences only about 16 of the initial 30 assets first studied by Search (see graphs). Furthermore, 76% of young people experience 20 or fewer assets.

The "asset gap" exists in all types and sizes of communities. In fact, youth in 95% of the communities studied [with our original 30 asset model] reported an average of 15 to 17 assets. Thus, in virtually every town, suburb, and city in America, far too many young people are struggling to construct their lives without an adequate foundation upon which to build. What has happened? Many of the ways society has provided these assets are no longer in place because of major societal changes, including the following:

40 DEVELOPMENTAL ASSETS

	ASSET TYPE	ASSET NAME	DEFINITION
EXTERNAL ASSETS	**SUPPORT**	1. Family Support 2. Positive family communication 3. Other adult relationships 4. Caring Neighborhood 5. Caring School Climate 6. Parent involvement in schooling	Family Life provides high levels of love and support Parents and child communicate positively; child is willing to seek parents' advice and counsel Child receives support from three or more non-parent adults Child experiences caring neighbors School provides a caring, encouraging environment Parents are actively involved in helping child succeed in school
	EMPOWERMENT	7. Community values youth 8. Youth given useful roles 9. Community service 10. Safety	Child perceives that community adults value youth Youth are given useful roles in community life Child gives one hour or more per week to serving in one's community Child feels safe in home, school, and neighborhood
	BOUNDARIES AND EXPECTATIONS	11. Family boundaries 12. School boundaries 13. Neighborhood boundaries 14. Adult role models 15. Positive peer influence 16. High expectations	Family has clear rules and consequences; and monitors whereabouts School provides clear rules and consequences Neighbors would report undesirable behavior to family Parent(s) and other adults model prosocial behavior Child's best friends model responsible behavior Both parents and teachers press child to achieve
	TIME	17. Creative activities 18. Youth programs 19. Religious community 20. Time at home	Involved three or more hours per week in lessons or practice in music, theater, or other arts Involved three hours or more per seek in sports, clubs, or organizations at school and/or community organizations Involved one or more hours per week Out with friends "with nothing special to do" two or fewer nights per week
INTERNAL ASSETS	**EDUCATIONAL COMMITMENT**	21. Achievement motivation 22. School performance 23. Homework 24. Bonding to school 25. Reading for pleasure	Child is motivated to do well in school Child has B average or better Child reports one or more hours of homework per day Child cares about her/his school Child reads for pleasure three or more hours per week
	VALUES	26. Caring 27. Equality and social justice 28. Integrity 29. Honesty 30. Responsibility 31. Restraint	Child places high value on helping other people Child places high value on promoting equality and reducing hunger and poverty Child acts on convictions, stands up for her/his beliefs Child "tells the truth even when it is not easy" Child accepts and takes personal responsibility Child believes it is important not to be sexually active or to use alcohol and/or other drugs
	SOCIAL COMPETENCIES	32. Planning and decision-making 33. Interpersonal competence 34. Cultural competence 35. Resistance skills 36. Peaceful conflict resolution	Child has skill to plan ahead and make choices Child has empathy, sensitivity, and friendship skills Child has knowledge of and comfort with people of different racial backgrounds Child can resist negative peer pressure Child seeks to resolve conflict nonviolently
	POSITIVE IDENTITY	37. Personal control 38. Self-esteem 39. Sense of purpose 40. Positive view of personal future	Child feels she/he has control over "things that happen to me" Child reports high self-esteem Child reports "my life has a purpose" Child is optimistic about her/his personal future

- Most adults no longer consider it their responsibility to play a role in the lives of children outside their nuclear family.
- Parents are less available for their children because of demands outside the home and cultural norms that undervalue parenting.
- Adults and institutions have become uncomfortable articulating values or enforcing appropriate boundaries for behavior.
- Society has become more and more age-segregated, providing fewer opportunities for meaningful intergenerational relationships.
- Socializing systems (families, schools, congregations, etc.) have become more isolated, competitive, and suspicious of each other.
- The mass media have become influential shapers of young people's attitudes, norms, and values.
- As problems—and solutions—have become more complex, more of the responsibility for young people has been turned over to professionals.

For several decades, Americans have invested tremendous time, energy, and resources in trying to combat the symptoms of these changes. It hasn't worked. It's time for a new approach—an approach that focuses energy, creativity, and resources into rebuilding the developmental foundation for all youth. As we begin shifting our thinking, we can anticipate creating communities where all young people are valued and valuable, problems are more manageable, and an attitude of vision, hope, and celebration pervades community life.

15 CHARACTERISTICS OF ASSET-BUILDING COMMUNITIES

What are some of the core features of a town or city that seeks to reclaim developmental assets for all of its children and adolescents? Proposed here are 15 benchmarks.

1. All residents take personal responsibility for building assets in children and adolescents.
2. The community thinks and acts intergenerationally.
3. The community builds a consensus on values and boundaries, which it seeks to articulate and model.
4. All children and teenagers frequently engage in service to others.
5. Families are supported, educated, and equipped to elevate asset building to top priority.
6. All children and teenagers receive frequent expressions of support in both informal settings and in places where youth gather.
7. Neighborhoods are places of caring, support, and safety.
8. Schools—both elementary and secondary—mobilize to promote caring, clear boundaries, and sustained relationships with adults.
9. Businesses establish family-friendly policies and embrace asset-building principles for young employees.
10. Virtually all 10-to 18-year olds are involved in one or more clubs, teams, or other youth-servicing organizations that see building assets as central to their mission.
11. The media (print, radio, television) repeatedly communicate the community's vision, support, local mobilization efforts, and provide forums for sharing innovative actions taken by individuals and organizations.
12. All professionals and volunteers who work with youth receive training in asset building.
13. Youth have opportunities to serve, lead, and make decisions.
14. Religious institutions mobilize their resources to build assets both within their own programs and in the community.
15. The community-wide commitment to asset building is long-term and sustained.

THE IMPACT OF DEVELOPMENTAL ASSETS

Based on Search Institute's intial study of more than 250,000 youth across the nation, which focused on the initially identified 30 assets, this chart shows that the more assets young people experience, the less likely they are to engage in a wide range of risky behaviors. In addition, youth with more assets are more likely to grow up doing the positive things that society values.

PATTERNS OF RISK-TAKING BEHAVIOR

PROBLEM ALCOHOL USE
National Percentage: 22%
(Six or more uses in the past month or got drunk once or more in past two weeks)
- 0-10 Assets: 44%
- 11-20 Assets: 23%
- 21-25 Assets: 9%
- 26-30 Assets: 3%

SEXUAL ACTIVITY
National Percentage: 32%
(Sexual intercourse, two or more times in life)
- 0-10 Assets: 51%
- 11-20 Assets: 34%
- 21-25 Assets: 17%
- 26-30 Assets: 7%

VIOLENCE/ANTI-SOCIAL ACTIVITY
National Percentage: 26%
(Two or more acts in the past year)
- 0-10 Assets: 51%
- 11-20 Assets: 28%
- 21-25 Assets: 13%
- 26-30 Assets: 5%

SCHOOL TROUBLE
National Percentage: 13%
(Skipped school two or more days in the past month and/or wants to drop out)
- 0-10 Assets: 30%
- 11-20 Assets: 12%
- 21-25 Assets: 4%
- 26-30 Assets: 1%

POSITIVE BEHAVIORS

SUCCESS IN SCHOOL
National Percentage: 18%
(Get mostly A's in school)
- 0-10 Assets: 5%
- 11-20 Assets: 13%
- 21-25 Assets: 28%
- 26-30 Assets: 51%

VOLUNTEER SERVICE
National Percentage: 37%
(Volunteer one or more hours per week)
- 0-10 Assets: 15%
- 11-20 Assets: 34%
- 21-25 Assets: 57%
- 26-30 Assets: 75%

CHAPTER 5

The Faces Of Resiliency

Students Challenge Their Community to "Flip The Page" from Negative Youth Stereotyping to Messages of Strength and Support

by Nan Henderson, M.S.W.

The Orleans Southwest Supervisory Union is comprised of two high schools, two middle schools, and five elementary schools within and around the community of Hardwick, Vermont. Located about 60 miles northeast of Burlington, Hardwick is a small community that appears as peaceful, connected, and concerned for its youth as any that could be found in the United States. Residents rarely lock their doors, crime is virtually nonexistent, and a meeting of community leaders about positive youth development that I facilitated packed a large conference room in a local restaurant. Indeed, the feeling of "community" and "caring for one another" in Hardwick is actually palatable just walking down the street.

This description of Hardwick underscores my amazement at the following report. Dr. Helen Beattie, a school psychologist for the supervisory union, asked principals of the secondary schools to select a "representative" group of students to work with her in a supervisory union-wide initiative to integrate resiliency building and asset development into schools. Dr. Beattie wrote the following description of her experience talking with these students.

On November 7, 1996, sixth through twelfth grade students from throughout the Orleans Southwest Supervisory Union met to review Search Institute survey data. One introductory activity was a brainstorming session in which I asked the students this question: "How do you feel you are perceived by adults and the community 'at-large'?" The students brainstormed this list of responses:

Partiers	Troublemakers	Punks
Crunchies	Druggies	Slackers
Lazy	Unsafe Drivers	Hormonal
Ditzy Blond	Know-It-Alls	Hyper
Reckless	Inexperienced	Unreliable
Rebellious	Irresponsible	Moody
Sulky	Unmotivated	Emotional
Worthless	Poorly Educated	Mouthy

Dr. Beattie said that about halfway through this activity one of the students stopped the group process and commented, "These are all negative." Other students agreed, but the brainstorming continued in the same vein. Dr. Beattie then conducted the next part of the activity:

Next, I directed the students, "List how you would like to be perceived by adults and the community 'at-large'—how you know your-selves to be." The students then brainstormed this list:

Responsible	Confident	Explorers
Seekers	Intelligent	Trustworthy
Creative	Smart	Resourceful
Independent	Dedicated	ActiveAlive
Well-rounded	Equal	Individuals
Logical	People	Normal
Hard-working	Grown-ups of the future	

Dr. Beattie and her students laminated the results of this activity in a display that was shared throughout the community in an invitation to "Flip The Page" for youth in Hardwick. She asked the students to share their thoughts about how the community can make that shift so students receive the messages of strength and support that comprise their second list. Dr. Beattie reported on their ideas:

I asked the students this question: "How can students, adults, and the community 'at-large' help 'flip the page'?" These were their responses:

- Bring everyone in the community together to improve the community (e.g., through activities like planting trees or flowers).
- Increase interactions between youth and elders through music, drama, and community dinners.
- Engage students in community service on a regular basis.
- Bring community mentors into the school on a regular basis.

- Publicize the good things about youth.
- Let youth share their vision of an ideal community.
- Organize student-led forums or dialogue nights.
- Develop a community center as a place for people of all ages to gather.
- Engage parents and community members in the organization and staffing of extracurricular activities.
- Encourage teens and adults to be positive role models.
- Provide opportunities for teens to tell adults how they feel they are being perceived—adults might not realize how they are stereotyping teens.

The challenge to "Flip the Page" was brought to students, school staff, and community members throughout the district with the goal of defining a common vision and identifying the means to achieve it.

This report from the students of Hardwick suggests that all communities need to explore these questions with their youth. It is shared with the hope it will be the catalyst for similar discussions and goal-setting in families, classrooms, community agencies, churches, and all youth-serving organizations. It also illustrates again the resilient nature of youth—that they can self-identify their own strengths in the midst of many messages of deficit—and their inherent wisdom about how communities can change to benefit all citizens.

Nan Henderson, M.S.W. is an international speaker, writer, and president of Resiliency In Action, a publishing and training company in Southern CA. She has authored several articles and coauthored four books on fostering resiliency, including Resiliency In Action: Practical Ideas for Overcoming Risks and Building Strengths in Youth, Families, and Communities *and* Resiliency In Schools: Making It Happen for Students and Educators. *She can be contacted at nhenderson@resiliency.com or at by calling 800-440-5171. More information is available at www.resiliency.com.*

Hardwick students share an illustration of an "ideal vision for our community." They are, from left to right (back row), Ginger Scott, Hazen Union junior; Dan Mercier, Hazen Union eighth grader; Kory Keene, Hazen Union freshman; (front row) Leona Stein, Lakeview Union sixth grader; Joshua Shepard, Hardwick Elementary sixth grader; Travis Reynolds, Craftsbury Academy junior; Micah Mutrux, Craftsbury Academy junior; and Anthony Wiley, Hazen Union senior.

CHAPTER 6

CCDO: Lessons from My Life to Guide All Youth Development

by John Seita, Ed.D.

John is totally unable to accept the close relationships of a foster home placement. As we discussed this, John told of his continuing wish to return to his mother. He strongly implied that he would continue to act out and get into trouble until he was returned to her. Although he recognized that his mother had some undesirable characteristics, he was quick to make excuses for her and seemed to be saying, "She's all the family I have." (Seita, Mitchell, & Tobin, 1996, p. 30)

I was moved roughly 15 times in a few years following removal from my mother's home. It is no wonder, then, that I rejected every attempted placement. No one should be surprised that I was angry and aggressive and alternately passive, quiet, and withdrawn. Perhaps I was simply responding to a harsh, rejecting, insensitive world filled with what seemed to be calculating professionals bent on identifying what was wrong with me and not much focused on what was right with me.

I have thrived despite these early tragedies, and I am here to tell my story. More important than the personal tragedies are the lessons learned about what facilitated my evolution from an angry, hurting, and institutionalized youth to an adult who, as Werner & Smith (1977) suggest, loves well, lives well, and expects well.

The intent of this article is to describe these lessons and in doing so, to propose a set of guiding principles that evolved from my own experiences, which are similar to the results of recent studies on resiliency and protective factors. These principles of "Connectedness, Continuity, Dignity, and Opportunity" (CCDO) could serve as the national standard that undergirds all action and practice on behalf of children, adolescents, and youth.

These lessons constitute what some call strength-based approaches (Brendtro & Ness, 1995; Benard, 1994; Burger, 1994; Seita & Brendtro, 1995) and are linked to protective factors and resiliency (Werner & Smith, 1977; Benard, 1997; Williams, 1997). In my own case, CCDO occurred more by chance, rather than by intention. My sad

and grim sojourn has been documented in the book *In Whose Best Interest?* (Seita, Mitchell, & Tobin, 1996) and will not be reprised here.

My sojourn, however, is illustrative and adds to the growing body of literature about protective factors and resiliency. I have labeled my journey as one of "pluck and luck." Most youth need more than pluck and luck. They need to experience purposeful efforts at creating CCDO.

A Shifting Perspective on Youth

Historically the approach in working with youth has been to label them, and to identify and attack what were thought to be deficits and so-called pathologies. In this collective, but misguided, wisdom kids are viewed as dysfunctional, deviant, disruptive, disordered, disturbed, delinquent, debased, and depraved (Brendtro, Brokenleg, & Van Brockern, 1990). Rarely was the strength in many of these societal outcasts acknowledged. The choice was made to see what was thought to be wrong with troubled youth, rather than to seek and understand what was right.

Today this approach is changing with the recognition that what has been viewed as a pathology is often a healthy response by a hurting youth to an unhealthy life ecology, which might more accurately be described as oppositional strength.

Legitimate and understandable responses to an unhealthy life ecology, however, are often not healthy for youth or for society in general. Yet, this society has been feckless at best and immoral and criminal at worst in exercising its collective responsibility for youth. "No one is certain what solutions, if any will work," writes Gleick (1996, p. 31) regarding the collective unfocused inaction on behalf of youth. Efforts need to be focused, channeled, and guided. CCDO is one way to channel and guide the policies and practices that affect youth, our communities, and our organizations.

CCDO—Not Just Another Model

Not surprisingly, because of my background, I am often asked about particular methods of intervention, so-called model programs, and the latest school curriculum. In reality, the search for model youth programs is not unlike looking for the mythical unicorn—it is a search that is bound to be disappointing. Models are simply temporary and contextual mechanisms for understanding and working with youth and are often categorical, reactive, and problem oriented. CCDO, on the other hand, is proactive, holistic, and transcends time, context, and personality because it is an unchanging set of core principles that guides our actions.

Definitions of each aspect of CCDO are provided below and expanded upon with personal illustrations.

Connectedness: Strong, positive relationships with others, especially with one person.

> Mr. Lambert was a child care worker. I didn't know where he came from or really much about him except that he seemed sincere and reached out to me. He shared genuinely his beliefs about character, values, respect, and honesty and love in relationships. I took all of it in like a sponge and pestered him with questions. He shared many of the subtleties of life that one only learns at the elbow of a caring and experienced mentor. In essence, this strong bond of connectedness formed the solid personal infrastructure for my life as a successful adult. (Seita, Mitchell, & Tobin, 1996, p. 42)

> Adults who work with children have long been aware of the awesome power of relationships. This was a dominate theme in the early writings in education, counseling, and youth work. However, as professional literature became more scientifically oriented, relationships were increasingly ignored. Now there are signs of a renewal of interest in the synergistic power of human relationships. (Brendtro, Brokenleg, & Van Brockern, 1990, p. 58)

Continuity: A sense of continuous belonging to a group, family, or spiritual entity.

> Old friends, they mean much more to me than the new friends because they see where you are and they know where you've been. (The late Harry Chapin, songwriter and anti-hunger activist.)

Continuity represents a sense of roots, of personal history. Moreover, continuity considers a person's legacy, family, and future. Continuity can also be enhanced by a bond to a higher power or something greater than oneself.

For example, my first night away from home when I was first placed in an institution as an 8-year-old, when no one else was awake, I kneeled beside my bed weeping and in a near state of shock and started to pray. I prayed for hours, perhaps half the night. Hundreds of "Hail Marys" poured out of me. I had learned how to pray and believed that the Virgin Mother would somehow deliver me from this undeserved fate. Of course it didn't happen that night, but praying did stabilize me in my moment of crisis. Youth can be encouraged to explore their spiritual selves and connect with a higher spiritual power without promoting a specific dogma or doctrine.

Dignity: Respect and courtesy.

Dignity is revealed in explicit and implicit attitudes and behaviors on behalf of children, and more importantly, through interactions with children. Valuing children as equals deserving of honesty, appreciation, and respect not only sends messages important to how children view themselves today, but shapes the outlooks and behavior of these children as adults. The following story reflects the small messages that are sent to children that suggest their diminished status.

> Larry Brendtro, former president of Starr Commonwealth for Boys (Starr Commonwealth, at the time, was a residential program similar to Boys Town), came up to me while I sat in the Emily Jewel Clark building on Starr's campus awaiting an appointment with a counselor. I sat there with pants too short, and wearing what we in the cottages called "ankle busters" (short, cheap, and thin sox that barely reached the ankles on my size 13 feet). Larry thoughtfully remarked that perhaps staff should also wear such threadbare and short sox and as if to join me in some sort of secret solidarity society lowered his sox to ankle mast also. Larry's actions were humorous, but also pointed and well understood by me at the time. (Seita, Mitchell, & Tobin, 1996, p. 90)

> Human service professionals have a long history of patronizing, infantilizing, and dehumanizing the very persons they are pledged to serve. While they may be unaware of their basic disrespect, young persons are not. (Brendtro, Broken Leg, & Van Bockern, 1990, p. 67)

Small messages and signals that adults send youth are powerful, impactful, and long remembered. What adults tell children through action, inactions, structure, and verbiage all contribute to how children process the world now and in the future. Subtle messages of disempowerment often abound.

Being directed to hand out clothes with nothing on or wearing "ankle busters" for sox certainly does not rank with having no food in the house, being abused by a caretaker, or living in a drug-infested environment. This does, however, represent an insidious pattern of marginalizing children and diminishing their value and potential growth. Moreover, if the goal is to foster the development of healthy, independent, and contributing children, then examples such as this are not to be ignored or dismissed out of hand.

Opportunity: The chance to capitalize on one's strengths. Opportunities need to be provided for youth that are consistent with their interests and talents but that also fill a role for society. Almost all youth have something that they do well. Adults should strive to identify what those sometimes hidden abilities are and seek to foster and promote them. As an adolescent, my hidden ability was basketball. Mr. Wilson, a child care worker at a residential treatment facility, nurtured my talent for basketball even before I knew it existed.

Mr. Wilson really expected the best of me and constantly encouraged my basketball efforts. He would never let me give up, no matter what the odds seemed to be. We were playing on the outdoor cement court one late afternoon when I was about 16. One exchange saw me playing what he called "tenacious defense" as he was forced further and further from the basket. I hounded him far out of shooting range. I can still see in my mind's eye a vision of him falling out of bounds, his back turned to the court, and 25 feet from the basket. Just as he was about to land on the grass beyond the out-of-bounds line, he turned, spun in midair and launched the ball toward the basket. The high arching shot seemed to float in the air for an eternity. I was astonished when it softly nestled through the net and went in. He then turned to me, and with a smile in his face and in his eyes, said, "See, never give up." (Seita, Mitchell, & Tobin, 1996, p. 46)

I eventually excelled at basketball and found basketball as a way to start my college education. Certainly there are other dimensions of opportunity: the opportunity to be afforded a quality education, to be trained in the skills of one's choice, to have economic opportunities. The range of opportunities are endless except for those who most often need them. Happily for me, opportunities were near and abundant. Sadly, for many youth today, that is not often the case.

CCDO In Action

In closing, the following suggestions are excerpted from Seita, Mitchell, & Tobin (1996) and may be used to implement CCDO on the individual/family level and the organization/school level.

Families: Families have a primary role for caring for and nurturing our children. Indeed, families remain the most likely place to offer and receive CCDO. The following suggestions are intended to guide families in their attempts to create a family environment that is protective.

- Create and maintain family traditions.
- Support spirituality, in whatever form it manifests itself.
- Provide all family members with opportunities to build upon his/her strengths.
- Celebrate the accomplishments of family members.
- Value each individual family member for his/her unique attributes.

School/Organization/Community: A clear understanding of the principles of CCDO can help all of us relate to children. What follows are some simple suggestions on issues that may improve educational, organizational, and other community settings:

- Design curriculum to meet the needs of the total child in his/her life ecology rather than only within the walls of the school and its traditional domain.
- Create an ethos that meets the needs of all consumers of services including nontraditional families.
- Develop, practice, and evaluate policies that support teachers and other staff to view their roles as extending beyond the classroom/school.
- Create an organizational culture that practices a value system which respects the dignity of all students.
- Encourage and reward staff who reach out to families in their homes, work, and in other nontraditional settings.
- Respect, nurture, and understand cultural differences, backgrounds, and spiritual beliefs.

Connectedness, Continuity, Dignity, and Opportunity is not just another model. It is a better way, based upon principles to engage children and youth, for organizations and communities that serve children than simply asking, "What is the best program?"

References

Benard, B. (1997). Fostering resiliency in urban schools. In Williams, B., *Closing the achievement gap*. Alexandria, VA: the Association For Supervision and Curriculum Development.

Brendtro, L., Brokenleg, M., & Van Bockern, S. (1990). *Reclaiming youth at risk*. Bloomington, IN: National Educational Service.

Brendtro, L. & Ness, A. (1995). Fixing flaws or building strengths? *Reclaiming Children and Youth: Journal of Emotional and Behavioral Problems, 4*(2).

Glieck, E. (1996). The children's crusade. *Time, 147*(23).

Burger, J. (1994). Keys to survival: highlights in resilience research. *Journal of Emotional and Behavioral Problems, 3*(2).

Seita, J. & Brendtro, L. (1995). Reclaiming the unreclaimable. *Journal of Emotional and Behavioral Problems, 3*(2).

Seita, J. (1994). Resilience from the other side of the desk. *Journal of Emotional and Behavioral Problems, 3*(2).

Seita, J. Mitchell, M., & Tobin, C. (1996). *In whose best interest: One child's odyssey, a nation's responsibility*. Elizabethtown, PA: Continental Press.

Werner, E. & Smith, R. (1977). *Kauai's children come of age*. Honolulu, HI: University Press.

John Seita, Ed.D., is an Assistant Professor in the School of Social Work at Michigan State University and the author of numerous articles on resiliency in youth, program evaluation, and working with youth who are resistant to relationships. He is also a frequent speaker and can be reached through the Reclaiming Youth Network @ www.reclaiming.com/speakers.

CHAPTER 7

The Resiliency Route to Authentic Self-Esteem and Life Success

A controversy is boiling about what is known as "feel-good" self-esteem.

by Nan Henderson, M.S.W.

A controversy has developed about what is known as "feel-good" self-esteem. At the heart of the controversy is the assertion that making oneself or someone else feel "special" by using methods such as looking in the mirror and saying "I am somebody," doesn't do any good, and may do harm. One result, say some researchers, is that this type of "self-esteem building" produces "counterfeit positive self-assessment" (Rosemond, 2002) that can set people up for disappointment in the "real world." This may be especially true for young people, who develop an unrealistic opinion about their "specialness," only to be disillusioned "when life's inevitable disappointments present themselves" (Smith & Elliott, 2001). In that disillusionment, kids may turn to alcohol, other drugs, violence, or other unhealthy escapist behavior.

I believe what people of all ages need is the "resiliency route to authentic self-esteem and life success." This type of self-esteem is not the mere fluff of meaningless affirmations. It is based on recognizing actual accomplishment, identifying and understanding how we have and can use our strengths, and living a life filled with expressions of our unique "talents and gifts."

Acquiring this "authentic self-esteem" starts by shifting our internal focus for ourselves–and for others, including our children–to a thorough appreciation and application of how we (or they) have "done as well as we've done."

Every day of life, everyone draws upon what researchers call the innate capacity for overcoming adversity. When dealing life's small hassles, such as getting stuck in a traffic jam or diffusing an argument with a coworker, or making the necessary arrangements to take care of a suddenly sick child, adults draw upon this internal capacity for resiliency. Children do this when they struggle through a difficult math lesson, figure out a way to get home when they miss the bus, or cope with an irritable parent. When a major life crisis hits, people draw upon this capacity in a much bigger way.

The first step on the resiliency route to self-esteem is to believe the resiliency research: that everyone, of all ages, has an innate capacity for bouncing back.

The second step is to identify individual personal patterns of doing this. Ask yourself, or facilitate your child or your friend or your client asking:

1. How have I done as well as I have done? What are the two or three biggest challenges (including crises or traumas) I have overcome in my life? What did I use to overcome them? Who helped me overcome my challenges?
2. What do I use every day to effectively cope with the typical stresses in my life?
3. How can I use these strategies, supports, internal qualities to cope with what I am currently facing in my life?

In other words, what specific qualities, supports, skills, attitudes, aptitudes, and talents has any individual used to make it this far?

After making this list, it helpful to look over the list of Personal Resiliency Builders (see chapter eight)–qualities researchers have identified as especially useful in overcoming adversity—and identifying those most commonly used when facing a crisis, large or small. It is truly self-esteem building for anyone to see that they do have a few or even several of these research-based Resiliency Builders. These are, in fact, personal lifelines to overcoming adversity.

Give yourself (and others) credit for what you and they have gone through and overcome–and especially for whatever was used to do it! Even if you (or someone you love) currently faces a terrible problem, suspend focusing there, and take some time to thoroughly assess and appreciate what has already been accomplished in overcoming other difficulties. Then, ask of yourself or another: How can these strengths be used to overcome current life challenges?

This is a powerful approach. A school counselor told me recently how she applied it. A high school student, Sandy, was referred to this counselor because she was failing in two subjects, math and science. Normally, the counselor told me, she would immediately confront a student with the problem–in this case two failing grades–after making some brief small talk. Instead, after the small talk, she opened her session with this question: "Sandy, I have learned a little about your life. Tell me, how have you managed to do as well as you have done?" Sandy, the counselor reported, immediately burst into tears. "Never in all my years has anyone acknowledged what it has taken just to get to school," she said. Most of the rest of the session was spent identifying all the strengths Sandy had used to "do as well as she had done." Towards the end of the session, the counselor said, "Let's talk about how you can use all these strengths you have shared to bring your grades up in math and science."

The third step is to expand the list of resiliency builders–ways we've overcome life's challenges–to include other strengths. "What are my strengths? How can I capitalize on them? What one, two, or three things can I do better than 10,000 other people?" are additional questions we should ask or help someone else ask (Buckingham & Clifton, 2001).

This composite list of resiliency builders and other qualities, talents, skills, and aptitudes paint the most important, but most often overlooked and undervalued, picture of who we are.

For the last 30 years The Gallup Organization has been conducting research into the best way to maximize a person's potential (see the next chapter for more information on this study). Two of the findings are "each person's talents are enduring and unique," and "each person's greatest room for growth is in the areas of his or her greatest strength." One of the conclusions of this research is: "The real tragedy of life is not that each of us doesn't have enough strengths, it's that we fail to use the ones we have"(Buckingham & Clifton, 2001). I would add another tragedy, connected to the first: We obsess about and overestimate the power of weakness, and we fail to recognize and underestimate the power of strengths.

Admittedly, using the resiliency route described here is not always easy to do. Our culture is obsessed with "what is wrong"–with our bodies, our homes, our leaders, our financial status, our material accumulation, and our children. And everyone is very specific in naming all that is wrong: "My thighs are too fat," "My carpets are dirty,"

"My income is too low," or "You are too lazy," "Your room is too messy." Rarely is anyone as constant and specific in giving oneself or others the credit that is due.

The approach I am suggesting here does not mean ignoring real problems–such as alcoholism, other self-destructive behavior, or an abusive, violent temper. But it does mean:

1. Giving ourselves and others credit for all we have overcome, all the ways we have demonstrated resiliency, and naming these accomplishments and the strengths we used in securing them as specifically as possible.
2. Spending time focusing on how we (or others) have done as well as we've done, suspending the common obsession with what hasn't yet been accomplished.
3. Identifying other strengths–important lessons learned, virtues, talents, skills and capabilities, how we help or serve others, all the best things about being who we are.
4. Maximizing these strengths as the best path to success, and using them to solve current life problems.

The final step on "the resiliency route to authentic self-esteem and life success" is finding ways to live in personal strengths, to use them to the utmost as much as possible. "Too many individuals hide their 'sundials in the shade'" conclude the authors of the Gallup research (Buckingham & Clifton, 2001). Rather than obsessing about correcting all the weaknesses, everyone should put their strengths to work, they advise. "Become an expert at finding and describing and applying and practicing and refining your strengths."

The happiest and most productive individuals are those who do just this, states Seligman (2001), past president of the American Psychological Association (APA) and a leading resiliency researcher. Seligman and several colleagues are spearheading a shift in psychology based on a recognition of the power and importance of human strengths. They have formed a new branch of psychology called Positive Psychology within the APA to create "a science of human strength to compliment the science of healing" (Seligman, 1998).

Ironically, social scientists are finding that achieving healing is more likely to occur through employing a focus on clients' strengths. People dealing with the serious problems mentioned above have historically struggled in therapies and programs that ignored their strengths. Fortunately, "the strengths approach" to helping people heal is gaining greater acceptance as a more powerful and successful approach.

"People are more motivated to change when their strengths are supported," concludes Dennis Saleebey (2001), editor of *The Strengths Perspective in Social Work Practice*. People I have interviewed who have left gangs, recovered from alcohol and other drug addiction, made it successfully through college despite a childhood of abuse, or overcome other significant traumas have told me the same thing. "The people who helped me the most were the ones who told me 'what is right with you is more powerful than anything that is wrong with you,'" a young man who successfully completed college despite a childhood of living in one foster home after another told me.

That is the most important message to communicate in successfully walking "the resiliency route to authentic self-esteem and life success."

References

Buckingham, M. & Clifton, D.O. (2001). *Now, discover your strengths.* New York: Free Press.

Henderson, N. (1999). Preface. In N. Henderson, B. Benard, N. Sharp-Light (Eds.), *Resiliency in action: Practical ideas for overcoming risks and building strengths in youth, families, & communities.* Ojai, CA: Resiliency In Action, Inc.

Rosemond, J. (2002, January 7). Unmerited praise doesn't help kids. *The Wichita Eagle.*

Saleebey, D. (Ed.). (2001). *The strengths perspective in social work practice* (3rd ed.). Boston: Allyn & Bacon.

Seligman, M. (1998, September 3). Speech delivered to the National Press Club. Washington, D.C.

Seligman, M. (2001). Review of the book, *Now, discover your strengths.* Printed on back cover. New York: Free Press.

Smith, L.L. & Elliott, C.H. (2001). *Hollow kids: Recapturing the soul of a generation lost to the self-esteem myth.* Rocklin, CA: Prima Publishing.

Nan Henderson, M.S.W. is an international speaker, writer, and president of Resiliency In Action, a publishing and training company in Southern CA. She has authored several articles and coauthored four books on fostering resiliency, including Resiliency In Action: Practical Ideas for Overcoming Risks and Building Strengths in Youth, Families, and Communities *and* Resiliency In Schools: Making It Happen for Students and Educators. *She can be contacted at nhenderson@resiliency.com or at by calling 800-440-5171. More information is available at www.resiliency.com.*

CHAPTER 8

Gallup Research Shows the (Underestimated) Power of Strengths

by Nan Henderson, M.S.W.

This article is reprinted from the on-line newsletter, Resiliency In Action News To Use, *and is available to download at no charge at www.resiliency.com.*

Gallup has been researching what leads to human success for the past 30 years, surveying almost 200,000 people working in thousands of "business units" around the world. The research has also involved conducting more than two million interviews with "the best" of the world's professions–including teachers, doctors, lawyers, salespeople, soldiers, nurses, housekeepers, pastors, and executives. Gallup's results challenge common assumptions about what contributes to life success.

Key findings are:

1. Success occurs in individuals' lives because they grow in the areas of their strengths, rather than obsessing about and trying to repair their weaknesses. While it may be necessary at times to "manage" a weakness, most of our attention should be focused on growing strengths.

2. People develop their strengths by first identifying their natural "talents," then learning information and building skills to maximize them.

3. In all countries where individuals were surveyed, strengths were overlooked, taken for granted, and underestimated.

4. The most productive, satisfied employees are those who report they have "an opportunity to do what I do best" every day. But only 20 percent of those surveyed said they have this opportunity.

These findings are reported in the book, *Now, Discover Your Strengths* by Gallup Executives Marcus Buckingham and Donald Clifton. What relevance does this research have for educators, parents, and social service providers? The authors state that strengths are more powerful than weaknesses–a finding very connected to the research on human resiliency.

School, they suggest, should be "a focused hunt for a child's areas of greatest potential" (p.31). "The keystone of high achievement and happiness is exercising your strengths" rather than obsessing on weaknesses, notes resiliency researcher Martin Seligmann, Ph.D., past president of the American Psychological Association, (on the back cover of the book). While this "building-on-strengths" approach is too seldom prevalent in schools, Buckingham and Clifton note this "building-on-strengths" focus is also not the norm in most corporations. They report that it is, however, something "the most successful managers" do.

Though the book was written primarily for a business audience, most teachers, parents, and counselors can also benefit from the suggestions on how to use a strengths approach to maximize life success. These are summarized on the following page.

Take the Gallup StrengthsFinder Survey On-Line and Access Additional Resources

Since the publication of *Now, Discover Your Strengths,* Gallup has also developed websites devoted to helping young people and adults identify their strengths, and to help schools become strengths-based organizations.

The strengths survey is available (for a fee) at www.StrengthsQuest.com. Gallup states that more than 2 million people worldwide have taken this scientifically developed and tested instrument. A personalized profile is immediately generated after taking the assessment on-line that identifies five top strengths of the person who takes the survey. This website also has numerous free resources, including articles, curriculum, research studies, and activities.

Gallup's website for educators can be accessed by going to www.gallup.com, and clicking on "Education Division." There, educators can access Gallup's program for students, ages 10 – 14 called *StrengthsExplorer*, and a program for older high school students called *StrengthsSpotlight*. Numerous resources for educators are available at this website as well.

How to Put the Strengths Approach Into Practice: Suggestions from *Now, Discover Your Strengths*

1. Ask yourself or those you are trying to help, "What are your strengths?" "What one, two, or three things do you (or could you) do better than most people?" "Where can your strengths take you?" "What do you need to maximize them?"

2. Any or all of the following clues can be used to help yourself or others identify innate talents that can be developed into strengths:

- *Yearnings* that "exert a consistent pull" (a desire to write, paint, or play a sport, for example);
- Experiencing "*rapid learning* in the context of a new job, challenge, or environment–immediately your brain seems to light up as if a whole bank of switches were suddenly flicked to 'on'" (p. 72);
- Identifying positive activities that bring you psychological strength and *satisfaction.*

Though some weaknesses need "managing", most of your personal and professional development (or the development of others) should focus on acquiring knowledge or skills that will build strengths. This is the place of "each person's greatest room for growth (p.8)."

References

Buckingham, M. & Clifton, D. (2001). *Now, discover your strengths.* New York: The Free Press.

Henderson, N. (2002). *The resiliency quiz.* Ojai, CA: Resiliency In Action.

Nan Henderson, M.S.W. is an international speaker, writer, and president of Resiliency In Action, a publishing and training company in Southern CA. She has authored several articles and coauthored four books on fostering resiliency, including Resiliency In Action: Practical Ideas for Overcoming Risks and Building Strengths in Youth, Families, and Communities *and* Resiliency In Schools: Making It Happen for Students and Educators. *She can be contacted at nhenderson@resiliency.com or at by calling 800-440-5171. More information is available at www.resiliency.com.*

Personal Resiliency Builders: Individual Qualities that Facilitate Resiliency

Note: This list is a menu of personal qualities that help people of all ages bounce back from life adversity. No one has all of these; everyone has a few that are their individual lifelines for overcoming.

Put a check by the top three or four resiliency builders you use most often. Ask yourself how you have used these in the past or currently use them. Think of how you can best apply these resiliency builders to current life problems, crises, or stressors.

(Optional) You can then put a + by one or two resiliency builders you think you should add to your personal repertoire.

[ ] Relationships -- Sociability/ability to be a friend/ability to form positive relationships
[ ] Humor -- Has a good sense of humor
[ ] Inner Direction -- Bases choices/decisions on internal evaluation (internal locus of control)
[ ] Perceptiveness -- Insightful understanding of people and situations
[ ] Independence -- "Adaptive" distancing from unhealthy people and situations/autonomy
[ ] Positive View of Personal Future – Optimism; expects a positive future
[ ] Flexibility -- Can adjust to change; can bend as necessary to positively cope with situations
[ ] Love of Learning -- Capacity for and connection to learning
[ ] Self-motivation -- Internal initiative and positive motivation from within
[ ] Competence -- Is "good at something"/personal competence
[ ] Self-Worth -- Feelings of self-worth and self-confidence
[ ] Spirituality -- Personal faith in something greater
[ ] Perseverance -- Keeps on despite difficulty; doesn't give up
[ ] Creativity -- Expresses self through artistic endeavor, or uses personal creativity in other ways

" Amazing"Classroom Results from Using "the Strengths Approach"

I received the following letter from a sixth grade teacher in Riverside, CA, who decided (after attending a resiliency training) to put the "building on strengths" approach into practice with her "very difficult group of students."

January 21, 2002

Dear Nan:

I was teaching a very difficult group of sixth graders last year and was running out of energy and hope. [I attended your resiliency] training, which gave me some new inspiration, and I took the tools from that day and trained my whole class. I had them go through the list of personal resiliency factors from the training [see list below] looking for their top three. We discussed them beforehand, and talked about how each might play a factor in helping them to bounce back from difficulties in their lives.

I teach in a low-income neighborhood with many gang involvement opportunities. I was unsure of the impact this little exercise would have. I had several students whose initial response was, "Ya, right. I don't have any of these!" However, after a few days of class discussion, assignments to share with parents, and one-on-one time, every student had chosen at least two that they already had. We then discussed how to make them stronger, and [how to] choose one or two more to work on in the coming year.

My classroom became a much different place. I firmly believe that looking at resiliency had a huge part in that. Before the training, I was focusing on what was wrong with my class. After our work together, each student had at least two "strengths" or as one student put it, "I have two things I do right!"

This same student was a huge behavioral challenge for me. I was so fearful of her entering Middle School. As of the last time we spoke, she was each of her teachers' favorite student! She sits right in front, and is getting high marks. Her SAT9 scores (that ever important academic component) went up 259 points overall! Another student who was always getting in fights is the student who is welcoming new students to school, and is taking all her friends to church!

The trick, I believe, was in focusing on what the individual students already had going for them. Now I am about ready to work with this year's class. I waited till I felt like I would be able to pick out strengths for each one. I can't wait to see the results! By the way, the rest of my class from last year is doing great as well.

They were an academically low-functioning group, and many of them are on the honor roll this year! The next step I would like to take is to meet with many of them, to see if their resiliency traits have grown, and if they have added more to their list.

I am very grateful for the training, and the talks we had that day. I am hoping to attend a Training of Trainers soon. I feel that Resiliency is the missing piece in the Asset puzzle, and I will begin sharing about resiliency in staff meetings once a month this February. My colleagues [have] actually asked me to tell them more! It seems most teachers are tired of the negative messages we are always hearing.

This is a long thanks to let you know that your message made a difference in my teaching and in the lives of my students.

Sincerely,
Keira Flionis 6th Grade Teacher,
Rosemary Kennedy Elementary Alvord Unified School
District, Riverside, CA

P.S. Thanks, too, for making The Resiliency Quiz available [see Part Four, chapter 11, or go to www.resiliency. com for a copy]. With a few changes, I will be using it with my students this year, as well as with the staff.

PART SIX

RESILIENCY AND FAMILIES

CHAPTER 1

Focusing Therapy on "What Families Do Right:"
An Interview with Steven Wolin, M.D.

by Bonnie Benard, M.S.W.

Steve Wolin, M.D., is clinical professor of psychiatry at the George Washington University Medical School, a longtime researcher in the department's Center for Family Research, and Director of Family Therapy Training. In addition to a private practice in psychiatry, Steve also directs Project Resilience, a private organization through which he and his wife, Sybil, provide training and consultation nationally and internationally (5410 Connecticut Ave. N.W., Washington, D.C. 20015, 202-966-7540, www. projectresilience.com).

The Wolins are the authors of The Resilient Self: How Survivors of Troubled Families Rise Above Adversity *(1993, New York, NY: Villard Books). I found this a compelling and beautiful book that documents the innate human capacity for transformation and change. Besides creating a vocabulary of strengths to counter the predominance of our deficit language in the helping professions, this book challenges all helping professionals to shift their paradigms from the "damage" to the "challenge" model. —B.B.*

BB: When I first discovered you, you were doing research with Linda Bennett. What was really interesting to me and very different than a lot of the research studying children in alcoholic families, was that you actually identified some of the positive things, even in very troubled families, that supported the kids. Could you speak to what these were?

SW: The research that you're referring to was very significant in my life. It was occurring in the mid-1980s, and was published in that time period, also. I started out being interested in transmission of alcoholism across generations; basically I was looking at the damage of alcoholism being continued over generations. The control group that I needed was a group of families that have the same alcoholism in the parent generation but no transmission. So I made a comparison of transmitter families to nontransmitter families.

I wasn't very interested in the beginning in that control group because I wanted to know what factors had gone wrong in the families where transmission occurred. I had to ask the nontransmitter families the same questions to be accurate in the study and for the people who were going to be doing the evaluation of the answers—they were blinded as to whether transmission occurred.

So we had to ask everybody: How did life go in this family? How did you handle the alcoholism of your parents? I was interested in what broke down in family life, especially family rituals, dinner time, holidays. (I was going to find that these important characteristics of family life broke down when transmission occurred more often than in those cases where no transmission occurred.)

But what was more important, was I was stunned by the information I was getting from the nontransmitter families, the control group. They had really interesting stories to tell about what they had done to prevent transmission from occurring. That's what changed my life.

But more important than their answers, actually, was my asking that question for the first time in my clinical life and being so overwhelmed with the amount of information. This has changed me forever. Now, I'm always asking people, "What have you done that worked out well?" "What have you done that was good for this family, especially during difficult times?" These questions, ten years later, are not very unusual questions for family therapists to be asking. Now lots of family therapists are interested in solutions and what has gone right. But for me as a researcher it was really a marker, a crucial experience that I had.

BB: This seems to be a phenomenon of resiliency researchers: They start out doing research that's much more into studying the problem, risk, or damage and are transformed through the stories of the people they're studying. I'm thinking of a video I saw of Robert Coles who had a very similar experience through listening to children.

SW: Yes. His famous story about what happened when he interviewed Ruby Bridges. Of course he's very much interested in the children under stress and keeps asking them how are they managing with the struggle of their lives. He's always finding interesting strength-oriented things that they're saying.

Again, my work with Linda Bennett was the critical experiment in my life. It changed my perspective so that I could start to ask the question, "What does the family do right in the face of pretty adverse circumstances, in this case parental alcoholism?"

There were four very specific findings:

The first one was this phenomenon of deliberateness. [Many] studies show that deliberateness is a very important quality inside families and in children. Deliberateness is a two-part characteristic: plan-fullness—making a plan—and carrying the plan out. It is an ability to take initiative, have a notion of what they're doing, and conceptualizing a positive future for themselves. These [nontransmitter] families were highly deliberate. They had at least one parent and several children who were extremely careful about how family life went because they sensed what the trouble was and knew they had to protect these zones of family life. So being deliberate was crucial. In fact, there is a book that's about that by Bill Doherty, a colleague of mine and a family therapist, called, *The Intentional Family: Simple Rituals to Strengthen Family Ties* (1999). It's all about deliberateness. He's using our research as a background to show that [families who make plans and carry them out, do much better than the families who don't]. The same thing goes with kids we talked to in that study who reported, for example, planning their future as early as age eight. They were visualizing a positive future for themselves, then taking steps to put their pennies under their pillow cases, etc.

> "People are saying to me, 'Oh, this is exactly what I do, but I didn't know there was a name for it, [or that] it was legit to do.'"

The second characteristic of these nontransmitters was distance. We were measuring the frequency of visits by children who were already out of the home and the

> "We need to . . . push this vocabulary of strength so that people believe it's as valid, deep, and substantive as the other stuff."

distance that they lived away from their still-drinking parents. You've got to remember that to be in this study the alcoholic still was drinking. [The nontransmitters] were having either two or fewer visits a year with their still-drinking parents, and lived more than two hundred miles away. These families had figured out that since drinking was going on, they had to take active steps to protect themselves using distance. That's where independence comes in as one of the protective factors. Being able to obtain both physical and emotional distance has been shown in many, many studies as a resiliency component.

The third finding was spouse selection. Since in the families that I'm talking about, the kids were now young adults, a whole bunch of them were already in serious relationships or married. So we were looking at these children of still-drinking alcoholics, and saw how important spouse selection was to them. Many described the care with which they were selecting the families that they were marrying into. They were clearly looking around for a surrogate family. The ones who married into non-alcoholic families did better. The ones who married non-alcoholics did better. The ones who married carefully thinking about these aspects of family life did better. Even the ones marrying into families more structured than the chaotic families they came from did better. Sometimes they made mistakes, but in general the statistics held up.

The fourth characteristic was the family ritual characteristic. We found [that families who focused on family rituals]—both the origin family and the [new families created by the kids when they were older]—did better. These families focused on a healthy dinner time, holidays, and celebrations without alcohol, and on routines set up so the family could count on it (one of the things that happens within alcoholic families is a tremendous destruction of all important ceremonies, celebrations, and rituals). Those four characteristics were often in the minds of children of alcoholics and even in their healthy parent's mind as they tried to give a positive legacy to the younger generation.

BB: Fascinating. You know that deliberateness/planfulness and spouse selection are exactly two of the major findings in two different studies Michael Rutter did in Great Britain.

SW: Yes. We chronicled a bunch of these in our book. The Beardsley study on children of depressed mothers showed that kids did better if they had a positive sense of the future, which is the same point again, this planfulness, and they didn't overly attribute to themselves their mother's depression. Some kind of independent deliberate position that occurs inside of kids is preventive for them.

BB: Are we finally moving to a more broad-based, strengths-oriented movement?

SW: I wouldn't say that the clinical activities are there yet, but I would say that I encounter lots of receptive audiences where the people are saying to me, "Oh, this is exactly what I do, but I didn't know there was a name for it, and I didn't know it was legit to do it." So there's a lot of affirmation that lots of therapists, when the door is closed, turn to the client's strength because that's basically what they have to work with.

BB: It also says something about their deep common sense and wisdom that in many ways, our institutions, and maybe a lot of our specialized programs, try to train us out of.

SW: We understand that there is a whole damage orientation that is not only in society, but in professional academies, and we understand where that comes from. One of the results of this is that there is very powerful language of damage that has risen up over the years, so that it's so easy to describe people and their "borderline personality disorder" and that they are "fragmented inner objects" and things like that. It sounds very deep and important when you talk about pathology.

> *"Whether you're a clinician, parent, teacher, or preventionist you can learn to talk about strength in ways you haven't before, which will make a meaningful difference in the life of a young person. To do that you have to believe there are strengths. This is mindset that we share."*

But when you talk about a strength such as creativity or the various aspects of someone's insight, it sounds almost pedestrian and banal. We need to get out there and push this vocabulary of strength so people really believe it's as valid, deep, and substantive as the other stuff. And, of course, it's a lot better in certain ways to work with.

I had a very interesting experience. I was on a panel at a substance abuse conference, and the man following me was a world-famous endocrinological expert with an expertise in fetal alcohol syndrome. He had always presented all the damage statistics and scary possibilities for mothers who drink in terms of what was going to happen with their babies. In my presentation before him, I had presented some of the statistics that showed that even in most situations there were a lot of people who were figuring out how to do things well. I showed that transmission of alcoholism in families wasn't the majority of circumstances, that in the majority of famlilies in fact, it was not transmitted. I didn't mean that it wasn't a problem, but people ought to know that they are not walking time bombs. They're not doomed.

So he got up at the end of my presentation, [looking] a little pale, and said [to the audience], "You know I don't think that I can present my presentation anymore as I would have done. Because, after listening to this guy, I realize that every one of my slides is going to be a scare statement to you about the dangers of drinking for mothers when, in fact, it's probably representing one tenth of one percent of deliveries, even with people who do exactly what happens when the bad things happen." He said, "It's not that these bad things don't happen, but I guess that I do have to tell you that it's by far the minority of cases where this will occur. We don't even know why it doesn't happen in the other ones. We've only studied the ones where it happens."

I think that for researchers to really be willing to shape their studies and their reports and give equal time to strength and the people who are doing well in the face of difficult things that happen—there's a lot of stuff they have to go through [to be able to do this], because they're afraid that they are going to lose their funding.

BB: That if you say there are strengths, the policy response is, "Oh, then we don't need to do anything. We don't need programs to help people." What message would you give to parents in light of all the research you've done?

SW: The main application of our work on resilience is talking about strength—talking to adults about strength. Our big push is that whether you are a clinician, parent, teacher, or preventionist you can learn to talk about strength in ways you haven't done before, which will make a meaningful difference in the life of a young person. In order to do that you have to believe there are strengths. This is mindset that we share.

But also, from our perspective, you have to have names for these strengths so that you can point them out to young people when they are using them. I do it all the time in my clinical work. I'd like to describe a couple of examples of how I do it in my clinical work with parents and with kids, because that's where I actively work with this stuff.

For example, I did a case consultation at the local children's hospital with a mother and daughter. I won't describe to you the problems, but what was important was that I was able to get the daughter to talk about how she handled gossip in the school. This daughter was in a lot of trouble and was the recipient of a lot of malicious gossip. Girls were coming up and saying, "Oh, you're a whore," and boys were coming up to her and asking if she would agree to have sex with them. This kid is 14.

There also had been a lot of trouble between mother and daughter and a lot of accusations about how the daughter is not taking good care of herself. The mother is suspicious about everything that the daughter does, etc., etc. The daughter has run away a lot. As you can imagine, it was a tense situation. In getting the daughter to talk about how she handled this malicious gossip, I was able to get her to focus on and identify what she evaluated in the social situation; that is, how she used her insight and independence, and how she was creative with her moral strength. I got her to actually say to her mother by saying to me, that she had the strength, that she was strong. And I said to the mother, "Well it's a very interesting set of things she's told us about herself. Have you ever heard it before?" She said, "No." She [said she] had never thought about her daughter as having those faculties that she used on the street and in the classroom when the girls were calling her names.

I [asked] the mother, "How about you? Have you ever been the victim and the recipient of malicious gossip?" [She] thought for a second, kind of turned a little pale, and said, "Well. Yes. There are some co-workers of mine who have accused me of being a lesbian behind my back." [The] daughter, who had not raised her eyelids to her mother probably in months, certainly not in the session, almost dropped her mouth and looked at her mother for the first time. I said to the mother, "Well that's pretty interesting. What did you do?" She described to me how she had gone to her supervisor, complained, gone over what the possibilities were, and decided to not tell certain people.

So I said to the mother, "How do you think you're handling it compared to your daughter?" She said, "Actually, I've learned a few things from [her]." She described how more sophisticated her daughter was in evaluationing these difficult gossip rumors than she had been. The daughter was, of course, tickled pink.

So I then closed this little sequence by pointing out the strength that this daughter had. Then the daughter said for the first time, "You know, mom, if you told me more about your life, I'll bet we could get along a lot better."

BB: What a wonderful story! Why do you think people have such a hard time—like the girl seeing her strengths, the mother seeing hers, as well as looking and seeing her own daughter's strength?

SW: To be focused on a strength is a stretch. It's unfortunately not natural. First of all we think it's bragging if we say we have one. We think it's kind of silly if we complement somebody because they have one. We are embarrassed by strength. We

> *"I am very actively involved in psychoeducational practice in family therapy. I'll spend a lot of time teaching family members about their strengths . . . teaching parents to talk to their kids about their strengths...talking to siblings about the different strengths in each other."*

are embarrassed by the sort of confrontation about how hard life is and giving somebody a pat on the back for the good job they've done. It doesn't go well. Then between parent and child, we have certain expectations of our children even though we've not met them in ourselves. We think we can criticize them easily for the things they have not done perfectly rather than focus on the hard work that they've been doing.

BB: You've nailed a lot of the issues in parent/child communications right there. What do you see as the greatest challenges facing families during this time of transition, not traditional nuclear [families], but people who would define themselves as a family?

SW: Of course I see a lot of divorced families in my practice, so I have to believe that understanding strength in the face of fragmented, non-nuclear, non-traditional families—this is one of the great challenges of today—and being able to accept differences among each other [is useful].

It's very hard to be generous inside the family. It's a hard change to come by. Our lives are busy, we're struggling, and we have so few resources from the community to give us strength. It's very hard to feel filled up, very hard to feel like you have a lot to give. It's much easier to feel like you need a lot. So if everybody's walking around feeling needy and nobody is saying, "I have to give at least as much as I take in order for this family to be filled up," families will never be appreciated as positive institutions.

Here's a wonderful little example: A colleague of mine saw a family in which everyone was very self-centered. Everybody was bitching about what they weren't getting and at the end of the third session, a little eight-year-old girl pulls him by the sleeve and says, "Tell me the truth doc. Whose side are you on here?" And he said, "Well Suzy, to tell you the truth I'm against all of you. Because when I look around in this family, all of you are first for yourself, and it seems like I'm the only one of you whose on the side of the family."

I think it's true a lot. It's very hard to find people who are on [the family's side] as an institution and feel they have something to give it.

BB: I know I have always been in a position where I felt like I have all these expectations from my work life that are in direct opposition to my family—things like time. It's always amazing to me that people expect you to work weekends, nights, and so on.

SW: And that they don't realize that you have to be flexible. Things come up in families all the time. People get sick, they have an accident. You have to have flexibility in your life to be able to be an active member of your family. It's very hard to come by flexibility when people are saying, "You know we need this by yesterday," and fax machines, and so on, that require everyone to shape up...to be there at every moment.

That's why family members especially need to see their strengths in dealing with all this stress. I use the notion of resilience in talking about strengths very actively. Like the case I just described to you about the mother and the girl and the gossip, I am very actively involved in psycho-educational practice in family therapy. I'll spend a lot of time teaching family members about their strengths. I'll spend a lot of time teaching parents to talk to their kids about their strengths. I'll also spend a fair amount of time talking to siblings about the different strengths in each other.

My favorite session is the session where several adult children will get together and talk about what it was like growing up in their families. But they come often to tell horror stories. My goal in the session is to change them to talking with admiration about each other's strengths. I want them to say, "Oh, I didn't know that about you Suzy. I didn't know that you knew how to do that." The idea that each of the children have different strengths that they're using, and that, hopefully, I'm going to be able to find something in every kid, and certainly, you know, I expect I will—that's what I'm going to go for.

You do have to understand that as a therapist I'm aware that people come in pain, so I'm not just focused on strength. I'm always trying to balance it. Our model shows that there is an equal amount of time for the damage part of the story, for the hurt, for the pain. We conceptualize people as being damage-first people and strength-first people in terms of how we're going to approach them in a clinical setting. Sometimes you just have to approach first from the damage part of their story, the trauma, the trouble, the pain in order to get their trust.

If you only present solutions to them and talk about how fabulous they are, they'll simply leave and say, "Oh you're on some kick, and you don't really know me." So those are the damage-first people and eventually you get around to showing them that there is more to the story than their damage story.

Then there are others who come in quite willing to talk about their strengths because they are either aware of them or they are not voluntary patients. Or there are whole families often very eager to talk about something they've done well as a family. I like to think about clients as being either damage-first or strength-first, but, in any case, I'm going to be finding a way for them to be talking about their strengths in the family sessions and get the other family members to acknowledge that they have these capabilities.

BB: This is very powerful work. Do you feel your field of family therapy is moving more and more to a strength focus?

SW: Yes, I would say that my phone doesn't stop ringing. It's a very healthy practice. People know that I am interested in positive qualities. I think I have a good reputation around town for that approach. And then my clients are often very willing to joke with me about my focus on strengths. Sometimes they come in and say, "Oh, we had this horrible weekend. I dare you, Steve, to find the strength in this story." They're actually playing with me.

I don't know if it's a movement, but I think it's certainly comfortable for me. I also know that a lot of my colleagues like it and don't yet do it. So I don't know how to accept it on this sort of sociological level, but I certainly think that it's in my blood now.

I think the whole solution-focused approach has a lot of these characteristics. The only difference between me and some of the other solution-focused therapists is that we have this specific vocabulary of people in terms of their bouncing back from adversity rather than what the solution-focused folks are doing. They are always just inviting the family to describe what they did that works. I always find that a bit too loose for me. Maybe I'm a bit of a control freak that way. But I feel that words give tremendous power to people, and that if I can give a name to something, they can walk away with it.

BB: I find that even just giving people some information about resiliency research is empowering.

SW: Right. It's like translating it for them. That's why I think that the good therapy, the good counseling is very psycho-educational because you are teaching people something.

BB: What I see in the education field—especially brain research/cognitive science—with people like Howard Gardner, and his multiple intelligences research, and now Daniel Goleman and emotional intelligence is that schooling has really had a very narrow focus and we definitely need to broaden it. Schooling itself must move towards a strengths focus—so that students will be acknowledged and validated for their unique skills and abilities.

SW: Absolutely. People who have street smarts, who have creative smarts, language smarts, and emotional smarts—all smarts which don't show up on SATs—must be acknowledged.

Bonnie Benard, M.S.W., has written widely and conducted workshops and trainings on resiliency for nearly 20 years. She currently works in the Health and Human Development Program of WestEd 's Oakland, CA office, where she has helped develop a statewide survey of students' perceptions of the protective factors in their lives (www.wested.org/hks). She can be reached by email at bbenard@ wested.org.

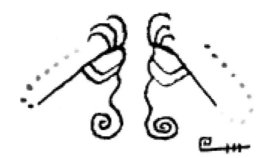

CHAPTER 2

Promoting Family Strengths

by Kelly A. Cole, Janet A. Clark, Sara Gable

reprinted with permission from the University of Missouri-Columbia extension program

Why are family strengths so important?

In our society, families take on many different structures. Although they may be formed in different ways, most families accomplish similar tasks, such as childbearing, providing for members' basic needs, providing emotional support, socializing members, establishing family traditions and delegating responsibility. By accomplishing these tasks, families influence the way individuals and society function. Few other social institutions have such a great impact on society. This profound influence makes evident the importance of strengthening families.

Family Diversity

American families are characterized by great diversity. The traditional family has undergone numerous changes in recent decades. Many of today's scholars refer to the current trend as the postmodern family. Factors that have led to this change include divorce, remarriage, adolescent childbearing, and changing social values. Descriptions of common family types are in the box below.

Family Resilience

According to the National Network for Family Resiliency (1995), resilience is the ability of an individual, or in this case a family, to use its strengths in order to positively meet life's challenges. It involves the family's ability to return to previous levels of functioning following a challenge or crisis.

Throughout the 21st century, individuals and families will be characterized by increased diversity, which could be experienced as stressful. Because of this, individual and family resilience may become increasingly important.

Resilience is exercised when family members demonstrate such behaviors as confidence, hard work, cooperation, and forgiveness. These behaviors contribute to the effectiveness of family protective factors—factors that help families withstand stressors throughout the family life cycle. For example, shared experiences such as family time, yearly vacations, holiday celebrations, and other traditions can help strengthen the bonds among family members.

When a family is confronted with a crisis, family recovery factors become critical. These are factors that help promote a family's ability to bounce back following a period of difficult family functioning. Events in which recovery factors may be especially beneficial include coping with a serious illness, an untimely death, the loss of a primary job or a natural disaster. Aids to recovery include the availability of family and community support, participation in recreational activities, optimism about the situation, and shared family experiences.

Building and Maintaining Healthy Family Relationships

In recent decades, a number of changes have contributed to a reshaping of American families. Examples include high rates of adolescent and unmarried childbearing, a high divorce rate, single-parent households, stepfamilies, and dual-earner families. Families need to be prepared to cope with these

---

- **Married nuclear families** (husband, wife, and children);
- **Joint-custody families** (divorced parents sharing child custody);
- **Cohabiting families** (unmarried men and women, and children, if any);
- **Single-parent families** (children raised by one parent as a result of divorce, death, desertion, or never marrying);
- **Voluntary child-free families** (couples who choose not to have children);
- **Involuntary child-free families** (couples who are unable to have children);
- **Blended and stepfamilies** (husband, wife, and children from previous marriage(s));
- **Families headed by gay men or lesbians** (may or may not include children); and
- **Grandparent-led families** (children raised by grandparents because of adult child's death, parent incarceration, financial problems, or other factors).

and other stressors and demands that may be placed upon them. Regardless of family type, there are times when all families need to be nurtured. Nurturing families in times of need can provide family members with a greater opportunity for building and maintaining healthy relationships.

A number of recommendations have been offered that can help families build and maintain healthy relationships. Selected recommendations follow.

Encourage open communication

- Communicate not only through words, but also through actions.
- Be aware of body language and tone of voice.
- Show that you understand what the other person is saying.
- Maintain good relationships with extended family members to increase sources of support and resources.

Maintain and strengthen relationships in the family

- **Parent-child:** Set and enforce family rules; be a patient parent; praise your children's efforts and accomplishments.

- **Marital:** Share housework and child care responsibilities; agree on family priorities and goals; value and nurture the relationship.

- **Siblings:** Develop sibling rituals and traditions; acknowledge one another as individuals; provide encouragement.

Manage crises and conflict

- Avoid taking things personally, which may help you avoid unnecessary conflict.
- When conflict does arise, resolve the problem before moving on.
- Direct attention to solving the problem rather than determining who is to blame.
- Understand what the conflict is about and model appropriate problem-solving strategies.
- Avoid holding grudges.
- Accept responsibility for your mistakes.
- Negotiations, compromises, or apologies may be necessary before reconciliation is complete.

Conclusions

Families have evolved in a number of ways over time, and these patterns of change can only be expected to become more common in the future. These transformations may be challenging for families, but the strategies outlined here can help minimize the stress these families experience. It is important to remember that all families have some strengths, although these strengths may be more evident in some families than in others. Individual family members play a significant role in determining how well a family functions. Although each member's actions are important, strengthening family relationships requires the commitment and cooperation of all family members. By working together, family members can build and maintain close relationships during periods of normal family functioning as well as during times of stress.

Characteristics of strong families

- Adaptability: Strong families are able to cope with everyday and unanticipated stressors.
- Appreciation: Because they care about other family members, individuals frequently do positive things for one another.
- Clear roles: Family members are aware of their roles and responsibilities and are able to remain flexible.
- Commitment to family: Family members are committed to the family as a system, and members recognize each individual's worth and importance to the family.
- Communication: Family members are open and honest with one another, and they are willing to listen to other members' views; conflicts are managed and resolved when they arise.
- Community and family ties: Strong families are connected to the community and they are involved in community organizations.
- Encouragement of individuals: Individual development is encouraged both inside and outside of the family system.
- Shared time: Both quality and quantity time are shared.

Strategies for strengthening families

- Spend quality time alone with each child at least once a week.
- Respond to children with patience and respect their feelings and abilities.
- Encourage family members by asking them to share their accomplishments.
- Visit and find ways to help at your child's school.
- Eat a meal together as a family at least once a day and involve family members in mealtime tasks.
- Hold family meetings that give all family members an opportunity to talk openly.
- Develop a family mission statement that includes your family's purpose, goals, and objectives.
- Develop and maintain family traditions and rituals.

This article can be downloaded at no charge from http://muextension.missouri.edu/xplor/hesguide/humanrel/gh6640.htm.

Parenting for Resiliency: How My Second-Born Child Taught Me to Use the "Power of the Positive"

by Tim Duffey, M.Ed.

One memory of my young fatherhood is emblazoned in my mind. The picture, as clear as if it were yesterday, is of me standing in the hallway of our home holding our screaming second-born child, a boy 30 months of age. This child held a special place in our hearts after having survived a serious bout with spinal meningitis when he was just five months old. Two days in Pediatric Intensive Care and eight additional days in the hospital pressed our family to new levels of endurance and tested our own resilience. That medical emergency bonded his mother and me to him in ways we had never encountered previously or since.

However, it was not our son's medical history that caused the image I remember so accurately. It was his behavior. In parenting seminars we had attended as young parents, we heard Dr. Charles Dobson, in his "Focus on The Family" video series describe this child's profile as "strong willed." On this particular day, "strong willed" was an understatement.

It had been clear from the beginning that this child had a personality distinct from our firstborn. He had a high need to be in close personal contact. Tantrums were a common occurrence. Within the first two years of life it was already evident that, in his view, limits were suggestions only—things to be tested. We established boundaries, he challenged them. If the answer was "no," he did it anyway. All of our parenting skills were being taxed to the limit.

I'd thought we had a pretty good bag of tricks as we approached parenthood. I'd earned a degree in sociology and psychology; my wife had a degree in child development. I had also received a masters degree in counseling and human development and had begun working in a large high school counseling center. Beyond that, we'd done our "homework"—utilizing parenting books, courses, tapes, etc. We'd discussed our parenting philosophy in depth before we started our family. We'd enhanced this philosophy through a parenting course at the local university, which focused on the writing of Dreikurs and Grey (1970). Through professional events, we came to know the work of Barbara Coloroso (1983) whose audio tape *Discipline: Kids are Worth It* has been played so many times by us and a myriad of friends and acquaintances that I am amazed the message is still audible. Following her guidance, we provided clear expectations, followed through with logical consequences, always strove to provide choices—an opportunity to "save face," and worked hard to encourage development of skill areas (gifts) we saw each child possess. These skills supported the parenting philosophy we had developed and were particularly important for this child's—our son Aaron's—excitement for life!

In my relatively short tenure in the school counseling center where I was working at that time, I had come to see a pattern of students with energy like our Aaron's. Frequently, they had frustrated nearly everyone near them with their approach to life. They steadily challenged rules and limits and were perceived to regard what applied to others as having little bearing on their behavior. Often, their parents had decided it was better to back off and give them room to make their own choices than to continue fighting to draw the line and enforce expectations. Too often, I saw these kids referred to as "juvenile delinquents," "troubled kids," or "high risk." The result often was a lowered expectation for performance and/or behavior; one they frequently lived down to.

That day in the hallway with screaming Aaron in my arms, I remember these thoughts racing through my mind. My son screamed because I would not allow him to continue throwing toys. I did not want my son to end up facing the same challenges I saw young people in my school facing. I knew then that we, as parents, had a choice. We could focus on the risk that his personality and energy held. We could talk about how, if he didn't change, he would end up in trouble with the law, be a juvenile delinquent, end up on probation, and be "no good." Or, we could find ways to direct that energy—to challenge him to use his strong sense of direction to his favor. His future options would likely depend in some large degree on our current attitude and choices. It was also clear that this would be hard work.

We renewed our efforts to set clear limits and consistently enforce them. We sought regular opportunities to show him our care and support in the endeavors of his choosing. We looked for means of directing his energy and enthusiasm for life, drawing from his natural gifts and talent. We continued to utilize consequences that we believed were fair and respected his ability to choose whether or not to encounter them. We sought periodic reprise and recreation for ourselves as a couple. We committed and recommitted to give it the best we had.

Some twelve years have passed since then. Just a few months ago, I watched this same child walk on stage as The Artful Dodger in our community theater's production of *Oliver!*. My eyes filled with tears as I struggled to comprehend where the years had gone. Where was my "little boy?" This young man, presuming to be my son, took the stage with a presence and strength that I sensed to my core. Theater has been one of the directions in which, with our guidance and support, he directed his incredible energy. He is a natural for it. The spotlight has attracted him for years, providing a positive time commitment and an amazing outlet for the creative energy housed in that young body.

Similarly, sports, public speaking, voice lessons, positive friendships, other caring, principled adults, family responsibilities, and participation in our congregation's youth group have contributed to shaping the raw materials I held in my arms some twelve years ago. Today I marvel at his ability to lead, his immense social awareness and sensitivity, and his gift for placing people at ease. We certainly did not do it alone. On the path to his current life success, contributions were made by many.

In the past few years as I have become immersed in the resiliency and positive youth development research, I have recognized that the thoughts running through my head on the day I held our screaming son in my arms were thoughts of the power of the positive—the power of resiliency. I knew then what I now have the language to communicate with others—that our attitudes and choices as adults are powerful determining factors for the future of our youth. The belief system and research base from which resiliency and positive youth development has grown affirms what I have long believed regarding our support of children and youth. Through Aaron, I have seen its impact first hand and I thank him for the lesson.

References

Coloroso, B. (Speaker). (1983). *Discipline: Kids are worth it* (Cassette Recording). Boulder, CO: Barbara Coloroso.

Dreikurs, R.,& Grey, L. (1970). *A parents' guide to child discipline*. New York, NY: Hawthorn/Dutton.

Tim Duffey, M.Ed., is Past President of the National Association of Leadership for Student Assistance Programs, and is currently a senior trainer for Search Institute. He can be reached by calling Search Institute Training, 800-294-4322.

CHAPTER 4

Selecting Parenting Programs that Foster Resiliency

by Nancy Sharp-Light, M.A.

My interest in writing parenting programs began in early 1978 while living on the Zuni Indian Reservation in Zuni, NM. As a teacher and a counselor, I worked with many students and their families to assist with a variety of issues, including poor school performance, behavior problems, and issues relating to family alcoholism. I found that most of the materials available did not address some very basic parenting issues and didn't relate to Zuni culture and tradition. I have since heard similar comments from parents and facilitators from around the country. Below, I share the basics of what I have learned about elements to avoid and elements to include in parenting curricula which either hinder or help the process of fostering resiliency in families.

In 1991, counselors from the Gallup Schools in NM asked me to write a program for parents that would include not only basic information about parenting but one that honored the personhood and culture of the parents. The curriculum overviewed in this article is the result of that request.

The awareness that parents need support, information, and skills, just like their children, is increasing. As a result, parenting curricula abound. The process of selecting one that fosters resiliency while being appropriate for cultural diversity can be overwhelming. It needn't be. Below are some guidelines to facilitate the selection process. An overview of one parenting curriculum that fosters resiliency called, *We're Doing The Best We Can*, is included. This program is designed specifically to help parents recognize their own resiliencies, provide them with new information and skills, and honor cultural diversity.

The Heart of Resiliency-Building Parenting Programs

The heart of an effective parenting curriculum begins with nurturing the parents. The same factors that foster resiliency in youth—caring/bonding, high expectations, meaningful participation and con-tribution, and life skills—foster resiliency in adults. If parents do not know how to nurture themselves, acknowledge their strengths, value their own accomplishments, accept themselves un-conditionally, and forgive themselves for mistakes, they will be less likely to model and teach these behaviors to their children. If a program concentrates too heavily on information and skill-building, it will not be as effective as one which begins with sessions focused on fostering the inherent resiliency in the parents and continues to support and reinforce this throughout the program.

Look For Balance

The most helpful curricula for parents have three points of balance: self-esteem building versus information-giving/skill-building; attention to a variety of individual learning styles; and the amount of time for facilitator presentation versus time for interaction among participants.

Do individuals perform better when they feel better, or feel better when they perform better? The answer to this is not either/or, but both. A heavy focus on either building self-esteem or information-giving/skill development can cause frustration. In fact, the two are complimentary. It is important to learn ways to improve self image. However, it is practice and skill development that helps to internalize and manifest positive self-esteem. Therefore, when assessing programs, look for those which have a good mix of self-esteem-building activities and skill-building activities.

Additionally, look for a program in which all three learning styles are used: auditory, visual, and tactile. Everyone—including adults—learns best in one of these ways. A curriculum must incorporate all three in order to accommodate each person's best learning style. Beware of a format that concentrates heavily on any one method, i.e., mostly lecture, whether by a facilitator or on a video, or multiple worksheets. The best format is "say it, show it, do it."

Finally, look for a balance between how much the facilitator is required to speak and how much time is allowed for participants to share and interact. Parents must be allowed ample opportunity to share their "stories" with one another. In this way, they learn they are not alone, that their experiences have value, and that they have the inner wisdom to create solutions appropriate for their families.

Guidelines For Selection

It is just as important to know what doesn't work as what does in selecting a parenting program. Assumptions upon which some parenting programs are based which can unintentionally sabotage resiliency fostering for parents is provided in Table 1. These assumptions can hinder parents' recognition and development of their strengths, capabilities, and capacity to do well.

Table 1

Assumptions That Sabotage Parenting Programs

1. There must be a problem or the parents wouldn't be there.
2. All that parents need is information about skills (rules and consequences, what to say, and when to say it, etc.).
3. Once parents have more information they will be able to put it into practice.
4. Parents know the resources available to them and how to use them.
5. There is a common language.
6. There is a shared level of education.
7. There is a common culture.

1 Many parents are tired of being blamed and shamed for the troubles of society. There is currently a great deal of negative publicity about parenting. If their child gets into trouble, even good parents are made to feel like bad parents. This attitude is a major reason why many parents will not attend parenting classes.

2-3 These two assumptions can actually create a sense of frustration, shame, and hopelessness rather than nurture self-honor, respect, confidence, and responsibility. An effective parenting curriculum must help parents realize their own resilience while learning new skills—exactly what they need to do for their children.

4 It is rarely the case that parents are aware of all the resources available. Even when they are, it does not mean that they are comfortable or skilled at asking for help. Discussions about resources and opportunities to practice asking for help (role playing, pairing up and reading a script, etc.) are useful.

5-6 The assumption that all participants use English as their first language, are proficient in their use of it, or that all participants have the same level of education is simply inaccurate. Much information, even when presented with the best of intentions, may not be understood by many. A rule of thumb relating to the level of language used is if "language" is being taught, the use of an expanded vocabulary, with definitions, is appropriate. However, if a concept is being taught, such as parenting and nurturing, the simpler the vocabulary the better. In one facilitator training a participant summed this up by saying, "Why use 'dollar' words when 'dime' words will do!" Participants, regardless of first language or level of education, shouldn't have to struggle with terminology. Rather, they should be able to focus on the concepts.

7 This country has a variety of rich and wonderful cultures. To present only one culture's methods of parenting or set of values can feel shaming or disrespectful to those whose lifestyles are different. During my 13 years on the Zuni Reservation and my subsequent work with families from other cultures, this has been the most commonly expressed reason for not attending parenting classes.

Table 2

Elements That Empower Parents

1. An initial focus on nurturing the parents.
2. Opportunities for dialogue, interaction, and sharing of experiences.
3. Opportunities and encouragement to practice new skills, through experiential activities.
4. Basic information on developmental stages, behavior management, and local resources.
5. In general:
   - a positive approach,
   - simple language,
   - sensitivity toward differences,
   - a sense of fun.

Elements which foster resiliency and should be in any parenting curriculum are listed in Table 2. Parenting curricula should also work from a strengths perspective just like resiliency building for youth. It is important for parents to have the opportunity to identify their own positive behaviors, strengths, and successes, rather than only concentrating on possible deficits and failures.

1 The best resource for a parent is another parent. The most effective parenting programs provide numerous opportunities for parents to share and interact. Any program offers information, but the ultimate value and benefit to the parents occur when they are in community with one another, sharing their experiences, hopes, dreams, problems, and solutions. Diverse cultures can learn from one another and those with similar backgrounds can provide support, "normalization," and pride for one another. Discussion time allows for meaningful participation, contribution, and a sense of belonging.

2-3 Opportunity for and encouragement to practice is critical to the learning process. This can be accomplished through a variety of practice activities including participant role-playing, interactive teaching "games," and suggested home-based activities between sessions. It is more likely that parents will be able to utilize new skills if they have, first, had a chance to internalize them through practice in a nonthreatening, non-critical situation. Activities which don't work for parents are as valuable a learning tool as those which do. Helping parents realize that mistakes are not a sign of failure, but of progress, reduces potential shame and teaches an important resiliency building characteristic—persistence.

4 Most parents agree with the saying, "children don't come with operating manuals." Therefore, it is important to include information on the normal stages of childhood development. This information provides parents with a reference of what behaviors to expect at any given age. Such knowledge can reduce anxiety and fear that something is "wrong" with either them or their child. It is particularly important for first-time and teen parents to have this kind of information. Sessions on how managing misbehavior and encouraging positive behavior are also vital for any parenting program. Facilitators can present techniques, but the content and context of the application should come directly from the parents.

5 Even though parenting is "serious" business, opportunities for fun, camaraderie, networking, and socialization are as important as the information. Humor is a great relaxer and can help break down walls of defense. Refreshments allow time for socialization, bonding, and networking. Small and large group discussions encourage acceptance, meaningful participation, and the creation of local support networks among parents.

Each of these elements of fostering parent resiliency model what parents should do to foster resiliency for their famlies and children.

"We're Doing the Best We Can"

The curriculum, *We're Doing the Best We Can* is one example of a resiliency-building parenting program. It is based on the tenant that every parent is already doing some things "right" and builds on this to expand parents' knowledge and skills. It has been implemented in several multicultural settings by a variety of organizations, including schools, social service agencies, and medical doctors who provide parent education. Two consistent comments made about this curriculum are how easy it is for facilitators to implement and how easy it is for participants to understand and utilize.

The program consists of six two-hour sessions. There are three sections—"Your Self," "Your Child," and "Your Family"—with two sessions devoted to each topic. All sessions include review/preview and short lecturettes followed by interactive learning activities. Suggested processing questions, and frequent opportunities for parents to discuss and share their ideas and experiences are included. Masters for all handouts and overheads are provided.

Curriculum Goals and Design

Part One: *Your Self* includes two sessions designed for parent self-reflection. Parents explore ways that they do/don't take care of themselves and how this affects their family relationships. Participants examine the methods their parents used to raise them, and possible reasons why—i.e. rapid changes in society, family, and education since World War II—what worked for their parents may not be working for them now.

Part Two: *Your Child* (sessions three and four) is designed to teach parents normal childhood development. They learn about what behaviors to expect from their children at different ages and examine how culture and the media affect the normal developmental process. They learn about the importance of consistency in their own behavior—setting and enforcing rules, consequences, rewards, and punishments—and explore techniques for managing and correcting misbehavior without shaming their children.

Part Three: *Your Family* (final two sessions) focuses on ways to encourage and support positive behaviors, how to schedule quality time, and ideas for activities to do during this time. Parents share their family and cultural traditions and discuss creating "new" traditions. Included is a video that shows parents of different ages and culture, sharing their stories of family traditions, the challenges, and the joys of their parenting experiences. It summarizes and exemplifies all the points of the program and is recommended viewing during the last session.

Curriculum Features

The following list describes some of the features of this curriculum.

1. User-Friendly: *We're Doing the Best We Can* is designed to provide facilitators with all the information needed in a simple, bulleted, list fashion. Very little prep time is required. No outside research is necessary.

2. Choose and Use Design: There is more information than can be presented within any two-hour session. So, facilitators can select what is most appropriate for their population. Charts and graphs are normally provided in two ways: an expanded

English version and one appropriate for the language needs of English as a Second Language (ESL) participants.

3. Cultural Relevancy: An appendix demonstrates how the curriculum can be adapted for different cultures. The included sample lesson is based on the child-rearing practices of the Navajo Indians of the Southwest. However, throughout the curriculum, sessions are designed so that the participants can, quite naturally, share their cultural traditions.

4. Activities and "Try-outs": All sessions include activities that are fun and teach at the same time. Each session ends with participants choosing one new thing to work on for one week called "try-outs"—simple activities such as having one sit-down meal with their family, self-care activities, making a point to say, "thank you" to a child for putting the top back on the toothpaste, etc. The purpose of the "try-outs" is to gently build positive habits, rather than force drastic, immediate changes. At the beginning of the next session, they share what worked and what didn't.

5. Flexibility: We're Doing the Best We Can is flexible and can be adapted to a variety of needs and populations. For example, one facilitator needed more time to examine childhood developmental stages with a particular group because there were many first-time and teen parents participating. Other facilitators have either expanded the program to eight or ten weeks, or divided the program into parts one and two.

Observations and Comments

In Albuquerque, NM, the program has been used as part of a Parents Anonymous support group working with issues of child abuse/neglect. The director said, "It [the program] emphasizes the empowerment of the parent in relation to his/her parenting. It's concrete and fun. In use with several 'macho, taciturn' men, particularly one Native American man, it was wonderful to see their efforts in writing/drawing something for their children." A parent who has taken the class twice said, "I could never get my kids and husband to do anything around the house. This class helped me realize that I was demanding their help, getting mad, and then doing everything anyway. Now I ask politely and wait and make sure to say, 'thank you.' They're actually helping me now. It works!" The facilitator for a program in one of the Gallup schools said her current group of parents ranges from a 16-year-old boy, to a teen mother, to a set of Native American grandparents. About the 16-year-old boy she said, "I knew him in grade school. He had a lot of behavior problems. Then he started using drugs. He's now in recovery and volunteered for the class. He says he wants to make sure he gives his kid what he didn't get." Another parent reported, "I didn't realize how much I was putting myself down in front of my kids and how it upsets them and makes them act bad. Now, I'm trying to catch myself and we all feel better." Parents of all backgrounds and levels of education comment that they appreciate the positive, simple, down-to-earth approach of *We're Doing the Best We Can.* They also express appreciation for the opportunity to share and network with other parents. They report a sense of confidence, pride, and well-being as a result of being involved in this program.

Improving the Parenting Experience for All

A parenting program should include a nonthreatening, caring, and supportive atmosphere in order to create the environmental conditions that will foster resiliency. It must provide opportunities for parent networking, meaningful contribution, and participation as well as basic parenting skills. It must help parents identify not only their personal strengths but those of their children and family as a whole. When parents feel good about themselves, and feel capable and knowledgeable, the parenting experience improves for both themselves and their children.

Nancy Sharp-Light, M.A., has been in education since 1972 in a variety of capacities including teacher, counselor, and district coordinator for substance abuse prevention programs. In 1988, she won the award for outstanding teacher of the year in New Mexico. She has authored 11 curricula, cofounded Resiliency in Action 1996, and now lives in Colorado Springs, CO. She can be contacted at nslight@msn.com.

CHAPTER 5

Resiliency and Gender

by Bonnie Benard, M.S.W.

According to Werner and Smith (1982, 1992) in their 50-year longitudinal study of resilient children on the island of Kauai, protective factors *within* the individual (such as "easy" temperament, good reasoning skills, self-esteem, and internal locus of control) consistently tended to make a greater impact on the quality of adult coping among the high risk females than among the high risk males. During infancy, an affectionate disposition and the absence of distressing eating and sleeping habits (as well as the older age and higher educational level of the father) correlated with successful adult adaptation in women. In childhood, girls who elicited a higher proportion of positive responses from their caregivers as well as from strangers also reflected this correlation. In adolescence, more potent protective factors for girls were problem-solving skills, smaller family size, and having a mother who was "gainfully and steadily employed" (1992, p. 184). At age 17-18 having "realistic educational and vocational plans and a positive self-concept" was an important protection. At age 31-32, the most powerful protections for women were, once again, temperamental: greater activity level and lower perceived distress and emotionality.

"*Outside sources of support* tended to make a greater difference in the lives of the high risk men than of the high risk women" (1982, p. 186). During infancy, the most powerful of these outside protective factors were the mother's educational level, positive maternal interactions, and family stability. In childhood, "The emotional support provided by the family, the number of children in the family, and the number of adults outside the household with whom the youngster liked to associate" were the more potent predicators of successful adult adaptation for the high risk boys (1982, p.185).

The power of relationship for boys lay in its transactional nature–in the individual's social responsiveness and social competence to reach out and make the connection, but also in the environmental availability of outside sources of social support to offer connection. In late adolescence, "The availability of a teacher as mentor or role model and the assignment of regular household chores and responsibilities were better predictors of successful adult adaptation for high risk men than for high risk women" (1982, p.185). In early adulthood, the number of sources of emotional support available in times of stress were better predictors for the men at age 31-32 than for the women.

Gender Differences in Resilient Outcomes

Across the lifespan to age 32, Werner and Smith's research found that boys were more vulnerable in the first decade of life to adversity, girls were more vulnerable in the second, and boys once again, in the third decade. Basically–and theses findings are consistent across other longitudinal studies–boys were more at risk for physical, learning, and behavioral problems during childhood while girls were more at risk for behavioral and coping problems during adolescence. Most researchers postulate that during childhood boys are not only physically more immature, but cultural sex-role expectations put them at a disadvantage psychologically, socially, and academically in that they live in a predominantly feminine home and school environment where control of aggression is a major issue. This trend is reversed, however, during adolescence when girls must deal with their sexuality and cultural sex-role expectations that no longer encourage autonomy and mastery but dependency.

"Just as aggressiveness tended to get boys into trouble in childhood, dependency may become a major problem for girls in adolescence" (1982, p.45). In fact, according to National Institute of Mental Health statistics, "While young boys have higher rates of treated mental illness than do young girls, by late adolescence, girls have as high, if not higher, rates as their male counterparts" (in Werner & Smith, 1982, p.45). Thus their research bears out that of Carol Gilligan and others on female adolescent's loss of "sense of self."

In terms of male vulnerability in their 30's–in spite of the fact that the women in their study were exposed to more transitions (into work, motherhood, and marriage)–Werner and Smith found a correlation with stressful life events in childhood. They claim, however, more studies are needed to determine, "Whether [women's] greater resilience as a gender stabilizes by the early 30s and continues into old age" (1992, p. 169).

In summing up, two major categories of individual protective factors, or traits, that correlate with *resilient outcomes for all individuals are social competence and sense of autonomy/independence*. In most measures of personality, females are usually found to have greater social competency (i.e., relational skills) and males, a stronger sense of autonomy (i.e., being in touch with their own power) and problem-solving skills. Werner and Smith and others have found, however, *resilient adults are usually found to have a balance of both.* Werner and Smith speak to healthy development as resulting in an "*androgynous model of competence... that includes being as well as doing, nurturance as well as risk-taking, for both sons and daughters*" (1982, p.162). This is a model in which males are in touch with their relational and caring selves and females with their sense of autonomy, identity, power, and problem-solving skills. Resilient children "appear to balance a strong social orientation and social competence with a great deal of independence, and they are quick and facile in information processing" (1982, p. 68).

Search Institute Research Also Shows a "Gender Gap"

The Search Institute has also found gender differences in its research on developmental assets in adolescence (this is the only developmental stage studied by Search) that correlate with positive behaviors and developmental outcomes. Using their inital data based of 30 developmental assets (both internal and external), Search researchers came to the overall conclusion that boys lag behind girls in asset development. "A difference of about two assets can be seen in each grade between six and 12 (in both the original research on 30 assets and the research on 40 assets)" (1997, p.66). However, when girls and boys are compared on each of the 30 assets, "There is only one in which boys excel beyond girls: *self-esteem* (53% for boys, 43% for girls)" (p.66). This gap, of course, is confirmed by the research of Werner and Smith, Gilligan, and other researchers of adolescent girl development who identify how "toxic" (Pipher, 1994) this culture is to girls.

According to Benson (1997), all other assets favor girls, especially those in the categories of *boundaries and expectations, constructive use of time, commitment to learning,* and *positive values.* He postulates that this is probably due to the fact that in most cultures, societies are more protective of girls. However, "Girls often perceive this inequality in boundaries as unfair or repressive, and families often pay a price for this: Conflict between child and parent is more pronounced for adolescent girls than boys" (p.67). I view this protection as possibly two-edged in that it can be *over* protection that results in not giving girls the room and freedom to develop their own sense of self and autonomy, thus contributing to the lowering of their self-esteem.

Crucial Need: Promote the Value of Caring

One asset the Search Institute found that is particularly low in adolescent boys is that of *caring.* "Only about one third of the boys graduate from high school carrying

with them the value of helping others." The rates are 33% for boys in grades 11 and 12 (compared to 54% of girls in these two grades) (Benson, 1997, pg. 68). What this means is that during the same years adolescent girls are experiencing a loss of their sense of self, boys are experiencing a parallel drop in their level of caring (from two thirds of sixth grade boys to one third of twelfth graders). Clearly, in this stage of developing one's sexual identity, cultural stereotypes–of caring and cooperation as "girls' stuff" and power and competition as "boys' stuff"–are exerting tremendous power.

As Benson concludes,

> The value of caring for others is the glue that holds relationships together, the energy source that fuels everything from attentive parenting to civic engagement and pursuit of the common good. Pro-social values are also needed to weather the demise of publicly funded services. Addressing this fundamental issue is crucial, and boys are the ones who need the most attention. (p.68)

Certainly, if we are to become a just and caring society, the values of caring and relationship have to become central in all lives, not just in the lives of women. Ironically, fostering caring in boys means elevating the status of the feminine and thus, validating the power of girls. Werner (1982) stated that the key to effective prevention efforts is reinforcing, within every arena, the "natural social bonds... between young and old, between siblings, between friends... that give meaning to one's life and a reason for commitment and caring....[To neglect the neglect these bonds is to risk] the survival of a culture" (p.163).

References

Benson, P. (1997). *All kids are our kids: What communities must do to raise caring and responsible children and adolescents.* San Francisco: Jossey-Bass.

Pipher, M. (1994). *Reviving ophelia: Saving the selves of adolescent girls.* New York: Ballentine.

Werner, E. & Smith, R. (1982). *Vulnerable but invincible: A longitudinal study of resilient children and youth.* New Your: Adams, Bannister, Cox.

Werner, E. & Smith, R. (1992). *Overcoming the odds: High-risk children from birth to adulthood.* Ithaca, NY: Cornell University Press.

Bonnie Benard, M.S.W., has written widely and conducted workshops and trainings on resiliency for nearly 20 years. She currently works in the Health and Human Development Program of WestEd 's Oakland, CA office, where she has helped develop a statewide survey of students' perceptions of the protective factors in their lives (www.wested.org/hks). She can be reached by email at bbenard@wested.org.

CHAPTER 6

Comprehensive Study of Divorce Emphasizes Child/Parent Resiliency

by Nan Henderson, M.S.W.

This article is reprinted from the on-line newsletter, Resiliency In Action News To Use, *wwwresiliency.com.*

"After studying almost 1,400 families and more than 2,500 children—some for almost 30 years—researcher E. Mavis Hetherington finds that 75% to 80% of children from divorced homes are 'coping reasonably well and functioning in the normal range,'" reported *USA Today* in its January 14, 2002 review of Hetherington's book, *For Better or For Worse: Divorce Reconsidered.*

Hetherington, a development psychologist, writes that much of the recent discussion about divorce, both academic and popular, "has exaggerated its negative effects and ignored its sometimes considerable positive effects." Ending marriage "is an experience that for most people is challenging and painful. But it is also a window of opportunity to build a new and better life." She also found that about 70% of parents wind up leading lives described as anywhere from "good enough" to "enhanced", i.e., better than those they had before the divorce.

The Surprise Findings on Children After Divorce

Hetherington told *People* magazine, reported in its March 4, 2002 issue: "I was amazed at how many children eventually bounce back. Although it's true that kids of divorce are more than twice as likely to be troubled while growing up, keep in mind that 10% of children from intact families also have difficulties with depression or antisocial behavior," she stated. "So for every young adult from a divorced family who is having problems, three others are functioning well. It's important to focus on the resiliency of kids—the majority of whom go on to have a happy life."

Hetherington, who has been married 46 years and has three grown sons and three grandchildren, stresses that she is not pro-divorce. "I harbor no doubts about the ability of divorce to devastate," she writes in her book. But, she told *People*, many of the children she interviewed who lived with lots of parental screaming and shouting told her they "used to pray that my parents would break up." She considers divorce "a legitimate decision" and notes that if children are in marriages "with parents who are contemptuous of each other, not even with overt conflict, but just sneering and subtle putdowns that erode a partner's self-esteem, that is very bad for kids."

The Most Important Protective Factors

What separates the children who do better after divorce from those who don't do as well? Hetherington told *People*, "The most important thing in a child's life during and after a divorce is a supportive, nurturing, responsive but firm adult…a competent and caring parent who focuses on the child's needs…We didn't see one well-adjusted kid who did not have this. Love is not enough. A structured environment gives an anxious child a sense of security."

Hetherington notes that parents who "load their emotional baggage on their kids" put "a horrible burden on them." Though parents should explain to children what is going on, parents err when they "tell their children too much." Instead of the parent comforting the child at this stressful time, the child, then, is expected to provide the comfort for the adult, and that is detrimental to children, she adds.

What about the Adults?

Hetherington writes that adults with "protective factors of maturity and autonomy" fare better than those who exhibit "the risk factors of impulsiveness and antisocialibility." *USA Today* summarized the findings from Hetherington's research on ex-spouses 20 years after divorce:

- Enhanced, 20%: Mostly successful at work, socially, and as parents.
- Competent Loners, 10%: Emotionally "self-sustaining; don't need lifetime companion."
- Good Enoughs, 40%: Divorce caused tumult, but didn't make lasting impression, good or bad.
- Defeated, 10%: Succumbed to depression, substance abuse, purposelessness.
- Seekers or Libertines, 20%: Seekers want to remarry quickly. Libertines want "the fast life."

Hetherington's findings challenge the work of other academics who have painted a far darker picture of the outcome of divorce. However, *USA Today* noted that her research as drawn "awe" from many of her peers, due to its length, the inclusion of a control group, the number of participants, and its thoroughness. The book claims it is "the most comprehensive study of divorce in America." Andrew Cherlin, a sociologist at John Hopkins University, states in the *USA Today* article, "[Hetherington] is the leading social scientist who studies the effects of divorce on children."

In a January 22, 2002 interview in *The Washington Post*, Hetherington says she wishes others wouldn't be so skeptical of her findings. "Why are [they] so afraid to say that in the long run, people end up living reasonably constructive lives?" she asked.

Hetherington's research is reported in her book, For Better or for Worse: Divorce Reconsidered, *which she coauthored with John Kelly. It was published in 2002 by W.W. Norton and Company.*

Nan Henderson, M.S.W., is an international speaker, writer, and president of Resiliency In Action, a publishing and training company in Southern CA. She has authored several articles and coauthored four books on fostering resiliency, including Resiliency In Action: Practical Ideas for Overcoming Risks and Building Strengths in Youth, Families, and Communities *and* Resiliency In Schools: Making It Happen for Students and Educators. *She can be contacted at nhenderson@resiliency.com or at by calling 800-440-5171. More information is available at www.resiliency.com.*

CHAPTER 7

Resilience at the Very Start of Life

by Renee Mandala, M.A.

As a professional doula and lactation counselor, I've shared the first weeks of parenting with over 500 new parents, and have attended the journey of labor with over 65 women. Doula is a Greek word meaning a minister or servant to the birthing family, and her role is to shepherd the family through the childbearing year. A doula provides continuous physical, emotional, and informational support to the mother before during and after childbirth. Women helping women at this time of life is an ancient practice which is slowly being restored in this country.

When a family is expectant or has just given birth, they are at a critical moment in their unfolding. It is a time of unbalance, when the family is attempting to regulate to a new normal. Successfully achieving the new balance is what makes a family resilient (Patterson, 1999). The "Challenge Model" developed by Wolin and Wolin (1993) points to how the birth of a baby, although a major stressor, provides the opportunity to respond "creatively and adaptively," and can ultimately be a strength-building experience.

A Vulnerable and Powerful Time of Life

At birth and in the early postpartum time, a woman is particularly open. Physically, she must be open to give birth (this is true even in surgical birth). Psychologically, she is transitioning into a new role in her life and therefore learning, exploring, and connecting to a new self she has not yet known. She is also highly sensitive to energy within herself and in her environment. Feeling "safe" takes on new meaning to expectant, birthing, and new mothers. Mammals have been known to stop their labor and relocate to safety if feeling threatened. The image of the protective "Mama bear" that no one wants to "mess with" describes a dynamic in humans as well. Ironically, this new-found strength helps many women to leave abusive relationships when they had not found the strength to so before.

Because birthing women are particularly aware and sensitive to words and energy around them, this is a time of great influence on the new family. Fortunately, a growing awareness is emerging that the way a woman is cared for in pregnancy, birth, and the postpartum time directly influences her mothering style, bonding, her ability to respond to, and love her baby.

As for babies, pre- and perinatal psychological research is demonstrating that life in the womb, the birth experience, and early infancy is perhaps the most impres-sionistic time of life. Wendy Anne McCarty, a leader in the field of pre- and perinatal psychology, points out that babies' experiences from the beginning of life have profound impact on all areas of their development and being. These early experiences imprint a person's core view of the world, including feelings about self, health , body, and how to relate to it all (1997).

Knowing that this early time is so impressionable necessitates a close look at how to work with new families. What do they need to foster their resiliency at this crucial time?

The Power of Focusing on Strengths

Reflecting on that question, I recall a training I at-tended for birthing professionals. The first thing every day, over cups of coffee and with our still-early morning voices, our trainers opened by leading us in song. By the end of the week-long training, we sang in rounds, some of us breaking out in harmony.

(Sung to the tune of "Frere Jacques")

"When you counsel, when you counsel,
 Never judge, never judge.
 Praise mother and baby,
 Praise mother and baby,
 Do suggest, don't command.
 Do suggest, don't command."

Singing it, I felt silly. But I also felt really good, and by the third day I was looking forward to the ritual. I loved that these educators used music to ingrain in us this way of being so foundational to our work. Praising mother and baby for all that is positive, for what they are doing that is work-ing, for their resourcefulness, mirroring their strengths: these will provide a lasting, powerful imprint on new motherhood.

Rather than doling out praise mechanistically, I look at each family to reflect to them what I see, authentically, that is contributing to their resiliency. "You appear to have such attunement with your baby," I may say as I observe a new mother-baby dyad. And I watch her response. Did that resonate with the new mother? She is exploring her connec-tion with this new being, having many thoughts and feelings about their new relationship. My intention is to sit with her in her questions, while allowing and respecting her learning process as vital to her transformation into motherhood.

Along the way, I listen with my heart, check my perceptions, and mirror to her what I observe and experience. My faith in her and in her process contributes to her own trust. In labor, or even surgical birth, we breathe together. I remind her to take one contraction, one breath, at a time. And we do the same in postpartum time, and while establishing lactation.

Learning from Doula Research

In a meta-analysis of randomized trials, the presence of a doula was shown to reduce the overall cesarean rate by 50%, length of labor by 25%, percent, oxytocin use by 40%, pain medication by 30%, the need for forceps by 40%, and requests for epidurals by 60%. Studies have also concluded that women birthing with doulas report greater satisfaction in their relationship with their partner after birth, have better perceptions of their babies at six weeks, report fewer infant health problems at six weeks, and have increased breastfeeding rates at six weeks. (Klaus et al., 1993).

How can something that costs less than a spinal epidural have such powerful effects on the birthing family? Henderson (1999) tells us that "caring and support" is the most powerful environmental resiliency builder, the crucial foundation for all other resiliency-building actions. Throughout labor and the vulnerable postpartum period, doulas, lactation specialists, and other birth professionals are in the optimum position to provide this strong protective factor. "I can't do it," my client says at eight centimeters of unmedicated dilation. "You *are* doing it," I answer. "I believe in you. I am here. I am going to stay with you until your baby is born." And she goes back to the work of having her baby. These messages also assist mothers and babies to establish lactation in the early days of life, and in meeting the myriad of challenges in the first weeks and months of new parenthood. Similar sentiments expressed by any caring family member or friend assist new mothers.

Other Resiliency-Building Advice for Professionals, Family, and Friends

Outlined below, under six general protective factor headings (Henderson, 1999), are specific suggestions that any caring person can provide a new mother, father, and baby.

1. Facilitate an attitude of optimism.
Giving birth in the US has become, for the most part, a medically managed process. For some, this is helpful. For others, it is unnecessary, and I believe undermining of the psycho-spiritual transition to Motherhood. The medical model, by its very nature, is focused on identifying pathology and treating for it. Much of what is done with women is not research-based, but takes place due to the viewpoint of the provider. Award-winning medical writer Henci Goer writes,

Obstetrician-gynecologists are surgical specialists in the pathology of women's reproductive organs. The typical obstetrician is trained to view pregnant and laboring women as a series of potential problems, despite the fact that pregnancy and childbirth are normal physiological processes that are no more likely to go seriously wrong than, say, digestion. Obstetric belief tends to become a self-fulfilling prophecy. It has been said that a healthy person is someone who hasn't undergone enough testing by specialists. (1999, p. 3)

Birthing women are taught to trust the diagnosis, the doctor, the drugs, the technology before their own inner knowing. Labeling is common in the field. "My baby is too big." "My pelvis is too small." "I am too old." "I am past my due date." "I didn't make enough milk last time." It is challenging to maintain an attitude of optimism in this milieu. How can caring family, friends, and professionals promote optimism for these women and help them listen to their natural instincts and abilities?

One way is to help women to identify care providers that are aligned with their perspectives of childbirth. The midwifery model of care holds the natural birthing process in high regard, and emphasizes a supportive rather than interventive care. Finding a provider, whether obstetric, family practice MD, or midwife, who is aligned philosophically can absolutely contribute to an attitude of optimism.

Another way is to refer them to research-based materials, such as Goer's book, *The Thinking Woman's Guide to a Better Birth*. This gem of a contribution is loaded with scientific data regarding obstetric management in a way that is accessible to us all. Doulas, midwives, and childbirth educators and offer similar information.

2. Communicate high expectations of success.
Realistic and yet high expectations for their success helps to create a structure within which birthing families unfold: "Yes, you will work very hard in labor, and I believe you can do it." "Yes, you will surrender yourself in many ways to parenthood, and I trust that you will find your way." The attitude that says "I believe you can!" combined with the creation of a web of environmental resources for support are the most important resiliency-building actions to take in the childbearing year.

3. Create a web of caring and pro-social bonding.
Most families birthing in the US today are in need of support in addition to their obstetrician and child birth education class. During pregnancy, families should evaluate their specific needs and make plans for the best support they can imagine. I meet with clients prenatally to explore emotions,

thoughts, hopes, and fears around birth and postpartum. After these meetings, with greater self-awareness, new parents often choose different plans or improve upon the ones they've made.

The protective circle of care and support that new parents create might include birth planning consultation, prenatal parenting class, "Birthing From Within" class, birth art work, pregnancy journaling, pregnant and mothers singing circle, midwives, LaLeche League meetings, birth and postpartum doula care, lactation support, supportive family members, community shared /organized meal preparation and delivery, individual and/or couples counseling. I always advise expecting parents to meet and interview potential service providers, and then to ask themselves: "Is this someone I (we) could show my most vulnerable self to?" The new parents also need to ask themselves, which family/friends and professionals in their community feels most caring, most supportive, and unconditionally accepting? These are the community members to provide the caring and support in the new families' protective circle.

4. Provide opportunities for meaningful participation and contribution.

I recently had the personally powerful learning experience of working with a single 19- year-old new mother. Her journey was rocky, and I had not been completely looking at her with the perspective of resilience. I sometimes found myself negatively judging her situation, rather than finding and feeding her strengths. I learned my own resiliency lessons, however, by seeing this young mother's innate strengths and good instincts pulling her through. Nine months after the birth of her healthy baby, I talked with her about her sound natural mothering instincts. By that time, at the local mother's support group, she was showing natural leadership abilities and great wisdom at her young age. We discussed the possibility of her becoming a LaLeche League leader because her contribution could be so helpful. Another contribution I discussed with her was organizing meal preparation and delivery to a family who have just given birth.

I've often asked former clients of mine if they would be willing to receive a call from a current client who is facing a particular similar challenge related to birth or new parenting. They are often honored to be asked, and are of great service to other families. I am planning a project to gather women to tell their birth stories to pregnant woman. Almost every new mother is excited to share her stories in service to others. These are examples of ways in which the giving and sharing of gifts strengthens resilience in new parents.

5. Teach life skills.
In years past, we lived in community with extended family close-by. Today's nuclear families are often isolated. Many birthing couples have never been around babies, let alone learned about childbirth and nursing from the sisters, cousins, aunties around them. We can support the resiliency in new families by creating avenues to expose them to pregnant, birthing and new mothers and fathers, as well as newborns. Prenatal group events with pregnant and nursing families are invaluable, as are new mother/parent groups. Certainly books and films are helpful.

Having extended family come to visit and assist with the new baby can be wonderful, if the visit feels truly supportive. Sometimes, however, new parents are more stressed than supported by visiting relatives. Increasingly, a postpartum doula fills this role. This experienced and trained woman support the new parents in finding their way in early parenthood by modeling things like how to bathe a newborn, how to swaddle, or how to wear a sling. She may give suggestions about care of the new mother and baby. Ideally, she does lots of reflective listening, mirroring strengths, and encourages the parents to find their unique ways of relating to their new child.

6. "TTT - Things Take Time" (Werner, 1999).
Often when I do a home visit after the baby's birth, the mother will say "oh, my house is such a mess." She is accurately reflecting a truth, beyond the home's physical appearance. In this moment, the family is disregulated , even chaotic in an inner and outer sense. Family, friends, and professionals can support the new family by not negatively judging the current dishevelment, and by validating that chaos is often a natural part of any transition.

I love hearing from families at the baby's one year birthday. They've accomplished so much by this time! It is truly a celebration for the family. Typically, they have not only survived, but surmounted the powerful resiliency-building challenge of giving birth and blossomed into their competence and great love for their child.

References

Goer, H. (1999). *The thinking woman's guide to a better birth*. New York: Perigee Trade.

Henderson, N. (1999). Fostering resiliency in children and youth: Four basic steps for families, educators, and other caring adults. In N.Henderson, B.Benard, B., & N. Sharplight (Eds.), *Resiliency in action: Practical ideas for overcoming risks and building strengths in youth, families, and communities* (pp. 161 - 167). Ojai, CA: Resiliency In Action.

Klaus, M, H., Kennell, J.H., & Klaus, P.H.(Eds.).(1993). *Mothering the mother*, Cambridge, Massachusetts: Perseus Books.

Patterson, J. (1999). Promoting resilience in families. In N.Henderson, B.Benard, B., & N. Sharplight (Eds.), *Resiliency in action: Practical ideas for overcoming risks and building strengths in youth, families, and communities* (pp. 151-159). Ojai, CA: Resiliency In Action.

McCarty, W.A. (1997). *Being with babies, Supporting babies: Innate Wisdom, Vol. 2.* Santa Barbara, CA: Wondrous Beginnings.

Werner, E. (1999). How children become resilient: Observations and cautions. In N.Henderson, B.Benard, B., & N. Sharplight (Eds.), *Resiliency in action: Practical ideas for overcoming risks and building strengths in youth, families, and communities* (pp. 11-20). Ojai, CA: Resiliency In Action.

Wolin, S. & Wolin, S. (1993). *The resilient self: How survivors of troubled families overcome adversity.*

Renee Mandala, M.A., CD(DONA) C.L.C., writes, teaches, and speaks, and offers birthing families a full array of services including prenatal preparation, birth, postpartum, and breastfeeding consultation. She has a master's degree in spiritual psychology and a decade of professional experience with birth. She can be reached at www.FullCircleBirth.com or 310-729-4542.

CHAPTER 8

The Faces Of Resiliency

Loretta Dejolie: A Teen Mom Builds a Better Life for Her Daughter

by Nan Henderson, M.S.W.

Emmy Werner has reported that life-span studies that have followed teen-age welfare mothers into later life have found they "do not end up permanently taking Aid For Families of Dependent Children." There are only three such research studies, she said; "very few people have bothered to study them over time." In her own longitudinal research of over 50 years, "Less than five percent [of teen-age moms on welfare] were still on some kind of government support when we saw them in their mid-30s. They moved up the socioeconomic ladder as they got more education and more vocational skills, and in their mid-30s were people who had decent and well-paying jobs. Over time, teen-age mothers do work themselves out of the dependency on AFDC, given two things: one, access to continued education, and the other, access to child care." (see "How Children Become Resilient: Observations and Cautions" by Emmy Werner, Ph.D., Part One, chapter three.)

Loretta Dejolie is a living example of Emmy Werner's findings. With the help of her mother, who provided the child care, and access to a school that provided an accessible and caring opportunity for learning, Loretta will no doubt follow in the footsteps of other teen moms who have gotten off welfare and are now doing well on their own.

Loretta Dejolie dropped out of school at age 16 when she was pregnant and had a baby girl, Amber, at age 17. Before she dropped out, Loretta was skipping school, getting Ds and Fs, driving around, drinking, and "being wild"—behaviors she had begun in junior high school.

At age 17, Loretta went back to school, got all As and Bs, and planned to go to college, considering a career in nursing. Loretta credits two family members with changing her life: her mother and her baby daughter.

Loretta said her daughter changed her life even before she was born. "I quit drinking and smoking months before I got pregnant, because I knew it was going to happen," Loretta explained. "And then as soon as I got pregnant, I knew that I had to stay quit because I might be having fun, but she might be paying for it. I knew I wasn't the only one anymore. I really wanted to make a better life for her."

Loretta said that she had no idea how hard being a teen parent would be. If she had to do it again, "I would have Amber later so I could give her a better life than I'm giving her now—a house, a better environment. I should have waited."

She said she had tried not to think about getting pregnant, "but I should have thought about it... Now, it is way too much." Amber's dad moved almost 200 miles away and he and Loretta have had an on and off relationship since Amber was born. He occasionally helps Loretta financially "a little bit."

She survives, for now, by receiving welfare. But she is determined to get off. "I get AFDC but I don't like it," Loretta said. "My goal is to get off... to get a good paying job. I went back to school right after Amber was born because I felt like I had to or we'd all be stuck here forever in the same old place. I really didn't want that for Amber. I know a lot of people that do that and they're not really happy with their lives. I don't want to be like that."

Loretta believes that the children of the people she knows on welfare pay a price. "I know how their kids feel," she said. "They feel bad. I can see anger and frustration in their faces." She has a different goal for her daughter. "I want her to be happy. I want her to have everything she needs and maybe some things that she wants. I don't want to be incredibly rich. I just want to be comfortable. And I hope she'll go to college and be whatever she wants."

When asked who else—besides her daughter—helped her grow from a wild teenage girl, ditching school, and flunking to a serious student getting As and Bs and planning to attend college, Loretta quickly answered, "My mother."

"She talks to me. She encourages me to go to school. She helps me a lot with Amber. She lends me money when I need it, if she has it. If I do something good, she praises me. She tells me she is proud of me."

Loretta's mother also wants something better for her daughter than she experienced, having dropped out of high school herself, and becoming a young single mom when Loretta's dad died when Loretta was just a baby. She has lived on her husband's social security, supported three daughters, and moved frequently. Loretta, her mom, her two sisters, and Amber all live in a motel.

Nan Henderson, M.S.W., is an international speaker, writer, and president of Resiliency In Action, a publishing and training company in Southern CA. She has authored several articles and coauthored four books on fostering resiliency, including Resiliency In Action: Practical Ideas for Overcoming Risks and Building Strengths in Youth, Families, and Communities *and* Resiliency In Schools: Making It Happen for Students and Educators. *She can be contacted at nhenderson@resiliency.com or at by calling 800-440-5171. More information is available at www.resiliency.com.*

**Loretta Dejolie and
her daughter, Amber**

Loretta, however, worked with her school counselor and researched scholarships and federal aid available for her to attend college. She also credits the school—an alternative high school—with her success. She said she was directed to try it by a counselor when she went back to re-register for school after she had Amber. The principal persuaded her on the spot to attend.

That was two years ago. And Loretta says she doesn't think she would have made it in the traditional high school she started in. Instead, she thrived in the alternative school.

"It is smaller. Everybody knows each other. The teachers are really nice...you can talk to them, too, if you are having problems—not just to the counselors. They pay more attention to you. They help you get through the assignments."

Loretta offered this advice to other teenage girls that are hanging out "and being wild" and ditching class: "If you want something better you have to try...you have it do it. Nobody can do it for you." It's a message she is role-modeling for her daughter.

CHAPTER 9

The Power of One Person:

A Crucial Message for Every Family Member, Teacher, Counselor, Neighbor, and All Caring Adults

by Nan Henderson, M.S.W.

One of the most vehement questions I get asked by both parents and educators when making presentations has to do with the potent forces of negativity that assail our children and youth. "What can I do, I'm just a mom (or a grandma…or an uncle…or one teacher)?" is a common lament. Fortunately, the resiliency research strongly challenges the mistaken belief that any single person can't have much impact in a young person's life in the face of the negative forces of media and peer pressure, or even in the face of child abuse, neglect, or other trauma.

I, too, used to think I didn't have much power to make a difference when I was working as a social worker in the 1980s. I was leading "support groups" for middle school and high school students experiencing a wide variety of stressors. Due to budgetary and other limitations, the groups lasted only one school term, and met only one time a week. I used to ask myself most weeks, "What good can one hour in a group do when those kids have to go back to their environments of negative peer pressure, family dysfunction and abuse, other adults in their lives that label and judge them, or back to neighborhoods of poverty and crime?"

What I didn't understand then, but do understand now, is the potent power of protective conditions that can be provided by any and all caring adults. Looking back, I realized I instinctively filled those groups with the six primary protective conditions I have since synthesized from resiliency research. (See chapter two of Part One of this book for a detailed list of protective conditions, and a diagram of The Resiliency Wheel.) Those six protective conditions are:

- Provide caring and support;
- Provide high (but realistic) expectations for success;
- Provide opportunities for meaning participation;
- Provide pro-social bonding (to positive activities, people, organizations, etc.);
- Provide clear and consistent boundaries; and
- Provide life skills training (such things as healthy conflict resolution, setting and achieving a goal, healthy refusal and other communication skills, study skills, etc.).

One Person Can Foster Resiliency Even in the Face of Adversity

The truth about the power of protective factors is this: Even though we as caring adults cannot eliminate all the "risk factors" in a child's life, we can—in whatever time we have—fill that child's life with protective conditions. Protective factors buffer and mitigate the impact of the "negatives" in a child's life, and propel children towards resilient, healthy outcomes. This is the power that every parent, extended family member, educator, counselor, neighbor, or caring adult has in the life of a young person. We are "agents of protective factors in their lives." Many researchers have documented the power of even one such agent to turn a child's life towards a resilient outcome, even in the face of enormous adversity (Benard, 2004, Werner & Smith, 1992, Wolin & Wolin, 1993, Wolin & Wolin, 1994).

In my own life, that one person was an extended family member, my grandmother. Werner (2003) also notes that in her research, "Teachers and school were among the most frequently encountered protective factors for children…From grade school through high school and community college, resilient youngsters encountered a favorite teacher who became a positive role model for them." She adds, "Even among child survivors of concentration camps, a special teacher had a potent influence on their lives, provided them with warmth and caring, and taught them 'to behave compassionately'"(p.vii).

I had the opportunity a few years ago to talk with Emmy Werner about my personal resiliency and my recognition that I might not have had such a resilient outcome from a childhood filled with great pain and adversity had it not been for my grandmother, Mary Sue Iverson. Interestingly, she was both my grandmother and, for 50 years, a public school teacher. At the time Emmy and I talked about my grandmother, we were driving through the rust-colored Native American lands of New Mexico, exploring the ancient cultures there which, unlike many modern cultures, understood and honored the power of grandparents and the extended tribe or clan.

Perhaps more forcefully than she has written about in her research reports, Emmy offered her opinion that grandmothers (and grandfathers) are significant contributors to resilient outcomes for many, and she was very interested in the information I shared about my own grandmother.

Born in 1900, my grandmother was the strongest person I have known, yet also the most consistently nurturing person I have ever known. I am certain her career as a public school teacher, which began at age 19 in a one-room schoolhouse in Arizona, contributed to the resiliency of many students. Even after she retired at age 69, for years she was the volunteer neighborhood tutor and mentor for dozens of neighbor children. But all I knew as a child was that every week-end, I could hardly wait to "get to grandma's." She was the one that made sure I had the necessary clothing and school supplies, help with schoolwork, appropriate discipline, money, encouragement, belief that I could do what ever I set my mind to do, and–later–college tuition, which enabled me to become the person I am today. She was that "one caring person" who, in Emmy Werner's words, told my brothers and I "we mattered." She did this not merely with her words but through providing bedtime stories each night at her house, countless hours of playing games, regular meals, camping trips, hand-made Halloween costumes, science project tutoring, the safety of her ordered life. Along the way, not in one-time lectures, but in how she lived, she instilled in us the values of what was right and what was wrong. She didn't say it everyday, but my brothers and I knew by her daily actions that we were deeply loved—the most powerful protective factor of all.

It took many years and a journey into adulthood for me to understand the seriousness of the abuse my brothers and I experienced from our parents, not because they didn't love us, but because of their own problems and illnesses. And until I encountered the resiliency research, I wondered how it was I had not ended up like them. But after studying the resiliency literature, it all made sense: First and foremost, my resilient outcome was due to the power of the time I had with my grandmother. True to Werner and Smith's (1992) research, the "buffers' of that "protective-factor-rich" relationship, made "a more profound impact on [my] life course than [did] specific risk factors or stressful life events" (p.202).

The Grandmother (or Grandfather, Aunt, or Uncle) Brigade

Jonathan Kozol (1997) wrote in an article, "Reflections on Resiliency," published in *Principal* magazine, about the "spiritual and moral" power of "grandmothers, sometimes grandfathers, and even great-grandmothers—a

powerful weapon that has gone largely unnoticed by our public schools." He called this weapon "often the greatest source of ...strength" in inner-city neighborhoods. "I don't think the public schools have made enough use of these women," nor have school principals recognized their value, he wrote. He recommended forming "grandmothers' brigades" in schools, and putting the grandmas in the school buildings to teach "the children and the school," not necessarily about academics–though many, like mine did, do provide homework help–but "a good deal about respect and moral authority and simple decency" (p. 6).

Whenever I am invited to speak to educators about involving parents in children's schooling, a popular topic these days, I encourage schools to be aware of the lesson I learned long before I read the academic research that supports it: It is important to recognize that for many children, grandparents (and/or aunts and uncles or other extended family members) are the ones that are providing the primary source of caregiving. Every effort should be made to reach out and partner with these often unnoticed and unrecognized sources of support, which are in many cases making the difference between a problem-filled and resilient outcome.

One of the myths of our culture, too easy to buy into, is that whatever any of us have to contribute to the well-being of children is not enough. Philosopher and theologian Wayne Muller (1996) addressed this in his book, *How, Then, Shall We Live?* He wrote,

We each have something to offer....

The gift of many [people]...[is] quietly building and preparing so children will do well. So many... decisions made and offered without children even knowing what was given, or that there was anything given at all. Still, the gift remains, embedded in the lives of countless children who were sent forth with love [and] caring....

These people I [am speaking] about are not saints–not in the traditional sense that they are somehow better or more holy than we. Rather, they are ordinary people following the natural impulse of kindness that rises within them. Each of us has a gift to offer to the family of the earth. While the size, shape, flavor, and texture of the gift changes from person to person, the certainty of that gift is, in my experience, undeniable. (pp. 243-244)

"But What About the Fact I Don't Have Much Time?"

"But what about the fact I don't have a lot of time?" is another common question from both family members and educators. Resiliency research supports that even small acts that take very little "clock time" have a powerful impact. As Gina Higgins (1994) reports in her book, *Resilient Adults: Overcoming a Cruel Past*:

> Several subjects in this study…strongly recommended that those of you who touch the life of a child constructively, even briefly, should *never* underestimate your possible corrective impact on that child….You do not have to pull a dove out of your sleeve to make a difference….So many of the resilient emphasized that their hope was continually buttressed by the sudden kindness of strangers….Remember, too, that the surrogates [those caring adults who positively impacted the lives of subjects in this study] of the resilient were generally available for only small amounts of clock time, and some faded after a limited developmental exposure. Yet there positive impact persisted for life. (pp. 324 – 325)

The problem with believing we must be able to "pull a dove out" of our sleeve to make an impact is that this mistaken notion keeps us from providing little acts of caring and kindness. Often, for children who don't have a consistent relationship with a grandmother, other family member, or long-term mentor, it is these little acts that add up over time and integrate into a "[larger] broader fabric" of resilience that, woven thread by thread, support a child's overcoming (Higgins, 1994). I tell my audiences, "Be that person that provides caring and support in the life of a child. Use whatever time or other resources you have. Don't tell yourself you are not enough."

The Good News that Goes Unreported

Over and over again, young people have told me stories of a single comment, a single act of kindness from a family member, a teacher, a "neighborhood mom or dad," a mentor of some kind that made a huge impact at that moment of need. Often the young person didn't even recognize its power at the time; they thought about it years later, and realized its potency.

I've become convinced that the good news that goes largely unreported is that our children are supported by an army of "single individuals doing what they can." A parent, a neighbor, a teacher, a mentor, a youth pastor, a grandmother, or uncle—any or all of these people in the life of a child make a huge impact towards resiliency that goes unrecognized and unsung. Does this mean we don't need to fund programs of caring and support for children and youth in schools and communities? We absolutely do need such funding! Professional caregivers need means of financial support, and it is not possible to put too many protective factors in the lives of children. What I am saying, though, is that every one of us can take advantage of momentary opportunities to provide kindness, listening, encouragement, and other expressions of love and caring—the most powerful resiliency builders of all. All of these are delivered by a single person who in a single moment can make a significant impact on the life course of a child.

References

Benard, B. (2004). *Resiliency: What we have learned.* San Francisco, CA: WestEd.

Higgins, G. (1994). *Resilient adults: Overcoming a cruel past.* San Francisco: Jossey-Bass.

Kozol, J. (1997). Reflections on resiliency. *Principal, 77* (2), 5-7.

Muller, W. (1966). *How, then, shall we live? Four simple questions that reveal the beauty and meaning of our lives.* New York, NY: Bantam.

Werner, E. (2003). Foreword. In N. Henderson & M. Milstein, *Resiliency in schools: Making it happen for students and educators.*

Werner, E. (1998). Resilience and the life-span perspective: What we have learned so far. *Resiliency in action, 3* (4), 1,3,7-8.

Werner, E. & Smith, R. (1992). *Overcoming the odds: High risk children from birth to adulthood.* Ithaca, NY: Cornell University Press.

Wolin, S. & Wolin, S. (1993). *The resilient self: How survivors of troubled families rise above adversity.* New York: Villard.

Wolin, S. & Wolin, S. (1994). *Survivor's pride: Building resilience in youth at-risk* (video). Verona, WI; Attainment Company.

Nan Henderson, M.S.W., is an international speaker, writer, and president of Resiliency In Action, a publishing and training company in Southern CA. She has authored several articles and coauthored four books on fostering resiliency, including Resiliency In Action: Practical Ideas for Overcoming Risks and Building Strengths in Youth, Families, and Communities *and* Resiliency In Schools: Making It Happen for Students and Educators. *She can be contacted at nhenderson@resiliency.com or at by calling 800-440-5171. More information is available at www.resiliency.com.*

PART SEVEN
RESILIENCY AND THE BRAIN

CHAPTER 1

Resiliency of the Brain, Mind, and Self:
What Every Caring Adult Needs to Know

An Interview with Theoretical Neuroscientist and Author,
Peggy La Cerra, Ph.D.

by Christine Golden, M.A.

Editor's Note: Peggy La Cerra developed the scientific models of the mind and life intelligence system presented in her ground-breaking book, The Origin of Minds: Evolution, Uniqueness, and the New Science of the Self *(coauthored with science writer Roger Bingham) after completing an award-winning dissertation in evolutionary psychology. When I had the opportunity to learn from Dr. La Cerra her model of the mind and self, I was impressed with the strong connection between her work and the findings of research on fostering resiliency. Specifically, Dr. La Cerra's recommendations based on her knowledge of the brain, the mind, and the self mirror the recommendations of resiliency researchers about how to effectively nurture resiliency in children and youth. She can be contacted via the website intentionalselfcreation.com.—N.H.*

How the self develops, and how internal and external factors influence its development, are crucial questions for educators and for all who serve and care for children. Speculation and theory about the development of the self have been offered since the time of Plato, and these notions form the foundation of our current educational (and parenting) practices.

Award-winning evolutionary neuroscientist and author, Dr. Peggy La Cerra, has put forth a groundbreaking new model (called the "Energetic Model of the Mind") that details how our minds and our internal representations of our self are created as a result of our interactions with other people.

I asked Dr. La Cerra about the importance and applicability of her model for educators and everyone who interacts with children. She presents a compelling case for using this new model of the mind as a lens through which we re-envision our approach to education and how we "raise" our children and youth.

CG: Dr. La Cerra, based on your research, what is the major point you want to communicate to parents and educators about what all children need to succeed?

PLC: I would hope to convey to parents and educators an appreciation that each child's—and every person's—mind is uniquely customized to his or her own life.

CG: Can you explain what you mean when you say our minds are uniquely customized?

PLC: Sure. Our minds are arising from neural networks in our brains that are being constructed as a result of our experiences. With each experience, our minds are modified

by this construction system. All humans have the same type of "mind construction system," and so we have a great deal in common. But, because each of us is following a unique experiential path through life, we all have unique minds. As cliché as it sounds, our minds are like snowflakes: all share common properties, but no two are the same.

CG: Does the idea that our minds are customized fit in with Howard Gardner's theory of Multiple Intelligences?

PLC: Yes, but I think his theory falls short of capturing the true nature of intelligence. Let me explain. Gardner identifies at least seven distinctive capacities or dimensions of intelligence. Overlapping his model and my own, an individual's mind would be seen as having been customized along each of these seven dimensions as a result of his or her life experiences. Multiple Intelligences theory broadens the scope of abilities that are included under the rubric of intelligence, affording educators an opportunity to acknowledge the importance of children's talents on dimensions such as "body-kinesthetic" or "auditory-musical." It's a step in the direction of acknowledging the uniqueness of the individual, but falls short of recognizing that minds are *absolutely unique, multi-dimensional*, and *changing moment to moment*. We need to recognize that categorizing and labeling children —whether the label is "auditory-musical" or "behavior disordered"—can to do more harm than good.

CG: A lot has been written about labeling. As educators, we are often asked to label students as "at risk" or "gifted" or "behavior disordered." Your model of the mind, then, supports the idea that labeling is damaging.

PLC: Absolutely. Our minds are being constructed on the basis of our experiences. Labels become embedded in the fabric of children's minds. They become part of the foundation from which a child's internal representation of his or her self is arising. Negatively labeling children—or anyone–does serious damage. But even positive labels can be harmful. As an educator, you're aware that children who have been tagged as "gifted" often suffer from perfectionism which can cause chronic stress. At its worse, perfectionism can lead to anxiety, depression, and difficulty forming secure relationships.

And there's another problem with labeling that's even more insidious. Labeling gives the false impression that the brain, the mind, and the self are static—caught in position on some dimension. Nothing could be further from the truth. The mind *never stops adapting* to its environment.

When a child has been negatively labeled, or has experienced psychological trauma or failure, his or her "self representation" reflects the effect of these experiences. But in the same manner, if a child begins accruing good experiences, *if even one caring adult supports the child and mirrors the child's intrinsic value and potential, the brain, mind, and self will begin to move in the direction of generating successful behaviors.* Once these new behaviors begin to lead to rewarding experiences, the self will begin to reflect this new record of success, and the child's self-esteem will rise.

Many exceptional educators have an implicit understanding of the ever-adapting nature of the mind. They resist labeling and provide a child with a wide range of options for future behavior. They create a supportive and encouraging social environment in which children learn well and play well with others. When these factors are present, any child is capable of enormous growth and radical change.

CG: It's easy to think of resiliency as being able to bounce back from hardship. But, if I understand this model of the mind, this idea of "bouncing back" is not really accurate.

PLC: When we talk about resiliency of the brain and its mind, it is easy to mistakenly envision a rather static organ, like a rubber ball, that has the capacity to bounce back. But our brains and minds don't ever return to a previous state. They are designed by nature to change with every experience in response to feedback from the environment. What we call "resiliency" is the mind responding in a way that will enable an individual to thrive in society at large. It is important to understand, however, that the child's mind is healthy and functioning appropriately even when he or she is having trouble. The mind and self are simply reflections of the child's experiences, good or bad.

What enables a child to be resilient is his or her overall history of experience in the environment, as well the quality of feedback he or she is currently getting from the environment. Teachers, and the classroom culture they create, *are* the environment in which children are growing and changing. If the feedback a child is getting in the classroom is mirroring his or her intrinsic value and potential, he or she will respond to those inputs and exhibit resiliency. The same can be said for the feedback a child is receiving within a family, neighborhood, or within any environment.

CG: It would seem then that your research underscores the importance of creating a positive classroom climate. What would a classroom culture look like in which students thrive both socially and academically?

PLC: Ideally, everyone involved in the children's education--teachers, parents, counselors, administrators, and the children themselves--would be on board with a new paradigm based on the following tenets:

- Every child is intelligent. A child's intelligence system--its brain and its mind--are customized to fit the child's unique life. One child's intelligence system is not comparable to another child's intelligence system.
- Grades do not reflect intelligence. They reflect performance on a particular task at a particular point in time.
- All those present in the classroom, the students, the teacher, and any others, are co-creating each other by their actions and words. Therefore, everyone commits to nurturing each other's highest sense of self, by acting with respect, kindness, and caring.
- Competition among individuals is discouraged, and emphasis is placed on cooperation and success for all.

In the ideal classroom (family and community), teachers, parents, and other caring adults are co-creating children who come to like themselves, *because they are treated as likeable.* They are creating children who feel seen and heard and valued because *they are seen and heard and valued.* They are creating children who know that they are capable of bringing their unique gifts to fruition in the world *because caring adults believe in them.* In the ideal classroom, family, and community, the first lesson learned is that we shape our selves and each other with our thoughts, actions, and words.

CHAPTER 2

From Negatively-Labeled Child to Award-Winning Researcher

by Christine Golden, M.A

CG: While I was interviewing Dr. La Cerra, I was reminded of an experience she had shared at a resiliency workshop about how she had been a victim of labeling in grammar school. I asked her to retell that story.

PLC: When I was six years old, my family moved and I started second grade at a new school. The class was divided into rows, each occupying a different section of the room. The first section had two rows of "above-average students," the second had three rows of "average students," and the third had a single row of "below-average students." The other students called this last row "the retarded row."

For a reason that was never made clear to me, Miss Wise (that really was her name) assigned me to the very last seat in the "retarded row," right behind four unfortunate boys. I was devastated. For months, I shrank in that seat, wishing that I could be anywhere else. I dreaded going to school in the morning, and avoided making eye contact with the other students when I got there.

I had no choice but to endure the pain of this situation, which went on for months. In January when school resumed, standardized tests were administered; and when the test scores were announced, mine were among the highest in the school! I did so well in fact that the school principal called me, my parents, and Miss Wise into her office to discuss my future placement.

Of course, I was immediately sprung from "the retarded row." But I never forgot my time there and how it made me feel about myself, or the tragic reality that there were four other children left to deal with the humiliation of that situation. The experience really impressed upon me that our sense of our self is being shaped by the social world.

What an awesome responsibility we have to be positive in our interactions with others, especially children. In my opinion, all school counselors, teachers and administrators should have a basic understanding of how our brains are creating our minds and our "selves," and resiliency training should be mandatory for anyone who works with children.

Interviewer's Note: For a complete description of the process by which the self forms, see Dr. La Cerra's book (co-authored with science writer Roger Bingham), The Origin of Minds: Evolution, Uniqueness and the New Science of the Self *(Harmony Books, Inc., 2002). Dr. Terrance Sejnowski of the Salk Institute for Biological Studies, said* The Origin of Minds *"stands out from all previous attempts to explain the self in its firm biological foundations." As a life-long educator, I believe the "Energetic Model of the Mind" has far reaching implications for education and could serve as a catalyst for wide spread educational reform. —C.G.*

Christine Golden began her teaching career 30 years ago. After earning an M.A. in Educational Administration, she was tapped for leadership roles in her school and community, earning her first principalship in 1989 while working on an Ed.D. in Educational Leadership at the University of Illinois, Champaign-Urbana. She is an advocate of the "Middle School philosophy," a proponent of the importance of creating a positive and caring classroom environment, and is currently working with Dr. La Cerra on a book that explains the "Energetic Model of the Mind" and describes how to use that information for intentional self creation. She can be contacted via www.intentionalselfcreation.com.

RESILIENCY AND THE BRAIN

Adolescence from a Strengths Perspective: A Guide for Parents and Other Caring Adults

by Shirley Trout, M.Ed.

Editor's Note: The following is an edited version of When It Comes from You: Research Report, *a manual which accompanies a parent education program by the same name offered by the Nebraska Council to Prevent Alcohol and Drug Abuse.*

"It was the best of times, it was the worst of times."
–Charles Dickens

Psychologist Michael Newcomb in his 1996 article, "Adolescence: Pathologizing a Normal Process" published in *Clinical Psychologist*, states that for far too long adolescence has been viewed as the worst of times, emphasizing the stressful and disruptive life changes that occur during this developmental period (Newcomb & Harlow, 1986; Newcomb, Huba, & Bentler, 1981, 1986). Little attention has been devoted to understanding adolescence as the potential best of times. What could be considered normal development has become problems and pathology (Newcomb, 1986).

Wagner (1996) agrees, noting that psychologists know a lot about the continuum of abnormal to normal, but little about the other end of the spectrum: surviving to thriving. In fact, he says, positive statements about adolescents are usually worded as improvements in problem behaviors (such as a decline of cocaine usage, or in teen pregnancy) rather than identified from a criteria that delineates optimal functioning. Lewinsohn and colleagues (1993) established prevalence rates for several diagnostic disorders among adolescents. Only 8% ever met the criteria for any type of substance use disorder, 7% met criteria for any form of disruptive behavior disorder, and less than 1% met criteria for any type of eating disorder. These three diagnostic groups reflect many of the most typically considered problems during adolescence in the categories of drug use, acting out, and eating disorders. Interestingly, the most common diagnosis was for unipolar depression, with a 20% lifetime prevalence rate (Newcomb, 1996). Yet no national campaign

has emerged, there has been no outpouring of federal funds, or federal office established to wage a war on depression among teenagers, despite the fact that suicide is their third leading cause of death (Dorgan, 1995).

Newcomb (1996) challenges those who work with adolescents to place these problems within a more balanced conceptualization of adolescence and focus efforts on processes that enhance optimal development among teenagers. To see a real effect on reducing these problems, preventing them from occurring initially, and enhancing or optimizing adolescent development, we must focus on resilience, buffering factors, and mediating influences (Newcomb & Felix-Ortiz, 1992).

Adolescence is a time of birth, preparation, independence, and evolvement; it is exciting and stressful (Erickson, 1968). The extremes of emotion and demands are vast and generate equally powerful responses that reverberate throughout our lives (Newcomb & Bentler, 1988a, 1988b). To create and forge a solid individual identity, teenagers must explore available options and potential ways of being. Adolescence is a truly vital, critical period, not only in the physiological sense of pubertal development (Caspi & Moffitt, 1991), but even more so as the psychosocial transition point and final training ground for young adulthood and later adult role responsibilities (Havighurst, 1972).

Figure 1
Cyclic Changes in Behavior Pattern

	Equilibrium, Good Adjustment	Breaking Up	Equilibrium, Expansion	Inwardization	Vigorous Expansion	Inward	Equilibrium
Age in Years	2	2 1/2	3	3 1/2	4	4 1/2	5
	5	5 1/2-6	6 1/2	7	9	9	10
	10	11	12	13	14	15	16

Source: Ames, Ilg, and Baker (1989). *Your Ten- to Fourteen-Year-Old.* New York, NY: Dell.

Adolescence is the time when every person transitions from the child of yesterday to the adult of tomorrow. Yet research shows time and again, that while this transition is, indeed, a time of stretching, exploring and questioning, it is not *normal* to be fraught with anger, deviance, and explosive behavior. Almost every researcher who has studied a representative sample of normal teenagers has come to the conclusion that, by and large, good coping and a smooth transition into adulthood are much more typical than the opposite.

In fact, adolescence should be approached as a time of excitement, exhilaration, and tremendous adventure. But it takes *knowledgeable and understanding parents, educators, and other caring adults* to help make that image a reality.

Recognizing the Transitions

Biological

If asked, most adults can readily identify a number of the biological and social transitions that are unique to the early adolescent. Biologically, the child is maturing physically in appearance and in her ability to one day reproduce or his ability to facilitate reproduction. This transition involves a new series of chemical reactions and activities that result in the release of hormones. As with any new learning, this new physical condition is not immediate, nor necessarily a smooth and gradual transition. It requires the body to become adjusted to an eventual stabilization of hormonal secretions over time. And the period before that time is known as early adolescence (Steinberg, 1996).

The result on the inside? Chemical fluctuations that are normal and expected, yet not the least bit predictable. The result on the outside? A child who experiences sudden shifts of mood and temperament that are just as foreign to the child as they are to his or her parent (Steinberg, 1996).

Social

Socially, it's not difficult to recognize the tremendous transitions modern society places on its early adolescents. During this time, the child moves from the relatively safe, nurturing environment of the elementary school to large, less-personal middle school or junior high. In traditional schools, this means children must adapt to a different teacher nearly every hour. They're suddenly surrounded by several more times the number of peers as in elementary school. And feeling or being considered too old to require a babysitter, they are often left unsupervised or unattended for hours at a time, with much greater freedom and far greater ability to be away from their home (Steinberg, 1996).

As their world changes, so do the relationships that are a part of this new world. Increasingly, parents are viewed as less necessary as peers become more important (Steinberg, 1996). The long-term independencies of parent/child relationships form the basis for expectations that affect adolescents' and parents' perceptions and interpretations of each other's behavior and, therefore, guide their actions and reactions toward one another. During the transition to adolescence, discrepancies between parents' and adolescents' expectations are especially likely to occur because multiple rapid changes during adolescence make past behavior an unreliable basis for predicting actions and responses and because those changes elicit new expectations that may not be appropriate yet. Those discrepant expectations generate conflicts, which in turn stimulate realignments toward more age-appropriate expectations (Collins et al., 1997).

Early adolescence is also a more expensive time for parents, as the child becomes more involved in--indeed is targeted by--the commercial world. Yet employment opportunities and earning power are limited, and it's typically unclear whether an early adolescent even *should* work, or whether he or she should "enjoy childhood" (Steinberg, 1996).

Cognitive

But while physical and social transitions are easy to identify and--to a certain extent--understand, far less is known by the typical parent about the early adolescent's *cognitive* transitions. By understanding this important area of development, parents and other caring adults can more thoroughly understand why some days, and even some *years*, seem fraught with emotional and family discord, while others are quite peaceful and seemingly "normal.

Figure 2
Piaget's Four Stages of Cognitive Development

Birth-2 years	Sensorimotor	Discovers relationships between sensation and motor behavior
2-7	Preoperations	Uses symbols to represent objects internally, especially through language
7-11	Concrete Operations	Masters logic and begins developing "rational" thinking
11+	Formal Operations	Develops abstract and hypothetical reasoning

Somewhere around age 11, dramatic mental events start to take place. Having mastered the world of objects, the early teenager must move on to manipulating abstract ideas--a transition from the security of concrete rules to a world of infinite possibilities and points of view. Enlarged mental perspectives create a sudden awareness of "ideals," and the adolescent may ruthlessly criticize his or her own family. Difficult as they are, these youngsters are covering necessary ground, learning to build with abstract ideas just as they once manipulated building blocks from their toy box (Healy, 1997).

It is during this time that students first develop powers of abstract reasoning. They begin to think of the world around them and themselves in new ways. For the first time, young adolescents can "think about thinking"--which often confuses them. This "reflexive thinking" allows them to form sophisticated self-concepts that are shaped by interactions between their experiences and new powers of reasoning. Understanding the development of abstract reasoning and reflexive thinking is especially important for successful teaching at the middle level.

Adolescence is the first time the child has the intellectual capability to appreciate the changes taking place. This cognitive ability allows adolescents to combine concrete objects and facts with abstract concepts and time. During puberty, the *outside* changes are happening so dramatically, the adolescent understandably has questions about changes taking place on the *inside*. With the changes occurring in the way he or she can think, this opens up a whole new world of alternatives. This, combined with radical new social roles, opens up a new array of choices and decisions that were not options prior to this time in the child's life.

In his provocative book, *Evolution's End*, author Joseph Chilton Pearce (1992) systematically unfolds the complexities of brain development from fetus to early adulthood. By getting even a basic comprehension of this development, early adolescent behavior not only becomes less confusing, but helps parents and teachers recognize and enjoy the special challenges of this important transitional time of life.

Pearce writes:

"Nature's imperative" involves an over-arching in brain development: That is, no intelligence or ability will unfold until or unless given the appropriate model environment. The character, nature, and quality of the model environment

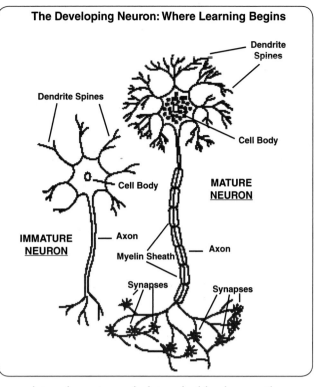

The Developing Neuron: Where Learning Begins

determines, to an indeterminable degree, the character, nature, and quality of the intelligence unfolding in the child.

"Myelinating" refers to some maturation or stabilization of neural structure as the brain develops. Several times in an infant-child's development the brain cleans house--releases a chemical that dissolves all unproductive, unused, or redundant axodendrite connections (and possibly various supportive cells as well), leaving the productive, developed neural fields intact. A field's imperviousness to this housecleaning chemical seems to involve a fatty protein called *myelin* (Giorgi). As learning takes place, myelin forms an insulating sheath around the long axon connections of the neural fields involved and corresponding muscular nerves. Myelin is impervious to the chemicals used in housecleaning; its sheathing somehow helps preserve that particular network, making that ability permanent. (p.20)

As learning develops, fewer connections can do the job. An initially slow, clumsy operation gets smooth and goes on "automatic pilot" when the myriad neural fields involved have myelinated enough to become a new intelligence or ability at our disposal. Repetition may stimulate myelination. The more frequent the response, the more myelin forms; the thicker the myelin sheathing, the quicker information can be conveyed; the more firm and lasting the learning, the more efficient and compact the particular neural network becomes. (p.22)

This explanation of the brain's developmental process becomes especially important in the early adolescent years because, as Pearce explains:

At around age 15 or so, the hemispheres have myelinated, and research indicates no further brain growth spurts or detectable change after that. Were the young person given the appropriate stimuli, a brain growth spurt would take place around age 15, ushering in the new block of intelligences obviously waiting.

All further development we undergo after 15 or so, our "higher education" and lifelong learning, is but an extension of or adaptation of the foundation of intelligences developed in those first 15 years. (p.192)

Keating (1990) described the unique transition in early adolescent cognition as it matures from the Piagetian description of concrete operations to formal operational (see Figure 2):

1. During adolescence individuals become better able than children to think about what is possible, instead of limiting their thought to what is real.
2. Adolescents become better able to think about abstract things.
3. During adolescence individuals begin thinking more often about the process of thinking itself.
4. Adolescents' thinking tends to become multidimensional, rather than being limited to a single issue.
5. Adolescents are more likely than children to see things as relative, rather than absolute (Steinberg, 1996).

Developmental Challenges

Steinberg (1996) explains that there are five basic developmental challenges that all people face as they grow and change: discovering and understanding who they are as individuals (identity), establishing a healthy sense of independence (autonomy), forming close and caring relationships with other people (intimacy), expressing sexual feelings and enjoying physical contact with others (sexuality), and being successful and competent members of society (achievement).

One reason the changes become so complex and so challenging for adolescents is that they must face these challenges in four specific yet different contexts: within their families, their peer groups, their schools, and their places of work and leisure.

Establishing Identity/Self Concept/Self-Esteem

During puberty, when adolescents are changing so radically on the outside, they understandably have questions about who they are--or are becoming--on the inside. Changes in social role opens up a new array of choices that were not available previously. It is during this time that the young person starts facing decisions about work, marriage and the future.

In light of these decisions, adolescents are constantly asking themselves, "What do I *really* want out of life?" "What things are important to me?" "What kind of person do I *really* want to become?" Generally, researchers and theorists have taken three different approaches to the question of how a person's sense of identity changes over the adolescent years.

The first approach emphasizes changes in *self-conceptions*--the ideas that individuals have of themselves in terms of traits and attributes. A second approach focuses on adolescents' changes in *self-esteem*, or self-image--how positively or negatively individuals feel about themselves. Finally, the third approach emphasizes changes in the *sense of identity*--the sense of who one is, where one has come from, and where one is going (Steinberg, 1996).

Researchers have identified three personality types replicable for study of adolescent behavior and development (Hart, Hofmann, Edelstein, & Keller, 1997). The types have been labeled as resilient, overcontrolled, and undercontrolled. The *resilient* type of child is self-confident, independent, fluent verbally, and able to concentrate on tasks; the *overcontrolled* child is shy, quiet, anxious, and dependable; and the *undercontrolled* child is impulsive, stubborn, and physically active (Hart et al., 1997).

Hart and colleagues demonstrated that the personality types have coherent patterns of relationships to adolescent development. The "resilient children" in this model have fewer concentration problems in school than do children of the other two types, with this advantage continuing into mid-adolescence.

Figure 5: The eight stages of development and their corresponding psychosocial crisis, according to Erickson (1959).

Stage	1	2	3	4	5	6	7	8
I Infancy	Trust vs. mistrust							
II Early childhood		Autonomy vs. shame, doubt						
III Play age			Initiative vs. guilt					
IV School age				Industry vs. inferiority				
V Adolescence					Identity vs. identity diffusion			
VI Young adult						Intimacy vs. isolation		
VII Adulthood							Generativity vs. self-absorption	
VIII Mature Age								Integrity vs. disgust, despair

Self-conceptions become increasingly complex throughout the adolescent years because of continual intellectual growth and development. Whereas an early adolescent is only beginning to process his "self" in complex ways, the older adolescent can understand how her actions may differ from where she wants to go in her life, or how she can be "different people" in different social groups (Steinberg, 1996). Hart concluded that because resilient children are better prepared to enter into and to benefit developmentally from social interactions, they manifest higher levels of friendship reasoning in childhood and adolescence. Finally, their ability to adapt to and to succeed in difficult contexts encourages the development of an internal locus of control (Hart et al., 1997).

In general, self-esteem tends to become increasingly more stable with age, suggesting that adolescents' feelings about themselves gradually consolidate over time and become less likely to fluctuate in response to different experiences (Alasker & Olweus, 1992). In the research conducted by Hart and colleagues (1997), the overcontrolled children showed consistent difficulties across childhood and adolescence in engaging successfully in social interaction. Moreover, the anxiety and fearfulness of the overcontrolled children was reflected in early and mid-adolescence in consistently low self-esteem scores.

The undercontrolled children differed significantly in adolescence from those of the other two groups in their levels of aggressive behaviors, and their developmental trajectories suggested that their negative, aversive interactions with others increased more rapidly than was true for those of the resilient and overcontrolled types. What is particularly interesting about the undercontrolled children is that they maintained high self-esteem (the estimated score for this group at age 15 was actually higher than the estimated score for those of the resilient type). This higher score suggests that their problems in adaptation reported by others do not necessarily influence their own self-conceptions (Hart et al., 1997). On the basis of their review of the literature, Baumeister, Smart, and Boden (1996) have suggested that high self-esteem is often associated with aggression in adolescents and adults (Hart et al., 1997).

Erickson (1959) identified eight stages of development and their correspondent psychosocial crises (see Figure 5). The fifth crisis he identified he termed *identity versus identity diffusion.* The key to resolving the crisis of identity versus identity diffusion, Erickson argued, lies in the adolescent's interactions with others. Through responding to the reactions of people who matter, the adolescent selects and chooses from among the many elements that

According to Kobak et al., adolescent attachments are characterized as secure, dismissing, or preoccupied.

The Secure Adolescent:

- interacts with their mother with less unhealthy anger and more appropriate assertiveness;
- is generally trusting in his/her relationships;
- is generous, forgiving of faults in self and parents;
- has more stable romantic relationships than their insecure counterparts

Furthermore, elevations in skin conductance have been shown in previous research to occur when individuals are being deceptive and when they deliberately attempt to inhibit their emotions in the presence of emotionally powerful and disturbing materials. Kobak found that individuals who were classified as dismissing showed marked increases in skin conductance when asked to recall experiences of separation and rejection by their parents.

SOURCE: Kobak, R., Cole, H., Ferenz-Gillies, R., Flemming, W., & Gamble, W. (1993). Attachment and emotion regulation during mother-teen problem-solving: A control theory analysis. *Child Development, 64,* 231-245.

could conceivably become a part of his or her adult identity (Steinberg, 1996).

Glenn and Nelson (1989) offer the analogy of a person facing a huge smorgasbord of choices. During adolescence, the young person must pick and choose what he or she is going to place into his/her own identity.

Erickson placed a great deal of weight on the role of the young person's society (and especially on those individuals who have influence over the adolescent) in shaping the adolescent's sense of self.

Working Toward Autonomy

Crittendon (1990) has defined autonomy as "capacities for taking responsibility for one's own behavior, making decisions regarding one's own life, and maintaining supportive relationships" (p. 162). Hill and Holmbeck (1986) have proposed that autonomy refers not to freedom *from* others (e.g., parents) but freedom *to* carry out actions on the adolescent's own behalf while maintaining appropriate connections to significant others (Collins et al., 1997). Autonomy is similar to--but not the same as--independence,

which refers to a person's ability to make his or her own decisions and then carry them out. Autonomy includes independence, but also refers to the emotional and cognitive ability to act for oneself.

A central task of development during adolescence is to transform the parent/child bond from the level of connection needed by children, to one more appropriate for young adults, leading to more positive adolescent and adult outcomes (Herman et al., 1997). Becoming an autonomous person--a self-governing person--is one of the fundamental developmental tasks of the adolescent (Steinberg).

Maintaining Healthy Attachment (Intimacy)

As has been stated many times already, the need for healthy relationships--healthy attachment--is not unique to the adolescent. During childhood, not having friends is association with a range of psychological and social problems (Hartup, 1983). And adult studies recognize that people who have others to turn to for emotional support are less likely to suffer from psychological and physical disorders (Myers, Lindenthal, & Pepper, 1975).

A child who has experienced supportive parents is likely to develop an internal representation of others as helpful and responsive, as well as a model of the self as worthy of respect and care. Children with secure representations are thus more prone to approach new experiences with confidence and trust. Children who have had experiences of rejection or neglect, in contrast, are likely to develop insecure attachment representations. These children are more vulnerable in approaching new people and situations, because they lack confidence that they will be responded to in a sensitive manner (Jacobsen & Hofmann, 1997).

Adolescents who have friendships typically have better mental health than peers who do not. Healthy adolescent development involves not only the ability to be a successful individual, but also the ability to maintain healthy and satisfying attachments with others (Steinberg, 1996). Children who have adapted well in early development generally continue to do so in adolescence, whereas those with more problematic adjustment persist in showing difficulties (Jacobsen, 1997).

Developing One's Sexuality

There are four developmental challenges concerning sexuality in adolescents (Brooks-Gunn & Paikoff, 1993):

1. The adolescent needs to feel comfortable with his or her body, its shape, size, and attractiveness;
2. The individual should accept having feelings of sexual arousal as normal and appropriate;
3. Healthy sexual development in adolescence involves understanding that sex is a voluntary activity for oneself and for one's partner. In other words, a person should neither feel forced into it, nor force another into it.
4. Healthy sexual development, for those sexually active, includes understanding and practicing safe sex, thus avoiding pregnancy and sexually transmitted diseases.

By age 15, about one third of all American males and one fourth of American females have had sexual intercourse. Among the most important predictors of adolescent sexual activity were having a steady boyfriend or girlfriend, using alcohol regularly, having parents with permissive values about sex, and being worried about one's future occupational chances.

In keeping with Newcomb's challenge to focus on what is *right* about adolescence, however, flip that seemingly alarming statistic and look at "the rest of the story." That is, whereas one third of the males may have engaged in sexual intercourse by age 15, that leaves 65 % of males who have not. And 75% of the American females in that age range have not. It is important for researchers, educators, parents--and even adolescents themselves--to keep in mind the full picture when identifying "characteristic" adolescent behavior. Hansen (1997) has identified "normative beliefs"--that which the early adolescent *believes* to be "normal" peer behavior--to be the most effective determinant of early adolescent onset or rejection of engaging in high-risk behaviors (see Part Two, chapter eight).

Reaching Achievement

Achievement is an important consideration in the study of adolescents in contemporary society largely because of the social importance placed on it (Steinberg, 1996). Industrial societies place an extraordinary emphasis on achievement, competition and success more so than on cooperation or development of satisfying interpersonal relationships (McClelland, 1961). It is also important because of the range and rapidly changing nature of the choices faced by today's young people.

Finally, achievement is an important issue because of the wide variation in levels of educational and occupational success. While there is a significant relationship between socioeconomic status and adolescent achievement (Steinberg, 1996), resiliency research is full of examples of individuals "rising above" their environment to achieve tremendous success in their lifetime. The two profound characteristics running throughout the resiliency success stories are 1) a healthy attachment with a significant, responsible adult, and 2) purpose or responsibility within the adolescent's environment.

Individuals differ in the extent to which they try to succeed. This is referred to as his or her *need for achievement* (Steinberg, 1996). Generally, researchers have found that adolescents who have a strong need for achievement come from families in which parents have set high performance standards, have rewarded achievement success during childhood, and have encouraged autonomy and independence (Rosen & D'Andrade, 1959; Winterbottom, 1958). Equally important, however, this training for achievement and independence generally takes place in the context of warm parent-child relationships in which the child forms close identifications with his or her parents (Shaw & White, 1965).

Studies have shown that adolescent achievement is directly related to the level of achievement that their parents *expect* them to attain (Steinberg, 1996). Resiliency research argues that in cases where the parent is *not* providing that encouragement, a significant responsible adult *outside* the family can accomplish the same level of need for achievement. With that inclusion, Steinberg's list of parental influences holds true.

Steinberg (1996) writes that parents who encourage school success:

1. set higher standards for their child's performance and have higher aspirations for their child;
2. support values consistent with good school performance and structure their home to support messages from school;
3. are more likely to be involved in their child's education.

Conclusion: Adolescent Transitions as Normal and Essential

While early adolescence is, indeed, a complex time of every person's life, it is by no means something to be feared or dreaded. In fact, the significant transitions that face the early adolescent are not only *normal*, but they are *essential* to healthy growth and development.

Youth at this age are facing change in just about every aspect of their existence: physically, socially and intellectually. Some of these changes are so apparent that even the child himself or herself recognizes that life, as they have known it, will never be the same. Yet other changes are happening within the person, and can only be understood by understanding, educated adults. The more the significant adults in any early adolescent's life understands about these natural and necessary transitions toward *autonomy* while balancing a healthy *attachment* to one's family or some other significant adult, the greater the likelihood that a child will engage in normal, nonexplosive years of healthy growth and development.

The result will be an autonomous young adult who functions well in society while maintaining a healthy attachment to family and other prosocial individuals and organizations. A healthy adult child is the reward for parents and others who understand the importance of this transitional time and help adolescents weather the storms which occasionally will interject themselves into a typically healthy family, school, and social environment.

References

Ames, L. B., Ilg, F. L., & Baker, S. M. (1989). *Your ten- to fourteen-year-old*. New York: Dell.

Alasker, F. & Olweus, D. (1992). Stability of global self-evaluations in early adolescence: A cohort longitudinal study. *Journal of Research on Adolescence, 1*, 123-145.

Barber, B. (1997). Adolescent socialization in context: The role of connection, regulation, and autonomy in the family. *Journal of Adolescent Research, 12*(1), 5-11.

Baumeister, R. F., Smart, L., & Boden, J. M. (1997). Relation of threatened egotism to violence and aggression: The dark side of high self-esteem. *Psychological Review, 103*, 5-33.

Best, K. M., Hauser, S. T., & Allen, J. P. (1997). Predicting young adult competencies: Adolescent era parent and individual influences. *Journal of Adolescent Research, 12*(1), 90-112.

Boss, P. G., Doherty, W. J., LaRossa, R., Schumm, W. R., & Steinmetz, S. K. (Eds.). (1993). *Sourcebook of family theories and methods: A contextual approach*. New York: Plenum.

Brooks-Gunn, J. & Paikoff, R. (1993). "Sex is a gamble, kissing is a game": Adolescent sexuality and health promotion. In S. Millstein, A. Petersen, & E. Nightingale (Eds.), *Promoting the health of adolescents: New directions for the twenty-first century* (pp. 180-208). New York: Oxford University Press.

Caissy, G. A. (1994). *Early adolescence: Understanding the 10- to 15-year-old*. New York: Plenum.

Caspi, A. & Moffitt, T. (1991). Individual differences and personal transitions: The sample case of girls at puberty. *Journal of Personality and Social Psychology, 61*, 157-168.

Collins, W. A., Laursen, B., Mortensen, N., Luebker, C., & Ferreria, M. (1997). Conflict processes and transitions in parent and peer relationships: Implications for autonomy and regulation. *Journal of Adolescent Research, 12*(1), 178-198.

Conger, K. J., Conger, R. D., & Scaramella, L. V. (1997). Parents, siblings, psychological control, and adolescent adjustment. *Journal of Adolescent Research, 12*(1), 113-138.

Crittenden, P. M. (1990). Toward a concept of autonomy in adolescents with a disability. *Children's Health Care, 19*, 162-168.

Dorgan, C. A. (1995). *Statistical record of health and medicine*. Detroit, MI: Gale Research.

Erickson, E. (1959). Identity and the life cycle. *Psychological Issues, 1*, 1-171.

Erickson, E. (1968). *Identity: Youth and crisis*. New York: Norton.

Giorgi, D. How the brain wraps up. *New Science, 112*(26), 486.

Glenn, S. H. & Nelsen, J. (1989). *Raising self-reliant children in a self-indulgent world: Seven building blocks for developing capable young people*. Rocklin, CA: Prima.

Hansen, W. B. (1997). *All stars youth curriculum*. Clemmons, NC: Tanglewood Research.

Hart, D., Hofmann, V., Edelstein, E., & Keller, M. (1997). The relation of childhood personality types to adolescent behavior and development: A longitudinal study of Icelandic children. *Developmental Psychology, 33*(2), 195-205.

Hartup, W. (1983). Peer relations. In E. M. Hetherington (Ed.), *Handbook of child psychology: Socialization, personality, and social development*, Vol. 4. New York: Wiley.

Havighurst, R. J. (1972). *Developmental tasks and education* (3rd ed.). New York: McKay.

Healy, Jane M. (1994). *Your child's growing mind*. New York: Doubleday.

Herman, M. R., Dombusch, S. M., Herron, M C., & Herting, J. R. (1997). The influence of family regulation, connection, and psychological autonomy on six measures of adolescent functioning. *Journal of Adolescent Research, 12*(1), 34-67.

Hill, J. P. & Holmbeck, G. N. (1986). Attachment and autonomy during adolescence. *Annals of Child Development, 3*, 145-189.

Jacobsen, T., Edelstein, W., & Hofmann, V. (1994). A longitudinal study of the relation between representations of attachment in childhood and cognitive functioning in childhood and adolescence. *Developmental Psychology, 30*, 112-124.

Jacobsen, T. & Hofmann, V. (1997). Children's attachment representations: Longitudinal relations to school behavior and academic competency in middle childhood and adolescence. *Developmental Psychology, 33*(4), 703-710.

Johnson, S. B. (1994). Counseling with children: Comments from a child psychologist. *The Counseling Psychologist, 22*, 458-461.

Keating, D. (1990). Adolescent thinking. In S. Feldman & G. Elliott (Eds.), *At the threshold: The developing adolescent* (pp. 54-89). Cambridge, Mass.: Harvard University Press.

Liedloff, J. (1975). *The continuum concept*. New York: Addison-Wesley.

Lewinsohn, P., Hops, H., Roberts, R., Seeley, J., & Andrews, J. (1993). Adolescent psychopathology, I: Prevalence and incidence of depression and other *DSM-III-R* disorders in high school students. *Journal of Abnormal Psychology, 102*, 133-144.

Litchfield, A. W., Thomas, D. L., & Li, B. D. (1997). Dimensions of religiosity as mediators of the relations between parenting and adolescent deviant behavior. *Journal of Adolescent Research, 12*(2), 199-226.

McClelland, D. (1961). *The achieving society*. Princeton, NJ: Van Nostrand.

Myers, J., Lindenthal, J., & Pepper, M. (1975). Life events, social integration, and psychiatric symptomatology. *Journal of Health and Social Behavior, 16*, 421-429.

Nelson, J. & Lott, L. (1994). *Positive discipline for teenagers*. Rocklin, CA: Prima.

Newcomb, M. (1996). Adolescence: Pathologizing a normal process. *The Counseling Psychologist, 24*(3), 482-490.

Newcomb, M. D. & Bentler, P. M. (1988a). *Consequences of adolescent drug use: Impact on the lives of young adults*. Newbury Park, CA: Sage.

Newcomb, M. D. & Bentler, P. M. (1988b). Impact of adolescent drug use and social support on problems of young adults: A longitudinal study. *Journal of Abnormal Psychology, 97*, 64-75.

Newcomb, M. & Felix-Ortiz, M. (1992). Multiple protective and risk factors for drug use and abuse: Cross-sectional and prospective findings. *Journal of Personality and Social Psychology, 63*, 280-296.

Newcomb, M. D. & Harlow, L. L. (1986). Life events and substance use among adolescents: Mediating effects of perceived loss of control and meaninglessness in life. *Journal of Personality and Social Psychology, 51*, 564-577.

Newcomb, M., Huba, G., & Bentler, P. (1981). A multidimensional assessment of stressful life events among adolescents: Derivation and correlates. *Journal of Health and Social Behavior, 22*, 400-415.

Newcomb, M., Huba, G., & Bentler, P. (1986). Determinants of sexual and dating behavior among adolescents. *Journal of Personality and Social Psychology, 50*, 428-438.

Pearce, J. C. (1992). *Evolution's end: Claiming the potential of our intelligence*. New York: HarperSanFrancisco.

Rosen, B., & D'Andrade, R. (1959). The psychosocial origins of achievement motivation. *Sociometry, 22*, 185-218.

Shaw, M., & White, D. (1965). The relationship between child-parent identification and academic underachievement. *Journal of Clinical Psychology, 21*, 10-13.

Schroeder, B. (1987). *Help kids say no to drugs and drinking*. Minneapolis: CompCare.

Steinberg, L. D. (1996). *Adolescence* (4th ed.). McGraw-Hill.

Trout, S. K. (1993). *Humor in your home doesn't mean your home is a joke*. Waverly, NE: Teachable Moments.

Trout, S. K. (1997). *Light dances: Illuminating families with laughter and love*. Waverly, NE: Teachable Moments.

Wagner, W. G. (1996). Optimal development in adolescence: What is it and how can it be encouraged? *The Counseling Psychologist, 24*(3), 360-399.

Wavering, M. J. (1995). Cognitive development of young adolescents. In M. J. Wavering (Ed.) *Educating young adolescents: Life in the middle* (pp. 111-130). Garland reference library of social science.

Wilmes, D. J. (1995). *Parenting for prevention: How to raise a child to say no to alcohol and other drugs*. Minneapolis: Johnson Institute-QVS.

Winterbottom, M. (1958). The relation of need for achievement to learning experiences in independence and mastery. In J. Adkinson (Ed.), *Motives in fantasy, action, and society*. Princeton, N.J.: Van Nostrand.

Shirley Trout, M.Ed., is the Director of Parent Education for the Nebraska Council to Prevent Alcohol and Drug Abuse, and the owner of her own publishing and training organization, Teachable Moments. She provices training on prevention, resiliency, adolescent development, parenting, and humor, and can be reached at strout@teachablemoments.com.

CHAPTER 4

Brain-Based Strategies
for Helping Challenging Youth

adapted from "The Resilient Brain" by Larry Brendtro and James Longhurst

Editor's note: Brendtro's and Longhurst's detailed article, "The Resilient Brain" appeared in the Spring, 2005 issue of the journal, Reclaiming Children and Youth. *The entire article is informative and can be accessed at www.pe4life.org/articles/the_resilient_brain.pdf. Below is an edited version of the practical suggestions included in the article for working with "challenging" youth—kids who have had less than optimum conditions in their lives. These strategies integrate brain-based and resiliency-building strategies. As the authors' note, all kids have "resilient brains that can be 'rewired' by positive learning experiences"(p.52).—N.H.*

Brendtro and Longhurst state in the introduction to their article "The Resilient Brain," "Resilience turns out to be a natural trait of all humans. This should not be surprising since our brains are specifically wired to cope with problems." They go on to note,

Recent advances in resilience science provide a roadmap for positive youth development, even in the face of adversity. Perhaps the most exciting finding is that the human brain is designed to be resilient. Resilience is universal across all cultures and encoded in human DNA. New imaging techniques are providing a better understanding of key brain-based processes impacting risk and resilience. It turns out the brain is in the business of overcoming risk. (p.53)

Below is a list of seven strategies from Brendtro and Longhurst, "blending brain science, resilience research, and best practices...for turning problems into opportunities...to develop...strength and resilience" (p.58):

1. "Disengage from destructive conflict."

This strategy involves several steps: It starts with never taking anger personally. It is useful to tell oneself that this young person is "a kid in pain" and to manage emotions in a stressful interaction so that this kid's pain is not added to, nor does his or her pain become our pain. Next, monitor and defuse emotional arousal in oneself and in the young person by being aware of internal and external cues of anger or fear that might be reaching disruptive levels. Time outs can help in intense emotional situations. Otherwise, listen with empathy and caring; provide forgiveness and kindness as a way of modeling to the young person how to "rebuild damaged relationships" (p. 58).

2. It is important, however, to "connect in times of conflict."

In stress or crisis, a child's brain is "signaling 'find somebody safe.'" This is an opportunity to take advantage of children's "natural brain programs motivating them to attach" to trustworthy persons at times they are upset or in trouble. Therefore, using discipline "by punishment or exclusion only creates further threat. Conflict and crisis present unparalleled opportunities to build trust, respect, and understanding" (p. 59).

3. "Reach out to guarded youth."

Instead of waiting for crises or problems to emerge, it is useful to practice "pre-emptive connecting with wary youth." This connecting needs to be unobtrusive to avoid any impression of favoritism. It is important to remember that this kind of connecting "does not require a major investment of time." In fact, it is more effective to bond in "natural moment-by-moment interactions." This is because forcing a quick intimacy can frighten or threaten kids who have been abused or traumatized. "Those with histories of negative encounters with adults are [positively and] strongly influenced by small cues of respect, humor, and good-will. The 'emotional brain' signals, 'This person is safe'" (p. 58).

4. "Avoid a judgmental tone."

The skill here is being able to offer needed suggestions while at the same time "communicating positive regard." It is important not to ignore problems, but "criticism conveying anger or disgust only drives youth away." Correction must be delivered at the same time as expressions of caring and positive regard. "To avoid adversarial encounters, respond to needs and search for strengths" (p.59). It is also often possible to find strengths in "negative" or acting out behavior and frame correction in an overall message of strength. For example, it is both strength-affirming and correcting to say to a runaway, "You were trying to care for yourself by getting to a place that was safer than home feels right now. And that's a strength. We just have to figure out a better place that truly is safer."

5. "Understand behavior"—intense emotions often cloud rational/good decision-making.

It is counterproductive to try to reason with kids about "consequences of behavior" when their "emotional brain" is still in charge. Intense emotions of any kind overwhelm children's rationality, and demanding rationality "may frustrate them further." This is "especially true in instances where the current experience triggers past pain or trauma. As we understand behavior from [this] perspective, we become sources of safety and encourage the 'thinking brain' to assume control" (p. 59).

6. "Clarify challenging problems."

The human brain "is designed to make meaning out of chaos and confusion. Kids need understanding adults who can help them "sort out 'what happened.'" Using the brain's innate "inclination to find meaning in events" helps youth learn from difficult experiences. "By exploring what happened in some conflict, such as getting kicked out of class, we help a youth develop more effective coping strategies. Resolving problems is the foundation for building resilience" (p. 59).

7. "Restore harmony and respect."

Conflict and discord "trigger painful emotions in the brain." By providing youth with external support and affirming and building their inner strengths, "we help youth resolve problems and restore harmony." By contrast, "traditional discipline" is based on pain-based methods that are counterproductive and ineffective in motivating change. "Restorative methods seek to restore broken bonds and build a climate of mutual respect" (p.59).

Larry Brendtro, Ph.D., is president of Reclaiming Youth International and former president of Starr Commonwealth, Albion, MI, where he continues to serve as dean of research and professional development. He can be contacted by e-mail: courage@reclaiming.com.

James Longhurst, Ed.D., is vice president for clinical and psychological services at Starr Commonwealth, which serves troubled children and youth in MI and OH. He can be contacted by e-mail: longhurstj@starr.org.

CHAPTER 5

The Brain-Building Power of Music:
Research Briefs on the Power of Music to Improve Academic and Life Success
Reprinted from the American Music Conference

Editor's Note: The following summary of some of the research documenting the power of music on brain functioning, cognitive development, academic success, and life success is reprinted from the resource- and research-rich website of American Music Conference (AMC), www.amc-music.org. AMC is a national non-profit educational association founded in 1947 "dedicated to promoting the importance of music, music-making, and music education to the general public." The findings below validate brain-based learning expert Eric Jensen's conclusions that "Music is part of our biological heritage and is hard-wired into our genes...Music-making contributes to the development of essential cognitive systems which include reasoning, creativity, thinking, decision-making, and problem-solving." Jensen makes these comments on another excellent website that details the benefits of music, www.songsforteaching.com.—N.H.

The pace of scientific research into music making has never been greater. New data about music's relationship to brainpower, wellness, and other phenomena is changing the way we perceive mankind's oldest art form, and it's having a real-world effect on decisions about educational priorities. The briefs below provide a glimpse into these exciting developments. For a more in-depth treatment of current music science, visit The Interbational Foundation for Music Research, at www. music-research.org.

Music Improves Math, Science, and Language Arts

1. Middle school and high school students who participated in instrumental music scored significantly higher than their non-band peers in standardized tests. University studies conducted in Georgia and Texas found significant correlations between the number of years of instrumental music instruction and academic achievement in math, science, and language arts.
Sources: University of Sarasota Study, Jeffrey Lynn Kluball; East Texas State University Study, Daryl Erick Trent.

2. Students who were exposed to the music-based lessons scored a full 100% higher on fractions tests than those who learned in the conventional manner. Second-grade and third-grade students were taught fractions in an untraditional manner by teaching them basic music rhythm notation. The group was taught about the relationships between eighth, quarter, half, and whole notes. Their peers received traditional fraction instruction.
Source: Neurological Research, March 15, 1999.

3. Music majors are the most likely group of college grads to be admitted to medical school. Physician and biologist Lewis

Thomas studied the undergraduate majors of medical school applicants. He found that 66% of music majors who applied to med school were admitted, the highest percentage of any group. For comparison, 44 % of biochemistry majors were admitted. Also, a study of 7,500 university students revealed that music majors scored the highest reading scores among all majors including English, biology, chemistry, and math.
Sources: "The Comparative Academic Abilities of Students in Education and in Other Areas of a Multi-focus University," Peter H. Wood, ERIC Document No. ED327480; "The Case for Music in the Schools," Phi Delta Kappan, February, 1994.

4. Music study can help kids understand advanced math concepts. A grasp of proportional math and fractions is a prerequisite to math at higher levels, and children who do not master these areas cannot understand the more advanced math critical to high tech fields. Music involves ratios, fractions, proportions, and thinking in space and time. Second-grade students were given four months of piano keyboard training, as well as time using newly designed math software. The group scored over 27 % higher on proportional math and fractions tests than children who used only the math software.
Source: Neurological Research, March, 1999.

5. A McGill University study found that pattern recognition and mental representation scores improved significantly for students given piano instruction over a three-year period. They also found that self-esteem and musical skills measures improved for the students given piano instruction.
Source: Dr. Eugenia Costa-Giomi, "The McGill Piano Project: Effects of three years of piano instruction on children's cognitive abilities, academic achievement, and self-esteem," presented at the meeting of the Music Educators National Conference, Phoenix, AZ, April, 1998.

6. Data from the National Educational Longitudinal Study of 1988 showed that music participants received more academic honors and awards than non-music students, and that the percentage of music participants receiving As, As/Bs, and Bs was higher than the percentage of non-participants receiving those grades. *Source: National Educational Longitudinal Study of 1988 First Follow-Up (1990), US Department of Education.*

Music Raises Test Scores and Improves Emotional Well-Being and Life Success

1. Research shows that piano students are better equipped to comprehend mathematical and scientific concepts. A group of preschoolers received private piano keyboard lessons and singing lessons. A second group received private computer lessons. Those children who received piano/keyboard training performed 34% higher on tests measuring spatial-temporal ability than the others, even those who received computer training. "Spatial-temporal" is basically proportional reasoning--ratios, fractions, proportions, and thinking in space and time. This concept has long been considered a major obstacle in the teaching of elementary math and science. *Source:* Neurological Research, February 28, 1997.

2. Young children with developed rhythm skills perform better academically in early school years. Findings of a recent study showed that there was a significant difference in the academic achievement levels of students classified according to rhythmic competency. Students who were achieving at academic expectation scored high on all rhythmic tasks, while many of those who scored lower on the rhythmic test achieved below academic expectation. *Source: "The Relationship between Rhythmic Competency and Academic Performance in First Grade Children," University of Central Florida, Debby Mitchell.*

3. High school music students score higher on SATs in both verbal and math than their peers. In 2001, SAT takers with coursework/experience in music performance scored 57 points higher on the verbal portion of the test and 41 points higher on the math portion than students with no coursework/experience in the arts. *Profile of SAT and Achievement Test Takers, The College Board, compiled by Music Educators National Conference, 2001.*

4. College-age musicians are emotionally healthier than their non-musician counterparts. A study conducted at the University of Texas looked at 362 students who were in their first semester of college. They were given three tests, measuring performance anxiety, emotional concerns, and alcohol related problems. In addition to having fewer battles with the bottle, researchers also noted that the college-aged music students seemed to have surer footing when facing tests. *Source:* Houston Chronicle, January 11, 1998.

5. A ten-year study, tracking more than 25,000 students, shows that music-making improves test scores. Regardless of socioeconomic background, music-making students get higher marks on standardized tests than those who had no music involvement. The test scores studied were not only standardized tests, such as the SAT, but also in reading proficiency exams. *Source: Dr. James Catterall, UCLA, 1997.*

6. The world's top academic countries place a high value on music education. Hungary, Netherlands, and Japan stand atop worldwide science achievement and have strong commitment to music education. All three countries have required music training at the elementary and middle school levels, both instrumental and vocal, for several decades. The centrality of music education to learning in the top-ranked countries seems to contradict the United States' focus on math, science, vocabulary, and technology. *Source: 1988 International Association for the Evaluation of Educational Achievement (IAEEA) Test.*

7. Music training helps underachievers. In Rhode Island, researchers studied eight public school first grade classes. Half of the classes became "test arts" groups, receiving ongoing music and visual arts training. In kindergarten, this group had lagged behind in scholastic performance. After seven months, the students were given a standardized test. The "test arts" group had caught up to their fellow students in reading and surpassed their classmates in math by 22 %. In the second year of the project, the arts students widened this margin even further. Students were also evaluated on attitude and behavior. Classroom teachers noted improvement in these areas also. *Source:* Nature, May 23, 1996.

8. "Music education can be a positive force on all aspects of a child's life, particularly on their academic success. The study of music by children has been linked to higher scores on the SAT and other learning aptitude tests, and has proven to be an invaluable tool in classrooms across the country. Given the impact music can have on our children's education, we should support every effort to bring music into their classrooms." *Source: U.S. Senator Jeff Bingaman (NM).*

CHAPTER 6

Why Children Need Play and Movement to Learn Well and Live Well

by Nan Henderson, M.S.W.

The American Academy of Pediatrics (AAP) issued a strongly worded report in 2006 warning of the "repercussions" of reduced child "play time." The Academy detailed the many cultural factors combining to reduce children's "free-time play...and physical outlets" but emphasized research confirms play "contributes to optimal child development for all children." The report concludes, "We must advocate for the changes [needed] so children have more opportunities for play" (p.2).

One of the driving forces behind the elimination of play is the pressure to increase academic success, especially since the implementation of the No Child Left Behind Act of 2001. A growing body of research, however, documents that play and physical movement are absolutely necessary for optimum brain development and learning. The AAP concluded that a change in activity, such as that provided by recess and physical play, "enhances children's cognitive capacity. A change in academic instruction or class topic does not offer this clear-cut change" (p.5).

Commenting further on the implications of this report for educators, the AAP said, "Play is integral to the academic environment....It has been shown to help children adjust to the school setting and even to enhance children's learning readiness, learning behaviors, and problem-solving skills" (p. 4).

Play..."Important as Sleep, Rest, and Food"

One reason for this, the AAP concluded: "Play is important to healthy brain development." The Academy based this statement on a growing body of brain research that only recently began utilizing "sophisticated brain-imaging technology, made possible by advances in computer science...This technology takes scientists into a world of three-dimensional color TV graphics with high spatial and temporal resolution" (Frost, 1998, p. 4). The picture that emerges:

Zap: neurons in the brain's amydala send pulses of electricity through the circuits that control emotion. You hold him on your lap and talk...and neurons from his ears start hard-wiring connections to the auditory cortex. And you thought you were just playing with your kid. (Begley, 1996, p. 55)

This enhanced research picture has revealed to neuro-scientists both predicted and "unanticipated results [of play]

to education and child development," notes University of Texas at Austin Parker Centennial Professor Joe Frost (1998), whose research provided pivotal data for the AAP report.

Play, the frivolous, unimportant behavior with no apparent purpose, has earned new respect as biologists, neuroscientists, psychologists, and others see that play is indeed serious business and is perhaps equally important as other basic drives of sleep, rest, and food. Hopefully, this unprecedented explosion of information about the importance of play for brain growth and child development will influence families, schools, and other social and corporate institutions to rearrange their attitudes and priorities about play, recess, physical education, music, games, art, and rich, personal interactions between caregivers and children. (1998, p. 1)

These factors: play, movement, fun, art, creativity, and loving personal interactions filled with "sharing pleasurable time together," along with "effective and developmentally appropriate discipline" are "the true predictors of childhood serving as a springboard toward a happy, successful adulthood," concludes the AAP. These factors are best served by "true toys, such a blocks and dolls, in which children use their imagination fully," scheduled as well as completely unscheduled time, a balance between child-directed and adult-directed movement and play, and the absence of "pressure to excel in each area" (AAP, 2006, pp.15 – 18).

Frost (1998) details the "linkages between brain development and play during childhood that now have considerable support from neuroscientists," noting:

- All "healthy young mammals play."
- "Play programs neural structures...and [the] resulting, increasingly complex neural structures influence [the development of] ever more complex play." The most vigorous animal play happens "precisely the time when its brain cells are frenetically forming synaptic connections, creating a dense array of neural links..."
- "The early games and frivolity of animals and humans equip them for the skills they will need later in life."
- "During the first years of life it is playful activity... that makes a positive difference in brain development and subsequent human functioning."
- "Play deprivation results in aberrant behavior."

- Only neuroscientists can see physical evidence (through brain scans)…"of the profound relationships between achievement and the endless games of the very young--patty-cake, peek-a-boo, and sing-song rhythms are in reality storehouses or machines for programming the brain for language, art, music, math, science, kinesthetic, and interpersonal abilities and intelligence." This relationship is not immediately obvious to "the casual observer." (pp.8-10)

So important, in fact, is "play and unscheduled free time" to healthy child development, the AAP termed them "protective factors" that "increase resiliency" (p.16).

Playful Movement to Improve Student Learning

Such research is shifting the attitudes of some educators about both the inclusion of recess and physical education in the school day—if nothing else, as a means to increase learning success. A pilot study at Central High School in Naperville, IL is indicative of emerging new approaches to utilize physical education and play to improve student learning. The *Chicago Tribune* reported September 13, 2006 on research at Naperville Central High using movement as an intervention with slow readers. Freshmen students with "below-average reading scores" were divided into two groups: One group participated in a 7 a.m. physical education class, then immediately took "a remedial literacy class." The second group "with similar [reading skills] had their reading class several hours after gym." For the students that took early morning PE followed immediately by the literacy class, "standardized reading scores [rose] the equivalent of 1.4 grade levels" (Breslin, 2006).

The *Tribune* article included a report of an Illinois 2004 study of nine-to-eleven year olds that found, "Students who scored higher on fitness tests were more likely to do better on standardized tests in reading and math." In addition, "Another study in California of more than one million students had similar results" (Breslin, 2006).

Antronette Yancey, director of the Center to Eliminate Health Disparities at UCLA, concludes in the *Tribune* article, "To compromise physical education in service of test scores and learning is completely backward thinking."

Many educators and other learning experts advocating for physical education say, however, that schools need to change PE so the focus is on "fun games that develop a lifelong love of fitness." In Naperville Central, for example, students can square dance, scale a climbing wall, or even chase rubber chickens on a field, "giggling and sweating as they do." In one recent class, the assignment for students was to hold hands in a contorted circle, then untangle themselves, using team work to solve the problem. The process also resulted in a lot of laughter.

"You do a lot of different things that are fun in here," sophomore Jordon Poll told the *Tribune*. "It's less like straight exercise and more about learning to cooperate more, not just running a boring mile."

Harvard psychiatrist John Ratey, a vocal advocate for physical education and movement in schools, is including a study of the Naperville program in his upcoming book on exercise and the brain. "I've said for years that exercise is like Miracle-Gro for the brain," Ratey said. "Now we're learning so much more about it, and just how much exercise causes a huge increase in growth factors in the brain" (Breslin, 2006).

The Council on Physical Education for Children (2001) concluded that both "unstructured playtime" such as recess and structured "physical education programs" are essential in schools. Both can contribute to brain development, learning achievement, and a reduction in stress and distractibility, as well as develop motor skills and life skills. As such, they are crucial to both student school success and in the long run, to life success.

References

American Academy of Pediatrics. (2006). *The importance of play in promoting healthy child development and maintaining strong parent-child bonds.* Elk Grove Village, IL: American Academy of Pediatrics.

Begley, S. (1996). Your child's brain. *Newsweek. Feb. 29*, 55-58.

Breslin, M.M. (2006). Naperville Central tests notion that exercise makes learning easier. In the *Chicago Tribune On-Line Edition.* Retrieved from http://www.chicagotribune.com/features/health/chi-0609130073sept13,1,4955337.story.

Council on Physical Education for Children; National Association for Sport and Physical Education. (2001). *Recess in elementary schools.* Reston, VA: National Association for Sport and Physical Education.

Frost, J.L. (1998). Neuroscience, play, and brain development. Paper presented at IPA/USA Triennial National Conference, June 18-21, 1998; Longmont, CO.

Nan Henderson, M.S.W., is an international speaker, writer, and president of Resiliency In Action, a publishing and training company in Southern CA. She has authored several articles and coauthored four books on fostering resiliency, including Resiliency In Action: Practical Ideas for Overcoming Risks and Building Strengths in Youth, Families, and Communities and Resiliency In Schools: Making It Happen for Students and Educators. She can be contacted at nhenderson@resiliency.com or at by calling 800-440-5171. More information is available at www.resiliency.com.

CHAPTER 7

Brain Gym:
Fun Tools for "Whole Brain Integration" with Amazing Learning Outcomes

by Nan Henderson, M.S.W.

Brain Gym is a set of simple movements developed by Paul Dennison, a California educator and reading specialist who began testing these techniques three decades ago in learning disability clinics. He was inspired early in his career to look for help for children and adults who had been identified as "learning disabled." His search led him to the study of Kinesiology, the science of body movement and its relationship to brain function. According to Dennison, The Brain Gym movements stimulate a flow of information along neural networks in the brain improving the relationship between the two sides of the brain, the back and front areas of the brain, and the top and bottom structures of the brain. Dennison and his wife Gail Dennison have pioneered this new field of "Educational Kinesiology," which is based on the knowledge that movement enhances learning. Brain Gym is usually practiced for about 10 minutes a day, and has been shown to bring about "rapid and often dramatic improvements" in concentration, memory, reading skills, writing skills, organizational ability, listening, and physical coordination (Brain Gym International, 2006).

Reading, music, and special needs educators rave about the positive impact of the brain gym approach (to see a few hundred such testimonials search "Brain Gym" at amazon. com). Brain Gym International, headquartered in Ventura, CA, reports the program has been utilized in "thousands of public and private schools" in 80 countries. For the past 15 years Brain Gym has been selected each year by the National Learning Foundation "as one of today's leading technologies for education."

What are Brain Gym Activities Like?

The complete Brain Gym program includes 26 activities. Some, like the following three, are widely recommended; others are used for specific learning needs.

- **BRAIN BUTTONS** (an exercise for improving blood flow to the brain to "switch on" the entire brain before a learning activity begins, which helps improve concentration skills):

  1. Position one hand so there is as wide a space as possible between the thumb and index finger.

  2. Place your index and thumb into the slight indentations below the collar bone on each side of the sternum. Press lightly in a pulsing manner.

  3. At the same time put the other hand over the navel area of the stomach. Gently press on these points for about two minutes.

- **CROSS CRAWL** (an exercise that helps coordinate right and left brain by increasing the information flow between the two hemispheres—useful for spelling, writing, listening, reading, and comprehension):

  1. Stand or sit. Put the right hand across the body to the left knee as you raise it, and then do the same thing with the left hand on the right knee just as if you were marching.

  2. Simply do this either sitting or standing for about two minutes.

- **HOOK UPS** (an exercise for calming nerves before a test or special event—nervousness from any situation can be helped by a few "hook ups" which will calm the mind and improve concentration):

  1. Stand or sit. Cross the right leg over the left at the ankles.

  2. Cross your right wrist over your left wrist and link up the fingers so the right wrist is on top.

  3. Bend the elbows out and gently turn the fingers in towards the body until they rest on the sternum in the center of the chest. Stay in this position.

  4. Keep ankles and wrists crossed and breathe evenly in this position for a few minutes.

Educators Comment on the Power of Brain Gym

Educator Jon Peterson, writing in *New Horizons for Learning*, an on-line journal cosponsored by the Office of the Washington State Superintendent of Public Instruction, offers a compelling account of the power of Brain Gym with first grade students who exhibited characteristics of ADD/ADHD. He reports on a boy named "Jeff" whose mother agreed to do five to ten minutes of Brain Gym activities with him every day for eight weeks. At the end of that time, Jeff's mother said of her son:

> He is calmer and much more focused. He does not get bored and frustrated like he used to. He's eager to participate in family activities, like hiking and bicycling. When we have a workday, he does more than he needs to do. His whole attitude has calmed down. He has had a total change in his ability to concentrate. His endurance is better.... He plays games better [and now] he can wait his turn. I see the results. (Peterson, 2006)

Peterson goes on to explain that movement activities like Brain Gym, change "old patterns" in the brain. When students like Jeff are stressed and anxious, "their systems are out of balance and their brain patterns have downshifted into lower, survival brain areas," Peterson writes. "The movements and activities of Brain Gym…strengthen the neural connections throughout the entire brain, including into and through the prefrontal cortex." This is the area of the brain with "the most impact on focus, attention, impulse control, and decision-making." Therefore, "when more neural pathways are opened and developed into the prefrontal lobes through very specific movement, the individual's mind/body system works with greater ease and harmony." The result is that kids like Jeff, those with ADD/ADHD, are then able to relax and focus, "attend to what is going on, control impulses, think about consequences, and make good decisions" (Peterson, 2006).

Cecilia Koester, a former special needs classroom teacher and author of *I Am the Child: Using Brain Gym with Children Who Have Special Needs,* now a Brain Gym consultant, explains how the process works this way:

> Children who have special needs "switch off" more frequently than the average child. Perhaps the stress from neurological damage or simply a more sensitive nervous system creates a need for movements, such as Brain Gym, as well as skills of coordination. The intention behind Brain Gym is to stimulate the brain so the child has equal access to all dimensions of the brain. (Koester, 2006)

She reports that she has "seen miraculous improvement in both children and adults" with the Brain Gym program, including "three children with whom I've worked [that] have gone from blindness to sight." Other "miracles" reported by Koester include a child who couldn't walk until he used the Brain Gym program at age five; a nine-year-old boy diagnosed as autistic who began to use functional speech after three months of using Brain Gym, and another five-year-old boy whose intense and frequent seizures significantly decreased as a result of using the program.

Though K-12 educators extensively utilize the Brain Gym approach, according to Brain Gym International, Brain Gym can help "all areas of performance" for people of all ages. More information is available at the Brain Gym website, www.braingym.org.

References

Brain Gym International. (2000). *A chronology of annotated research study summaries in the field of educational kinesiology.* Ventura, CA: The Educational Kinesiology Foundation.

Brain Gym International. (2006). *Welcome to brain gym, educational kinesiology.* Retrieved from http://www.braingym.org.

Dennison, P.E. (2006). *Brain gym and me: Reclaiming the pleasure of learning.* Ventura, CA: The Educational Kinesiology Foundation.

Koester, C.F. (2006). *Have you heard of brain gym?* Retrieved from http://www.iamthechild.com.

Koester, C.F. (2000). A summary of a brain gym research project on reading, *from Brain Gym Journal.* Retrieved from http://www.iamthechild.com.

Peterson, J. (2006). ADD, ADHD and Brain Gym. *New Horizons for Learning.* Retrieved from http://www.newhorizons.org.

Nan Henderson, M.S.W., is an international speaker, writer, and president of Resiliency In Action, a publishing and training company in Southern CA. She has authored several articles and coauthored four books on fostering resiliency, including Resiliency In Action: Practical Ideas for Overcoming Risks and Building Strengths in Youth, Families, and Communities and Resiliency In Schools: Making It Happen for Students and Educators. She can be contacted at nhenderson@resiliency.com or at by calling 800-440-5171. More information is available at www.resiliency.com.

CHAPTER 8

A Summary
of a Brain Gym Research Project on Reading

by Cecilia (Freeman) Koester, M.Ed.
Reprinted from Brain Gym Journal, December 2000

Given my deep desire to get Brain Gym into the schools, as well as the enormous amount of conversation about the need for longitudinal research on the effects of Brain Gym on academic skills, in 1998 I set out to do a year long research project at an elementary school.

To accomplish this task, I engaged the assistance of Brain Gym Consultant Joyce B. Sherwood. The report for this pilot project offers data supporting the finding that students in grades three, four, and five who used Brain Gym throughout the year improved their reading test scores on a statewide standardized test (the Stanford 9) twice as much as did the students in the control group who did not use Brain Gym as a part of their learning. These are remarkable results--both academically and statistically.

Having formerly worked as a classroom teacher in a special day class for severely challenged students on this particular campus, I approached principal Paul Jablonowski at Saticoy Elementary School in Ventura, California with the request to conduct this project with some of his students. I received his consent and was met with open arms and great enthusiasm for the project by the twelve teachers whose classrooms would be involved. These teachers agreed to the following:

1. To meet for one hour after school every Monday throughout the school year.

2. To do a minimum of 15 minutes of Brain Gym each day, integrated into the daily activities of the classroom rather than in a one-time block.

3. To allow students selected by each teacher to leave class one time each month for a 30-minute session of Brain Gym within a small group, facilitated by a Brain Gym consultant.

4. To invite Brain Gym consultants to do classroom consultations a minmum of two times during the school year.

5. To allow students' test scores to be gathered for data comparison. An equal number of student scores were gathered from the school files to serve as a control group, with the permission of the teachers in those classrooms.

Throughout the school year, enthusiasm and follow through remained high. All of the above agreements were carried out. We arranged a special parents' night which drew an astonishing crowd of 120 to inform the parents about Brain Gym and explain how their children were using it in the classroom. In addition, the participating classroom teachers papered their walls with suggested Brain Gym materials, instructed students in the task-appropriate use of the Brain Gym movements, and reminded the young people about which Brain Gym activities to do prior to undertaking a homework assignment. The teachers learned the Brain Gym exercises and subsequently taught their students. As I passed through the halls when we were only three months into the project, I saw children using Brain Gym throughout the school day, even without teacher direction.

The students who continued to have difficulty with their reading skills were seen by a Brain Gym consultant in small groups of two to four. These groups were facilitated to remediate specific difficulties related to such areas as attention and comprehension, fine- or gross-motor coordination, or specific academic skills.

The results of this pilot project were phenomenal. Students' self-esteem improved, the classroom climate became more calm, the students reported how much easier their reading had become, and the teachers expressed deep gratitude for this simple, effective tool that enhanced their teaching strategies.

I also gathered test data from the Stanford 9. Students in each grade level who experienced the Brain Gym activities improved their test scores twice as much as did the students in the control group who did not practice Brain Gym.

Given these results, I believe that all reading programs would benefit by infusing Brain Gym into the school day. Whether the approach is phonics, guided reading, or reading recovery, testing should inform instruction rather than the other way around. Classroom teachers everywhere need to be encouraged to add Brain Gym activities to their teaching strategies.

One grateful parent volunteer summarized community responses with the following letter:

> To Whom It May Concern: I am writing in regard to the Brain Gym Program that is being taught at my child's school. These small, but effective techniques have helped my daughter excel in class immensely. Her ability to focus, concentrate, and complete class assignments increase after each morning's pace exercise. The class as a whole, in which I volunteer two times a week, seems to calm down and show improvement with listening as well as performing the days' tasks.
>
> I am sure as time goes by, children will only benefit from this Educational Kinesiology brought to our schools....Getting in touch with your mind through the body sounds fantastic. What a wonderful way to begin a life, positive, healthy, and strong—the perfect way to create a successful adult.

Cecilia K. Freeman, M.Ed., is a former classroom teacher and one of the leading experts in the educational use of Brain Gym. Though her specialty is working with children and adults who have special needs, she also works with general education students. She is the author, with Gail E. Dennison, of I Am the Child: Using Brain Gym with Children Who Have Special Needs. *Cecilia consults nationwide, doing teacher in-services as well as teaching "Brain Gym for Special Education Providers." She can be reached through her website: iamthechild.com.*

SAVE MONEY BY ORDERING MORE BOOKS DIRECTLY FROM

Resiliency In Action

Four ways to order:

- Call Toll-FREE (800) 440-5171
- Order on line at www.resiliency.com
- Fax the order form below to 805-969-0460
- Mail the order form below to Resiliency In Action

> P.O. Box 1433
> Ojai, CA 93024

Special Discounts for Purchasing A Quantity of *Resiliency In Action*

Buy 15 books and get a 25% discount off the list price of $36.95.
Buy 50 books and get a 30% discount off the list price of $36.95.
Buy 100 books or more and get a 40% discount off the list price of $36.95.
Buy 1,000 books AND GET 50% OFF THE LIST PRICE OF THE BOOK!

Shipping and handling charges are 10% of the discounted price total of your order (20% outside the U.S.). Books must be paid for at time of ordering to get this special price. Call 800-440-5171 to place your order or e-mail resadmin@resiliency.com.

MAIL OR FAX THIS FORM

NAME_____PHONE_____
ORGANIZATION_____
ADDRESS_____CITY_____STATE_____ZIP_____
E-MAIL_____

I am ordering_____copies of the 2nd Edition of *Resiliency In Action: Practical Ideas for Overcoming Risks and Building Strengths in Youth, Families, and Communities.*

Enclosed is a check for_____ ($36.95 X number of copies) **PLUS shipping/handling charge: No charge for 1 – 2 books, or 10% total order for 3 or more books** [Shipping and handling for CANADA is 20%; FOREIGN shipping and handling is 25%.]

OR Please charge my ☐ VISA ☐ MASTERCARD for books plus shipping/handling charges (see above)
Card number_____Exp.date_____
Billing Address for the card_____City_____
State_____Zip Code_____

MAIL TO:
Resiliency In Action, P.O. Box 1433,   **FAX TO:** 805-969-0460
Ojai, CA 93024-1433   **For more information call:** 800-440-5171